Hella Town

The publisher and the University of California Press Foundation gratefully acknowledge the generous support of the Peter Booth Wiley Endowment Fund in History.

Hella Town

OAKLAND'S HISTORY OF DEVELOPMENT AND DISRUPTION

Mitchell Schwarzer

UNIVERSITY OF CALIFORNIA PRESS

University of California Press
Oakland, California

© 2021 by Mitchell Schwarzer

First paperback Printing 2022

Library of Congress Cataloging-in-Publication Data

Names: Schwarzer, Mitchell, author.
Title: Hella town : Oakland's history of development and disruption /
    Mitchell Schwarzer.
Identifiers: LCCN 2020054657 (print) | LCCN 2020054658 (ebook) |
    ISBN 9780520381124 (cloth) | 9780520391536 (pbk) | 9780520381131 (epub)
Subjects: LCSH: City planning—Social aspects—California—Oakland. |
    City planning—Political aspects—California—Oakland. | Oakland
    (Calif.)—History—Political aspects. | Oakland (Calif.)—History—
    Social aspects.
Classification: LCC F869.O2 S38 2021 (print) | LCC F869.O2 (ebook) |
    DDC 979.4/66—dc23
LC record available at https://lccn.loc.gov/2020054657
LC ebook record available at https://lccn.loc.gov/2020054658

Manufactured in the United States of America

30 29 28 27 26 25 24 23 22
10 9 8 7 6 5 4 3 2 1

For the Ohlone peoples,
who have long tended the land
now known as Oakland.

Contents

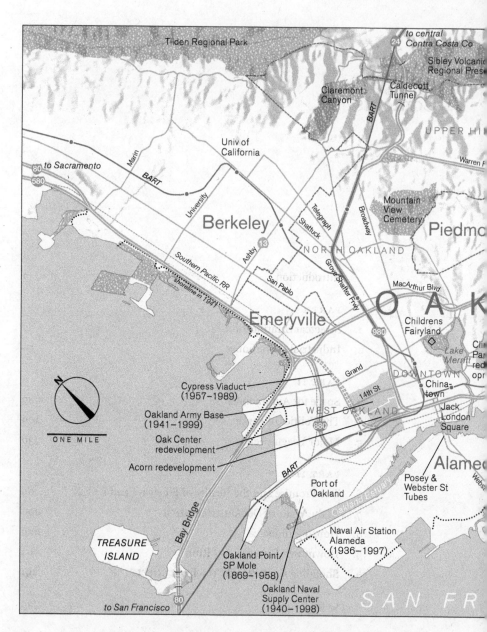

Map 1. Streets, Highways, and Major Features. Map by Dennis McLendon.

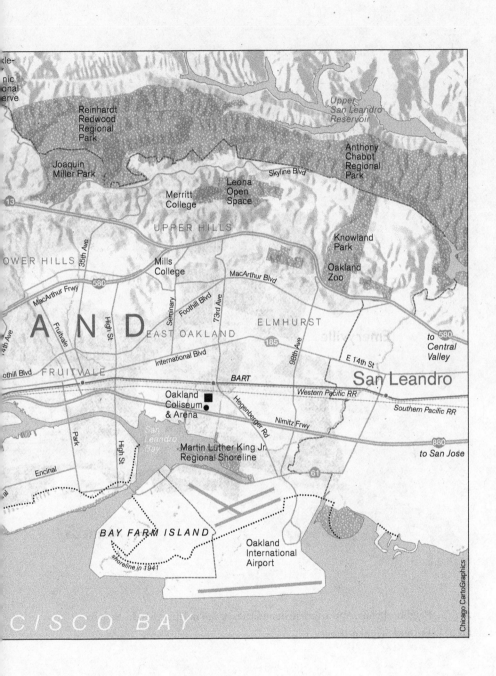

Reinhardt
Redwood
Regional
Park

Joaquin
Miller Park

13

OWER HILLS

35th Ave

Mills
College

UPPER HILLS

Merritt
College

Leona
Open
Space

Skyline Blvd

Upper
San Leandro
Reservoir

Anthony
Chabot
Regional
Park

Knowland
Park

Oakland
Zoo

MacArthur Frwy

580

AND

Fruitvale

High St

Seminary

Foothill Blvd

73rd Ave

MacArthur Blvd

EAST OAKLAND

ELMHURST

185

98th Ave

to
Central
Valley

580

14th Ave

othill Blvd

FRUITVALE

International Blvd

E 14th St

San Leandro

BART

Western Pacific RR

Southern Pacific RR

Oakland
Coliseum
& Arena

Hegenberger Rd

Nimitz Frwy

880

Park

High St

San
Leandro
Bay

Martin Luther King Jr.
Regional Shoreline

to San Jose

Encinal

61

al

BAY FARM ISLAND

Shoreline in 1941

Oakland
International
Airport

CISCO BAY

Chicago CartoGraphics

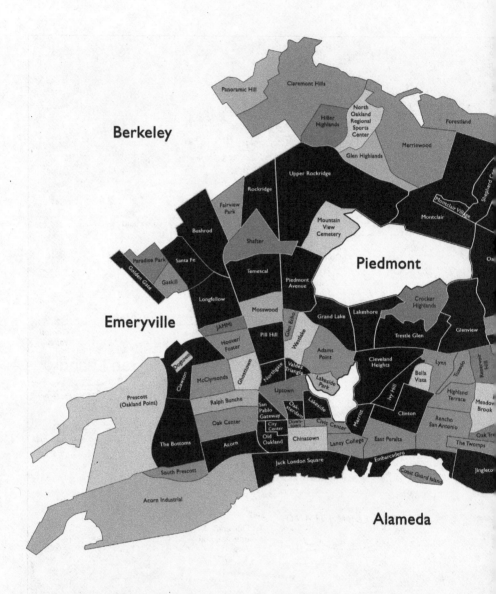

Map 2. Neighborhoods. Approximate boundaries of 146 neighborhoods. Map by Ozan Berke and Stephen Texeira.

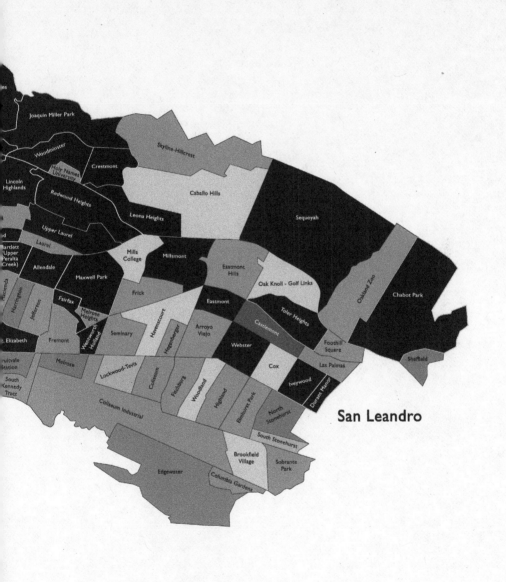

Joaquin Miller Park

Woodminster

Holy Names University

Lincoln Highlands

Crestmont

Skyline-Hillcrest

Redwood Heights

Caballo Hills

Leona Heights

Upper Laurel

Sequoyah

Laurel

Bartlett Upper Peralta Creek)

Allendale

Maxwell Park

Mills College

Millsmont

Eastmont Hills

Oak Knoll - Golf Links

Oakland Zoo

Chabot Park

Harrington

Jefferson

Fairfax

Frick

Eastmont

Toler Heights

Melrose Heights

Wentworth-Holland

Seminary

Havenscourt

Hegenberger

Arroyo Viejo

Castlemont

Foothill Square

Elizabeth

Fremont

Webster

Cox

Las Palmas

Sheffield

Fruitvale Station

Melrose

Lockwood-Tevis

Coliseum

Fitchburg

Woodland

Highland

Iveywood

Durant Manor

South Kennedy Tract

Coliseum Industrial

Bancroft Park

North Stonehurst

San Leandro

South Stonehurst

Edgewater

Brookfield Village

Columbia Gardens

Sobrante Park

Introduction

"There is no there there," Gertrude Stein's notorious statement about Oakland, appeared in her 1937 memoir, *Everybody's Autobiography*. Stein lived in Oakland from age 6 to 17. In 1891, she moved with her family to Baltimore, and in 1935, now a noted author and socialite, returned for a lecture tour. Speaking at the English club at Mills College, she grudgingly agreed to visit her former stomping grounds around 13th Avenue and E. 25th Street. In the intervening 44 years, the landscape had been recast from an occasional farmhouse, surrounded by rose bushes and peach and eucalyptus trees, to corridors of single-family dwellings. The Steins' family house and expansive grounds were gone. Gertrude was disoriented and later penned the famous remark. Regardless of the fact that she was expressing the kind of disappointment that most people would feel upon revisiting a home long departed and witnessing that everything had changed, her words have since underpinned a false impression that Oakland is lacking in something, in someplace.[1]

It is worth recalling that in 1935 what may have distressed Stein had uplifted the builders of the district as well as its residents and businesses. Starting in the 1890s, Oaklanders experienced a profound increase in their personal mobility through the aegis of electric streetcars, which turned the walking city into a radial metropolis. After the 1906 Earthquake, which

Figure 1. Stein's old neighborhood. In the vicinity of 13th Avenue and E. 25th Street. Photo by Mitchell Schwarzer, 2020.

destroyed San Francisco, Oakland's growth accelerated. New industries capitalized on California's growth. Housing construction ramped up, and macadamized roads were laid for the latest mass phenomenon—automobiles. At the time of Stein's visit, the Great Depression had dampened investment, but it resumed with a vengeance during the Second World War.

Had Stein been able to come back 44 years after her lecture tour visit, in 1979, she would have experienced a city transformed once more. Scattered apartment buildings broke up single-family house rows, many of whose windows were now secured by metal bars. Buses ran where streetcars had. Upslope, an eight-lane freeway coursed across the base of the hills, and higher still, on what had been cascading carpets of wildflowers, the latest subdivisions were being erected. Down by the waterfront, the manufacturing belt was emptying. Once-vibrant commercial arteries were marred by unoccupied storefronts and vacant lots. Another process of city change was taking place: disinvestment yielding deterioration.

When Stein visited her former neighborhood, she had recently returned to America after having spent over 30 years in Paris. Approaching a city like Oakland with European preconceptions of stability, hierarchy, and monumentality invariably leads to disappointment. Place in California is better understood as a verb and not a noun, a process of moving and making and remaking. If Oakland appears faceless at times, that is less a flaw on its part and more an inability of an observer to appreciate the fits and starts of urbanization in a California city. Instead of a grand canvas showing finished pieces in flawless order, cities like Oakland, Sacramento, Los Angeles, and even the European-seeming San Francisco expose snapshots of city formation and deformation, driven by economics, technology, and politics: one where the Civil War jump-started cotton production in California farmlands, leading to cotton manufacturing alongside the waterfront; another where an innovation in transportation, the electric traction streetcar, cast commercial strips across the flatlands and lower hills; and another still where the racist approach to guaranteeing mortgage loans on the part of a federal agency, the Home Owners' Loan Corporation, brought deprivation to minority neighborhoods.

Land-use and building patterns are a puzzle that can only be deciphered by going back in time, following the patchy moments when plans get realized, or not, when the variable trajectories of real estate acts become apparent, and when the changing priorities of governmental and business entities make themselves felt. After progressing northward from the waterfront, Oakland coalesced a retail district on lower Washington Street and an office center around 14th and Broadway. While a new office district arose along Lake Merritt's western end, the retail district continued to move north along Broadway, and then disintegrated. Numerous plans were hatched for a civic center on the lake's southern side; Oakland ended up with three dispersed collections of governmental buildings, and only one by the lake. When land was available, Oakland leaders failed to set aside a large central park in the vicinity of Lake Merritt. Park acquisitions took place primarily in the upper hills, far from where most of the population lived.

It is from those lofty heights where we can get a comprehensive visual picture of Oakland's land-use and building patterns: the waters claimed from the bay for manufacturing and the Port of Oakland; the transporta-

tion-industrial corridors paralleling the waterfront; the high-rise offices
and residences downtown and by the lake; the sea of low-rise housing stretching from those districts across the flatlands, lower hills, and
upper hills, punctuated here and there by hospitals, church spires, and a
tall office or apartment block. Equally, we can construe the city's natural
geography: a sweep of terrain fronting an estuary of San Francisco Bay
and shielded by the San Francisco peninsula from the direct winds and
fog of the Pacific Ocean; a landscape canvas ascending from the bay's salt
marshes to alluvial plains to undulating hillsides and finally steep canyons
and peaks topping out at 1,760 feet.

.   .   .   .

Hella Town: Oakland's History of Development and Disruption exam-
ines Oakland's built environment from the 1890s to the early twenty-first
century, from the time when population growth, industrialization, and
mechanized transportation unleashed the conditions for the modern city,
to the contemporary moment when the region's galloping information-
age economy has produced a dire housing shortage amid lopsided priva-
tization of urban development. Over this span of more than 125 years, I
track the uneven pace of development, the booms and busts, the buildups
and breakdowns of a great American city. I analyze how transportation
improvements charted its growth, how built functions—housing, workplace, shopping, and civic culture/recreation—were realized, and how
those functions were subject to elite control and inequities tied to race.[2]
Development, the act of adding to (and/or subtracting from) the physical makeup of a city, invariably brings forth disruption. How development proceeds, gradually or rapidly, thoughtfully or recklessly, openly or
behind closed doors, determines the severity of the disruption as well as
who comes out ahead and who gets left behind.

The title, *Hella Town*, draws from two local memes. Most Bay Area residents call San Francisco "the City"; by contrast, many Oaklanders refer
to their home as "the Town," Oaktown, an acknowledgment of its smaller
size and status, and its gritty, down-to-earth vibe. The term "hella" popped
up within East Bay youth culture after the 1970s, a shortened version of

helluva or *hellacious*, signifying "very" or "extremely," an adverb like the Southern California "totally" that gives an adjective or noun both emphasis and a distinct regional flavor. Together, the words hella and town, *Hella Town*, describe an Oakland that has struggled to measure up to its adjacent metropolitan center but, at the same time, an Oakland prideful in its upstart status, an Oakland not only warmer in weather but warmer in personality, an Oakland as an exceptional convergence of religions, ethnicities, races, social classes, and sexual orientations. Back in 1987, hip-hop artist Too $hort rapped on the song "Oakland": "Oakland, Oaktown, Oakland, Oaktown, straight from the west, Oakland is the best, baby it's so fresh ..."

To know why Oakland can be hella fresh or "hella disrespectful," another song by Too $hort, we need to start with the economic geography that underlies the town's advent. From colonial through contemporary times, land development has been central to the formation of an American society. Once surveyed, recorded, and put up for sale, land is developed and disrupted, recast into a more valuable resource and more intensive activity. An acre occupied by forest becomes, say, a farmstead. It might give way later to residences and, afterward, storefronts or office buildings. Each change cements the land to rules of law, political machinations, and a marketplace of expectation, exchange, and exploitation. Access is crucial: in both senses of the word. First, people benefit by being able to get to a particular location with increasing ease and speed—a plot of land links into a network that ramps up connections to other people and places. Second, people purchase, occupy, or benefit from the connected plot of land—control is taken by certain individuals or segments of society while others are kept out.

In *Hella Town*, I give special emphasis to how emergent transportation technologies and systemic racism configured access to urbanized land. Circulatory infrastructures, from public mass transit to private automobiles, and long-standing biases against people of color, were perpetuated at individual and societal levels, and operated as synergistic factors in the growth of the built environment and its patterns of neighborhood change and succession.

On one side, how people got around—walking, horse-drawn omnibuses, electric traction streetcars, automobiles, buses, freeways, BART, bicycles—regulated physical access to the town's acreage, determining the distance that could be covered on a daily basis and the disposition of the trip undertaken: fast or slow; relaxed or tiresome; isolated or in closer contact to both the cityscape and other people. Each type of transportation infrastructure influenced where development took place, what kind was favored, and how it was built with respect to density and lot coverage.[3] These networks were never fully public or private: managed by private companies in the railroad and streetcar era of communal travel, and later under the jurisdiction of governmental entities, while enabling privatized freedom of movement in automobiles. Circulatory vessels between the vital urban organs, the corridors were themselves contested as to their function, sometimes accommodating a range of users and uses, other times limiting their purview to rapid vehicular passage. Entire districts could be targeted or bypassed, given help to build up or purposely disempowered: a branching of the town, as symbolized by the coast live oak, into limbs of growth, stasis, regeneration, and decay.

Transportation has long been central to Oakland's identity. In 1852, it was founded as a sailing and trading port. Over the course of the late nineteenth century, it grew into a commercial and industrial center on the basis of its interface between shipping and railroads. In the twentieth century, that interface was extended by highways, rapid rail transit, and a pioneering container seaport as well as a jet airport. Over and over, Oakland was wired to faraway destinations, other parts of California, the Bay Region, and its internal geography. It has remained a destination for migrants, both national and international. Yet in a place that has of late counted as one of the nation's most ethnically and racially varied populations, barriers to land access have persisted. On the other side of the coin, then, the story of access was more complicated than being able to take BART or own an automobile. Technological innovation, in and of itself, did not inherently lead to a level playing field in the urban scene. It oftentimes reconfigured enduring societal pecking orders.

In American cities, residential property values were customarily set according to a scale ranging from undesirable to exclusive that corresponded to use, class, and race.[4] Was a particular plot distant from industrial plants, commercial strips, and poor neighborhoods? Could legal contracts or, when they could not be enforced, social sanctions or brute force, keep white residents apart from Asians, Latinos, or African

Americans? High home values in all-white neighborhoods—one of the key markers of wealth and status, and a sign that one had attained the dream of substantial property—depended upon a contrast with lower values in poorer, mixed, and majority-minority districts, much as the idea of whiteness itself depended upon other, subordinate racial categories. Building upon earlier transportation technologies like the streetcar, the automobile accentuated these tendencies; cars contributed to an enhanced sense of individual freedom and potency expressed through socio-spatial sequestration. From the 1920s onward, most new automotive routes led to (and catalyzed the settlement of) the hills or suburbs, areas that would long be off-limits to people of color, who were left with the older flatlands—that were separate but not equal.

Such inequities were endemic to California before the twentieth century. Oakland was founded on land that had been occupied for millennia by Native Californians: Chochenyo-speaking Ohlone peoples subsisting as hunter-gatherers and small-scale agriculturists. Starting in the late eighteenth century, their villages were pushed aside by Spanish colonialists who drew the Ohlone to newly established Christian missions, causing a demographic and cultural collapse. During the 1840s and afterward, the Mexican inheritors of the Spanish Mission Era found themselves dispossessed of the land by Anglo settlers. The lands they had taken from the Ohlone and used primarily for cattle ranching were divvied up by speculators for profits in farming and urban activities. Earlier genocidal practices against the Ohlone continued, including the almost complete eradication of their villages and burial mounds. Their survivors, alongside Mexican Californios, were consigned to low-paying jobs, segregated residence in barrios, and negligible opportunities for advancement. East Asian Californians from China, Japan, the Philippines, and elsewhere, who came during the Gold Rush and afterward, found themselves similarly oppressed and segregated, their competitive actions within the marketplace thwarted by legal statutes and outright violence. Chinese immigrants occupied a social stratum in California somewhat comparable to blacks in the Jim Crow South, forced to pay extra taxes, denied the right to testify in court, and after 1882, subject to the harsh provisions of the Chinese Exclusion Act.

Ideologies of white supremacy saw this imperium as just and rational.

Peoples from lands outside Europe were products of less advanced or even primitive cultures and, accordingly, best subordinated to white leadership and example. Whites were insiders. Others were outsiders. A racialized blueprint to land settlement was in place before the urban development of modern Oakland, and operational thereafter.

Black migrants arrived to California from the South in large numbers only during the military buildup leading to the Second World War. From that point on, demographic change was swift. By 1980, Oakland had become almost majority black and one of the centers of black culture and politics in the United States. Due to their numbers, blacks represented a threat to white hegemony. Throughout much of the century, the town was torn asunder by its white political establishment into two parts: one white and one black and minority; one wealthier and one poorer; one whose communities were restricted and one whose were nonrestricted; one, blue- and green-lined, endowed with finance and improvements, and one, redlined, deprived of those advantages. Racist practices colored all aspects of housing, employment, criminal justice, and education, as blacks were prevented from attaining the kinds of safety, jobs, neighborhoods, and routes of upward mobility that whites took for granted. Black residents had the unenviable distinction of police harassment and recurrent housing dispossession, worsened by government programs like highway building and urban renewal. The disappointment upon finding out that Oakland, that California, wasn't altogether different from the South, that urbanization instigated by business growth and new transportation networks wasn't breaking down ghetto walls, accounts for the town's gestation of political radicalism and community activism.

In theory, expanding transportation infrastructures should have opened up more of Oakland for all Oaklanders. In practice, those technological advances repositioned segregationist real estate practices across dispersed geographies. As streetcars gave way to automobiles and buses and later freeways and BART, the geographical lines between white and nonwhite, established and newcomer, changed in turn. Over the twentieth century's first half, the town's relatively small (under 10 percent) minority populations lived mostly in the nineteenth-century city alongside poorer whites, while more affluent whites settled in new, racially restricted, streetcar subdivisions along the lower hills. From the 1940s through the 1970s, amid an automotive-enabled exodus of whites to suburban locales within and without the town, and in an era of negligible immigration, blacks were able to leave the West Oakland ghetto and settle across the North and East Oakland flatlands. From the 1980s through the early twenty-first century, immigrants from East Asia, Latin America, and East Africa established themselves across those flatlands while white migrants (most called gentrifiers on the basis of their higher incomes and education levels) found their way to practically all parts of the town.

· · · · · · ·

While my methodology for assessing city-making in Oakland stresses the relationship, with respect to land access and urban development, between transportation innovations and racist practices, several other parameters of analysis are crucial to understanding the unique path Oakland took during these times. To start off, the proximity of the town to the city worked to both the former's favor and disservice. Oakland's stretches of flat land on the continental side of the bay across from peninsular San Francisco led to it becoming a transportation hub. From 1869, when the nation's first transcontinental railroad reached its western terminus at Oakland Point, the town was a center of networks enabling economic development for the region. About a century later, the Bay Area's freeways and rapid transit corridors met in Oakland; BART's four lines cross downtown; several interstate and state highways merge and diverge just east of the Bay Bridge. Because of the considerable amount of land devoted to right-of-ways, though, these passageways did not always benefit Oakland's citizens: rather, they often cleaved and debased the neighborhoods they passed through. Their evolution underscores Oakland's variable status within a rapidly growing, sprawling, and polycentric region, contending with its closest neighbors, the far-flung suburbs and, most of all, San Francisco.

"The smoke of Oakland filled the western sky with haze and murk, while beyond, across the bay, they could see the first winking lights of San Francisco," wrote Jack London in *The Valley of the Moon* (1913). Here the Oakland-bred writer described a journey westward down from the Contra Costa hills into the checkerboard of fields and towns that made up Oakland, coming upon a view of the manufacturing waterfront just short of the pot of gold at the end of the rainbow, the flatlands in sight of the Golden Gate but anchored on the continent and overshadowed by its glamorous neighbor. Oakland's smoky skies, proof of its bustling factories, showed that it was not a satisfied second city but a relentless competitor, convinced that its expanses of flat land and transportation connections would lead to eventual preeminence. Its leaders equated progress with equaling or overtaking the far larger and wealthier city across the bay. They took immeasurable satisfaction in becoming the dominant Bay Area container port and in sporting, for decades, more major league teams than San Francisco.

If Oakland never counted many more than 400,000 residents, it consistently punched above its weight. Because it became the center of the populous East Bay, no city of its size in the United States attained as big a reputation: in politics, business, and sports. But as time went on, Oakland's rivalry with San Francisco could lead it to unrealistic goals. Fisherman's Wharf became a tourist mecca in the city; the town's retort, Jack London Square, never coalesced. The BART rail system catalyzed a boom of office construction in downtown San Francisco; Oakland's attempts to mirror that success fell short.

Part of the reason lay in the fact that the town was thwarted in its efforts to grow larger, unable to annex nearby East Bay cities and forge a greater Oakland. Its relationship with those adjacent places nonetheless proved pivotal. A small swath of the lower hills, Piedmont, incorporated as an independent municipality entirely surrounded by Oakland. Many of the town's business elite resided in the well-off enclave, gaining from its excellent services while not contributing nearly enough to Oakland's civic improvement. Berkeley, the university city to Oakland's north, cultivated a vibrant cultural and political scene that profoundly influenced its neighbor: the Arts and Crafts and Modern movements in architecture; environmentalism with respect to parks, creeks, and the bay; the creation of regional agencies targeted to functions like water supply; the student-led Free Speech and anti–Vietnam War protest movements; lifestyle and gastronomic trends, from Zen Buddhism to California cuisine. After midcentury, the suburbs of Alameda and Contra Costa Counties drew Oakland's residents, industries, and stores; over the final decades, tiny once-industrial Emeryville, wedged between Oakland and Berkeley, turned itself into the inner East Bay's suburb-style shopping hub.

Analogous to Los Angeles, its larger and longtime industrial rival on the Pacific Coast, Oakland operated during those times as a Rust Belt city in the Sun Belt. Deindustrialization hit Oakland hard. Manufacturing plants shut down or relocated out of town. Swaths of the city corroded. The once-humming flatland corridors began to resemble downtrodden midwestern cities like Detroit. During those same times, however, while most of California and the Bay Area continued its virtual nonstop growth, other parts of Oakland benefited, as evidenced by a flurry of deluxe lakeside apartment buildings and mile after mile of hillside houses and planned unit developments that could be mistaken for nearby affluent Marin County. Again, race relations drove this contrast; the Rust Belt of laid-off factory workers and declining neighborhood quality was concentrated in the city's flatland neighborhoods populated largely by black and other minority residents; the town's Sun Belt of white-collar salaries and bay views was a reality for the whiter hill districts. In the novel *Humpty Dumpty in Oakland*, posthumously published in 1986, Philip K. Dick describes a white businessman visiting a black realtor in search of a property for a used car business: "Her specialty was business property in the non-restricted—he added in his mind, *run-down*—part of Oakland...What was a used-car lot, if not the embodiment of non-restricted Oakland?"

For the first three-quarters of the twentieth century, the city's movers and shakers lusted for growth—at almost any cost. The adoption of land-use zoning in the 1930s encouraged greater density and classified a disproportionate amount of land as commercial and industrial. Even when industry faltered, many of Oakland's business leaders paradoxically viewed the suburbs as fertile territory for industrial growth: despite their financial and political independence. But starting earlier, other public entities—the Port of Oakland, the East Bay Regional Park District, the State of California—augmented the private sector's historic control over urban development. Franklin D. Roosevelt's New Deal, Dwight D. Eisenhower's National System of Interstate and Defense Highways, and Lyndon B. Johnson's Great Society brought about groundbreaking transportation infrastructure, residential complexes, civic buildings, and parklands. Their immense scale was highly disruptive, felling thousands of buildings and forcing tens of thousands of residents to relocate.

Through this period, the leading local actors in the fashioning of Oakland's built environment were almost always white and often Republican businessmen with an outsized role in politics. Building the physical city was an elite affair—private entrepreneurs or governmental entities with the power and purse-strings to plan projects, buy land, finance buildings, secure permits, and see matters through to construction. The vast majority of building projects discussed in this book were realized in this top-down manner. In the century's final quarter, this building culture began to democratize. Under pressure from community activists, the federal government grew sensitive to demands for involvement in future development. Black Democrats were elected to the city council and mayor's office and took up leading positions in city agencies as well as the port. Nonprofit associations, neighborhood groups, and concerned citizens took larger roles, addressing underrepresented communities, amending proposed projects—even as the town's business activity cratered.

I structure the narrative of *Hella Town* around urban functions: transportation infrastructure, workplace, housing, commerce, parks, and civic attractions. The first two chapters, Part I, take up the period between 1890 and 1945. "Streetcar Stratification" tells the story of how electric traction streetcars spawned subdivisions and commercial arterials across town segmented by class and race; at the same time, the meeting of streetcar lines downtown created conditions for intense commercial activities and a fiction of a unified city. "Industrial Powerhouse" looks into how Oakland became one of the nation's larger manufacturing centers, home to both resource-based businesses and advanced industry.

The middle three chapters, Part II, analyze efforts over the course of the twentieth century to secure parklands, craft world-class civic structures, and modernize and expand the road infrastructure for automobiles. "Space for Automobiles" lays out the bridges, tunnels, street reconfigurations, and mass transit retrenchments that made up the vehicular conquest of urban transportation. "The Politics of Parks" scrutinizes why a growing Oakland never built a large urban park accessible to its citizens, and how the East Bay Regional Park District endowed the town with expansive semi-wilderness parks. "Major League Venue" looks at how civic complexes, museums, sporting arenas, and concert halls vaulted it into the national limelight, while at the same time sidelining the involvement of minority communities.

The final five chapters, Part III, concentrate on the period after the Second World War when governmental involvement in urban development ramped up and systemic racism continued to play a leading role in city-making. "The Promise and the Reality of Freeways and BART" describes the formation of the town's rapid circulation networks and the consequences of their reorientation of mobility from neighborhood and city to individual dwelling unit and region. "In the Wake of Deindustrialization" highlights the evisceration of the city's manufacturing economy, racial employment disparities, and the business community's fixation on making Oakland a largely white-collar logistics center for global communication and trade—especially via the Port of Oakland. "Housing Injustice" explores the divergent tracks of affluent whites and poorer blacks and other people of color with respect to residential opportunities. "Downtown Renewal and Ruin" interrogates the related aim of business leaders to upmarket the central business district for high-rise office buildings and a huge regional mall. Finally, "Shopping Centers and Storefront Streets" explores Oakland's mixed efforts to keep up with the suburbs by building car-oriented retail complexes and, later, its more successful revival of older streetcar strips amid an influx of immigrants and gentrifiers.

As Oakland recovered from the Great Recession of 2008–10, it became an up-and-coming place, as discussed in the Coda. Its natural beauty—a unique tree canopy of towering conifers and exotic palms, a varied topography offering vistas of mountains, waterways, and cityscape—was recognized widely. So too was its mild Mediterranean climate, mid-sized urbanity, idiosyncratic neighborhoods, and relative affordability. Construction cranes soon crowded the skyline. San Franciscans flocked in. Media reports, movies, and books covered the revitalization, but pointed out the displacement and resentment attendant to it. In *There There* (2018),

Tommy Orange follows a BART train as it courses toward Fruitvale: "the graffitied apartment walls and abandoned houses, warehouses, and auto body shops appear, loom in the train window, stubbornly resist like deadweight all of Oakland's new development." Reactive to anything resembling the midcentury era of massive disruption and dislocation, other Oaklanders adopted stances on development pioneered earlier in Berkeley and San Francisco—low-impact visions rooted more in the village than the metropolis.

The facts emerging recently from the ground, the rumors and retorts wafting in from the media, followed a momentous and tumultuous twentieth century. Throughout, waves of people came and went, buildings rose and fell, neighborhoods transitioned. The town was shot in different directions, parts successfully gaining something greater, other parts finding their hopes deflated. What Gertrude Stein saw of Oakland in 1935, what any one of us observes of a city at a given moment, is but an ill-lit fragment of vast processes of historical change, the tip of what has happened. *Hella Town: Oakland's History of Development and Disruption* seeks to illuminate and explain aspects of the iceberg beneath.

Part I

1 Streetcar Stratification

In 1919, the Fred T. Wood Company advertised lots for a promising 126-home subdivision, Lakeshore Terrace, nestled in the foothills just above Lake Merritt and a couple of miles from downtown. Like all of Oakland, the land had undergone fateful changes over the prior century. The Spanish Empire had granted much of what we now know as Oakland to Luis Peralta, who later passed his 45,000-acre Rancho San Antonio on to his sons. After the annexation of Alta California, then a part of Mexico, to the United States in 1847, the Peralta family lost most of their holdings to Anglo-Americans. Toward century's end, Lewis Leonard Bradbury, who made his wealth in Mexican gold mining and California real estate, purchased the tract that came to be called Lakeshore Terrace; maintaining homes in Oakland and Southern California, Bradbury erected the famous Bradbury Building in Los Angeles, which opened a few months after his death in 1892.

Amid a building boom that coincided with America's entry into the First World War, Bradbury's oak-studded grasslands were ripe for development. Fred T. Wood was a California native who had arrived in Oakland in 1904 to work in real estate. He modeled his subdivision on an earlier, nearby effort, Lakewood Park. In a brochure, we read that the latter's

Figure 2. Lakewood Park tract. The intersection of Rosal and Balfour Avenues, across Lakeshore Avenue and alongside the upcoming Lakeshore Terrace, 1918. Photo courtesy of Oakland Public Library, Oakland History Room.

property values had doubled and tripled since development began there four years earlier. Logically, Lakeshore Terrace would attain similar success as a subdivision of choice for higher-income residents: "Lakeshore Terrace is in the heart of the head-of-the-lake district, an established residence section of the highest type." The brochure extolls the fact that the south-facing slopes are protected from north winds, affording maximum sunshine and the warmest climate, as well as perfect drainage, and that the approach on Lakeshore Avenue, a broad boulevard of easy grade, is shaded by plane trees. Since Wood purchased the land at half its assessed value, he claimed to have added improvements of the finest kind: streets endowed with cement gutters, curbs, sidewalks, sewers, water mains, and gas and electric conduits. To top it off, we are informed that a streetcar runs from Lakeshore Terrace to downtown, and a Key Route interurban, whisking one to San Francisco in 40 minutes, is practically at the subdivision's doorstep.

Lakeshore Terrace was part of the greatest groundswell of residential construction in Oakland's history. During the first third of the twentieth century, the country estates of Oakland's lower hills and farms of its flatlands were recast into houses and businesses by real estate entrepreneurs like Fred T. Wood. The engines behind this transformation were streetcars running on steel rails and powered electrically by overhead wires. Streetcar service freed people to reside farther from the city center in neighborhoods of their choice—to an extent.[1] The new subdivisions would be highly stratified along class and racial lines. Affluent whites had the lion's share of the new dwelling opportunities, while poorer whites and people of color were limited to older buildings and districts. Upper-middle-class subdivisions were designed and advertised differently than working-class subdivisions. They were located farther from industry, set apart through pastoral aesthetic traits, and linked to office jobs in downtown Oakland or San Francisco. Legal barriers fortified their exclusivity. Lakeshore Terrace came with "full building and race restrictions." Only people of Caucasian descent were allowed to purchase homes here and in most upscale Oakland neighborhoods.

Streetcars unglued the diverse functions of Oakland's downtown. The electrified transit system allowed residents and businesses to relocate to more favorable and spacious locales. While homes rose up in the foothills and remote flatlands, industries followed the waterfront corridors north and south of downtown and shopping strips spread along the streetcar lines radiating out to these new areas. Downtown transformed into a largely commercial entity. Office buildings, department stores, hotels, and movie palaces were the new components of a dense zone of business operations and consumer attractions. For a time, downtown's increased density and vibrancy produced the impression of a unified city. But hotels and department stores too catered to stratified markets.

Long before comprehensive planning and zoning regulations came into effect in the 1930s, distinct functional and social sections characterized streetcar Oakland: an industrial waterfront; a sea of houses across the flatlands and lower hills, divided according to class and racial lines; along the transit lines penetrating each of these zones, commercial strips; an unprecedented, intense urbanity downtown amid the streetcar system's crossing points. This stratified cityscape would persist and even intensify after 1945. Other transportation improvements (e.g., automobiles, freeways, BART), coupled with other, racially based discriminatory practices (e.g., redlining, urban redevelopment, white migration to the suburbs), continued to divide the town into zones marked by function, class, and race.

ELECTRIC TRACTION

In the years after its founding in 1852, Oakland slowly grew into a village on an estuary of San Francisco Bay. In 1860, more than a decade after the Gold Rush began, only 1,543 people resided there. Then, in 1869, the town became the Pacific terminus of the nation's first transcontinental railroad, an almost 2,000-mile line connecting California to the eastern rail network at Council Bluffs, Iowa. Rail met sail at Oakland Point, the foot of 7th Street in West Oakland, from where passengers completed their train journey to San Francisco on transbay ferries. Industries, which we will discuss in the next chapter, gravitated to the West Oakland rail yards and shipping wharves, and Oakland soon passed Stockton and Sacramento to become California's second-largest city after San Francisco—counting 34,555 residents by 1880. Growth centers succeeded one another; first downtown, then West Oakland, and later other parts of the city. Villages developed on stops of the Central (and later Southern) Pacific railway: Clinton, Fruitvale, Melrose, Fitchburg, Elmhurst—what would later be called East Oakland.[2] Yet aside from Clinton, they were for many years too small to be called either industrial towns or commuter suburbs.[3]

If steam railroads propelled long-distance travel and trade as well as commuter suburbs, the iron horses were impractical for intra-city commutes, and hence intensive city building. Streets could hardly bear the weight of trains, whose engines produced noise, smoke, and sparks that were both a nuisance and threat to nearby structures. The time it took speeding trains to come to a full stop so people could disembark resulted in stations spaced at least one to two miles apart. The train corridor was best situated in a separate right-of-way. Other means of transportation would be needed for city-making.

Through the early 1890s, most travel within Oakland was either by foot, on horseback, or in horse-drawn vehicles. Among the latter, most prominent were omnibuses, a version of stagecoaches, later converted to trams running along iron or steel rails and allowing for faster speeds and smoother rides. The horse-trams traveled four to five miles per hour, a little faster than walking. Nonetheless, they pushed out the boundaries of the walking city. Eighteen miles of lines of horse-car lines were built from downtown to West Oakland and Clinton.

San Francisco pioneered and made extensive use of steam-powered cable cars, a mechanized advance over horse-drawn omnibuses. Aside from a couple of brief experiments in 1889 and 1890, though, cable car technology, practical only for straight runs, was too inflexible and expensive for the flatter terrain being developed at lower densities in Oakland. Instead, electric streetcars (also called trolleys) would push Oakland's next phase of urban transportation. A couple of decades into the harnessing of electricity, Frank Sprague, a naval officer, had linked electric traction motors on individual streetcars to overhead wires that sucked power from electric generating stations.[4] His system debuted in Richmond, Virginia, in 1888. The streetcars glided at an average speed of 10 miles per hour and could reach 15 miles per hour, three times faster than horse-drawn trams.[5] Using the motor as a brake, they could easily decelerate. They were fine at climbing and descending hills, an important advantage over the horse-car.[6]

Electric traction streetcars took America by storm. In 1890, two years after Sprague's initial run, 154 electric street railway systems operated on 1,263 miles of track, more than half equipped by his firm. By 1902, 22,000 miles of electrified streetcars accommodated more passengers than steam railroads.[7] From 1890 to 1920, annual trolley ridership in the nation grew from 2 billion to 15.5 billion.[8] A 1902 editorial in the weekly New York magazine, *The Independent*, didn't hold back: "We are entering the trolley age. We shall speedily develop the trolley system to reach every section of our hill and valley homes. These systems will spider-web the counties and the States and bring the whole country into a network of intercommunication."[9] In *Streetcar Suburbs*, Sam Bass Warner highlighted the horse-car and electric streetcar's impact on urban geography in Boston. Between 1870 and 1900, as Warner tells us, streetcars produced a new kind of fragmented city, one split between the old center and radiating rings of industrial and commercial subcenters and residential suburbs.[10] Once their transit was electrified, cities began to sprawl up to 10 miles in every direction.[11]

Oakland was no exception. The city's first streetcar line began operations on Grove Street in 1889. A year later, the Oakland Consolidated Railway debuted and, by 1894, there were 98 miles of electric railway.[12] Around a dozen separate transit companies sprang up, all of them private, and many duplicating lines: Oakland Railroad Company; Oakland and Berkeley Rapid Transit Company; San Pablo Line; Oakland, Brooklyn, and Fruitvale Railway. Still, the costs of laying track and wires, building power stations, and assembling rolling stock encouraged centralized administration, and one of the town's leading businessmen figured out the advantages that would accrue to economies of scale.

Francis Marion Smith—known as Borax Smith—began to buy up companies and consolidate lines. By 1902, the miner turned business mogul had unified Oakland's streetcars into the 75.4-mile system of the Oakland Transit Consolidated. His story embodies Oakland's streetcar-driven development. Born in Wisconsin, Smith moved west to prospect for minerals and, by 1881, when he settled in Oakland, had amassed a fortune from borax mining. Smith set about using his newfound wealth for building projects. In 1891, he erected a mansion for himself on 53 acres along Park Boulevard between E. 22nd and E. 28th Streets, a gaggle of gables, turrets, and chimneys in the Queen Anne style. Two years later, he expanded his Pacific Coast Borax Company refinery in Alameda, hiring Ernest Ransome to construct the first reinforced concrete building in the United States.[13] Ransome, an English-born engineer, had earlier patented a crucial, twisted spiral rod to prevent steel reinforcements from losing their grip as concrete hardened.[14]

In 1895, Smith branched out, forming The Realty Syndicate (TRS) with Frank C. Havens. Soon one of country's largest real estate operations, through the early teens TRS came to control 13,000 acres in the lower and upper hills from Berkeley to East Oakland. Originally from New York, Havens had arrived in California with ambitions as far and wide as Smith's. In 1902, he had a mansion built in Piedmont, soon to be a separate and almost entirely residential city encircled by Oakland. Between 1910 and 1914, his Mahogany Eucalyptus and Land Company planted millions of blue gum trees along the high ridge of the East Bay, envisioning the creation of a 14-mile stretch of eucalyptus tree farms.[15] As it turned out, gum trees under two and a half feet in diameter were useless for timber. After only two years, they were abandoned to grow into fire hazards. Havens likely used "Mahogany" in the company name because he had fantasized that the valuable tropical tree would grow in temperate California.

Together, Smith and Havens crafted an ambitious four-part plan for transportation, residential, and industrial development. Their aim was to make piles of money from city building. Their efforts anticipated many aspects of comprehensive city planning: the interlocking of building and infrastructural projects, and the encouragement of their mutually reinforcing effects. The first step was to acquire and consolidate diverse street railway companies into a single system serving Oakland and the inner East Bay cities. Next, given the poor quality of passenger service across the bay to San Francisco, Smith and Havens forged a new transbay interurban/ferry service. Then, building upon the streetcar and interurban operations, and using the model of Henry Edwards Huntington's Los Angeles Railway as a promoter of suburban land development, they employed TRS for the subdivision and sale of residential lots along the streetcar and interurban routes. Finally, they acquired tidelands around their interurban/ferry terminal for a grandiose warehouse and factory district.[16] In the first three instances, Smith and Havens succeeded beyond their wildest dreams. In the fourth, their efforts hardly progressed, but set forth a model for turning marshlands along the bay into industrial zones.

Until 1903, the steam trains of the Southern Pacific railroad (SP) monopolized the important transbay service between the Alameda and Oakland wharves and San Francisco's ferry terminal; the Oakland mole was the busiest railroad terminal in the West. That year, Smith launched competing electric interurban trains: the San Francisco, Oakland and San Jose Railway. The company changed names several times, and from 1923 onward became known as the Key System Transit Company. Interurbans, popularized in the Midwest at the turn of the century, were larger, heavier, and faster than streetcars.[17] They could easily be linked together into multiple-car trains on busier routes. Although they traveled at only two-thirds the speed of steam railroads, they came four to five times more frequently and did not require large stations or separation from the urban fabric.[18]

On San Francisco Bay tidelands just south of the Emeryville city line,

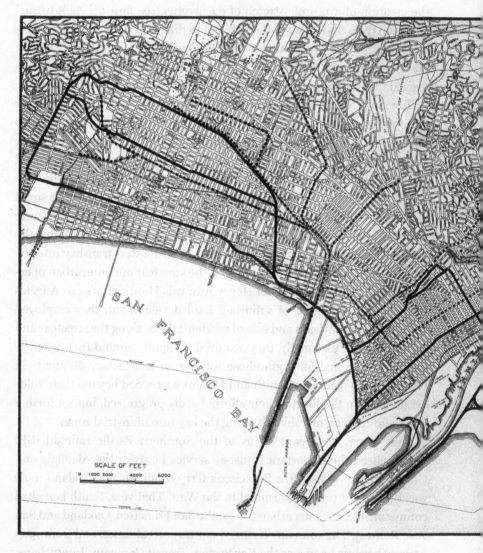

Map 3. East Bay Interurban Lines. Southern Pacific Company and Key System Transit Company lines, 1927. SOURCE: Wikimedia Commons. Creative Commons Attribution Non Commercial Share Alike 4.0 International License.

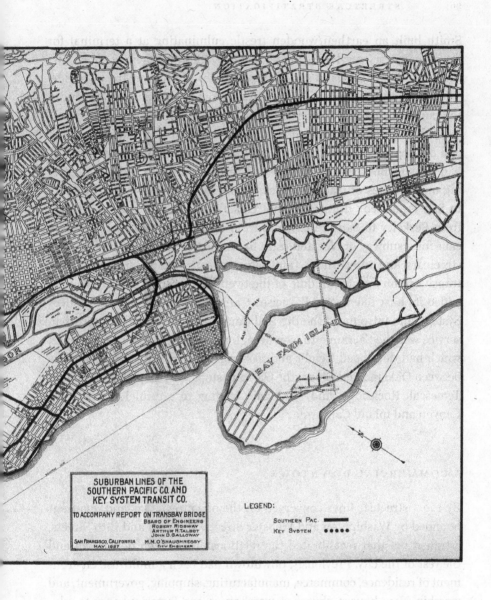

SUBURBAN LINES OF THE
SOUTHERN PACIFIC CO. AND
KEY SYSTEM TRANSIT CO.

TO ACCOMPANY REPORT ON TRANSBAY BRIDGE
BOARD OF ENGINEERS
ROBERT RIDGWAY
ARTHUR N.TALBOT
JOHN D.GALLOWAY

SAN FRANCISCO, CALIFORNIA   M.M.O'SHAUGHNESSY
MAY, 1927   CITY ENGINEER

LEGEND:

SOUTHERN PAC. ▬▬▬
KEY SYSTEM ●●●●●

Smith built an earthen/wooden trestle culminating at a terminal for interurban/ferry service.[19] It extended 3.6 miles into the bay, much further than the SP Oakland and Alameda moles, shortening the ferry ride. The inaugural interurban line of 16 cars ran to Berkeley and reduced the commute to San Francisco from 58 to 38 minutes. Annual cross-bay ridership increased from 12.7 million in 1901 to 20 million by the end of 1903.[20] Between 1904 and 1911, Smith opened five more interurban lines to Berkeley, Piedmont, and various parts of Oakland, operating on 101 miles of track. He focused the interurbans on the commute to San Francisco's downtown, not Oakland's. It became as easy to get from Berkeley to San Francisco as from Berkeley to Oakland;[21] despite calls for a subway or elevated train to connect the two East Bay centers, streetcars and interurbans (and later buses) remained the sole mass transit option into the middle of the twentieth century. In 1911, SP electrified its East Bay to San Francisco transit lines in response to the Key System, and introduced the Big Red Cars.[22] Another, smaller interurban service was the Sacramento Northern, formed in 1929 from earlier lines, which had developed freight and passenger service on a 183-mile route between Oakland and Chico; the Oakland stops were at 40th and Shafter, Temescal, Rockridge, and Montclair, leading to a tunnel at Shepherd Canyon and inland California.[23]

A COMMERCIAL DOWNTOWN

By 1900, streetcar lines converged on the downtown Oakland quadrant bounded by Washington and Webster Streets, and 12th and 16th Streets, a transit net that recalibrated the relationship between downtown and the rest of the city. Previously, downtown had been a multi-use environment of residence, commerce, manufacturing, shipping, government, and worship. Now, houses, churches, warehouses, and factories began to relocate into more homogenous zones on undeveloped land beyond downtown: single-family residential districts; apartment clusters; industrial swaths along the waterfront and railroad tracks. Those same transit lines enabling suburbanization also facilitated greater numbers of Oakland and East Bay residents to work, shop, and entertain themselves downtown, in

Figure 3. Downtown Esquire Theater. "3" Streetcar on San
Pablo Avenue near 17th Street, Tribune Tower in distance,
1943. Photo courtesy of Oakland Public Library, Oakland
History Room.

what became known, due to its increasingly commercial character, as the
central business district.

Streetcars set in motion a two-pronged form of urban development.
Dwellings and manufacturing plants spread horizontally across the
breadth of Oakland. Downtown, commercial structures shot up vertically.

Office buildings, department stores, hotels, and movie theaters were
recent phenomena, dynamic products of an industrializing economy.
Space for administering manufacturing plants, farms, mines, and transportation operations had once been limited and located on-site. In the
decades after the Civil War, escalating economies of production laid the
groundwork for modern business practices, creating far larger company
operations—the modern corporation—and independent professional
services that employed secretaries, clerks, managers, directors, lawyers,
draftsmen, designers, engineers, editors, and reporters. Likewise, middle-

men, jobbers, factors, commission agents, importers, and exporters grew
in importance, providing transshipment links between farmers and manufacturers, rural stores and industries abroad and in large cities. Bankers,
bookkeepers, accountants, and insurers also handled increasingly complex
financial transactions. The downtown office building provided space for
these activities, the cost of its land purchase and construction measured
against potential rental income. New infrastructural networks—railroads,
streetcars, telegraph and telephone wires, improved mail delivery—facilitated the emergence of the office district by linking office buildings to
manufacturing plants along waterfront and railroad corridors. The first
Industrial Revolution of steam engines and railroads had broken the
home/workshop into geographically separate dwelling and work spheres.
Now, the second Industrial Revolution, driven by electrification, the internal combustion engine, and advances in metals and machining, spawned
distinct geographical zones for production and administration, dividing
work between blue- and white-collar jobs.

As the city began to function differently, its appearance changed.
Churches had dominated Oakland's skyline since the 1860s: the spires of
First Presbyterian on Franklin Street and those of First Congregational
on 12th and Clay Streets, both reaching over 100 feet in height. From afar,
the city's commercial buildings barely registered, as they were but one to
three stories.

In 1905, Oakland's first office highrise, the Union Savings Bank, rose at
1300 Broadway. Whereas older buildings were constructed with load-bear-
ing walls, architect Walter Matthews—who designed Borax Smith's osten-
tatious home—built up to 11 stories and 160 feet by using a steel frame,
a first for the city, and serviced by elevators. Soon after the Earthquake
and Fire of 1906, 11 Oakland banks formed the Oakland Clearing House,
an attempt to ease the expected growth of business in the downtown district.[24] Banks henceforth impelled downtown's skyward development. In
1908, when the First National Bank relocated along Broadway, from 10th
to 14th Streets, its new building reached seven stories.[25] This time, architect Llewellyn Dutton employed a reinforced concrete frame, another constructional milestone. Shaped like a flatiron to correspond to the place in
the city grid where San Pablo Avenue veered off at a diagonal to the north,
First National Bank Building anchored the busy streetcar intersection that

would become the center of downtown.[26] The new bank/office buildings not only towered above the older cityscape, their stone and terra-cotta claddings contrasted with older wooden-frame construction, portending an era of permanence and prosperity.[27]

In subsequent years, other tall buildings crowded the urban core.[28] City government joined the skyscraper age. Oakland has had five city halls, and by 1909 the fourth iteration, a ramshackle wooden affair at 14th and Washington Streets, was scheduled for replacement on the same site. The next year, a nationwide competition drew 28 entries and a unanimous decision for New York architects Palmer & Hornbostel. In 1914, Oakland's final city hall was completed as a 320-foot skyscraper, the first of its kind in the nation and the tallest building in the city until 1959—a testament to the town's sense of itself as a regional powerhouse independent from San Francisco. Its architects married the form of a monumental civic building with that of an office tower: a low-rise, three-story base contained judicial and legislative functions, while the high-rise shaft served administrative offices and was topped by a thin, distinctive tower and cupola.[29] Although other distinctive skyscrapers were added to Oakland's skyline in this initial period of highrise construction—notably, the 22-story Tribune Tower at 401 13th Street—Oakland's downtown remained smaller than San Francisco's, both in the number of tall buildings, their height, and the amount of office space. San Francisco was home to the headquarters of California's great mining, shipping, transportation, agricultural, and financial companies. Even industries maintaining major operations in Oakland, such as Del Monte and Southern Pacific, headquartered on the west side of the bay.

The streetcar nexus generated other high-intensity functions downtown. Social clubs (Athenian-Nile, Bellevue, Elks) and dance halls (Sweet's Ballroom, Rose Room Ballroom) multiplied across downtown. So did venues for groceries. Around 1917, Oakland's wholesale terminal market was given permanent, indoor quarters in a group of buildings designed by Charles McCall, who used canopies, truss roofs, and clerestories to cover and light the rows of wooden produce stalls.[30] A somewhat forgotten aspect of Oakland's commercial past were the numerous food markets feeding off this wholesale district at Franklin and 3rd Streets. They included the Produce Exchange Commission Market (1903)

at 11th and Webster Streets; Housewives Food Market (1908), which
moved from 6th and Clay Streets to 825 Clay Street in 1952; Oakland
Free Market (1917) at 9th and Clay Streets (later Swan's Marketplace);
Capwell's Central Market (1927) at Telegraph Avenue and 19th Street; and
Twentieth Century Market (1928) at 13th and Jefferson Streets. Drawing
streetcar customers from around the city, the market halls represented a
brief period where residents of outer Oakland neighborhoods shopped for
food downtown. They were also the last gasp of the old traditions of the
bazaar and its system of individual proprietors. Change was on the way.
Already by the 1920s, the new American model of centralized ownership
and single point of purchase would lead to the onset of the supermarket
age, with Oakland a leading force as discussed in chapter 10, "Shopping
Centers and Storefront Streets."[31]

Retail stores in pre-industrial times served a population who produced
much of their own food, furnishings, and clothing. The transformation of
the home into a purely domestic space and the onset of wage labor at the
workplace brought about an upsurge in urban consumption, which drove
the creation of specialty boutiques as well as department stores: multifaceted emporia that sold clothing in addition to drygoods and household
items. The downtown blocks of Washington south of 14th Street filled with
small shops and mid-sized department stores: J. C. Penney's, National
Dollar Stores, Money Back Smith's, Hale Brothers. In a phenomenon that
would repeat itself many times into the twentieth century, growing sales
volume led to a demand for larger, modernized stores as well as aims to
escape the congestion on Washington Street. Oakland's two largest mass
retailers—Kahn's and Capwell's—illustrate the steady northward movements of the retail district.[32]

In 1879, Israel Kahn, a German-Jewish immigrant from Darmstadt,
built Kahn's Department Store at 10th and Broadway; in 1893, his sons
relocated to 12th and Washington; and in 1912, they rebuilt once again,
hiring Charles W. Dickey to design a six-story store at 16th and Broadway,
a site basically considered out in the country.[33] Epitomizing the grandeur
embellished on department store retailing at the time, the latest Kahn's
featured a magisterial 120-foot-high, glass elliptical dome in an atrium
at its center.[34] Such interior spaces are what made the department store
into one of the cornerstones of modern urbanity. Like cathedrals of an

earlier era, a trip to the department store was a voyage into a world of heightened spaciousness and precious objects—albeit, in this case, goods for purchase.

Capwell's, Oakland's largest department store, pushed the retail zone even further north.[35] Michigan-born H. C. Capwell had built his first store at 10th and Washington Streets in 1889, calling it the Lace House; in 1912, his business, now called H. C. Capwell's, relocated to an imposing, five-story building at Clay and 14th Streets next to City Hall. Capwell was a prominent Oakland businessman, helping to found the Security Bank and Trust and later serving as president of the city's Board of Trade and Chamber of Commerce. In 1929, after a merger with San Francisco's Emporium, Capwell's was on the move again, leaping past Kahn's to the corner of Broadway and 20th Street. Ernest Van Vleck, architect of the earlier Lord and Taylor and Saks Fifth Avenue stores on New York's Fifth Avenue, designed a megastore, six stories high and containing over 600,000 square feet of floor space; at the time, it was the largest department store west of the Mississippi River. Especially for women, going to Capwell's by streetcar meant going to a safer city within the larger city, part of a day spent shopping for dresses or housewares, dining, or socializing. The basement hosted a luncheonette with pink tile walls, a post office, and a bargain store, while the mezzanine offered travel and repair services. Four stories of retail goods culminated in a roof garden restaurant with adjoining children's playroom. To make the trip easier, Capwell's also provided a garage for a thousand automobiles—a sign of disruptive transportation changes to come.[36]

For an American city, the erection of a large hotel cemented its status as a cosmopolitan center. Hotels boasted high-class restaurants, travel agents, banqueting halls, and meeting rooms. They introduced technological innovations that would later find their way into apartments and houses: the elevator, the telephone, the private bathroom off the bedroom. In 1875, the 120-foot-tall Palace Hotel and its 755 guest rooms had brought this status to San Francisco. Yet no such grand hotel was built in downtown Oakland until 1912, when the 500-room Hotel Oakland opened at 260 13th Street, halfway between the lake and the city's center at 14th and Broadway. Designed by Bliss and Faville, the eight-story building's twin cupola-towers were the first clearly identifiable landmarks on the city's twentieth-century skyline. Guests entered through a large, floral courtyard and lobby covered by a barrel-vaulted ceiling. Banquet and meeting rooms functioned as the city's social, business, and political center, accommodating a stream of business and civic meetings, and hosting Charles Lindbergh and Presidents Wilson, Coolidge, Hoover, and Roosevelt.[37] In 1926, a second major hotel, the 11-story, 300-room Hotel Leamington, opened at 1800 Franklin Street, further uptown and designed by W. H. Weeks. In comparison to the Hotel Oakland, where hostelry efforts had concentrated on marble flooring and mahogany furniture, priorities had changed; the Leamington's rooms were equipped with radios and electric clocks, and the basement and sub-basement accommodated guest parking.[38]

In a time of few domestic entertainments, going to the movies amounted to a special outing. Around two-dozen movie theaters were built in and near downtown Oakland. They were equipped with concession stands, held promotional nights and giveaways, were advertised by marquees of flashing lights, and, of course, showed newsreels and one or two feature films. In terms of size and spectacle, three stood out. They featured elaborate and sometimes mysterious stone and terra-cotta facades, grand entrance lobbies, huge auditoriums, and orchestras of up to 50 musicians. In 1923, the 3,000-seat Fox Theater, designed by Weeks and Day, opened at 1730 Broadway, containing a full stage for legitimate and vaudeville theater as well as movies. Like department stores, such large theaters favored locations on the northern stretch of downtown, extending the commercial zone toward well-to-do residential districts. In 1928, the Fox chain opened an even larger, 3,200-seat theater on Telegraph Avenue and 19th Street, and the earlier Fox was renamed the Orpheum. Two years into the Great Depression, the Paramount-Publix chain opened the Paramount Theater even further north on Broadway, an architectural gem described more fully in chapter 5, "Major League Venue." Like the office buildings, department stores, and grand hotels, Oakland's movie palaces produced an impression of downtown as a place of unearthly delights, its signs and towers lit brightly at night by arrays of incandescent bulbs and neon tubing, an electrified city filled with electrifying attractions.

The downtown buildings, many embellished with terra-cotta and glazed tiles, spires, domes, and exotic ornaments, announced Oakland's arrival as a substantial city. In 1900, its population had stood at 66,960 residents; by 1910, it had more than doubled to 150,174; and by 1930, it reached 284,063. Oakland grew its population not only by attracting migrants but also by increasing in size. In 1909, the city added a vast set of lands to its south—Fruitvale, Melrose, Fitchburg, and Elmhurst—thereby almost doubling its footprint to 60.7 square miles. That was to be the last increase in landmass, however. Although Oakland and the East Bay cities resisted a 1912 attempt on the part of San Francisco to incorporate them as boroughs, its own efforts to fashion a Greater Oakland across the East Bay were similarly fought off.[39]

THE ONSET OF SPRAWL

How did streetcar Oakland expand out of the downtown? As theorized by Homer Hoyt in 1939, cities develop not in concentric rings, the model developed by Ernest Burgess, but rather in radial sectors or wedges impelled by the high-end residential, or wealth, corridor. Beginning in the central business district, where higher-income residents work, Hoyt argued that the wealth corridor followed superior transit lines toward higher ground, a pleasant (and nonindustrial) waterfront or a free and undeveloped countryside.[40] In Oakland, his theory is borne out by the movement of affluent residents from downtown along the Broadway axis to the north and the Grand Avenue axis northeast to the lower hills: in the direction of Rockridge, Piedmont, Adams Point, and other neighborhoods near Lake Merritt like Grand Lake, and away from lower-class housing, the waterfront, and industry.[41] In so doing, affluent homebuyers led the way for other types of development along the wealth corridor, including leading education institutions and places of worship.

The vectors of religious buildings correspond to the transition toward streetcar-led settlement of the foothills. In 1891, the Church of St. Francis de Sales was newly built at San Pablo Avenue and 21st Street. It succeeded St. Mary's Church, downtown at 7th and Jefferson Streets, as the largest parish church of Oakland. The new building established the Roman Catholic Church along what was then the primary, horse-car route to the expanding, flatland residential districts of North Oakland. Over the next two decades, however, electric streetcars allowed the wealth corridor to relocate north-eastward, toward the lake and lower hills. Numerous churches and Temple Sinai, a Jewish synagogue, left the downtown along those new wealth corridors on Broadway, Harrison Street, and Grand Avenue.

Apartment houses for more prosperous Oaklanders paralleled these religious movements. Two types of buildings epitomized the phenomenon: garden apartments, two to four stories in height, for the middle class; and along the lake, highrises for the upper class.[42] Between 1908 and 1916, more than a dozen buildings rose up—including, in 1913, the Raymond at 1457–61 Alice Street, the city's first brick apartment house.[43] By 1922, after a wide avenue was completed from Oak to Harrison Streets,[44] development inched right up to the lake and become grander in stature, including the eight-story Regillus, completed in 1924 at 200 Lakeside Drive. Other landmark apartments rose around the lake: the seven-story, Lombard-style Edgemere Manor, or Peacock Building, at 2122 Lakeshore Avenue (1927); the 15-story, art deco Bellevue-Staten in Adams Point (1930). Most notable was a 12-story Spanish-Churrigueresque edifice at 244 Lakeside Drive. Completed in 1927, it has been referred to as the Bechtel Building after its owner Stephen D. Bechtel Sr., longtime president of the Bechtel Corporation.[45] From 1933 to 1960, while residing in Oakland, Bechtel directed the company's worldwide operations from an office in San Francisco. His (and his son's) projects included the Hoover Dam; the San Francisco–Oakland Bay Bridge; a pipeline through the Yukon Territory and Alaska; and the BART system.

One of Bechtel's neighbors in the building was Joseph R. Knowland, longtime publisher of the *Oakland Tribune* and the city's consummate power broker through the mid-twentieth century. Born in Alameda, Knowland was elected to the US House of Representatives in 1904 and served until 1915; the previous November he was defeated in a bid for a seat in the US Senate. Not to be undone, a year later, he became publisher of the *Tribune* and went on to serve on the boards of scores of local business organizations. Knowland's Republican-leaning *Tribune* dominated the Hearst Company's *Oakland Post-Enquirer* and sometimes the San Francisco papers as well, achieving an outsized prominence in the shaping of Oakland business, politics, and urban form.[46] In 1953, his son William Knowland became majority leader in the US Senate; that same year, another Oaklander, Earl Warren, was appointed chief justice of the

Figure 4. Key Streetcar "10" on Piedmont Avenue. At 41st Street, ca. 1930s. Photo courtesy of Oakland Public Library, Oakland History Room.

Supreme Court. Never before or since had Oakland attained such heights of national, political power.

Further afield, older transportation arterials—7th Street to West Oakland, San Pablo Avenue northward, and E. 14th Street eastward—were the principal routes where working-class housing was built in conjunction with nearby manufacturing plants. In all cases, on their trajectories out of downtown, streetcar routes birthed neighborhood commercial districts targeted to the types of residents who settled nearby. Lots directly facing the trolley lines were less desirable for housing due to the traffic and noise of the steel cars as well as the visual effects of their overhead wires. They were taken up mostly by retail stores and service establishments. On the longest and busiest arterials, like Telegraph Avenue and E. 14th Street, commerce developed along fairly continuous strips that stretched for many miles. Intersections where streetcars stopped, usually every couple of blocks, attracted businesses oriented to everyday needs: bakeries, produce stores, pharmacies. In between, specialty stores—paint or furniture stores or sometimes lower-priced residences—filled the gaps.

Commercial subcenters emerged nearby transit stations. In 1904, the Santa Fe Railroad built a passenger station in Emeryville, just west of San Pablo Avenue near Park Avenue. Emeryville, which incorporated in 1896 as a tiny city of little more than two square miles, nonetheless successfully competed with Oakland and Berkeley for industrial plants and entertainment venues. Interurban routes passed close to the small city on their way to the Key System pier, and the area became a hub of manufacturing and commerce, with banks, bars and restaurants, and a ballpark for the minor league baseball Oakland Oaks.

In 1929, two hotels were built between downtown and the Santa Fe Station on San Pablo Avenue: the 97-room Roosevelt at 29th Street and the 172-room California Hotel at 36th Street. The California Hotel was notable both for its size and its orientation to both streetcars and automobiles. Like most commercial development until then, the massive five-story building was built to lot-lines, and its ground floor hosted a range of commercial establishments. The hotel advertised as well a motorists' patio, a separate route for driving guests that connected the parking garage behind the building directly to the lobby.[47] Through the 1950s, for black travelers, denied lodgings in prestigious downtown hotels, the California Hotel became a favored place of accommodation as well as a music venue.

Other subcenters grew up around intersections of streetcar lines where transfers were common, such as the Dimond District, served by several routes along Hopkins Street and Fruitvale Avenue. In 1910, the district still retained the atmosphere of a small village; 10 years later, after the introduction of the electric traction trolleys, there were over 40 stores.[48] In 1927, the Dimond Egyptian Theater opened at 3422 Fruitvale Avenue, near the northern terminus of the Fruitvale car line. A replica of Grauman's Hollywood Egyptian, the theater had a capacity of nearly 1,500.

Across Oakland, the towers, signs, and marquees of movie theaters could be seen from long distances, signaling the approach to a center of a commercial district and its banks, drugstores, produce markets, bakeries, shoe repair shops, hardware stores, and restaurants. Practically every district in the city sported a theater with eye-catching details. The Fairfax and Seminary Districts along Foothill Boulevard in East Oakland had not one but two grandiose palaces: the Capitol and the Fairfax. Both were designed by the Reid Brothers in the mid-1920s, both were styled with Spanish Colonial ornaments, and both were housed as part of large commercial blocks that hosted other small storefronts. The two theaters, one at Fairfax Avenue and the other almost at Seminary Avenue, were separated by about a quarter mile. Although close to one another, they never consolidated into a single, intensive commercial district. Rather, the interval between them filled over the years with commercial buildings, apartments, and some single-family houses. Theaters, like all commercial buildings, were speculative ventures, capitalizing on hopes for future development. Changing economic cycles, in this case the Great Depression, could put an abrupt end to real estate plans.

Oakland never developed a secondary downtown, akin to St. Louis's Midtown, Chicago's Uptown, or New York's multiple secondary centers. That's not to say speculators didn't try. Two districts came closest. The stretch of E. 14th Street from Fruitvale Avenue to High Street was already a dense commercial corridor when, in 1925, the New Fruitvale Theater opened at 3720 E. 14th Street, offering 1,200 seats for moviegoers and identifying the arterial with an expanding Fruitvale District. Nonetheless, the locational geography that animated streetcar strips spread significant commercial buildings over large-enough distances to discourage creation of a dense, secondary downtown. In 1924, about a mile to the west of the New Fruitvale Theater along E. 14th Street, Montgomery Ward had opened a colossal building at 29th Avenue. It was Ward's second mail-order center west of the Rockies, an eight-story, reinforced concrete edifice that also housed a retail store. Ward's location pulled commercial development away from the most intensive stretches of E. 14th Street, around both the intersection with Fruitvale Avenue and the vicinity of the New Fruitvale Theater. A small medical district even coalesced around Ward's: the seven-story, 90-bed East Oakland Hospital at 27th Avenue and the six-story Fruitvale Medical Building at 3022 E. 14th Street. Because so many dispersed commercial districts emerged along E. 14th Street, none were able to grow into a secondary downtown. Compared to cities with subways and elevated trains, concentrating pedestrian traffic at specific points usually at least a half mile apart, the electric streetcar and interurbans' closely spaced stops on E. 14th Street and elsewhere favored strips of predominantly low-rise buildings with intermittent bursts of higher-intensity construction.

The other district with passing pretensions of becoming a secondary downtown was the Grand Lake District, where storefronts had been developed between 1924 and 1930 along Grand, Lake Park, and Lakeshore Avenues—nearby Lakeshore Terrace. Much of the hype had to do with the construction in 1926 of the Grand Lake Theater, whose 1,900 seats made it the largest neighborhood theater in the city. Designed by the Reid Brothers, the theater's pretensions were confirmed by its 52-foot-tall rooftop sign, lit by 2,800 coordinated bulbs to look like a fireworks explosion. In 1930, Zura Bells, a realtor for the Fred T. Wood Company, predicted a wave of office skyscrapers, department stores, hotels, and large apartment buildings in the district, less than two miles from the heart of downtown. The theater, she wrote, "is there because of the great residential wealth and buying power which surrounds it ... this district will be changed definitely to one of tall buildings."[49] The wave never came, or at least in the manner forecast. Periodic flooding from underlying creeks as well as the deepening effects of the Great Depression doused enough economic insecurity on those tall dreams to keep Grand Lake from exploding skyward.

TRANSIT SUBDIVISIONS

The platted blocks astride the streetcar lines were the domain of residential building: mostly single-family houses. The idea of a detached house surrounded by grass and trees stemmed from rural antecedents. In the urban context, however, the house lot lost its prior function as the site of food production/processing and manufacture of tools, clothes, and other items. Most lots were too small to allow anything beyond limited gardening or mechanical tinkering. In more affluent settings, the lots grew in size, but those households, earning their keep via white-collar salaries, purchased—rather than produced—a family's domestic needs. Indeed, the new houses built across Oakland were dependent on transportation routes leading to stores, jobs, and other services. Builders favored lots within two to four blocks of a streetcar line; as the distance grew into what people would consider an overly long walk, the number of unbuilt lots increased.

Fortunes were made in real estate. Hard-to-reach land had once been accorded low values. Once the streetcar lines arrived, prices skyrocketed. From the early 1890s through 1912, Oakland subdividers created over 50,000 new residential lots close to the new streetcar lines.[50] Borax Smith, Frank Havens, and TRS were leaders, developing over a hundred tracts along those lines.[51] They were experts at finding undeveloped lands, assembling streetcar lines to service them, and then entering into contracts with outside real estate firms to subdivide and market the lots.[52] As reporter Bill Stokes noted: "Huge tracts of land could be bought cheaply, cut up into city lots, tapped by a coordinated transportation service and then sold at a profit. The streetcar service would sell the land, the land owners would support the car service and, eventually, improved light, water, and power facilities might be called for."[53]

Development companies extensively marketed the new subdivisions, running advertisements in newspapers, planting banners and flags around their perimeters, and offering free streetcar transportation and food/entertainment on open-house days.[54] Across the nation, it had long been common to site a magnet attraction at the end of a streetcar line to show that progress was rapid and inevitable and advertise the new subdivisions to riders.[55] In Oakland, before the streetcar era, Walter Blair had built a park and hotel at Piedmont Springs, the end of the line of his Piedmont Railroad, and J. H. Doherty had similarly financed the California Railway to serve the Laundry Farm District and Leona Hotel.[56]

Key System interurbans perfected the practice. In 1907, along the main trunk line leading to Piedmont and central Oakland, Smith erected the three-story, 130-room Key Route Inn in a distinctive English half-timbered style by architects Oliver and Foulkes. Called the "first of the pretentious hotel structures to be completed since Oakland's awakening," passengers could leave trains and go directly into the building and, if they chose, rent soundproofed rooms.[57] Eventually, both the B- and C-lines ran underneath the Key Hotel on their way, respectively, to Piedmont Park, site of the Piedmont Springs Hotel, and the Lakeshore Highlands subdivision. The F-line to Berkeley ran by Idora Park, an amusement park on Telegraph Avenue, opened by TRS in 1903. At the end of the E-line, Smith built the 300-room Claremont Hotel, an 800-foot-wide colossus whose 200-foot-tall tower became a landmark of the East Bay hills upon its opening in 1914. "Back in 1915," reporter Ralph Craib tells us, "when the Panama Pacific International Exposition was held in San Francisco, it was a fashionable Sunday outing for the ostrich-featherhead ladies and high-collared dandies to take the ferry ride on one of Borax Smith's ferries and spend the afternoon in the pleasant grounds of the big white wooden hotel. People who go to Palm Springs today would have gone to Berkeley then."[58]

Although Smith created an enviable mass transit system for the East Bay, his focus remained on short-term ventures and profits, not the long-term needs of the East Bay cities or even his own company. In fact, the streetcar companies were never intended to make significant profits or even run in the black; most profits came from subdivision activity. This led to the questionable practice of overbuilding new lines in advance of population. In economic downturns, when subdivision sales decreased, such as the Panic and Recession between 1910 and 1914, TRS revenues could not cover the expansion and modernization for the transit system. The universal five-cent streetcar fare too became a burden.[59] Lastly, Smith relied on dubious accounting and bonds, oftentimes investment certificates bearing 6 percent interest, known as "long-term sixes." By 1912, he was deeply overcapitalized, and from 1914 to 1923, representatives of various groups of creditors took control the San Francisco–Oakland Terminal Railways, as it was then called.[60]

THE RANKS OF NEIGHBORHOODS

Oakland, as much as Los Angeles, became a realm of small houses. In 1920, reporter Robert Peter Giles characterized Oakland as "a community of home owners. Federal statistics show that 57% of the people of the section reside in their own homes. It is the highest percentage of home ownership claimed by any city in the United States."[61] That year, 41,000 single-family homes could be found in the city. Housing starts had been increasing since 1900, leading to a peak shortly before the First World War. The upward trend caught fire once more in 1918, and rocketed to a crescendo in 1925. A gradual downturn followed and then, after the stock market crash of 1929, the housing market collapsed for almost a decade.

As with land subdivision, housing construction evolved from a small-scale, random affair to a professionalized operation. In the past, cash-poor, working-class households, accustomed to laboring with their hands, had built their own homes or bought a home as a work in progress, occasionally hiring subcontractors—excavators, masons, tinsmiths, plasterers, glaziers, bricklayers, and painters—for improvements or additions they couldn't accomplish themselves.[62] Residence, work, and recreation were tightly intermingled. Architectural historian Marta Gutman describes late nineteenth-century Oakland Point in West Oakland as a jumble of mixed-use buildings built by small builders and workingmen themselves: "Old mansions, flats, cottages, hotels, rooming houses, and a few tenements stood cheek-to-jowl with factories, coal yards, stables, food processing plants, laundries, and many saloons."[63]

Examined closely, the houses revealed their happenstance processes of formation. Focusing on working-class cottages in Oakland and Berkeley before 1900, urban geographer Paul Groth found a disparity between their somewhat formal front facades and their in-process rear sides. Back rooms were an assemblage of self-built additions with scavenged parts, often in many stages of construction. The cottages were spatially irregular, with rooms serving multiple purposes. Streetscapes showed little uniformity: setbacks were varied; lots were differently sized.[64]

By 1900, close to half of the nation's population had become urban residents. From this point onward, Groth gleaned a shift away from informality and transience, and a turn toward standardized building practices and centralized decision-making. The minimal bungalows were now built all at once in a form that appeared to be complete and permanent. Their interior spaces were specialized, bedrooms set apart from public spaces. Their streetscapes were more uniform, with standardized lot sizes, setbacks, and architectural composition.[65] Speculators, realtors, and builders had figured out that lots sold faster and for more money in subdivisions with dwellings for the working and (increasingly middle) classes that aspired to the protocols of the affluent.

From the 1910s through the 1920s, the bungalow became the standard bearer of those dwelling aspirants.[66] Bungalows were usually professionally built homes that combined practicality with uniformity. Although small in size, they had open floor plans where rooms were used for circulation, resulting in fewer corridors.[67] In subdivisions like Melrose Highlands and Steinway Terrace, wage-earner bungalows had short street

Figure 5. Maxwell Park. Newly constructed bungalow
homes, ca. 1922. Photo courtesy of Oakland Public
Library, Oakland History Room.

frontages, shallow setbacks, and narrow side yards. Developers marketed
utilitarian considerations: termite-proof foundations, sanitary plumbing,
quality wiring, and electricity for a growing number of appliances. They
trumpeted convenient streetcar service and macadamized streets, quality
nearby schools and restrictions against the construction of shacks.[68] Tens
of thousands of such humble bungalows offered working-class Oaklanders
an entry to the American dream.

In order to jump-start housing construction at mid-range prices, subdividers initiated more improvements, building an attractive framework
for a community before homeowners arrived.[69] Between 1905 and 1915,
Wickham Havens, Frank Havens's son, developed a rustic allure for Oak
Glen Park by preserving a number of trees along a creek. Across town
in East Oakland, in 1912, he marketed the 21-acre Havenscourt subdivision as consisting of "nothing unsightly, just splendid paved avenues,
planted with oranges and palms—beautiful lawns with flowers and trees.
Park and park spaces, and hundreds of pretty bungalows." Alongside such
positive exclamations came other, exclusionary promises: "no saloons, no
Chinese, no Japanese, Negroes or Filipinos, no telephone poles or wires in
the streets."[70]

Between 1920 and 1923, J. P. Maxwell, a hardware store owner, laid out

Maxwell Park, a 487-home community nearby Mills College. Its realtors, Burritt and Shealey, advertised the beautiful hillside views, warm climate, good schools, and proximity to the Southern Pacific Electric trains leading directly to the Oakland mole and San Francisco. They called attention to the individually styled houses; in point of fact, a cast of like elements—doors, windows, bays, roof pitches, porch parapets, wall angles, entry hoods—were configured differently for different houses to convey an impression of variety.[71] They touted the fact that Maxwell Park was restricted as to Orientals, Asiatics, and Africans. Middle-class bungalow living, anticipating the later rush to the suburbs, was motivated by the paired promises of improved material circumstances and divisive social geographies.

Racial restrictions were related to efforts aimed at limiting residence in higher-end communities to persons of the same, privileged economic class. As a case in point, Rockridge Properties, sold by Fred E. Reed of the Laymance Realty Company, was launched shortly before the First World War, and marketed through its location on a car line leading past the golf links of the Claremont Country Club. Ads boasted of the large lots, 60 to 100 feet in width with deep setbacks, rules for landscaping, streets lined with Canary Island palms, panoramic views, and an entrance glorified by a pair of stone pylons. The community included three levels of subdivisions—Rockridge Place, Park, and Terrace—whose prices rose with elevation and amenities. Houses were large and came in varied styles: Spanish Colonial, French Provincial, English Tudor and, later, Art Deco. There were many restrictions: on side fences, to keep the landscape open and park-like; ownership limited to single-family homes; minimal purchases at $20,000 in the most prized sections.[72] Well-to-do homeowners wanted to escape the teeming hordes of workers and constant barrage of commerce elsewhere in the city.[73] For the owners and managers of industry, social life and domestic space was, paradoxically, anti-urban, revolving around smooth, green lawns of their homes and those of nearby country clubs, and rooted in the desire to live at a good distance from their products and the workers who built them.

Besides high home prices, from Havenscourt to Maxwell Park to Rockridge, the prevailing method for achieving social exclusiveness was race—whether an aspiring resident was considered of the "Caucasian race" or not.[74] Since race is a cultural, not a biological, category, who was white or nonwhite changed over time and with respect to location. In the eastern United States, it was identified at first with Protestants of Northern European descent, and was positioned not only against blacks but sometimes against Catholics and Jews, regardless of their European origin. In California, the earliest racial statutes were directed against Chinese immigrants and Chinese Americans; pioneering ordinances in the 1870s and 1880s aimed to prohibit their laundries in San Francisco, and thus their livelihood and residency.

From the 1880s through the early 1920s, a great wave of immigrants from Southern and Eastern Europe overturned the customary demography of the nation's white population. Many native whites called for an end to immigration, and crafted new approaches to separate themselves from the new arrivals: one was a purchase arrangement restricting access to housing for whites alone. For the next few decades, restrictive covenants became the most important means of enforcing homogenous neighborhoods.[75] They involved an agreement between buyers and sellers, taking the form of an appendix or article in the deed, that specified conditions on the sale, rental, leasing, or alteration of a property. Their racial component became enforceable in court after the 1926 *Corrigan v. Buckley* decision, upheld by the Supreme Court. They were backed by the National Association of Real Estate Boards and, after 1933, by federal housing policy. "The usual pattern was to have concentrations of these restrictive agreements in areas around black neighborhoods," as professor of government Michael Jones-Correa writes, "relatively sparse coverage elsewhere in the city, and much more widespread application in newer suburban developments."[76]

In Oakland, blacks, Asians, and Mexicans were targeted; the town's Portuguese and Italian Catholics as well as Jews were by and large exempt. To white homebuyers, buying in a community where one's neighbors would all be white was an assurance that social mixing—despite the increasing heterogeneity in the white population—would be limited and that property values would be maintained. In some lower hill neighborhoods, where covenants didn't apply, rallies were held to prevent Asian or black families from buying homes.[77] The only way a nonwhite could reside in a restricted subdivision was as a domestic servant. "Whites Only" listings for houses appeared in the *Oakland Tribune* as late as 1964.[78]

Restrictive covenants followed a tradition of residential exclusivity going back to the nineteenth century. The nation's first residential parks had been Llewellyn Park, outside Newark (1857), and Riverside, outside Chicago (1869). They were the forerunners of America's suburban ideal, creations of realtor/developers who acquired raw land, established community guidelines for physical design and social character, and hired other professionals to complete the project. Bay Area prototypes were in Hillsborough and Mill Valley and, then, in 1914, St. Francis Wood was launched in San Francisco. Developed by Mason-McDuffie—the same firm which later built up Berkeley's Claremont District—St. Francis Wood set a standard for design quality and strict community regulations.

Oakland's Lakeshore Highlands above Lake Merritt was the first residential park in the East Bay. Beginning in 1918, Walter Leimert, who had founded the Walter H. Leimert Co. in 1902, promoted and coordinated the development of 1,054 properties on 200 acres; all homeowners were mandatory members of the Homes Association.[79] Entered through gates off Lakeshore Avenue, Lakeshore Highlands boasted quality architectural design and landscaping as well as an interurban line. It pioneered the use of model homes to sell lots and houses. It targeted higher-wage professionals. An advertisement, hawking appreciating values and accelerated transit, called attention to a new relationship between Oakland's homes and San Francisco's workplaces: "Read the picture on the opposite page. There you can see San Francisco—the city of offices and business. Now note, just across the beautiful bay of San Francisco, Lakeshore Highlands, nestling on the sloping terraces from Piedmont to Lake Merritt, in Oakland. San Francisco, the business place, and Lakeshore Highlands, the permanently restricted residential park of beautiful homes." The words express the core values of America's suburban ideal: easy transportation access to professional workplaces and a socially exclusive domestic environment. As this and other realty ads promised, for the aspiring class of managers and professionals, a home distinguished by fine architecture and sylvan landscaping, spaciousness and up-to-date appliances and furnishings, and a community of all-white neighbors, somehow all went together.

In the community's *Declaration of Restrictions*, Clause XV—Limitation of Ownership read: "No person of African, Japanese, Chinese or of any Mongolian descent, shall be allowed to purchase, own or lease said property or any part thereof except in the capacity of domestic servants of the occupant thereof." The clause was deleted only in 1979, 29 years after the US Supreme Court, in *Shelley v. Kraemer* (1948), declared that courts could not enforce racial covenants on real estate. Delays in rescinding (and also prohibiting the enforcement of) racial covenants affected scores of subdivisions across Oakland and the East Bay, where getting a supermajority vote for racial justice was difficult in America's lingering racist climate.

CITY PLANNING AND ZONING

Through the period under discussion, private entrepreneurs or speculators launched most urban developments, be they transit lines, subdivision plats and houses, or office buildings. Few public regulations or mechanisms of oversight were in place to regulate such activities, and many projects were poorly conceived and oriented to short-term profits. At the higher end, for residential parks like Lakeshore Highlands, developer/realtors were driven increasingly, however, toward uniform and predictable outcomes, results that extended profit and product expectations into the long term. Unlike TRS's ambitious, if scattershot approach, Walter Leimert realized that lasting profits in home sales could only come about through the widespread involvement of professional experts and institution of planning regulations.

City planning originated with such businessmen, who viewed it as a way to shape the urban environment architecturally, socially, and for greater profits.[80] Gradually, individual land speculators gave way to larger real estate companies who employed architects, engineers, and landscape architects to design improvements as well as marketers to target certain geographic areas and economic strata.[81] If in 1880 or even 1900, a subdivision included little beyond houses, by 1924, an array of improvements— water mains, sewers, landscaping, entrance gates, restrictive covenants— had become standard practice. Surveying emerged as a profession by the turn of the century, laying out subdivision boundaries, streets, and lot lines as well as the arrangement of utility easements and landscaping.[82] It was impelled in large part by increasing governmental regulations—the first iterance of public involvement in city planning.[83]

Governmental land use controls originated not out of utopian visions, but from statutes regulating nuisances and noxious industries. Property owners wanted protection from each other as well as marketplace forces and undesirable social groups. Their dominant concern was maintaining expectations and, by extension, house values.[84] To this end, zoning emerged as a means to safeguard higher-quality subdivisions from industry, and then apartments, commerce, and other uses deemed detrimental to the quality of life and maintenance of those pecuniary levels. From 1909 to 1915, Los Angeles crafted a zoning ordinance to separate residential and industrial uses. Hundreds of American cities adopted similar pioneering decrees: Berkeley in 1916, San Francisco in 1921.[85]

Zoning in Oakland proceeded piecemeal and in response to localized problems. In 1914, the city designated 10,000 acres along the shoreline for industry—segregated from more affluent housing. In 1921, in response to a concern that stores would soon surround Lake Merritt and mar its natural beauty with commercial signs, the lands around the lake and along Grand Avenue were zoned as an exclusive residential district. One part of the new zone, in Adams Point, prohibited apartment buildings, another key concern for homeowners anxious to keep their neighborhood exclusively single-family.

By 1930, Oaklanders moved toward a consensus that the city needed a comprehensive zoning survey instead of a piecemeal approach that responded to angry residents' concerns. Too little land had been set aside for single-family dwellings. Apartment buildings were encroaching into those neighborhoods. Billboards were proliferating. Off-street parking spots were in short supply.

Politics too were changing. Oakland had an initial progressive era under Mayor Frank Mott in the early 1900s, where, as we shall later see, parklands were acquired, sewers built, and the waterfront opened for commercial development. Mott was followed in 1915 by John. L. Davie, whose laissez-faire approach scaled back the city's involvement in urban development. In 1931, after 15 years of conflicts between the pro-zoning Oakland Realty Board and the anti-zoning Mayor Davie,[86] and with Fred Morcom newly installed as mayor, a preliminary zoning ordinance was finally passed, creating five zones for the entire city: (A) single-family residence with a 35-foot height limit; (B) multiple-family residence with an

80-foot height limit; (C) wholesale, retail, amusement, and other business; (D) heavy industry; (E) light industry.[87] Four years later, a comprehensive ordinance bumped the number of districts from five to nine: adding a two-family residence; breaking the multifamily residence into apartments limited to three stories and those up to eight stories; and dividing the business district into three categories: commercial (on smaller streets), general business (on principal streets), and central business district.[88] These zoning ordinances, enacted during the Great Depression, expressed a tempered wave of progressivism—J. R. Knowland and allied business interests realizing that a tighter governmental framework for development could increase confidence in development plans.

Zoning was less a means of planning a livable city for everyone than a mechanism to limit property conflicts and maintain a semblance of spatial division and order, especially for the single-family homes of the white middle and upper classes. Still, given Knowland and the chamber of commerce's hunger for growth, much of the land along streetcar lines remained commercial, even though the city could never support such extensive commercial corridors. Huge swaths of the waterfront flats were similarly zoned for industry despite the fact that significant parts of them were largely occupied by working-class housing; junkyards and other "industrial uses" became a fact of life in some of these poorer neighborhoods. In the middle-class flatlands and parts of the lower hills, the pro-growth mentality led to the insertion of two-unit and multiple-unit zones in areas with predominantly single-family housing; pressure to replace single-unit dwellings with multiple-unit apartments became omnipresent. Oakland zoning, therefore, when targeted to the less affluent parts of town, did not correspond to the existing city, but to an economic engine as envisioned by promoters: a city of escalating population, business activity, tax revenues, and social hierarchies expressed in geography.

Through the first four decades of the century, ascendant transportation technologies (e.g., electric traction streetcars), coupled with higher real estate prices and exclusionary practices (e.g., restrictive covenants, zoning), facilitated a way for those with means and power to break away from the pack. Much newly built housing was developed by professional realtors and builders with varying levels of improvements, and targeted to more affluent households of the "Caucasian race." In a process that has come to be known as filtering, poor and minority households had to settle for older, "vacated" buildings and neighborhoods.[89] Apart from affluent areas where zoning was compatible with land uses and political power was potent, Oakland's older, working- and lower middle-class districts would continue to be subjected to disruptive plans for supposedly more beneficial uses, plans that disregarded current occupants and structures in favor of profits and higher values for the moneyed class. A city of haves and have-nots resulted: protected enclaves, on the one hand, and sectors subject to rampant speculation and disruption, on the other.

2 Industrial Powerhouse

In 1913, the German city planner Werner Hegemann was lecturing and consulting across the nation, including Sacramento, San Francisco, and the East Bay. Wherever he went, Hegemann advocated for a kind of master planning that could replace the American tendency toward piecemeal responses to sudden growth. His time in the East Bay produced the *Report on a City Plan for the Municipalities of Oakland and Berkeley* (1915), which applied rational planning methods to the historical and cultural uniqueness of those cities.[1] Since Hegemann realized that transportation infrastructure was key to the region's rise, the *Report* analyzed how harbors, railroad corridors, and streets might propel Oakland to new heights and, by generating industrial jobs, improve the everyday lives of its citizens.

Hegemann called for a modern harbor apart from what had developed incrementally along the estuary, adopting ideas put forth by Thomas Rees of the Army Corps of Engineers for a 10-mile (1,200-foot-wide) channel dredged from Richmond to Oakland in order to provide deepwater approaches, adequate piers and slips, and, as a bonus, a set of artificial islands with parks in front.[2] The German city planner was impressed with the scale of the region's train and streetcar networks, but worried that Oakland was but a tributary of the Key System's passenger river to San Francisco. He proposed an elevated electric train between Alameda, Oakland, and Berkeley that would cut travel times between the key East Bay centers by two-thirds and a dedicated freight rail line servicing waterfront industries.[3] Hegemann was aware that the juncture of deepwater shipping and overland rail transportation had proven enticing to manufacturing enterprises.[4] "These spacious railroad streets are the real streets," he remarked, "the skeleton on which the practically unbroken settlement extending over eighteen miles, or more, along the east side of the bay, has been built up."[5]

While few of these precise recommendations were carried out, the *Report* alerted Oakland to the reciprocal relationship between an urban industrial economy and its distribution networks. It came at a fortuitous moment. Until this time, Oakland's port and railroads had largely served the state's resource-based economy: the processing of wood, stone, mineral compounds, and agricultural products into houses, streets, hides, textiles, and food products. These industries established a rapport between city and countryside; products moving back and forth; managers, workers, and salespeople shuttling among fields, rural processing houses, and urban factories and offices. By the time the *Report* was published in 1915, the American economy had just emerged from a recession. The European war stimulated purchases of American goods and increased government spending on military hardware—catalyzing an expansion that lasted through 1918. Over the next few decades, Oakland and the East Bay became, alongside Los Angeles, the West's great industrial belt.

The character of Oakland manufacturing leaned to advanced industrial products made of glass and metals: lightbulbs, radios, calculators, automobiles, ships. Some of the impetus came from California's historic resource industries, especially mining. The invention of dynamite—the first commercial plant in the nation was in San Francisco—as well as cable cars, pumps, and hydraulic equipment laid the groundwork for innovations in other sectors. Another impetus was the phenomenon of branch plants of eastern industries, an expression of the new dominance of large corporations over the American business landscape as well as California's growing market presence. Finally, the distance of California from other population centers fueled enthusiasm in the state for transportation and communications technologies that could better bridge that gap.

Oakland's industrial fortunes would depend upon several interrelated factors: access to and extraction of raw materials; a growing and nearby customer base; the availability of investment capital; engineering/business expertise; transportation linkages and costs; and unpredictable external events.[6] Certain key resources were perennially in short supply, such as coal and iron ore, and they would influence production involving steel. The know-how to make machines composed of precisely calibrated parts and connections was concentrated at eastern facilities and universities, and decisions about industrial locational geography were made at those eastern sites as well. The state's remoteness from other parts of the country meant that transportation costs, as measured by everything from minor alterations in fuel pricing to major innovations in technology, were a constant concern to Oakland's industrial outfits. As Hegemann realized, the convergence of transcontinental rail and oceanic shipping upon which Oakland industry was predicated had produced benefits that should not be taken for granted. New transportation convergences and modes were continually unfolding, and Oakland had better take a leading role in their development.

Would modernizing railroads, wharves, and roads be enough? Might up-and-coming networks, like aviation, be necessary to boost Oakland's competitive advantage? Would the town's historic and heroic equations of "rail meets sail" and well-paid manufacturing employment persist amid the century's stream of disruptive changes to transportation networks, supply chains, and corporate locational decisions?

RAIL YARDS AND THE PORT

In 1929, Ralph Fisher, president of Oakland's Board of Port Commissioners, declared: "Our agricultural hinterland, our central distributing position, our location between rail and ship, between air and water, have placed unusual advantages in our lap."[7] Over the years, Fisher's was but one of a myriad of statements attributing Oakland's rise to prominence to its unique geography. Boosters flaunted the "fact" that the city was nearest to the center of the Pacific Coast population.[8] Despite the hyperbole, they weren't far off the mark. San Francisco Bay is not only one of the best natural harbors on America's Pacific Coast; the rivers feeding the bay link it to the Central Valley, a 400-by-70-mile swath of the best farmland in the nation. When irrigated with waters from the rivers cascading down from the Sierra Nevada Mountains, the valley's fertile soil and Mediterranean climate allow farmers to grow cotton, wheat and rice, and a range of fruits, nuts, and vegetables that are almost impossible to duplicate anywhere else in the country. In the mid-nineteenth century, the lower reaches of those rivers were the epicenter of the Gold Rush, the boom that launched California's modern development.

Oakland was founded on the eastern shore of the bay directly across from San Francisco, isolated on its peninsula from land routes to the east. This location made it a logical end point for railroad lines linking San Francisco Bay to other parts of the nation. In 1869, the initial Central Pacific Railroad line was constructed from Stockton over Altamont Pass to the Livermore Valley, up again over Dublin grade and down through Niles Canyon to the San Francisco Bay, and finally up its eastern side through San Leandro to Oakland Point, a couple of miles west of downtown and directly across from Goat (later called Yerba Buena) Island.[9] The fact that Oakland Point was the shortest ferry route to San Francisco was crucial; in 1870, San Francisco was California's premier seaport and urban center, with a population of 150,000; Oakland counted a mere 8,000 souls.[10]

Oakland grew as its transportation networks multiplied. Other railroads arrived in the East Bay city: the Central and Southern Pacific (SP) (north to Portland, south to Los Angeles, and east to Ogden, Utah); the Santa Fe (to Los Angeles and Chicago); and the Western Pacific (WP) to Salt Lake City. All were obliged to transfer passengers and freight heading to San Francisco onto ferry terminals, at the end of moles (linear railroad wharves extending out onto the bay), in Oakland and Alameda. Train depots were dispersed along the shoreline. In 1910, Western Pacific built a downtown station at 3rd and Washington Streets.[11] That same year, Santa Fe built one on the south side of Emeryville, near the Oakland line. In 1912, SP constructed a grandiose passenger station at 16th Street where it met the waterfront. Architect Jarvis Hunt designed the station as an interurban transfer point, where cross-country trains would arrive on the ground floor and passengers would be shuttled to an elevated track for interurban service to the Oakland mole.[12]

Figure 6. Oakland Point and Southern Pacific Mole. Rail/Ferry Terminal; Albers Milling Company, *left*, ca. 1920. Photo courtesy of Library of Congress, Historic American Building Survey HABS CAL, 1-OAK, 1-14.

The yards in West Oakland, begun by the Central Pacific Railroad in the early 1870s and inherited by Southern Pacific, epitomized the railroad's prominence in the town's economy. Situated a couple of blocks south of 7th Street, between Kirkham Street and the waterfront, they were Oakland's largest single employer for decades: 4,000–5,000 workers by the 1920s. They headquartered construction operations of Southern Pacific—the bridge and building department for the western region. Stations, roundhouses, and other buildings (including hotels) across the West were planned here.[13] Since Oakland was the western terminus for many routes, sleeper and coach cars were overhauled, cleaned, and repaired at the yards. At the height of operations, this meant around 100 passenger cars per day, plus 20 freight cars. The vast site included sorting yards for trains; commissaries supplying smaller stations in the west; roundhouses and machine shops for locomotive repair; blacksmith, machine, and car shops for construction, maintenance, and repair of freight and passenger cars; planing mills providing finished lumber; gas works to generate acetylene for locomotive headlights and passenger car-lamps; a tie-creosote plant; and even a shipyard, which built SP ferries.[14] The railroad, a set of machines arranged into an infrastructure connecting other machines, signaled Oakland's industrial identity.

Unlike its railroads, the port developed slowly.[15] Compared to San Francisco, Oakland's waterfront possessed more abundant supplies of fresh water, pasture, and wood, along with better weather.[16] But the estuary was not an ideal location for ship traffic. At low tide it had a depth of only a few feet; over the years, the channel had to be repeatedly dredged of silt to provide sufficient draft for shipping. Two drawbridges to Alameda impeded the movement of boats and ships.[17] But what hindered the port's development most of all was the fact that much of the land along the estuary was held in limbo for decades due to a questionable deed granted to the city's first mayor and Southern Pacific railroad lawyer, Horace Carpentier. Through 1910, Southern Pacific controlled much of the waterfront and prevented competitive facilities.[18] As historian Woodruff Minor explained: "Oakland's newfound prominence as a rail terminus should have guaranteed its prominence as a seaport. Ironically, the railroad's stranglehold on the waterfront inhibited such development, and the practice of transshipping goods across the bay assured the dominance of the Port of San Francisco."[19]

After freeing up of waterfront land for maritime and industrial expansion, an expression of Oakland's growing autonomy, the city went about improving its port. In 1926, voters approved amendments to the city charter, creating a permanent Board of Port Commissioners that controlled the affairs and funds of the Port of Oakland—established the following year. The port quickly built a set of modern terminals on 2,305 acres. Growth in the size of vessels, and requirements for buildings and equipment for loading, unloading, storage, refinement, and transfer of goods, led to new public break-bulk transit sheds at 9th Avenue, at the foot of Grove and Market Streets, and farther out along the bay toward the Oakland mole, in what later would be known as the Outer Harbor, at 14th Street;[20] alongside the berths, an 80,000-square-foot transit shed was capable of holding a large cache of canned fruits and vegetables, bales of cotton, and sacks of coffee.[21] Tonnage at the port tripled during the 1930s and doubled again during the 1940s.[22] Yet through 1960, it functioned primarily for exports; most imported goods came in through San Francisco.

RESOURCE ECONOMY

At the turn of the twentieth century, California's industrial growth had been impressive. While the state ranked twenty-first in size of population, it was thirteenth in manufacturing output.[23] Oakland's industry relied on the extraction and processing of natural resources from the city's rural hinterland. Cattle who grazed upon the land provided meat, dairy products, and hides for tanneries; forests contributed timber for lumber mills that went into the building of houses, furniture, and carriages; the bay was harvested for fish, seafood, salt, and other minerals that were processed into chemical compounds; hillsides were quarried for Franciscan sandstone that was used for concrete sidewalks and building foundations as well as macadamized streets; truck farms and orchards produced vegetables and fruits, much of which was then canned; wheat, oat, and barley fields supplied grains for flour mills and breweries.[24] For instance, the Excelsior Redwood Company received redwood logs by sea and rail from Northern California forests in Humboldt County, and cut them into doors, windows, moldings, and other milled work. The Remillard Brick Company dug into the East Bay's abundant clay earth for the stuff with which to make bricks.[25] The Albers Milling Company capitalized on the Central Valley farming of wheat, barley, oats, and rye to grind grains for flour and meal. Its 366,200-square-foot facility near Oakland Point was once the largest grain-handling plant on the Pacific Coast.[26]

Agribusiness and agri-industry grew up with California. In 1858, Josiah Lusk began operating a 350-acre farm in North Oakland, on what would later become Claremont Avenue, growing fruits and vegetables. Seven years later, after harvesting a huge crop of raspberries and wanting to avoid spoilage, he started a cannery to preserve the overproduction—J. Lusk Canning Company.[27] In peak canning season, running roughly 18 weeks, from July to October, up to 900 workers prepared 3,000 cases a day, much of the fruit packed in glass jars as well as tin cans.[28] Before the turn of the century, both the manufacture of tin cans and canning process was mechanized, leading the world into a new realm of factory-preserved foods.[29] California led the way, canning a range of fruits from apples and apricots to cherries, pears, and peaches; vegetables, like asparagus and tomatoes, were also canned.[30] Despite the invention of the refrigerator railcar in 1878, allowing longer-distance transport of fresh fruits and vegetables, canning flourished. After 1915, the Panama Canal shortened shipping routes, and California solidified its position as the canning center of the nation. Most canneries were in vicinity of Stockton, San Jose, and Oakland; the latter's proximity to farms and growing districts in Alameda County was the reason for its prominence. From three million cases of fruits and vegetables canned in 1900, the California industry grew by 1960 to 55 million cases of canned fruit and two million of canned vegetables.[31]

Market expansion and consolidations drove the industry. In 1899, instigated by Francis Cutting, head of the F. P. Cutting Company in Oakland, and Mark Fontana, of Fontana & Co., 18 companies, roughly half of the canning establishments in the state, merged into the California Fruit Canners Association (CFCA).[32] Originally from Massachusetts, Cutting had been the first canner to use tin containers, while Fontana, who had emigrated from Italy, pioneered large-scale canneries. In 1916, the CFCA merged with four, large remaining companies to create the mammoth California Packing Corporation, or CalPak, operating over 60 canneries in California and the West.[33] Its headquarters were in San Francisco and, between 1919 and 1949, nationwide consumption of its products doubled.[34]

The Del Monte Foods label, appearing by then on 50 CalPak products, was the association's premium brand. "Del Monte" had originally been the property of Tillman & Bendel, an Oakland-based firm that, in 1886, first used it to identify a blend of coffee prepared for the Hotel Del Monte in Monterey. When Frederick Tillman formed the Oakland Preserving Company in 1891, he extended the Del Monte brand for their premium, canned products.[35] The Oakland Preserving Company's buildings—a brick cannery, warehouse, and coal shed—were located at 110 Linden Street near the estuary. It was one of two Oakland canneries that had merged with 16 other companies to form the CFCA.[36] During the 1915–16

World's Fairs in San Diego and San Francisco, the CFCA popularized the Del Monte line.[37] It later became so identifiable with CalPak that by 1967 the corporation changed its name to Del Monte.[38]

California canneries enjoyed tremendous growth from 1910 to 1930, and hatched numerous associated businesses making cans or cardboard boxes. In 1927, canneries employed 10 percent of the state's industrial labor force.[39] CalPak canneries were constructed up and down the East Bay waterfront. In Emeryville, a cannery originally built for Western Canning Company became CalPak Cannery #35 in 1927. The five-acre operation was the largest cannery in California during the 1920s, employing close to 1,500 workers for whom CalPak offered housing in company cottages and daycare for employees' children. Products included peaches, olives, cherries, pears, apricots, and tomatoes. At its height, the cannery put out 600,000 cases of canned fruits and vegetables annually.[40] It famously produced fruit cocktail, a concoction invented by Dr. William Cruess, chair of the Food Technology Department at the University of California, Berkeley. Fruit cocktail was a medley of diced peaches, pears, grapes, pineapple tidbits, and halved cherries in sugar syrup that became the company's best seller after cling peaches.[41] The canned olive was also invented at an Oakland CalPak cannery.[42]

In 1927, CalPak opened a cannery at 1071 29th Avenue after purchasing the H. G. Prince Company, founded in 1868. Called Cannery #37, it became the site for a jam, preserves, and juice drinks operation as well as the canning of tomatoes, cherries, and stewed prunes. In season, a hundred trucks a day of tomatoes arrived from the Central and Salinas Valleys, leading to the employment of over a thousand workers. Off-season, employment levels fell to 350 employees. Another CalPak factory at 380 5th Street manufactured nut margarine from coconuts, peanuts, milk, and salt.[43] Overall, California's canning industry was a steady, fairly inelastic business, its fluctuations produced by annual changes in the harvest and gradual transformations in consumer taste.

Another valuable crop flourished in California. Cotton had been introduced to the San Joaquin Valley during the Civil War when southern fields became unavailable to northern industries. Planters quickly realized that, when irrigated, the loamy soil and hot, dry climate produced a superior grade of product. In 1883, a Scotsman, William Rutherford, founded

Figure 7. Roving and Spinning Room. California Cotton
Mills, Jingletown, late nineteenth century. Photo courtesy of
Oakland Public Library, Oakland History Room.

the California Cotton Mills on the waterfront a couple of miles east of
Oakland's downtown. By the end of the decade, its workforce had grown
to 190 employees, many of them Portuguese immigrants who lived near
the plant in one- and two-story workers' cottages built for them. As was
customary at the time, the single-story factory buildings were constructed
with brick-bearing walls and wooden interior framing supporting distinctive, north-facing sawtooth roofs that admitted plentiful, yet cool light.

By the early twentieth century, California's cotton production expanded
to the northern Sacramento, Coachella, and Imperial Valleys.[44] The
California Cotton Mills encouraged this agricultural expansion through
a marketing campaign that included giveaways of cottonseed to farmers
and mill owners. In 1917, taking advantage of newfound wartime demand,
it undertook a significant plant enlargement.[45] By now, steel framing had
solved the problem of building multiple factory floors that could be lit
with natural light. California Cotton Mills' four-story addition, crowned by
a conspicuous clock tower, was a quintessential "daylight factory," where
pier-to-pier windows framed in steel sash admitted copious amounts of
light to each of the interior floors.[46]

Not only were early twentieth-century factories taller than their nine-teenth-century predecessors, their facilities were more efficient. Notably, the new cotton factory included a separate electric power station. Electric power enabled the illumination of streets and edifices and reordered the manufacturing plant. Gone were steam engines and their maze-like assemblage of mechanically connected pulleys and belts. Electric motors, connected merely by wires to an onsite or offsite power plant, allowed factories to locate their machines and other operations flexibly in a large open space. Employing as many as 1,200 workers during its peak period in the late teens and twenties, the California Cotton Mills plant produced cotton sheeting, batting, bolting, cloth, duck, burlap, canvas, rope, cord, towels, mops, twines, and parachutes—a greater variety of cotton prod-ucts than any comparable plant in the nation. In possession of some of the largest dryers and looms in the United States, at the height of operations it utilized up to one-quarter of the cotton grown in California.[47]

There were less obvious things to harvest from Oakland's hinterland. In 1913, five businessmen came together to open the nation's first liquid bleach factory at 809 High Street in East Oakland. At first, a one-story wood-frame building, hard by the railroad tracks, housed the electrolysis operations necessary to convert brine from salt ponds in the San Francisco Bay into the twin compounds, chlorine and sodium hydroxide, that make up liquid bleach. Originally called the Electro-Alkaline Company, sales grew dramatically after William and Annie Murray devised a way to dilute the powerful industrial bleach for domestic use.[48] A two-story reinforced concrete addition was added in the 1920s, about the time the name of the company was changed to the Clorox Chemical Company, an amalgam of the two key chemicals, chlorine and oxygen. By this time, the plant was producing 48,000 amber-colored bottles of bleach a day, and soon Clorox opened branch plants in Chicago and Jersey City. Similarly, in West Oakland at 26th and Kirkham Streets, the West Coast Soap Company uti-lized caustic soda, neutral soda, soda ash, volcanic ash, salt, borax, and tallow, 90 percent of which came from California, its tubs bubbling like miniature volcanoes, to produce cleaning powders and soaps, like Powow Cleanser and Blue Bird Washing Machine Soap.[49]

Oakland's resource-based industries represented a new stage in the rapport between city and countryside. For much of human history, agriculture functioned as a labor-intensive economic sector distinct from urban manufacture. Now, farming and resource extraction was integrated into a commercial and industrial economy fostered by cities like Oakland. While some raw materials continued to be sold as commodities, most others were processed into breakfast cereals, canned peaches, canvas sheets, or liquid bleach. Indeed, synergy between resource extraction/cultivation and processing prepared Oakland for its next industrial stage: electronics manufacturing, sometimes in conjunction with large eastern corporations.[50]

ESCALATING ELECTRONICS

During the First World War, Oakland industry took off. By 1917, factory employment in the East Bay cities had risen to 35,000, almost tripling in three short years.[51] Four years later, Oakland was the greatest freight terminal west of Chicago, attracting hundreds of new wholesale and manufacturing firms.[52] After a sharp yet short recession in 1921, the economy grew appreciably for the rest of the decade. By 1925, there were 50,000 industrial workers in the East Bay, a fourfold increase over the prewar years.[53] In 1910, there had been 460 manufacturing plants in Oakland. That number increased to 1,415 by 1929 and, despite the subsequent Depression years, jumped to 3,714 large and small industries making 1,948 different products 10 years later.[54] Most companies were homegrown. Others were branch plants of eastern companies. From Oakland's point of view, the step from a resource-based economy to one engaged in electronics was desirable. Such goods held the promise to advance economic productivity and improve practically every aspect of everyday life.

Manufacturing in United States was traditionally centered in a belt stretching from New England and the Mid-Atlantic through the Midwest.[55] By the early twentieth century, falling transportation costs and increasing economies of manufacturing scale had allowed companies to sell to California consumers from those eastern factories. But as telecommunications and rail transportation improved and California's internal market grew, the fastest-growing large corporations faced a decision. Rising consumer demand out west put pressure on their main plants to increase production. Should they be enlarged or relocated nearby in newer, bigger facilities? Or might branch factories be established faraway in the midst of new consumer markets like California?

Through the 1950s, the latter trajectory prevailed more often than not. Precision machining allowed for the production of interchangeable parts that could be shipped long distances.[56] The capital-intensive nature of such industry was also less affected by California's comparatively higher labor costs.[57] In Oakland's favor was something Hegemann had highlighted: its combined rail and sea access to resources essential to industry, because for many bulky items, ship transport was less expensive than the railroads. Finally, many of the branch plants took advantage of California natural resources or access to other raw materials, like coconut or palm oil and cane sugar, imported through Bay Area ports. Over time, the list of national companies opening East Bay branch plants came to include H. J. Heinz; Libby, McNeill & Libby; Peets Brothers Soap; Procter & Gamble; and Colgate-Palmolive. As a case in point, in 1916, the Shredded Wheat Company, based in Niagara Falls, New York, opened a 67,000-square-foot Oakland plant at 1267 14th Street. Famous for its large sign, "Shredded Wheat Visitors Welcome," the company benefited from the nearby growing of Pacific soft wheat that could then be turned out into Shredded Wheat cereal or Triscuit crackers.[58] In yet another constructional innovation commensurate with electrification and the steel frame, the three-story Shredded Wheat plant, along with its grain silo, was built completely out of reinforced concrete. Compared to the use of wooden beams and boards for interior structure, monolithic concrete floor slabs and flared columns provided far superior fireproofing and easily supported the much heavier loads of both material and machinery in an open, unobstructed, and thus more efficient workspace.[59]

Inexpensive electricity derived from California's growing array of dams enabled not only the lighting of streets and buildings but also the creation of machines geared toward industrial production, commercial and domestic utility, and communications and entertainment. Through the early twentieth century, the familiar names of the industry, like Western Electric, Westinghouse, and General Electric (GE), set up shop in the East Bay.

Created through a merger of three companies in 1892, GE represented

Figure 8. Pacific Coast Shredded Wheat Company. 12th and Union Streets, West Oakland. Photo by Mitchell Schwarzer, 2020.

the leading edge of technological innovation in the early twentieth century, employing hundreds of scientists and inventors, and manufacturing electric meters, motors, steam turbines, locomotives, household appliances, and electric lights.[60] By 1910, the company controlled 80 percent of the light (or lamp) market in the United States. Since electrification was rapidly expanding across the nation, GE chose to diversify production beyond its Harrison, New Jersey, lamp factory, embarking on a system of dispersed manufacturing plants. At the time, the company was developing a new tungsten bulb, the Mazda light bulb, named after the Persian god of light, that burned whiter than comparable bulbs using carbon filaments and was adaptable to most lamps.[61] One location where GE decided to manufacture the fragile glass Mazda bulbs, whose filaments were finer than a human hair, was a new factory at 1648 16th Street in West Oakland. The Oakland Lamp Works was GE's nineteenth branch lamp manufacturing division.[62] Within a couple of years, the 150,000-square-foot brick complex was churning out three million Mazda light bulbs a year for GE's western territories. The factory site doubled in size a few years later, and employed 650 workers by the mid-1920s.[63]

Starting in 1922 and continuing through the 1940s, GE built the 24-acre Oakland Works at 5441 E. 14th Street, encompassing 21 buildings for the manufacture of copper wire, switchboards, transformers, and motors. This complex included a two-story, Classical Revival studio for GE's radio station, KGO, which included space for studios and a control room. A nearby building housed the powerful generators and transmitters. In 1924, KGO, known as the Sunset Station, began broadcasting from Oakland at 1,000 watts via two 150-foot steel towers supporting the antenna.[64] It was advertised as the most powerful station west of Schenectady, New York, and was initially on the air with music and educational programs on Tuesdays, Thursdays, and Saturdays from 8 to 10 p.m.[65]

Electricity ushered in a host of new consumer goods that brought the world into the home: radio, phonographs, and eventually television. Two major recording companies set up shop in Oakland. In 1924, the Victor Talking Machine Company, based in Camden, New Jersey, opened its ninth branch plant in Oakland on 20 acres of what had been the short-lived Durant Airport, at E. 14th Street and 78th Avenue. The 40,000-square-foot, two-story concrete building, with brick façade, contained a record stamping plant for 78-rpm recordings and a studio for musicians and orchestras.[66] Two years later, Columbia Phonograph Company, another eastern record manufacturer and recording studio, opened an 8,000-square-foot facility on 57th Avenue and E. 14th Street to augment its overworked main factory and studio in Bridgeport, Connecticut. The Oakland plant, geared to customers west of the Rockies, manufactured Royal Blue Records, a blue laminated product marketed to attract visual attention. The business models for both Oakland facilities included recording units for nearby leading Pacific Coast artists. Yet, in the 1930s as the industry centralized operations in New York and Los Angeles, where talent had migrated, and as radio developed into a critical competitor to the recording industry, regional branch plants for recording records in places like Oakland became impractical.[67]

Oakland's industrial prowess attracted other companies that were intent on expansion but hindered by their location in smaller western locales. In 1910, Peter Jensen, a Danish engineer, founded the Commercial Wireless and Development Company in Napa, which distinguished itself through the development of loudspeakers and a product emanating from it—the electrical phonograph. Seven years later, after acquiring the Sonora Phonograph Distributing Company, it relocated to San Francisco and was renamed the Magnavox Company, for "great voice." By 1919, with sales increasing, Magnavox relocated production facilities to Oakland, a two-story building at 2701 E. 14th Street where it manufactured amplifiers, loudspeakers, telephones, anti-noise intercom systems, noise-cancelling microphones, and radios—including the world's first single-dial radio.[68] Floor space was tripled by an expansion in 1922. The company's research and development and manufacturing were based in Oakland until 1930 when, as a result of reorganization, Magnavox moved its headquarters to Chicago and then Fort Wayne, Indiana—shuttering its Oakland facility.[69]

Like Victor Talking Machine and Columbia Phonograph's closures of their Oakland plants during the Depression, Magnavox's abrupt departure was an early sign of the impact that the networked nature of American manufacturing would have on Oakland. Operations could relocate for many reasons: the centralization, in the former case, of the recording industry; the decision of companies founded on the West Coast, as with Magnavox, to seek out the advantages of industrial production in the Midwest.

Oakland hatched its own electronics businesses that over time took on a national scope. In 1913, Rodney and Alfred Marchant started the Marchant Calculating Machine Company with a production facility initially at 7th and Market Streets. By 1916, the company had acquired a two-acre site in Emeryville at 4th and Powell Streets, where a daylight factory was constructed beginning in 1918; the company headquarters located to downtown Oakland in the Cathedral Building.[70] Seeing itself as the "Master of Mathematics," Marchant was America's first mechanical calculator made for commercial use, its machines taking the place of scores of skilled clerks.[71] Marchant went on to build electromechanical calculators, also known for their reliability and sophistication, and by the 1920s the company was producing 12,000 machines a year.[72] In 1958, the firm was acquired by the Smith Corona Typewriter Company, and the new company was renamed Smith Corona Marchant; the Marchant division operated from a new building at 6701 San Pablo Avenue, on the Oakland-Berkeley line.

Alongside firms like Palo Alto's Federal Telegraph Corporation, a pioneer in radio and vacuum tube technology, and inventors like San Francisco's Philo Farnsworth, creator of electronic television, Oakland's electronics industries were part of the Bay Area's early twentieth-century technology hub that set the stage for the later development of Silicon Valley.[73] These modern, multi-unit enterprises grew through both horizontal expansion (via mergers) as well as vertical integration of key company functions within the confines of a new building type—the factory. They were the inheritors of a revolution in industrial production begun in the 1850s with the telegraph and telephone. The speed and volume of production was brought about by new sources of energy (steam and then electrical power) and ascendant technological knowledge and application.[74] Equally, improvements in transportation and communication as well as demand, through population growth, transformed distribution and resulted in the dispersion of the gigantic industrial enterprise across the continent. An American industrial colossus resulted, a yardstick whereby the core identity of cities like Oakland would be measured throughout the twentieth century. Yet, as with the earlier resource-based industries, upturns, downturns, takeovers, mergers, relocations, new competition, transportation innovations, and product obsolescence buffeted electronics plants. Events nearby or faraway could lead to the need to add manufacturing space or sell off assets. Wars, stock markets, patents, and successful marketing could make or break a business. Two sectors epitomize the impact of these larger forces: shipbuilding and automobile assembly.

GLASGOW OF AMERICA

At the onset of the twentieth century, the nation's steel shipbuilding centers were Philadelphia; Camden, New Jersey; Newport News, Virginia; and Quincy, Massachusetts. The next largest production center was the Union Iron Works in San Francisco, later acquired by the Bethlehem Steel Corporation.[75] Yet during the two world wars, armed with plentiful contracts from the US government, the Oakland waterfront joined the ranks

Figure 9. Moore Dry Dock Company. Ship under construction along Oakland Estuary, 1939. Photo courtesy of Library of Congress Prints and Photographs Division HAER WA-167-44.

of the nation's shipbuilding centers. Four major shipyards (and 12 minor ones) emerged in Oakland and Alameda on 342 acres during the First World War.[76] Three were located on the estuary: the Moore Shipbuilding Company, the D. J. Hanlon Shipyard, and Bethlehem Steel Corporation's Alameda Yards; the fourth, operated by the Union Construction Company, was situated along the West Oakland waterfront near the Southern Pacific mole. Each of the yards included a set of buildings and structures: shipways; drydocks; fabricating and machine shops; water and gas pump houses.

In 1905, Robert and Joseph Moore along with John Scott formed the Moore & Scott Iron Works in San Francisco, initially contracting solely for ship repair. A couple of years after the facilities burned down following the 1906 Earthquake, the company relocated to the Oakland estuary, purchasing the W. A. Boole & Son shipyard at the foot of Adeline Street. The company turned to building steel oil tankers, ferry boats, and oceangoing merchant vessels, and contracting from firms like the Cunard Steamship line. During the First World War, Moore received a coveted government contract for 10 merchant vessels. By the end of the wartime effort to build a "bridge of ships," in 1921, his company had launched 48 vessels for the federal government's US Shipping Board and 14 other hulls for private companies like the SP railroad and Standard Oil Company. Renamed Moore Shipbuilding in 1917, the 60-acre yard employed 13,000 workers at the war's peak, a time at which Moore brought more steel to Oakland than any industry up to that point.[77]

In 1915, at the foot of 5th Avenue, Dan Hanlon established the D. J. Hanlon Shipyard. Hanlon had been a longshoreman and, in a rare case of rising from manual labor to ownership, was able to save some money and convince others to contribute to his dream of running a shipyard. He was wildly successful.[78] Between 1916 and 1920, the yard expanded onto 36 acres of mudflats, as it built the first electrically controlled drydock and increased its workforce from 500 to 4,000. On orders from the US Shipping Board, Hanlon launched freighters, steamers, and cruisers.[79]

On the eve of America's involvement in the war, San Francisco's venerable Union Iron Works had become a unit of the Bethlehem Shipbuilding Corporation, a subsidiary of Bethlehem Steel, the second-largest steel producer in the country. In 1916, Bethlehem acquired the United Engineering Company, located at the foot of Webster Street in Alameda; at the time, the city of Alameda was building up its maritime and shipbuilding industry, in large part because it had more available waterfront land than Oakland. The new Bethlehem shipyard became known as the Alameda Works to distinguish it from Bethlehem's Potrero Works in San Francisco.[80] At the height of wartime operations, between 1918 and 1919, the Alameda Works expanded to almost 80 acres and was noted for its Machine Shop, the largest on the West Coast; five stories high, it measured 552 by 164 feet; due to its power demands, a Pacific Gas & Electric substation was erected nearby. Over 8,000 workers constructed 58 P-50 cargo ships and tankers at the Alameda Works for the US Shipping Board.[81]

Finally, the Union Construction Company, known for the construction of gold dredges and placer mining equipment, opened a 64-acre shipyard in 1918 on the West Oakland waterfront. Through 1921, it employed up to

3,000 workers who built ten freighters, four tankers, and four gunboats for the federal government.[82]

What a difference a war makes. Before the conflict, from 1901–16, 21 vessels with 22,212 gross tonnage were launched by Oakland-Alameda shipyards. Between 1917 and 1921, the figures skyrocketed to 140 vessels with 851,285 gross tonnage. At their height of operations around 1919 and 1920, Oakland/Alameda shipyards had an 18.5 percent share of total American shipbuilding and employed over 40,000 workers.[83] But as wartime government contracts dried up, military shipbuilding ground to a halt. The Hanlon yard was taken over by Alameda's General Engineering and Drydock Company, and converted to repair operations after delivering its last ship in 1927.[84] Union Construction attempted to keep its large plant busy by building steel frames for buildings and bridges, but closed by the end of the decade.[85] Bethlehem's Alameda Works first downsized to a repair yard and drydock, and then lay idle during the Great Depression. Moore built ferryboats, a hangar at Oakland airport, two bridges over the Oakland estuary, and caissons for the Bay Bridge; its employment ranged from 800 to 2,400 in the interwar years.[86] Steel shipbuilding in California had relied upon government action that, in turn, depended on the nation's involvement in distant foreign conflicts; it was extremely sensitive to the presence or absence of such engagements.

Compared to East Coast yards, Bay Area shipbuilding was hindered by the scarcity of nearby sources of coal and iron ore. It was not until the development of hydroelectric power after 1900 and oil refineries after 1910 that sufficient power, apart from imported coal, was provided for California industries.[87] Iron ore continued to be brought in by ship through midcentury. In 1920, California's ingot production was 0.8 percent of the national total, and by 1940, it had risen only to 1.25 percent.[88] Approximately 85 percent of domestic iron ore production emanated from the Lake Superior region in the Midwest, and much of the rest came from the Appalachian mountain region. Steel production on the Pacific Coast was thus limited by high transportation costs for imported raw materials. Since the population west of the Rocky Mountains remained a small slice of the American pie, importing iron ore and then shipping finished steel products to other parts of the country invoked double transport costs and made little sense.[89]

Along the Pacific Coast, scrap metal was widely used to make up for the lack of ore and coal.[90] Mid-sized East Bay iron and steelmaking industries serviced local markets. Oakland Iron Works turned out steam engines and machinery. Union Machine Works, Bay City Iron Works, Vulcan Foundry, and Phoenix Iron Works provided steel for local industry and building. The area's largest yard was the Judson Iron Works, founded on the Oakland/Emeryville bayfront by Egbert Judson in 1883 as the Judson Manufacturing Company. By the 1920s, Judson was operating with three open-hearth furnaces, producing a bar iron, foundry casings, girders, spikes, bolts, rivets, nuts, and tacks. Its steel was used for docks and piers, bridges, and power plants as well as buildings, including Oakland City Hall.[91]

In 1936, reacting to the Japanese conflict with China and Hitler's remilitarization of the Rhineland, the Merchant Marine Act created the Maritime Commission, which instituted a subsidy for the construction of merchant vessels. A shipbuilding renaissance took place along the shores of the bay.[92] The five large US shipyards in the Northeast were inundated with orders, and were soon augmented by several others on the Gulf and Pacific Coasts, including the Kaiser Company shipyards in Richmond, Marinship in Marin County, Bethlehem's Union Iron Works in San Francisco, and, on the Oakland estuary, the renamed Moore Dry Dock Company and Bethlehem Steel Corporation's reopened Alameda Yards.[93]

From 1940 onward, Bethlehem Steel's Alameda Yards built P-2 troop transport ships, oceangoing tugs, and tankers, and also repaired more than a thousand vessels.[94] By 1944, 6,200 employees were working at the Alameda Yards. Moore Drydock Company primarily received orders for cargo ships. Operating eventually on 128 acres, Moore launched the *Sea Arrow*, *Sea Star*, and *Sea Panther*, 495-foot cargo carriers.[95] At the height of the Second World War, while building 65 C-3 freighters, eight landing craft, and two submarine tenders, and repairing over 2,000 other ships, Moore employed 37,000 workers—the highest employment numbers in Oakland history.[96]

Leading up to the war, Oakland became home as well to three military bases and thousands of military and civilian jobs. First, the vacant site of the Union Construction Company was repurposed into the Oakland Port of Embarkation and General Depot, or Oakland Army Base. In operation by 1941, and augmented in size, the base supplied army troops in the Pacific campaign (and later wars in Korea and Vietnam). Fifty-five miles of railroads connected Camp Knight, seven quarter-mile warehouses, and other buildings to ten wharves.[97]

A year later, south of the Army base, the Naval Supply Center was established on 392 acres filled from mudflats. From 1942 to 1953, through the Second World War and Korean War, it was the largest supply base of its kind in the world. The depot handled 58 million tons of supplies and equipment: everything from paper clips to ship radar installations; food, clothing, books, magazines, medicines, equipment, weaponry, and machines. A 34-mile railroad along with 17 buses handled movement among the 146 hangers, warehouses, and offices, and seven wharves. Sixty-eight seacraft carried supplies to ships anchored in the bay. Employment began at 656 employees and reached 16,000 by 1945; it fell after the war and rose again to 11,000 in 1951 at the height of the Korean War.[98] The third major military installation in Oakland was located in the East Oakland hills, the Naval Hospital at Oak Knoll; opened in 1942, by the end of the war it had a capacity of 6,000 beds in 111 barracks-like buildings.

The Second World War military buildup contributed to California's population growth and more than doubled the state's industrial sector.[99] For Oakland and other Bay Area cities it amounted, as historian Marilynn S. Johnson tells us, to a second Gold Rush.[100] Not only did the war revive shipbuilding and introduce a significant military component to Oakland's economy, the city's population grew from 302,000 in 1940 to 343,000 in 1945. The war also brought about a demographic sea change. Much of the town's population increase was due to the Second Great Migration of African Americans from the South. In 1940, the census counted 8,462 Negroes in Oakland. By 1950, this population had increased to 47,610.

Until the war, white Oaklanders owned most industrial businesses and held the vast majority of industrial jobs. Employment shortages in the wartime industries now stimulated the migration of blacks from Arkansas, Louisiana, Oklahoma, and Texas to California. After President Roosevelt's executive order in 1941 requiring equal opportunity employment at wartime defense contractors, trade unions were required to hire black workers.[101] They were able to move into well-paying occupations previously denied to them and other minorities. Still, labor disputes between black workers and unions persisted throughout the war years.[102] Although 20 percent of the wartime workforce, blacks were usually given jobs separate from whites, and had an extremely hard time attaining skilled positions or management tracks.[103] White workers in some trades, like boilermaking, steamfitting, and pipefitting, kept out black workers.[104] As we shall discuss at greater length in chapter 7, "In the Wake of Deindustrialization," these discriminatory practices worsened in peacetime. The town's burgeoning black population would face a harsh postwar employment landscape because of manufacturing decentralization and race-based exclusion from most (and certainly better-paying) jobs.

DETROIT OF THE WEST

In 1913, automobile registrations in California reached the 100,000 mark, immediately behind New York; this was despite the fact that California ranked only thirteenth in population among the states. Midwestern automobile manufacturers began to look west and, at its ship-railway nexus, Oakland quickly became a major assembly site.[105] Already in 1911, the short-lived California Motor Car Company, the city's first, began turning out "Pacific Specials" from a small plant at High Street and San Leandro Boulevard. As reported in *Sunset Magazine*, "A new and important industry—one of the most progressive and promising since the foundation of the Union Iron Works—has recently been established in the city of Oakland...a large plant dedicated to the manufacture of automobiles."[106] Three large assembly plants were soon constructed across East Oakland: Chevrolet, Fageol, and Durant Motors. Associated components plants set up shop nearby: Coast Tire and Rubber Company produced tires, inner tubes, and rubber goods; American Thermophone Company built thermostatic devices for automobiles and buildings. By the mid-1920s, 40 separate factories producing automobiles or automobile accessories led business leaders to proclaim the town as "Detroit of the West."[107]

In 1916, following the Ford Motor Company's growing network of branch plants, General Motors built Chevrolet branch plants in St. Louis, Fort Worth, Toledo, and Oakland. The expansion reflected the company's hopes for its increasingly successful 490 touring car, introduced a year earlier as a competitor to Ford's Model T.[108] Previously, freight railroad rates, computed from the rail center in Chicago, had given a competitive advantage to midwestern fabricators.[109] Now, the increasing perfection of the assembly line made it harder for smaller automobile manufacturers to compete with large companies.[110] For those giants, the branch plant strategy was an attempt to improve distribution of cars to dealerships around the country as well as save on freight transportation. Compared to the Midwest, Oakland production benefited from cheap hydroelectric power, the lack of the need for heating in winter, and an availability of skilled workers.[111] Still, only assembly would be done in California, as raw materials—steel and rubber—continued to be shipped in by rail and often by sea.

From 1904 to 1917, a Michigan carriage maker, William Durant, began a series of purchases and mergers of automobile companies that epitomized the remarkable growth and equally remarkable turmoil of the nascent industry. Durant first revived Buick Motors, then founded General Motors, was subsequently forced out of General Motors, founded Chevrolet Motors (with Swiss race car driver Louis Chevrolet), regained control of General Motors and, once more, lost it again.

In 1916, while GM/Chevrolet was under Durant's leadership, the company opened a seven-acre site on Foothill Boulevard between 69th and 73rd Avenues for the first large automobile assembly plant in California. Fittingly, it was located on the final stretch of the Lincoln Highway as it wound its way from New York to the Oakland waterfront. In 1917, its first year of full production, the Chevy plant assembled 10,089 cars. Using an assembly line, pioneered a few years earlier by the Ford Motor Company, "the body of the machine passes on its way from one hand to another until, dripping with enamel, it disappears in bake ovens. Scores of young women are stitching the tops and seat covers, upholsterers are busy on the cushions, electricians installing magnetos; and so the machine takes form until it runs out of the building under its own power."[112] In 1922, responding to a demand for enclosed cars, General Motors opened a 164,000-square-foot Fisher Body Company plant along adjacent Hillside Street.[113] Soon, Chevrolet and Fisher Body employed almost 1,000 auto-workers in five large buildings, and by 1928, the original Chevrolet factory had been enlarged three times, to half a million square feet, increasing its

Figure 10. Chevrolet assembly plant. Aerial view at 69th Avenue and Foothill Boulevard, ca. 1920s. Photo courtesy of Oakland Public Library, Oakland History Room.

workforce to 1,300 and putting out close to 85,000 vehicles annually.[114] By the 1930s, the associated General Motors plants had the largest steady payroll of any industrial institution in Oakland.[115]

Oakland's second large manufacturer of automobiles and related vehicles made its mark in the East Bay. In 1916, just as Chevrolet was setting up shop in East Oakland, Frank and William Fageol, who had moved to the Bay Area in 1904 from Iowa, began car manufacturing behind their Rambler dealership in North Oakland.[116] Two years later, the Fageol Motors Company opened a modern plant on a ten-acre site a few miles from the Chevrolet plant, at 107th Avenue and Hollywood (now MacArthur) Boulevard.[117] It too was just off the route of the Lincoln Highway. Part of the two-story reinforced concrete factory was made famous by a 1934 photograph by Imogen Cunningham, *Fageol Ventilators*. It shows a grid of 12 steel ventilators rising from the roof like a set of organ pipes transmitting, in this case, the pitch of automotive progress.

At first, Fageol produced the Touring Car, running on a six-cylinder engine made at the Hall-Scott Company of Berkeley—the most expensive automobile of its time. Mainly, Fageol churned out small trucks and tractors, known for their sturdiness and improved features like an automatic oiling system for the chassis and a compound gear set.[118] Manufacturing tractors made sense in California not only because of the enormous size of the state's agricultural industry but also because agriculture, as with other California industries, suffered from a chronic lack of labor and relied heavily on capital investments for mechanization. A local orchardist, Rush Hamilton, helped design Fageol's tractors for efficient plowing, disking, and hauling. From 1921 to 1922, the company unveiled its first buses.[119] Demand for the trucks and tractors led the company to start a second factory in Cleveland, Ohio, in 1920, yet losses beginning in the late 1920s and continuing into the Depression years forced Fageol to enter bankruptcy in 1932. In 1939, while operating in bankruptcy, T. A. Peterman, a Tacoma-based lumber dealer, purchased Fageol Motors, renaming the factory Peterman (and later Peterbilt) Motors Company—known for heavy-duty trucks.[120]

The last of the major automotive assembly plants to start operations in Oakland was a spin-off from General Motors. In 1921, no longer working for the company, William Durant started Durant Motors, and a year later opened a 20-acre, 300,000-square-foot plant in Oakland along E. 14th Street between 107th and 109th Avenues—capable of an annual capacity of 50,000 vehicles. The building's design perfected the linear nature of the assembling room invented in the previous decade: "The chassis materials are assembled on the first floor, while the body work is done on the second floor, at the same rate of speed. When the completed chassis arrives at the end of its assembly line, the completed body is ready to be lowered on it and made fast. Then the complete car is ready for the testing room."[121] Alongside the company's Midwest factories, the Oakland facility assembled models like the Durant Fours and Sixes, and later the new economical Star car of the associated Star Motor Company, helmed by Durant's colleague and former Chevrolet manager Norman De Vaux. Durant Motors operated the factory until 1930, yet cars like the Star never panned out; Ford responded to this Model-T competitor by lowering its prices. Durant Motors was renamed De Vaux–Hall Motors and limped on until 1933. In 1936, the facilities were sold to General Motors—they became part of the Chevrolet Trucks and General Motors Truck and Coach Division.[122] A year later, the combined Foothill and E. 14th GM assembly plants churned out over 100,000 vehicles.

MUNICIPAL AIRPORT

In 1920, the ever-industrious William Durant broadened his sights to the sky, and founded the Durant Aircraft Company. He acquired land for Durant Field, a grassy plain at the foot of 82nd Avenue in East Oakland, intending to start an aircraft assembly plant. As he reasoned, ships, railroads, and automobiles had been the successive drivers of Oakland industry. It was only natural to assume that aircraft would have a similar effect in the future.

While aircraft production never took off in Oakland, in 1925, the chamber of commerce called for the creation of a municipal airport in order to win airmail contracts from the US Postal Service. One year later, the city council voted to acquire a 682-acre tract on Bay Farm Island, at the far southeastern end of the city. A year later still, the newly formed Board of Port Commissioners of the Port of Oakland was tasked with developing the airport.[123] Soon, an administration building and two industrial-style hangars (90 feet by 200 feet) rose, followed by four more hangars. Hangar Four was the most massive nonmilitary hangar ever built in the United States: 55 feet tall, and 300 feet by 142 feet in plan. Parking was provided for 1,500 cars, and a hotel, with 37 rooms and a restaurant, opened. It was the first airport hotel in the world.[124] There were as of yet no fixed runways. A grass landing field, illuminated by border lights at night, allowed for planes to choose a number of different directions since they needed to take off and land into the wind. Anthony Fokker, the famed German aircraft designer, praised Oakland Municipal Airport as the best in the world.[125]

By the early 1930s, Oakland Municipal Airport had swelled to 845 acres, the largest in the nation. The initial development of airports wasn't impelled by passenger travel. Airfares were considerably more expensive than first-class travel by train or ship. Air voyages were also dangerous; one out of a hundred passengers died in 1928.[126] Instead, the airport's progress was catalyzed by the needs of the post office and the feats of celebrity airmen and airwomen. In 1925, the Air Mail Act was passed by Congress, turning responsibility for carrying the mail to commercial air carriers, under control of the US Post Office. A year after that, on May 20, 1927, former mail pilot Charles Lindbergh flew from Roosevelt Field on Long Island to Le Bourget Field in Paris.[127]

California fell in love with airplanes, as it had earlier with automobiles. In 1929, its 172 airports and 1,129 licensed pilots numbered twice as many as New York's.[128] The Bay Area saw the founding of numerous airports besides that of Oakland: in Alameda, Berkeley, Concord, and Livermore as well as one at Mills Field on the peninsula south of San Francisco.[129] Similar to railroads and automobiles, western cities took to new technological developments that helped bridge the enormous distances within the West and between it and other places. Just as importantly, quickly embracing a new technology like the airport offered a city the promise of securing and maintaining regional prominence for years to come.[130]

In Oakland, these factors would play a role in the airport's development. Four days after Lindbergh's flight, James Dole of the Hawaii Pineapple Company offered $25,000 for the first flight between Hawaii and the United States mainland. Lieutenants Lester Maitland and Albert Hegenberger took up the challenge, and on June 28, 1927, flew in an Army Fokker C-2 airplane from Oakland Municipal Airport to Wheeler Field in Honolulu in 25 hours and 49 minutes. The flight brought great fame to the pilots as well as the airfield.[131] At the end of 1927, Oakland was chosen to be the western terminus of the transcontinental airmail route. The US Airmail Service delivered 22,386,000 letters that year. An intermittent route, with numerous stops along the way, had been established in 1924 between New York and San Francisco.[132] Four years later, the Boeing Air Transport Company (later to become United Airlines), based at the Oakland Municipal Airport, offered a 30-hour mail service to New York with two flights daily.[133] Airmail for the entire Bay Area, the latest transcontinental connector, now came through Oakland.

The town briefly possessed one of the largest and busiest airports in the nation. In 1931, Oakland Municipal Airport became the western headquarters for United Airlines and offered cargo shipments by Transcontinental and Western Air (the original full name of TWA) and passenger travel by Maddox Air and Western Air Express. The main weather station for the Pacific Coast Airways reporting chain was located in the airport administration building. Using mainly DC-2, DC-3, and Boeing 247 aircraft, annual passenger numbers increased from 4,000 in 1929 to 91,000 in 1940.[134] In 1937, a new traffic control tower was built adjacent to the United Airlines building. Plans were hatched for more hangars and, in 1940, the port purchased additional tidelands, bringing the airport's total to 1,200 acres. There were hopes for new and expanded runways, and a doubling of overall capacity.[135] But compared to its early years, many of these plans remained plans. At the time, an airport analyst, John Walter Wood, commented on the Oakland facility: "Along with so many other airports, less foresight has been shown in the planning and layout of the airport, which has had sporadic and unplanned growth, the placement of buildings and other facilities of the earlier, smaller landing area bearing little relation to the present airport now in the process of expanding."[136]

To be sure, airports are driven by a continual demand for longer runways, advances in air traffic control, and larger and more elaborate terminals. In all those respects, during the 1930s, San Francisco's airport, 12 miles south of downtown, was overtaking Oakland's. Although founded the same year as Oakland Municipal Airport, Mills Field (now SFO) had lagged initially. By 1933, though, many of the same regular airlines that were flying out of Oakland were also scheduling flights at Mills Field. Runway expansion began in 1935 and two years later a new terminal opened, an opulent Spanish Colonial design meant to woo wealthy travelers.[137] That same year, United Airlines announced Mills Field would be its new headquarters. By 1940, United Airlines and TWA, as well as Pan-American transpacific service, were based at the San Francisco airport. The Second World War worsened Oakland's predicament, as commercial operations were curtailed after the attack on Pearl Harbor, and ceased entirely between 1943 and 1945. The same restrictions were not placed on Mills Field, giving it a great advantage in the postwar boom in air travel.[138]

By the end of the Second World War, notwithstanding inertia at the airport, Oakland's industrial economy was healthy. Manufacturing and transshipment contributed to the creation of a wage economy that supported the West's second-largest—after Los Angeles—industrial sector and one of the nation's fastest-growing populations. While Los Angeles benefited from the discovery of nearby petroleum fields and went on to become a major producer of automobiles, aircraft, tires, glass, and chemicals, Oakland's industry gravitated to a balance between resource-based goods, electrical machines, shipbuilding, and automobiles. Its plentiful, well-paying jobs benefited most Oaklanders.

Compared to the southland behemoth or the industrial giants back east, Oakland's industrial complex was modest. Chicago provides a comparison with respect to the transition from resource to advanced industrial manufacturing amid the growth of the West. In *Nature's Metropolis* (1992), historian William Cronon relates the history of Chicago's emergence into an industrial powerhouse to its railroad-led rapport with a vast midwestern hinterland, one where logs, hogs, and grains were transported from Michigan or Iowa or the Dakotas to Chicago and turned into lumber, pork products, and cereals. Similarly, but augmenting rail with oceanic shipping, Oakland's industrial economy grew through relationships with the timberlands of the coastal Pacific, the grain belt of the Central Valley, and smaller sites of agrarian resources across the West and Pacific—as far as the Philippines. Still, the greater size of Chicago's hinterland, coupled with the Windy City's centrality within the United States, led it to create a larger industrial base for the production of steel, grain harvesters, apparel, machine tools, and other elements used in metal fabrication. While Chicago controlled the bulk of regional manufacturing, as compared to its ring of much smaller industrial cities like Gary, Indiana, Oakland never fully corralled Bay Area industry, scattered as it was across San Francisco, South San Francisco, Alameda, Emeryville, Berkeley, and Richmond.

Lastly, some troubling questions appeared over time, putting into doubt Oakland's industrial fortitude after the Second World War. Would shipbuilding retrench once again as it had after the First World War? Could more industries, following the path of Magnavox and 78-rpm recordings, be subject to pressures for geographic relocation? What would happen if Oakland's nearby agricultural hinterland was claimed by suburban development or if new means of transport, like trucks, allowed for a dispersal of farmland? Would automobiles and their road networks launch new zones for all types of industry beyond Oakland's borders?

Part II

Part II

Space for Automobiles

In 1898, only eight years after electric streetcars first ran on Oakland streets, Dr. L. E. Nickolson drove a steam automobile down those same roads. Within a few years, he acquired two more automobiles, each an improvement over the last. Oakland's first car-owner, Nickolson was hard on his mechanical workhorses, stating: "I have traveled in the three machines over 30,000 miles. I never could possibly do with two horses what I am doing now with my two machines and two horses would cost as much to keep as the two machines with the possibility of the animals being taken sick and dying on my hands at any time."[1] He and other doctors in Oakland used the steam automobiles for their house calls, claiming they could tend to more patients using a car than by horse. Replacing tires was easier, the doctors agreed, than shoeing a stallion.

At the turn of the century, 150 residents of Alameda County owned steam or gasoline automobiles. Twenty years later, efficiencies with regard to the speed of powering up a vehicle and the distance one might drive led gasoline engines to corner the market. Along the way, such automobiles became easier to use and more reliable, their chassis equipped with better springs and pneumatic tires and their motors ignited by electric starters.[2] Once a novelty, the internal combustion engine was turning into a mainstay. In 1919, the number of registered automobiles in Oakland reached 33,878, when most cars were still open air. By 1929, as enclosed automobiles became the norm, the number almost tripled.[3] The Alameda County seat continued its romance with the internal combustion engine, so that by 1946, Oakland counted only 2.8 persons per automobile, compared to 4.6 persons per car nationally.[4] Through these decades, motor vehicle registrations easily outpaced population growth.[5]

It was one thing to own an automobile. It was quite another matter to use it efficiently. Across the nation, road construction lagged behind automobile ownership. In 1914, seven vehicles took up each mile of paved road. By 1922, that number had bounded to 22.[6] The weight of motor vehicles, their speed, and the volume of their traffic meant that streets were in constant need of upgrading: paving and repaving; installation of proper curbs, gutters, and sewers; and a whole lot more. Transportation infrastructure, having developed in a time of horses and carriages, needed to be improved, and this turned out to be a hugely disruptive transformation of Oakland's circulatory system—not only the way people got around but also the way they related to each other and the built environment.

From the 1920s through the 1970s, an urban mobility infrastructure built on walking, mass transit, and shared street spaces—accommodating commerce and sociability in addition to circulation—was transformed into one attuned to exclusive vehicular passage. Oakland's blocks and buildings were re-engineered, overturning long-standing relationships between a building and its lot coverage and a house facade or storefront and its sidewalk. Since both downtown and streetcar commercial districts had been conceived before the car, their lot-line development and continuous building walls gave way for another of the automobile's needs—parking. To alleviate congestion, arterial streets were reconceived, equipped with traffic signals, converted into one-way routes, and, quite destructively, widened by one or more lanes. Finally, the coexistence of asphalt roads with Key System rails and crossings came to a head—streetcars would be the losers.

Oakland was split between the growing ranks of cars and dwindling mass transit. A driver's operative city—the places one frequents on a regular basis—expanded, leaving those without cars, often the poor and minorities, more isolated and cut off from commercial and employment opportunities. Highways, tunnels, and bridges were constructed to accommodate automotive culture's inflated horizons. Those networks reordered the geographical equation of American urbanity that had been in place since the mid-nineteenth century, shifting a person's ties from their neighborhood and downtown to their home and the metropolitan region. While a backlash against the automotive domination of urban space took place toward the turn of the millennium, decades of pro-automotive policies reverberated into the twenty-first century. Instead of becoming denser and more pedestrian- and transit-friendly, Oakland had accelerated its suburbanizing trends and neglected the substantial segments of the population prevented, due to racist practices, from equally participating.

DEMISE OF THE STREETCAR

The fortunes of the streetcar waned just as those of the automobile waxed. Nationwide, streetcar ridership peaked around 1925, thereafter undergoing a precipitous decline. Automobile owners enjoyed many advantages over streetcar riders. They could travel whenever and practically wherever they pleased. They could stop multiple times on an outing. They could transport bulky items. Aside from a house, a car became the most expensive purchase most consumers made. And like a residence, one's car was a symbol of accomplishment, identity, and style.

Motor vehicles had it over street railways in other ways as well. For one thing, the public sector assumed responsibility for building and fixing roads for them. Starting in 1919, state governments enacted gasoline taxes as a means to finance road construction, augmenting property and labor taxes as well as automobile registration and license fees; California got on board in 1923. The federal government soon figured out the efficacy of the new gasoline levy, and it eventually financed more than half the cost of new roads and highways in the United States.[7] By comparison, privately owned street railways were undercapitalized and beset by debts incurred during earlier times of expansion. The standard five-cent fare persisted longer than commonsense economics dictated, leading many companies to defer system-wide maintenance and modernization. Streetcar companies were responsible for maintaining right-of-way, including repaving damaged streets where rails ran: the only exceptions were the few cities where mass transit was partially or fully run by a municipality.[8] No wonder, as transportation historian Vernon Sappers commented about the East Bay's Key System, "the company would resist any effort made by cities to require the improvement of pavement around track areas, or the renewal of track if that necessitated new pavement or relocation of the track."[9]

By the mid-1920s, not only were automobile owners abandoning mass transit in droves, another internal-combustion-engine competitor to the streetcar had emerged—the bus or motor coach. Buses succeeded the informal jitneys operating during the teens in converted Model T automobiles.[10] In 1918, San Francisco's Municipal Street Railway launched some of the nation's first bus lines.[11] The East Bay's San Francisco–Oakland Terminal Railways Company (soon to be reorganized as the Key System) followed three years later, with buses accommodating 22 passengers on lines to Montclair and Mills College. The number of routes grew. In 1927, motor coaches were still but a fraction of the overall Key System; 46 compared to 517 streetcars and interurbans. A decade and a half later, motor coaches outnumbered streetcars 408 to 180.[12]

Why did buses powered with dirty diesel fuel replace cleaner-energy electric streetcars? For starters, launching a motor coach line was faster and less capital intensive than a streetcar line; there was no need for rails, trolley poles, overhead wires, or generating stations. Unlike street railways, burdened with long-standing regulations that required a motorman and a conductor, buses could run more economically with one operator who both drove and collected fares. New transportation infrastructure projects also recognized the cost advantages of building exclusively for vehicles, without accommodations for streetcars. In 1928, the Posey Tube connecting Oakland to Alameda was finished without rails; the first significant statement that streetcar lines were on their way out. Most importantly, buses aligned with the dispersed settlement patterns generated by the automobile, and because of the far lower capital costs for starting a line, buses were able to drive on many more roads and more easily forge new routes.

Through the 1930s, those Oakland streetcar lines burdened by declining ridership were abandoned or converted to buses. While gasoline rationing and decreased automobile production and sales temporarily revived streetcar fortunes during the Second World War, the reprieve ended after

VJ-Day. Automobile ownership rocketed skyward and mass transit usage plummeted. In 1947, the new *Transit Facilities and Mass Transportation Element* of Oakland's Master Plan recommended retaining streetcar service on just five arterials leading to the central business district.[13] That proved optimistic. For in 1946, National City Lines purchased the Key System. A holding company of American City Lines, National City Lines acquired considerable equity funding from a series of automotive-related industries: General Motors, Standard Oil of California, Phillips Petroleum, Mack Manufacturing, and Firestone Tire and Rubber. They bought up transit systems throughout California—San Jose, Sacramento, Stockton, Fresno, Pasadena and Long Beach—and everywhere replaced streetcars with buses. In 1948, electric streetcar service in the East Bay came to an abrupt end.

Initially, National City Lines promised some trolley coaches running on existing power lines. Such electrified buses had proved effective in hilly cities like San Francisco and Seattle.[14] But in the similarly undulating East Bay, across cities already equipped with the necessary electric infrastructure, plans for trackless trolleys, or electric buses, should have happened.[15] Yet although some trolley coaches were delivered to the system, they were never used. National City Lines declared them impractical due to the high costs of maintaining the power lines and generating stations.[16] Instead, gasoline- or diesel-powered GM coaches replaced electric streetcars on all lines where mass transit service was continued. Approximately 144 miles of double-track streetcar line were ripped out and streets repaved.[17] A system built up over half a century was taken apart in less than two years. Oakland's experience wasn't unique. Nationwide, there had been 40,000 electric streetcars in 1935. There were only 1,400 left by 1967.[18] The sole surviving streetcar lines were in cities that used underground transit tunnels, like Boston, Philadelphia, and San Francisco, corridors where the fumes of gasoline or diesel buses would be difficult to ventilate.

Was the rapid demise of electric streetcars the result of their internal structural deficits? Or part of a corporate conspiracy aimed at increasing market share for bus vehicles, gasoline, rubber tires, and lubricating oils?[19] As David St. Clair surveyed the evidence for a conspiracy, he found no smoking gun. Yet in light of the sound economics of trolley coaches and streetcars, the rapidity and sheer extent of the replacement operation remains worthy of further investigation. He concluded that "the activities of those alleged to have conspired to motorize and destroy public transit reveal a pattern that... is highly suspect, to say the least."[20]

Initially, interurban transbay service appeared more immune to the threats of automobiles and buses. Some of its right-of-way was not shared with vehicles and, starting in 1938, a double-track on the lower deck of the Bay Bridge leading to a new transit terminal in San Francisco replaced the rail-to-ferry routes. Regardless, rail operations scaled back. In 1940, the Key System took over Southern Pacific's interurban lines, and a year later, Sacramento Northern interurbans ceased passenger service on their 18 miles of track from Oakland to Lafayette. After the war, Key System interurban service suffered steep ridership declines, losing half of its passengers between 1945 and 1958.[21] Since vehicular traffic on the Bay Bridge far exceeded expectations, the prospect of devoting the entire lower deck to motor vehicles became irresistible—especially given plans for the new BART system, discussed later. On April 20, 1958, Key System interurbans made their last run to San Francisco.[22]

TRAFFIC CONGESTION AND PARKING WOES

A newfangled metropolis was emerging, unchained from the radial spokes of the rail age to the all-over sprawl of the automotive era.[23] In Oakland, houses sprouted on land left vacant during streetcar times, the lots more than several blocks distant from the transit lines. Subdivisions were platted on winding, steep hillsides where streetcars had never penetrated. On major arteries, automotive-related businesses sprang up: dealerships, repair garages, parts stores, and filling stations.[24] Upper Broadway north of downtown was thronged with showrooms and became known as Auto Row. The dealerships transformed the experience of urbanity as one crossed Grand Avenue from pedestrian to automotive, from sidewalks fronted by stores and movie theaters to a cityscape of vehicular attractions where human-scaled doors yielded to garage-scale ramps and the motorized dynamics of the street passed directly into those of the building. The high-ceilinged showrooms might be clad with historicist ornaments harkening to one bygone century or another, yet invariably they were faced in vast sheets of plate glass to make plainly visible the lineup of new vehicles inside to the perceptions of motorists outside.

The fact that railroads ended in central stations and streetcars converged at a few key intersections had led to the creation of the dense American downtown. Now motor vehicles were streaming into that mass of transit, building, and crowds. But how could drivers get there on a road network that had never been intended for such traffic volumes? And once there, where would they park?

In the 1920s, Miller McClintock, a transportation engineer who had studied at Harvard University, came up with a series of highly influential ideas on traffic control. His traffic survey was the first means for scientifically assessing the vehicular use and occupation of urban space. The survey counted vehicle numbers, speeds, and turns, and differentiated through and destination trips—a trip, say, going from Clinton to West Oakland through downtown or one leading to downtown as a destination. It noted the availability of curb parking. His friction theory was based on the idea that movement could be speeded up by separating corridors for pedestrians and vehicles. This attention to vehicular proclivities resulted in the greatest reconception of the street since the founding of cities millennia ago. Historically, streets had been multipurpose circulation routes shared by pedestrians, horses, other animals, carriages, and later mass transit omnibuses and streetcars. They were outdoor living rooms, linear plazas, accommodating circulation, commerce, entertainment, and sociability. Altogether differently, as the automobile age accelerated, traffic engineers like McClintock proposed streets as specialized channels for internal-combustion vehicles. If earlier, intermittent streetcars had already made streets less safe for other activities, motor vehicles now wrested this vast area of urban space for their use alone. "Efficiency-minded engineers," historian Peter Norton notes, "reconceived the street, from curb to curb, as public infrastructure for transportation."[25] Pedestrians were pushed off the street to a newly raised space, the sidewalk, and, when crossing streets, were herded into marked lanes whose occupancy would eventually be measured by a timer. The idea of "jaywalking," or unlawful pedestrian movement across streets, came about as a means to limit injuries caused to pedestrians by motor vehicles but also as part of a hierarchy of street space that put motor vehicles at the apex.[26] Roadways, the quintessential

Figure 11. Automobile congestion on E. 12th Street. Near 22nd Avenue in the San Antonio District, 1935. Photo courtesy of Oakland Public Library, Oakland History Room.

public space alongside the plaza and park, no longer offered unlimited access and use to anyone not using a vehicle—a seminal moment in the erosion of public space.

Even shorn of wayward pedestrians and their myriad activities, there simply wasn't enough street space downtown or in other key commercial corridors to accommodate escalating numbers of motor vehicles. Instead of the smooth driving promised in advertisements, automobiles were getting bottled up in traffic jams of their own making, caused by their enormous popularity. How could vehicular flow be bettered? In the 1910s and 1920s, street improvements, many of which have become so commonplace as to be practically unnoticeable nowadays, ensued:[27] the conversion of narrow streets from two-way to one-way routes; the reduction of turns at intersections to reduce accidents;[28] the installation of interconnected electric traffic signals to stagger vehicle flow and similarly reduce collisions at intersections.[29]

Parking motor vehicles was a related challenge. In residential neighborhoods, cars could be stationed at the curb, on driveways thrust onto lots and, in Northern California, where most houses had basements partially aboveground, they could be stored in enclosed garages excavated and built under houses.[30] In downtown Oakland, curbside parking was in especially high demand. Regulations were implemented against "sleepers," cars parking overnight and limiting the availability of spots during the morning rush. Later, the parking meter attempted to solve the problem of car owners leaving their vehicles at the curb all day long.[31] Meters appeared on the streets of Oakland after the Second World War.[32]

In the larger picture, curbside parking conflicted with the goal of traffic flow. Since parking at the curb took one or two lanes of traffic from streets, reducing curbside parking became a common conclusion of downtown traffic studies. Off-street parking, in commercial lots and garages, was the obvious solution. In 1918, in downtown Detroit, Max Goldberg had opened the first commercial parking lot; by 1961, there were over 19,000 off-street parking facilities in the United States.[33] Yet in the dense downtown fabric, where could the lots or garages be located? Initially, working with the turning radius of cars, architects carved parking garage ramps and platforms into older buildings, and squeezed lots onto the rare unbuilt space. In 1927, the Oakland Business District Association launched a survey, the counting done by Boy Scouts, to determine how many motorists parked at the curb or utilized parking lots or garages. The finding: Too many cars parked curbside. Shortly afterward, another civic group of businessmen and merchants, the Downtown Oakland Property Owners Association, addressed the critical need for parking spaces voiced by retailers, and began planning for a system of parking lots behind principal streets, parallel to major shopping thoroughfares like Washington Street and Broadway.[34] The scheme never materialized, as the Great Depression and Second World War temporarily reduced motor vehicle traffic and parking demands. But after the war, as automobile purchases and traffic rebounded, the question of parking was once again front and center.

Harland Bartholomew was a city planner based in St. Louis whose firm authored comprehensive plans as well as specialized reports concerning parking, street improvements, and highways. Like McClintock, Bartholomew was part of the first generation of transportation and city planners who worked across the nation and helped implement an automobile-first agenda for the American city. Bartholomew had worked with the

City of Oakland in the 1920s on such issues and was hired again a couple of decades later. His *A Report on Off-Street Parking and Traffic Control in the Central Business District* (1947) noted that the business health of the city's central business district—the maintenance of its high levels of retail sales and employment—depended upon shoppers and workers arriving, for the most part, by automobile and finding a place to park. "An automobile is as useless," Bartholomew sagely noted, "when it cannot be stopped as when it cannot be started. New traffic arteries and expressways to bring more traffic to the business district may well be wasted if adequate terminal parking facilities are not provided."[35] In 1947, there were 5,075 curb spaces and 7,793 off-street spaces in downtown Oakland. Bartholomew encouraged expanding the city's number of one-way streets, reducing curb parking by 500 spaces, and providing 7,500 additional off-street parking spaces. The additional off-street spaces were to be located in 16 ground-level parking lots, seven structured garages, and other ground-level lots under a new Eastshore Freeway.[36]

For the next several decades, parking lots and garages sprouted across downtown. Continuous, pedestrian-friendly building walls, lined with services and stores, were eroded. In 1958, two three-story buildings on 11th and 12th Streets, between Broadway and Franklin, were demolished for a new, 15,000-square-foot lot, the eighth such structure erected by the Downtown Merchants Association.[37] Such lots were regarded as temporary measures, yet many of them persisted for years, creating dead zones. Parking was considered a superior use for lots occupied by older buildings because, once demolished, their high property tax assessments could be replaced by lower rates. In 1958, behind City Hall, the city sponsored its first off-street parking garage, a 577-car, pre-stressed concrete structure with clear-span spaces for stalls and sloped floors to connect the ground level to an upper open deck.[38] Other garages were constructed for large stores like Breuner's and Capwell's, and the new Kaiser Building (1959), a combined office and retail center, included a massive five-story parking garage containing 1,339 spots. Compared to the street-level lots, parking garages sometimes had admirable architectural virtues, such as concrete forms that expressed the internal movements of vehicles up ramps. In 1962, Oakland's most dramatic parking garage was built on the site of the old courthouse annex. Meant to serve the new Alameda County

Administration building, the 730-stall garage spiraled up seven stories in a circular structure that culminated in a rooftop heliport.[39]

Parking became a priority for neighborhood retail streets as well. The 1947 Bartholomew plan proposed adding hundreds of off-street parking spaces to the Grand Lake shopping district. Five potential sites, each of which would have necessitated the demolition of dozens of houses, were identified, including ones along Longridge Road and behind Lake Park Avenue.[40] Although the proposal was not acted upon, in 1961, the City of Oakland undertook a study of 11 neighborhood business districts: Foothill Boulevard and 34th Avenue; Foothill Boulevard and Fruitvale Avenue; 23rd Avenue and E. 14th Street; Park Boulevard and E. 18th Street; Grand Lake; Piedmont Avenue; Grove and 55th Street. The next year, the neighborhood parking lot program got underway, and lots with anywhere from 30 to 400 spaces were built in most of the locations.[41]

Not all proposals sailed through. In 1969, a plan surfaced for a partially underground 114-car parking garage at the intersection of Grand and Bellevue Avenues, just outside downtown in the Adams Point District. The construction of numerous apartments in Adams Point now led nearby restaurants and offices to request a parking structure in Lakeside Park, the city's "central park." Vigorous opposition from conservationists and residents led to its defeat. [42]

WIDER STREETS

In the 1920s, planners recognized that one-way streets, traffic signals, parking meters, and parking garages/lots were not enough to solve the problem of traffic congestion. Too many cars, trucks, and buses were clogging the city's narrow streets. Many of them were double parking, further reducing capacity. Already prior to the First World War, New York City had enlarged important routes like Fifth Avenue to ameliorate mounting motor vehicle traffic, first enforcing building setback requirements to shift sidewalks toward buildings and, then, shifting the street toward the sidewalks—increasing space for vehicular traffic.[43] Miller McClintock had initially opposed street widening, arguing, in *Street Traffic Control* (1925), that widened streets would only attract more cars. Two years later, realizing that more and more cars were inevitable, he reversed his position. In the essay "How the City Traffic Problem Will Be Solved," he advocated for the provision of greater street area.[44]

In 1923, the Oakland City Council approved the Street Commission's plan to widen 20th Street between San Pablo Avenue and Harrison Street, a distance of a third of a mile. The city needed another east–west artery north of 14th Street on what had once been referred to as its northern fringe, a thoroughfare that could relieve congestion on other cross-town streets as well as funnel traffic from the new residential subdivisions being built in the nearby lower hills. Four years later, just as H. C. Capwell's department store was planning its relocation to Broadway and 20th Street, the latter street was widened from 40 feet to 60 feet by moving buildings back 20 feet on the southern side of the thoroughfare; the cost of $850,000 was paid from the city's general fund and, in what would be a common practice for street improvements, by locating an assessment district (and its additional taxes) onto properties lining the affected street.[45]

In 1924, the City of Oakland widened and improved the entirety of E. 14th Street from 50th Avenue to the San Leandro line, a relatively easy job since most of the route had yet to be intensively developed.[46] That year, in a lecture to Oakland city officials, Bartholomew recommended sweeping changes to other, older sections of Oakland's street system: more streets; wider streets; and streets taking on specialized roles like accommodating rapid transit lines, heavy truck service, or pleasure cars.[47] As a result, the Major Highway and Traffic Committee of One Hundred invited him to prepare a study on the issue, which led to *A Proposed Plan for a System of Major Traffic Highways* (1927). Bartholomew was distressed that the city had grown in an illogical, inefficient manner. Street extensions were inconsistent, complicated by topography, the insertion of new roads and transit lines, and the activities of real estate subdividers. Many streets came to abrupt ends or were twisted into narrow byways. There was no uniform width for arterials, collectors, or secondary streets. Bartholomew praised the fact that several 100-foot-wide arteries ran north, like Broadway and San Pablo and Telegraph Avenues. But most other arterials attained this width for only portions of their routes. There weren't enough wide, through streets connecting the arterials.[48]

Juxtaposing these street conditions against traffic volumes, Bartholomew put forth a plan for specialized streets across the surface of Oakland. Downtown, curb parking would be reduced, sidewalks narrowed so as to widen streets, and some buildings condemned for similar widening. Arteries leading downtown would be broadened. A bypass loop would be constructed to funnel through traffic around and away from the downtown core. A through route for trucking and industrial use would be established along the waterfront. In residential areas, crosstown routes would be built to connect disparate neighborhoods; for instance, Moss Street, Santa Clara Avenue, and Excelsior Street could be amalgamated into a major crosstown route.

Working with Bartholomew, the City of Oakland developed many of his ideas into *A Major Street Plan for Oakland*.[49] The 1928 plan set forth a comprehensive process whereby several streets—Foothill Boulevard, E. 18th Street, Fruitvale Avenue, College Avenue, and Hopkins Street—were widened and upgraded into crosstown arterials.[50] East 12th Street was developed as a new route serving East Oakland's growing bayside industries, and its section by the dam over the Lake Merritt Channel almost doubled in width from 120 feet to 220 feet. Seventy-seventh Avenue was extended a mile and a half to the new Oakland Airport. Part of Grand Avenue was conceived as a distributor street to funnel traffic around the northern edge of the central business district. Finally, improvements were suggested for Skyline Boulevard. It had been built as a largely gravel road in the 1910s to accommodate motoring enthusiasts desirous of marine panoramas and rolling foothill country. The new plan proposed paving and widening, and by 1933 the project reached from Montclair to Golf Links Road.[51] The proposals of *Major Traffic Highways* and *A Major Street Plan for Oakland* were consistent with contemporaneous efforts around the country. In 1929, landscape architect Saco Rienk de Boer guided the *Denver Plan*, where the city was adapted to the automobile through a system of circumferential bypass routes, radial feeders, diagonal highways, parkways, and widened streets.[52]

Street widening can be likened to cardiovascular surgery on urban arteries in order to clear up traffic blockages and produce clear-flowing vehicular vessels. But like surgery, street-widening projects were invasive with long recovery times and permanent complications. Hundreds of buildings were demolished, facades were sliced off, and entirely new building fronts constructed for their shallower interiors. Many buildings were hoisted up and shifted back on their lots or moved to other locations.[53] Wide sidewalks became a thing of the past. Street trees became less commonplace.

Since street widening required action on many contiguous lots and blocks, necessitating the acquisition of additional right-of-way, the process was time consuming, causing disruption for months or years. Property owners sometimes complained because of the disruption or threat of condemnation. Other times they protested the assessment district increases that piled onto their property tax bills. Sometimes their protests succeeded. In 1925, a 14-foot addition to Washington Street between 7th and 14th Streets was abandoned when property and storeowners claimed the widening would harm businesses. On the whole, though, most property owners saw an uptick in their property values when a street was widened and more dense commercial development replaced widely scattered residences. Given the growth of an auto-industrial complex, support for improved vehicular infrastructure was considerable. The chamber of commerce, automobile clubs, neighborhood improvement associations, and national planning leaders advocated converting narrow streets into modern boulevards, thoroughfares wide enough accommodate a citizenry who drove while commuting, on errands or simply on pleasure excursions. Like streetcars before them, the corridors of improved automotive arterials experienced increases in land values and became a magnet for development—albeit usually of an automotive-related nature.

BRIDGING THE REGION

Before the automobile era, four principal paved highways diverged out from downtown Oakland: San Pablo Avenue to the north toward Berkeley, Richmond, and the Crockett Ferry; Broadway northeast and, then snaking up over a thousand feet, to the tunnel leading to Central Contra Costa County; E. 14th Street to the south toward Hayward and San Jose; Foothill Boulevard heading southeast to Hayward, and over the Dublin Grade to Livermore and the east.[54] A sequence of small bridges led to Alameda. San Francisco could be accessed directly only by ferry. Then, in an eight-year span from 1928 through 1936, most of these linkages were remade, scaled up to the traffic loads and speeds of automobiles, buses, and trucks.

The Oakland estuary, or San Antonio Creek, snakes five miles from San Francisco Bay to the tidal canal that since 1902 has separated Oakland from Alameda and turned the latter into an island. A series of bridges spanned it. As automobiles became more popular and shipping traffic increased, the goal of simultaneous movement of boats and ships on the estuary and vehicles on bridges linking the two cities became impractical. When bridges were raised to allow a ship to pass, automobiles were halted. The problem was most severe in the lower reaches of the estuary alongside downtown where major shipyards had been developed during the First World War. In 1923, as a partial remedy, the Harrison Street railroad bridge was removed. Six years later, the swing bridge on Webster Street came down, having been, over the years, knocked into the water by steamers, set afire, repaired countless times, and condemned as an impediment to industrial development. To allow safe passage for larger ships in the estuary, an underwater tube for vehicles was proposed to replace the swing bridge. Its advantage would lie in the fact that a tunnel would allow for rapid and uninterrupted passage for vehicles, while aboveground it would consist merely of ventilation shaft buildings, freeing up the shoreline for maritime/industrial projects.

Completed in 1928, the George A. Posey Subway was the second major tunnel project in the United States, following by one year the considerably longer Holland Tunnel that connects New York to New Jersey. Compared to its predecessor back east, the Posey Tube had a wider (65-foot) diameter, used similar methods for mechanical ventilation of exhaust gases, and represented the first use of precast, reinforced concrete for an underwater tunnel. It was also, as historian Frank Lortie tells us, "one of the earliest major transportation facilities in California designed just for the car."[55] Accessed in Oakland on Harrison Street, the tunnel led to Webster Street in Alameda. Quickly exceeding capacity, especially after the military buildup in Alameda during the Second World War, plans commenced for a second nearby tunnel, and the Webster Tube opened in 1963.[56]

The most grueling route out of Oakland had long been the one to Contra Costa County over the East Bay hills. The traditional path led up Claremont Canyon to the ridgeline and then down Fish Ranch Road. After

Figure 12. Posey Tube. Tunnel interior between Oakland and Alameda, 1922. Photo courtesy of California History Room, California State Library, Sacramento.

1903, an alternative, funded by Oakland's Merchants Exchange, was built in the next canyon to the south, Temescal Canyon. Carriages and cars snaked several miles up Tunnel Road to an elevation of 1,040 feet before entering a quarter-mile timber-lined tunnel. The new passage was still inadequate for a modern metropolis, and plans for a more easily accessible tunnel were proposed during the mid-1920s. Two routes were suggested for the canyons to the south: one on Moraga Road and up Thornhill Canyon, and the other up Park Boulevard and Shepherd Canyon, with both connecting to a tunnel opening onto Redwood Canyon and Moraga. Another possibility was to dig a new Temescal Canyon tunnel at a lower elevation than the existing tunnel. In 1929, assured of state funding, Alameda and Contra Costa Counties agreed to create a Joint Highway District to design and manage the project. Like the East Bay Municipal Utility District and the East Bay Regional Park District, discussed in the next chapter, the Joint Highway District expressed the willingness of cities and counties in the East Bay to collaborate on projects of regional importance. The district decided to use the Broadway extension route, at the lower, 754-foot elevation. Ground was broken in 1934 and in late 1937 two concrete-lined bores, 3,168 feet in length with 22-foot roadways, opened to traffic.[57]

The new Broadway Low-Level (or Low-Elevation) Tunnel reduced travel times and brought Oakland into closer contact with an undeveloped hinterland; one could now drive from downtown to Walnut Creek in about half an hour. At the time, Walnut Creek covered only one square mile and had a population of 1,200. Lafayette and Orinda were even smaller.[58] The tunnel instigated a real estate boom and Central Contra Costa County became a subdivision builder's paradise. The growth was so rapid that by 1952 there were complaints of too much traffic through the tunnel, as the daily count of cars grew from 4,000, when the tunnel opened, to 30,000.[59] A third, larger, and traffic-reversible bore through the Oakland hills was added in 1964, ventilated with forced air and lit with fluorescent tubes.[60] The entire complex was renamed for Berkeley's Thomas Caldecott, former chairman of the Alameda County Board of Supervisors and instrumental in pushing the additional bore through.[61]

More ambitious was a bridge connecting Oakland to San Francisco. It arose out of the town's rivalry with the city. Starting in the 1910s, Joseph Strauss, an engineer, began talking up the idea of a bridge between San Francisco and Marin County and, in 1923, the state created a special district to oversee the realization of what would become the Golden Gate Bridge. Oakland leaders became concerned that San Francisco would soon increase its hinterland beyond San Mateo and Santa Clara Counties, and began promoting their own bridge traversing the bay as a means to put Oakland and Alameda County in a better position within the Bay Area.[62] At the time, the San Francisco Bay was under consideration by the War Department for a major naval base. Local jurisdictions, federal agencies, and the State of California became involved in a contentious set of discussions on the parameters of the bridge project and, especially, its potential location. President Hoover and California governor C. C. Young broke through the logjam in 1929, creating the Hoover-Young San Francisco Bay Bridge Commission and, a year later, recommending a double-deck structure from Oakland's rail hub to Yerba Buena Island and finally to a landing point slightly south of downtown San Francisco.[63]

The task was formidable. The bridge, including land approaches, would be eight and a half miles in length, four and a half miles of which would span open water—the longest and most massive bridge of its kind ever built. The design phase occupied two years and construction, assisted by Kaiser Industries, which broke ground in 1933, took an additional three years.[64] The completed San Francisco–Oakland Bay Bridge consisted of two spans linked by a tunnel through Yerba Buena Island: a novel combination of a cantilevered and truss bridge and a double suspension bridge supported by a central anchorage.[65] Funded by bonds, and designed and built by the State Department of Public Works (with 50 engineers supervised by Chief Engineer C. H. Purcell), the aluminum-gray bridge was dedicated in November of 1936, six months before the Golden Gate Bridge was completed.[66] To the citizenry of San Francisco and the East Bay, the bridge was more than an engineering marvel. It encapsulated the region's fusion into a single vehicular metropolis.

Vehicles from San Francisco heading to the East Bay descended from the cantilevered section to a toll plaza set on a peninsula jutting into the bay atop sand fill. From here they continued east, ascending again onto the 8,500-foot-long East Bay Distribution Structure, which lofted them over the Oakland rail yards, rail and interurban lines (16 grade crossings in all) to an interchange offering routes to the north, east, and south without any left-hand turns or right-angle crossings. Located in Oakland and Emeryville, the multilevel, concrete and steel-girder Distribution Structure was a monument in and of itself, containing ramps, viaducts, and overpasses.[67] Branching off the Distribution Structure, a new road, East Shore Highway (Highway 40), followed the shoreline north to Berkeley. Cypress Street led south through West Oakland and then via 7th Street to downtown. A newly amalgamated sequence of Oakland roads (Highway 50) headed east: 38th Street, followed by Moss Avenue, Santa Clara Street, and then Excelsior Avenue and Hopkins Street; these were renamed MacArthur Boulevard in 1942 in honor of General Douglas MacArthur. Improvements to this partially completed cross-city route were resumed after the Second World War, as Moss Avenue was widened from Broadway to Perry Street and Hopkins Street was widened and straightened to 55th Avenue.[68]

CROSSTOWN RUSH

East Bay drivers used the East Bay Distribution Structure as a means of not only getting on or off the Bay Bridge but also circumventing street congestion in Oakland and Emeryville. Operating until its replacement by the Eastshore and MacArthur Freeway approaches to the Bay Bridge between 1959 and 1966, the East Bay Distribution Structure anticipated the freeway's creation of a separate domain of vehicular travel, elevated above (or less commonly, depressed below) grade-level street traffic as well as rail lines. After the war, street widening and expansion resumed, in part for the reasons that had launched the idea decades earlier: arterials that could accommodate higher traffic volumes and open up new districts for development. To a greater extent than before, newly reconstructed arterials were specialized as to destination and function.

Harland Bartholomew returned to Oakland in 1947, and released (alongside his parking study) *A Report on Freeways and Major Streets in Oakland*. Once again, the St. Louis planner analyzed Oakland's overall circulation system and found it antiquated and in need of modernization. Bartholomew proposed the "improvement" of more than a dozen avenues to four lanes and 80-foot width.[69] He had several objectives in mind: to facilitate crosstown routes; to provide better access to and between freeways; and to allow new arterials to serve as feeders for areas of significant building construction.[70] Like streetcars at the beginning of the century, vehicular arteries were conceived as a stimulus to urban development. Historically, Oakland's cadastral pattern—of street and block layout and dimensions—developed along a series of arterials radiating out from downtown. Up until this point, following development patterns initiated by streetcar subdivisions, those arterials had been widened. Yet, as traffic grew beyond all expectations and automobiles afforded the possibility of diverse routes across the city, Oakland officials became aware that the city lacked adequate crosstown arterials to join those spokes at varying points across the city's surface. Following many of Bartholomew's recommendations, better east–west connections were forged in several locations between the primary radial spokes of North Oakland. In 1956, as part of the 27th Street extension and widening, two 41-foot roadways separated by a dividing strip created a diagonal shortcut from Telegraph Avenue to Grand Avenue, allowing southbound cars to avoid downtown on their way east.[71] In 1960, a four-lane crosstown route was created along 40th Street, the former route of Key System trains. The widening took place from Broadway west to San Pablo Avenue, and was intended to relieve Bay Bridge–related congestion on nearby MacArthur Boulevard.

Feeders for the new freeways were another priority from the 1950s through the early 1970s. West Grand was widened from Telegraph all the way to the recently completed East Shore Freeway; frontages on one side of the street were removed for 17 straight blocks.[72] Fifty-first Street was

Figure 13. Bancroft Parkway. Mayor Clifford Rishell at street widening near 98th Avenue in Elmhurst, 1956. Photo courtesy of Oakland Public Library, Oakland History Room.

widened from two to four lanes between Broadway and Grove Shafter Freeway ramps, just west of Shattuck Avenue.[73] In East Oakland, 14th Avenue, Park Boulevard, Lincoln Avenue, and 35th Avenue were widened from two-lane collector streets to four-lane arterials, connectors between the new Warren and MacArthur Freeways.[74] Similarly, a new four-lane 98th Avenue created a crosstown route from the airport to the zoo and hillside residential subdivisions.

Widened arterials were also envisioned as a means for organizing Oakland into single-use functional zones. East 12th Street along the waterfront and Skyline Boulevard atop the crest of the hills were enlarged to facilitate, respectively, anticipated industries/aerial BART structures and high-end residences/regional parks. Responding to fears of industrial relocation of the Chevrolet, Fisher Body, and Peterbilt Motors vehicular assembly plants to suburban locations, an alternative arterial was created to relieve congestion on commercial Foothill and MacArthur Boulevards. Bancroft Avenue was widened from 50nd Avenue to 67th Avenue and, from there to the San Leandro line, widened even further into a parkway. "The project," its backers claimed, "will convert Bancroft from a rundown, non-continuous street and railroad right-of-way into a major intercity thoroughfare and railroad parkway."[75]

The lakeside boulevard around Lake Merritt had initially been intended for carriages and strolling. The rise of the automobile altered that vision. New roads were now built for rapid car access to other parts of the city. In 1951, in order to accommodate greater traffic volumes between downtown and East Oakland, the 12th Street road system dam was upgraded again, this time to 12 limited-access lanes. Pedestrians could no longer cross directly from the Municipal Auditorium to the lake; instead, three underpasses were provided beneath the mini-freeway. A few years later, Harrison Street, as it skirted alongside the other side of Lake Merritt, was enlarged to four lanes in each direction. The short stretch of highway was aimed at meeting the expectation of higher traffic volumes around the developing office district by the lake; the new Kaiser Center would open in 1959.[76] Those on foot intending to cross between the lakeside park and its surrounding districts soon found their journey unpleasant and unsafe.

Across town, the streetscapes that resulted from such widening efforts had similarly deleterious outcomes from the perspectives of both aesthetics and walkability. On the 27th Street cut, a series of new, low-rise commercial buildings were constructed, laced with vehicular drives and parking lots and resembling a suburban automobile strip. On West Grand Avenue, the north side of the street was torn apart by house demolitions and relocations; yet, because the widened street now catered to new auto-uses, a drive down the avenue shows few intact blocks even on previously unaffected southern side. On 51st Street, which continued to be zoned residential, most of the houses on the south side remained intact, while the northern side, where demolitions and relocations occurred, was turned into a linear strip of landscaping. Pleasant walking streets, where sidewalks faced parks, houses, apartments, or stores, were recast into fast arterials where the pedestrian experience was framed by blank walls, parking lots, and vehicular access lanes.

This transformation occurred amid a segregating urban society. Overall, the triumph of automotive infrastructure exacerbated those demographic changes, producing modes of mobility and occupancy of street space reflective of class and race. White residents had higher rates of automobile ownership and privileged access to disparate points across the town

and suburbanizing region: jobs, regional parks, shopping malls, and subdivisions. Black and other minority residents depended more upon mass
transit—just as Key System streetcars and interurbans were being phased
out and replaced by less frequent bus service. Relegated to the inner city
by discriminatory statutes and outright intimidation when they ventured
into white America, they were forced to make use of rundown streets and
sidewalks as primary social, commercial, and recreational spaces. But
here too there would be issues.

Before the automotive age, overcrowded commercial sidewalks along
streetcar lines had been regulated by cities to improve pedestrian flow.
That would no longer need to be the case. With the demise of streetcars,
retail and service businesses, as we shall discuss in chapter 10, "Shopping
Centers and Storefront Streets," were despoiled across the town's aged
avenues. Corner stores on collector streets closed or turned to sales of
cheap liquor. Vacant storefronts multiplied on arterials like Grove Street
(now Martin Luther King Jr. Way) and Foothill Boulevard. Given the
rampant unemployment that came to plague the minority community by
the early 1960s, many of those thoroughfares became sites for unpermit-
ted or illegal transactions, some of which—illegal sales, gambling, drugs,
prostitution—carried prison terms. From the point of view of city leaders,
sidewalks were better left empty, and they became subject to aggressive
policing. Even benign forms of black civic expression, such as hanging out,
were recast as loitering, a municipal offense.[77]

During the Jim Crow era in the South, ordinances had required blacks
to cede the sidewalk to white passage—relegating them to the gutter.[78]
Now, hardly any whites walked the sidewalks of Oakland's minority
neighborhoods, but police patrols turned into a western version of white
passage, one where lights, sirens, guns, and handcuffs subjected minority Oaklanders to constant harassment. Over time, the town acquired a
deserved reputation for police brutality.[79] The racial contrast was striking.
While white suburbanites were experiencing a world without sidewalks,
shopping having shifted to highly controlled centers and malls, being on
the street or sidewalk while black in the Oakland flatlands subjected one
to suspicion and potential arrest. Yet from the point of view of many in
the black community, the sidewalks and streets were home, the poor person's living room and backyard rolled into one: "All citizens have a right to

stand," Black Panther co-founder Bobby Seale quoted Huey Newton after a confrontation with police in West Oakland in the mid-1960s.[80]

Since the construction of boulevards across Europe in the nineteenth century, wide sidewalks had stood for an ascendant urbanity, spacious thoroughfares for strolling along carriageways, for meeting and socializing, for taking in the resplendent scene from a café table. While Oakland's arterials never reached those heights of leisurely living, McClintock and Bartholomew's automobile-first plans made sure that free-flowing vehicular movement would trump all other uses. By 1961, writing in *The Life and Death of Great American Cities*, Jane Jacobs famously outlined the modernist and suburban effects of long blocks, superblocks, homogenous uses, and enlarged building scale on the life of city streets, bemoaning the associated loss of sidewalk vitality and security. The cumulative effects of such practices were highly noticeable on Oakland's cityscape. Being modern meant driving. Should it be surprising that those streets became less safe? There were fewer pedestrians and thus fewer eyes watching what was going on, other than those of the frequently overzealous police. Alongside other factors, foremost among them employment discrimination, the spike in crime in Oakland that began in the 1960s was attributable in part to the attenuation of the city's pedestrian vitality by decades of infrastructural projects geared to automobiles. Similar to how television provided a compelling residential alternative to the movie theater, the enhanced vehicular corridors contributed to a cityscape conducive to automotive domesticity; in each case, the city's privileged residents spent more time in privatized, glazed environments, cut off from the society and landscape around them.

CHALLENGES TO THE VEHICULAR PARADIGM

By the latter 1960s, some children of the suburbs who had moved back into the city began to take back street space from cars and vehicular traffic: a few blocks at a time, a few hours at a time. They held marches, demonstrations, and festivals that closed streets to vehicular traffic. They established flea markets in parking lots. They challenged the regional priority on automotive passage and parking.

A little earlier, as part of the late 1950s Clinton Park urban renewal plan, discussed in chapter 8, "Housing Injustice," street diverters were erected at numerous intersections in the neighborhood just east of Lake Merritt. Their goal was to reduce cross-town traffic through the neighborhood, preserving its spaces for residents. A few years later, the novel Oakland idea spread to Berkeley, and, in 1975, the Berkeley Traffic Management Plan expanded the use of diverters across the city.[81] A driver made a turn onto a secondary street and encountered a "No Thru Traffic" or "Dead End" sign. Landscaped mini-plazas with concrete-barrels or pylons diverted or altogether blocked movement across myriad Berkeley intersections.

In 1978, several San Francisco neighborhoods began to employ a different tactic to reduce traffic on their neighborhood streets. They turned from building parking garages or discouraging long-term parking through overnight bans and street cleaning to a program that issued permits to residents, allowing them to park curbside while commuters and nonresidents were limited to a few hours of free parking before they were issued a ticket. Over time, across Oakland, resident permit parking became commonplace around BART stations, hospitals, colleges, and busy shopping streets, places where nonresidents frequenting those facilities or businesses were grabbing and holding onto street parking for much of the day.[82]

Starting in the 1980s, an altogether different challenge to the buildup of rules governing streets took place in East Oakland. What has become known as the Hyphy Movement built upon California traditions of motorcycles, low-riders, dragsters, and cruising, but with a twist. This time, the protagonists were largely black, inner city, and frustrated with decades of municipal neglect and police provocation. Sideshows, where cars painted in garish colors and sporting big rims dance to hip-hop music, first began in the parking lots of declining shopping centers like Foothill Square and Eastmont Mall.[83] Initially, they were a way of showing off souped-up vehicles alongside crafts fairs. Over time, they became kinetic and hazardous, taking over streets like MacArthur Blvd. in Elmhurst or Maritime St. and Middle Harbor Rd. by the Port of Oakland, ignoring traffic laws amid an atmosphere of raucous partying, vehicular bravado, and occasional violence.[84] A means of reclaiming public space, a manner of spectacle as politics, a way of getting lit, events blared out, "I'm here too, do you see me?"[85]

Of course, the difference from millennial traditions of multi-use street space was that noisy, smoky, and stylized automobiles spinning dangerously out of control right next to pedestrian onlookers were now the dominating attraction. Oakland, which had long embraced the evolving norms of automotive culture, had now happened upon a devolution of the notion of driving as a means to quickly and orderly get from one place to another.

By the turn of the millennium, the tide was turning worldwide against automobile domination of urban street space. The concept "street calming" grouped a set of measures to accommodate users of the road other than cars. They involved road barriers, speed bumps, narrowed streets, reduced lanes (often with new bicycle lanes), and lower speed limits. The aim was to slow driving and re-create the street environment as a public space. European and Asian cities pioneered such efforts: Germans reducing road space for cars; Danes giving priority to pedestrians and bicycles; Japanese providing comprehensive rail networks and huge numbers of bike spaces at each station.[86] In 1999, Dan Burden set out the influential *Street Design Guidelines for Healthy Neighborhoods*, an attempt to reverse the nearly century-long American effort to increase traffic volume and vehicle speed and exclude all modes of nonvehicular movement from streets.[87] Many of its recommendations were tried out in Oakland.

Robert Raburn, president of the East Bay Bicycle Coalition, put forth a 1998 plan advocating for more designated bike lanes and making all streets more bicycle-friendly; a year later, backed by the city council's endorsement of a bicycle master plan, Grand Avenue's three lanes of traffic on each side were reduced to two, allowing for bike lanes. From that point onward, colorfully painted bike lanes spread across the city. Meanwhile, in 2003, the redesign of the commercial district around Clinton Park sacrificed numerous parking spaces in order to beautify the barren streetscape by constructing bulb-outs that introduced plantings distinguished by date palms. So too did Lake Merritt's earlier street widening projects prove unpopular in a part of the city dedicated to park usage and walking. In 2012, the concrete highway maze atop the 12th St. dam was remade: the roadways reduced to six lanes; a channel opened between the lake and estuary; and additional park acreage was created in front of the Municipal Auditorium, lying vacant since 2006 due to city budget cuts.

Curbside parking was once again questioned, but this time not from the perspective of enhanced vehicular flow. In 2005, San Francisco inaugurated Park(ing) Day, an annual event where parking spaces were temporarily converted to public parks. Five years later, some of those spaces were made permanent as the city kicked off the Parklet movement, a means of crafting microparks on retail streets.[88] In front of a sponsoring restaurant or café, a landscaped seating area, at least six feet deep or the width of a parked car, took the place of a couple of parking spots, endowing the sidewalk with activities of interest on both sides: store windows and interiors on one side, sculpted planter boxes and seating on the other. Oakland's first parklet debuted in 2012 in front of Farley's coffee shop at 33 Grand Avenue, bicycles hung from racks framing the seating area. Other parklets were later constructed on 40th Street in Temescal, 25th Street between Broadway and Telegraph, 20th Street downtown and MacArthur Boulevard in the Dimond District. One, on Martin Luther King Jr. Way near the MacArthur BART, took the form of a streetcar, a tribute to the days when electric traction streetcars rumbled along the streets of Oakland and sidewalks were filled with pedestrians of all ethnicities and social classes.

4 The Politics of Parks

In 1902, a reporter for the *Oakland Enquirer* took a walk in Oakland's foothills and admired the scene: "There near at hand, but somewhat beneath you, are the regular, neat streets, the artistically constructed and painted residences, shady trees and green lawns. While beyond are the placid waters of the bay, on which graceful ships with their tall masts and countless spars and ropes are tranquilly lying at anchor. Then turn around and enjoy the sight of green carpeted hills."[1] Four years later, city planner Charles Mulford Robinson saw the same setting when he came to Oakland, yet complained about the absence of public open spaces: "There is not a spot on all the long bay and estuary frontage where they are free to watch the ceaseless panorama of shipping. And on those hills, with their noble views and romantic glens there are no free pleasure grounds to which they have inalienable right."[2] Other than Lake Merritt, nothing broke up the vista of houses and industries.

Robinson's *A Plan for Civic Improvement for the City of Oakland, California* (1906) proposed to remedy the situation. A great park would wrap around Lake Merritt and take in the bluffs on its eastern side. It would continue uphill to a foothill tract around Indian Gulch (now Trestle Glen), and sometimes referred to as Sather Park for its picturesque groves of oak and eucalyptus that were informally used for hiking and picnick-ing. It would further extend a finger upslope through Dimond Canyon and finally ascend to the high ridgeline and its valleys of redwood groves. To Robinson, the park would "offer one of the most picturesque and romantic walks and drives that can be found near any large city of my acquaintance in this or other countries."[3]

Energized by *A Plan for Civic Improvement for the City of Oakland, California*, local park advocates argued for the value of open spaces for the town's spiritual and physical health. They pointed out that plentiful green-swards would improve its standing among the cities of the nation. They provided optimistic estimations of the financial value that parks accrued to the residential real estate in their vicinity. Though possessing few built structures, parks also generated considerable construction employment: for road networks, parking lots, picnic areas and recreational attractions, signage, trails, and extensive landscaping. Regrettably, the City of Oakland acquired few parklands. Its difficulties may be explained by the fact that despite their many benefits, parks fit like a round peg into the rectilinear drive toward urban development.

Compared to other urban functions, parks offered the intangible ben-efits of city life amid nature. And within the context of those functions, the creation of parks was communal, akin to public transportation and civic structures, and distinct from the individual impulses behind auto-mobiles, housing, industry, and commerce. Setting aside permanent open space took land off the tax rolls and out of the real estate and building contests. One mayor's embrace of municipal beautification often did not carry over into the term of the next mayor, as progressive and laissez-faire administrations alternated during the early decades of the century. Like civic buildings, discussed in the next chapter, park acquisitions required municipal outlays, chronically in short supply, but they did not lead to the monumental, built outcomes that politicians and donors craved. Land acquisitions for parks were neglected by Oakland, as they were by Los Angeles, because Oakland, like LA, grew up against a vast unbuilt terrain. The need for parks was more easily dismissed in such cities of single-fam-ily houses, confident of their stunning natural surroundings and unmind-ful that they could be lost in a short period of time.

Despite the setbacks, two remarkable types of parks emerged in

Oakland. In the first case, resistance to land acquisitions due to conservative supermajority voting thresholds led a visionary park superintendent to
work with less, assembling on existing park land a series of fantasy parks,
playgrounds, and zoo that represent an important chapter in California's
celebrated creation of themed environments. Even more impressively, the
state's water shortages and need for watersheds to service growing cities
led a consortium of East Bay cities to form a regional agency to provide
a reliable supply of water, and soon afterward another regional agency
to acquire and administer surplus lands as semi-wilderness parks. While
parks were sought by the City of Oakland in the populous flatlands and
lower hills and rarely acquired, they were secured in considerable numbers by the East Bay Regional Park District in the remote upper hills. Not
until the century's closing decades would the bayfront, denuded of industry and cleansed of sewage, become an open space option, but as with the
hill parks, there too automobiles were required to reach most sites.

FIRST PLANS

It was 1864 and Frederick Law Olmsted, who had recently designed Central Park in New York, had come to the East Bay. Invited to design a campus for the College of California in Berkeley, the noted landscape architect
soon received a commission to design a cemetery in Oakland.[4] Aware of
the inadequacies of the downtown graveyard, the Mountain View Cemetery Association had used bonds to purchase a 266-acre tract, two miles
to the north. Olmsted came up with a proposal to plant the hillside with
cedars from Lebanon, stone pines from Italy, and native cypresses and
oaks. He contrasted formal geometry with natural landforms, playing
the linear entry axis and its sequence of circular fountains against a circuit of paths curving along the topographic contours past gravesites.[5] All
the while, Olmsted did not regard a cemetery as an appropriate spot for
recreational outings. Only parks could satisfy that need. Then he had an
epiphany regarding his original commission. Why not shape parks as sin-
uous, green alternatives to the rectilinear, gray city? Strawberry Creek on
Berkeley's university campus could be the spine for a meandering pleasure
lane for pedestrians and carriages that would follow the uphill narrow-

ing of the flatlands' alluvial fan into the hillside canyons.[6] It was an idea before its time.

During the first half of the nineteenth century, America's city streets were treeless stretches of milled planks, bricks, and stone. Parks, a novel idea imported from the European palace garden, offered an antidote to the hardscape. By 1877, 20 American cities had created parks, and by 1902, that number had jumped to 716 cities.[7] The expansion was argued on health, aesthetic, and ethical grounds. As cities grew, residents found themselves farther from trees, meadows, lakes, and rivers. They spent their leisure time on streets and alleys, graveyards and amusement parks, places where it was hard to exercise and play sports, to breath fresh air, or to admire nature's wonders. Many park advocates were also reformers who held moral objections to pleasure grounds featuring dining, drinking, music, and entertainments ranging from puppet shows to circus acts.[8] Parks could steer adults and children alike away from such temptations or debaucheries and toward the healing powers of nature.[9]

In those decades, New York's Central Park, San Francisco's Golden Gate Park, and Philadelphia's Fairmount Park set the standard for large city parks—places that were also settings for museums, promenades, and statuary. After 1900, with Robinson at the lead, parks became a key element of the City Beautiful Movement. If, in the popular imagination, the City Beautiful is associated with neoclassical sculptures and civic monuments, planting green interludes across the breadth of the city was also one of its paramount objectives. Kansas City led the way. Between 1893 and 1917, city planner and landscape architect George Kessler developed a system of parks and parkways: starting with the large Swope Park, and including medium-sized parks, smaller squares, and boulevards connecting the green spaces.[10] Along the boulevards, land values rose between 200 and 500 percent. In a significant argument that would often be used in the future, parks not only offered curative powers to their users, they enhanced real estate values.[11]

Oakland was late to park acquisition. In the 1890s, blessed with abundant, undeveloped grasslands and woodlands across its hills, and deluded that those greenswards would persist alongside the growth of the city, its voters twice turned down park bond issues.[12] In 1905, the election of progressive Frank K. Mott as mayor brightened park opportunities. Mott grew up in Oakland, built up a hardware business, and served several terms on the city council. Once mayor, he brought Robinson to the city, agreeing with the city planner that Oakland's existing 38½ park acres were paltry.[13] While not implementing Robinson's grandiose plan, Mott began to acquire parklands, stating: "It is well known that no city of any pretentions these days hesitates about acquiring lands for park and recreation purposes."[14] In 1907, he pushed through a bond issue for park purchases. Lake Merritt was its centerpiece. The 155-acre tidal slough at the heart of Oakland had been named for Samuel Merritt, who in 1869 erected a dam at what is now 12th Street, linking downtown by road to what would become East Oakland.[15] Site of the nation's first wildlife refuge, it was not until 1891, when Mayor Melvin Chapman purchased the brackish waters, that the slough was walled into the permanent contours of a lake. Mott now added 45 acres of parkland alongside the lake—Lakeside Park—and acquired additional parcels for a recreational boulevard intended to encircle the lake.[16] The bond issue also created the city's first neighborhood parks: an expanded Bushrod Park in North Oakland; DeFremery Park in West Oakland; and, a few years later, Mosswood Park in North Oakland. A Park Commission was established, gradually filling the new parks, some of which were converted estates, with playgrounds, clubhouses, swimming pools, tennis courts, and baseball diamonds.[17]

WILDWOOD PARK

Mayor Mott turned next to Robinson's idea for a roughly 300-acre lake-to-canyons park, which reprised Olmsted's idea of taking advantage of Oakland's steep topography and its opportunities for long-distance vistas and riparian promenades.[18] In the years after his plan was published, the city could have purchased the land, for what was often referred to as Wildwood Park, for as little as $1,000 an acre.[19] But Mott got caught up in other projects like the construction of a Municipal Auditorium and new City Hall.[20] Although civic leaders, like department store owner H. C. Capwell, joined the push for the purchase of Trestle Glen and the Sather Estate from The Realty Syndicate, by 1913 land prices had risen to $6,000 an acre. A dynamic economy was leading to land banking by realty com-

Figure 14. Lone car in undeveloped Montclair. Upper Hills,
ca. 1925. Photo courtesy of Oakland Public Library, Oakland
History Room.

panies with an eye toward subdivision. When the Park Commission, in
1914, settled upon an option to buy much of the land, Mott and Oakland
leaders delayed final action, worried by the acquisition cost of $250,000
and its effect on outstanding city debts.[21] A year later, Werner Hegemann's
East Bay plan concurred with Robinson's urgency, writing: "The time will
have gone by when timid men without vision managed to bar the East
Bay cities from the rank among American park cities they deserve by their
unheard of possibilities of using their parks all the year around and of
blossoming not during one or two months but every month of the year."[22]
Hegemann noted that Oakland had only one-tenth the park area it should
have according to good American standards.

Mott was soon out of office, and the election of a new mayor, John
L. Davie, cast dark clouds over Wildwood Park. Originally from upstate
New York, Davie moved to Oakland in the late 1880s and was first elected
mayor in 1895. Voted in once again in 1915, and this time in office until
1931, the longest run for any Oakland mayor, Davie repeatedly opposed
increasing taxes to improve city services, reining in Oakland's civic ambitions.[23] Early in his term, Davie put a stop to any idea of purchasing land

for Wildwood Park on an installment basis. There were but a couple of park victories during Davie's early years; in 1917, the city purchased 12 acres of the Dimond Estate for Dimond Park; two years later, park advocate Edgar Sanborn was able to push through the purchase of 68 acres for Sequoia Park, which grew, after subsequent land purchases over the next few decades, into a 410-acre preserve—the eventual Joaquin Miller Park and later highlighted by the steps and cascades leading to the Woodminster Amphitheater, erected in 1941.[24]

Between 1918 and 1920, after gaining support from John McLaren, superintendent of parks in San Francisco, the Sierra Club and Contra Costa Club, the Oakland City Council and Chamber of Commerce, and local civic organizations like the Oakland Rotary Club, Lions Club, Kiwanis Club, and Building Trades Council, momentum appeared to be building at last to secure lands for Wildwood Park. A committee of Oakland Rotary Club members proposed an even more grandiose 600-acre pleasure grounds, encompassing Trestle Glen, the Sather Tract, Dimond Park and canyon, Sequoia Park, and Redwood Peak. They were racing against time. Across the Oakland foothills, barbed wire and signs were going up, blaring "Private," "No Trespassing," and "Keep Out."

The Wickham Havens Realty Company, inheriting some of the Sather Tract from Smith and Havens's Realty Syndicate, and noting the city's inaction, began developing the land. Nearby, the Walter H. Leimert Company, with Havens's initial involvement, platted the Lakeshore Highlands subdivision around Trestle Glen. Without its 60 acres connecting Lake Merritt to the uphill canyons, a lake-to-canyons park could never be realized. Predictably, Mayor Davie fought against buying land for the park. He insisted on a vote by the city's citizens who, he claimed, did not want more parks.[25] His steadfast opposition to Wildwood Park prevailed. In 1921, workmen ripped out the last old-growth oaks of Trestle Glen. Streets were graded. House frames were erected. Oakland would never possess a large central park.

In defeat, park advocates moved onto the next remaining wild lands that might be converted into parks. In 1922, led by Howard Gilkey, the city's landscape engineer, Lee Kerfoot, superintendent of parks, and Sanborn, now president of the park board, a bond issue to purchase 1,547 acres of mountain parks—including Dimond Canyon, Shepherd and Palo

Seco Canyons, and Redwood Peak—went to the voters. Again, as in 1898, the majority voted for the parkland acquisitions. Again, the two-thirds threshold was not reached, dooming the idea of conserving the city's canyons and redwood groves. In 1923, Oakland had 43 city parks on 335 acres, even though the average park size of cities on the Pacific Coast— San Diego, Los Angeles, San Francisco, Portland, Tacoma, Seattle—was approximately 1,800 acres.[26] As city planner Carol Aronovici complained at the time, opportunities have been neglected in Oakland and Berkeley. Their parks were small, scattered, and lacking in any vital rapport with the centers of their cities.[27]

Kerfoot and Sanborn kept trying. Davie kept stalling appointments to the park board until he could stack it with opponents of large-scale park expansion. A pitched battle took place in 1927 concerning two pro- posed parks, McDermott in West Oakland and Mandana, a fragment of undeveloped land within the old Wildwood Park perimeter. Stating, "I am against the waste of taxpayer's money in the purchase of land that is even worthless to real estate developers," Davie staked out a position against parks that butted up against residential backyards or industrial sites, as was the case with both the seven-acre Mandana property and the 15-acre McDermott site.[28] Earlier Davie had fought the vast Wildwood Park. Now he inveighed against small parks. Davie opposed against flat parks that had no scenic value and yet he also opposed Mandana Park for being little more than a collection of cliffsides. Just when it seemed as if the pro-park forces had triumphed over Davie's objections, a voting technicality voided the purchase agreement for Mandana Park. McDermott Park met a simi- lar fate.

By 1931, as Mayor Davie was ending his long reign, prospects for more Oakland parks were bleak. The city had acquired Sequoia Park in the upper hills, yet the tract was distant from most of the city's residents, who lived miles away in the flats or lower hills. No sizeable parks, other than the eight-acre Municipal Rose Garden, were added until 1939, when 17 acres in East Oakland were turned into the Arroyo Viejo Recreation Center. Incredibly, that modest tract was to be the largest park added to the city's residential flatlands. All significant park additions would be situated in the upper hills or along the bayfront (and set apart by high- ways and train tracks). For Oakland's poorer residents, living in cramped conditions with minimal private open space, the magnificent hill parks especially were a long way off. Located in the "white part" of town, many people of color felt uncomfortable venturing up to those remote and often unwelcoming locales; during the 1920s, several large gatherings of the Ku Klux Klan were held in the hills above Oakland.[29]

The City of Oakland never fashioned a grand and accessible urban park, akin to Golden Gate Park; to this day, crowds drawn to the narrow strips of parkland along Lake Merritt attest to the demand for such a place. When the opportunity presented itself, when undeveloped lands in both the flatlands and lower hills were available, a mentality geared to business and the individual, epitomized by Mayor Davie, tied the city's hands. That lack of vision and public service counts as one of Oakland's lasting failures.

WATERSHEDS

Water shortages are a chronic problem in California, where it rains almost entirely in winter months. Season to season, rainfall is also highly variable. Procuring water thus became an early and critical component of city-making in Oakland. At first, entrepreneurs dammed some of the creeks rushing down in wet months from the hills, impounding water in dams and reservoirs, and piping it to consumers wanting indoor plumbing and irrigated gardens. In 1868, the Contra Costa Water Company built an earthen dam on a North Oakland creek and created Lake Temescal. Eight years later, Anthony Chabot dammed the larger San Leandro Creek just beyond the city's southern border to form what is now called Lake Chabot. Akin to the early years of streetcar transit, a succession of private water companies arose, merged, or went out of existence: the California Water Company, the Oakland Water Company, the People's Water Company, and lastly, the East Bay Water Company, formed in 1916. The latter inherited Frank Havens's vast land holdings in the East Bay hills reaching into Contra Costa County, and quickly dammed San Pablo Creek in Contra Costa County, creating the huge San Pablo Reservoir, more than twice the size of Lake Chabot. Despite the increased capacity, a devastating drought in 1918 exhausted local reservoirs for almost six months. All water needs had to be met by wells.[30] The story of water in the East Bay had become one of spotty service, depleted sources, and rising rates.[31] The inadequate supply threatened Oakland and Berkeley's ability to sustain and attract industry, precisely at a time when manufacturing was coming into its own.

In 1919, Berkeley mayor Louis Bartlett helped form the East Bay Water Commission to address those concerns. Engineer Philip Harroun was hired to investigate options for both creating a public utility to administer the water supply and developing a new and far larger watershed to meet future needs.[32] Harroun was aware of the other water projects in the state: Los Angeles's Owens Valley Aqueduct, completed in 1913; and San Francisco's Hetch Hetchy project, on which construction of the O'Shaughnessy Dam had started in 1919. He recommended that the East Bay cities not participate in Hetch Hetchy, reasoning that an independent East Bay project would promise lower rates, more reliable supply, and improved water pressure and quality.[33]

Mayor Davie accepted the residential and industrial demand for increased water, and yet was opposed to the creation of a regional agency with jurisdiction over the city; he preferred a city-managed water agency, but did little to develop that idea. Instead, Berkeley mayor Bartlett advocated for public ownership and scientific management of water resources, and pushed for a public vote on the matter. His progressive vision prevailed. Following the passage of the California Municipal Utility District Act in 1921, the East Bay Municipal Utility District was created in the ensuing 1923 election. Its first task was to acquire a large and reliable water source beyond the East Bay. The search led planners to eight Northern Californian rivers: the American, Eel, Feather, McCloud, Mokelumne, Sacramento, Stanislaus, and Toulumne. One by one they were analyzed. Some were deemed to have insufficient volume, others not clean enough, and still others either too far away or already targeted for local irrigation.[34] The Mokelumne was the last river in the running. Falling from the Sierra Nevada Mountains in Alpine, Amador, and Calaveras Counties, it could be dammed and stored in a reservoir closest to the Bay Area, from where water could be transported via an aqueduct to the East Bay cities.[35]

The efficient and model project was completed in 1929, ahead of San Francisco's Hetch Hetchy project. Mokelumne water was impounded at the Pardee Dam, in the Sierra foothills at Lancha Plana east of Lodi, and then sent along a 94-mile aqueduct to the vicinity of Orinda, all by gravity. Running through filter plants, the water was subsequently pumped up through the Claremont Tunnel from where it divided into a Wildcat Aqueduct, running north to Berkeley, and a Sequoia Aqueduct, extending south, via Oakland's Central Reservoir, as far as 98th Avenue.[36] Through the twentieth century, well over 80 percent of EBMUD water supply came from the Mokelumne watershed.[37]

In 1927, a few years after the formation of EBMUD and during construction on the Pardee Dam and Mokelumne Aqueduct, voters approved a $26 million bond to acquire the East Bay Water Company and its 40,000 acres of watershed, dams, and reservoirs. Two years later, after an assessment of its new territories, the utility, administered by former governor George Pardee, declared 10,000 acres as surplus to its needs—primarily the ridge-top along the crest of the hills in Berkeley and Oakland and the front canyon lands to its west.[38] A great opportunity was at hand.

REGIONAL PARKS

Citizens and groups—the Sierra Club, Contra Costa Hills Club, Oakland Park League, Oakland Recreation Commission, and East Bay Planning Association—were ready. In 1929, led by Robert Sibley, an engineering professor at the University of California, they founded the East Bay Metropolitan Park Association, later changed to the East Bay Regional Parks Association. Irving Kahn, grandson of Israel Kahn, founder of Kahn's Department Store in downtown Oakland, agreed to finance research into the creation of parks on the surplus land—the 1930 publication of *Proposed Park Reservations for the East Bay Cities*.[39] Authored by the Olmsted Brothers, the nation's premier park planning firm who had just completed a report on state parks in California, and Ansel Hall, chief forester and senior naturalist of the National Park Service, the report favored the creation of "large (park) units of complete and self-contained scenic and recreational value."[40] It was expected that the bulk of the new parklands, stretching for 22 miles, would come from surplus EBMUD lands, and be administered by either the utility district or a new park district. A few parcels in private hands might have to be purchased.

Proposed Park Reservations for the East Bay Cities was written with a sense of urgency. Rapid growth and rising land values were closing off opportunities for securing large tracts of parkland. The EBMUD surplus lands could end up as subdivisions. The report warned that the progress of cities depends upon adequate parklands: "With the growth of a great metropolis here, the absence of parks will make living conditions less and less attractive, less and less wholesome. Insofar, therefore, as the people fail to show the understanding, courage, and organizing ability necessary to grasp the present opportunity, the growth of the region will necessarily tend to choke itself."[41] To this end, the text recapped an argument that had been made for over three decades with respect to both Berkeley and Oakland's park deficit. The park acreage in the East Bay cities was mournfully inadequate, just 900 acres, or one acre of park per 500 people. The standard ration around the country was five times as high, one acre of park for every 100 persons.[42]

East Bay park advocates were aware of the new phenomenon of regional parks and their role in checking suburban development. Extra-large parks on undeveloped lands outside of cities were planned to prevent outlying districts from becoming—as many cities already had become—tedious stretches of houses, factories, and stores.[43] In 1895, Essex County, New Jersey, became the first county to assume supervision over park administration and development, creating regional parks in the Watchung Mountains.[44] Those same years, in Boston, Charles Eliot developed a report calling for a Metropolitan Park Commission, based on the region-setting precedent of the Metropolitan Sewage Act.[45] By 1900, Boston's Metropolitan Park District had grown to encompass more than 9,000 acres, becoming the nation's first "regional" park system.[46]

After publication of *Proposed Park Reservations for the East Bay Cities*, planning and implementation proceeded rapidly. In 1931, a thousand people gathered at the Claremont Hotel to petition for EBMUD to transfer the 10,000 surplus acres into an institution that would administer them as parkland. After EBMUD declined to manage the potential parks, an assembly bill, drafted by former Oakland mayor Mott, authorized the establishment of the East Bay Regional Park District (EBRPD). It passed in 1933, and included the cities of Oakland, Berkeley, San Leandro, Alameda, Albany, Emeryville, and Piedmont—together constituting a population of close to half a million persons. Unfortunately, after the Contra Costa County supervisors refused to sanction the election, fearing that parks would lead to higher taxes, El Cerrito and Richmond were forced to drop out.[47] The achievement was nonetheless considerable. "Never before," writes historian Laura McCreery, "had a state government attempted to form a 'special district' to integrate preservation and recreation for the citizens of a fast-growing urban area."[48] In the November 1934 election the measure sailed to victory by a two-and-a-half to one margin. Although opposed by the Oakland Real Estate Board, it was supported by the mayors of the seven cities included in the district; Robert Sproul, president of the University of California; Aurelia Reinhardt, president of Mills College; George Pardee, president of EBMUD; and Earl Warren, district attorney of Alameda County and future chief justice of the United States Supreme Court.[49]

The proposed parklands would not be donated for free. Approximately 18 months of negotiations with EBMUD on purchase prices for the surplus lands followed. In 1936, the first purchase was made for three parks: the 2,166 acres of Wildcat Canyon above Berkeley (later renamed Tilden Regional Park, after Charles Tilden, the Alameda businessman who served as head of the district's first board of directors); 227 acres for Roundtop above Oakland (later renamed Sibley Volcanic Regional Preserve, after Robert Sibley—eventually expanded to 678 acres); and 50 acres for the old Oakland reservoir, Lake Temescal. Civilian Conservation Corps workers went to work, blazing trails and firebreaks. Lake Temescal included amenities found in the kind of city parks lacking in the East Bay—a swimming beach, planted lawns with picnic tables, and recreation buildings.[50] Roundtop became a nature park reserved for hiking.

Over the next couple of decades, park expansion consumed most of EBMUD's surplus lands. In 1939, 1,494 acres were purchased for Redwood Canyon above Oakland (later Redwood Regional Park), which was subsequently enlarged to 2,074 acres. Called a natural arboretum by John McLaren, Redwood remained a wilderness park with a few groomed meadows and picnic facilities. In 1951, the district acquired the 82-acre Roberts Regional Recreation Area, for intensive recreational purposes, including a swimming pool, ball fields, a merry-go-round, and picnic tables for 5,000 people; and two years later, it included the 3,000-

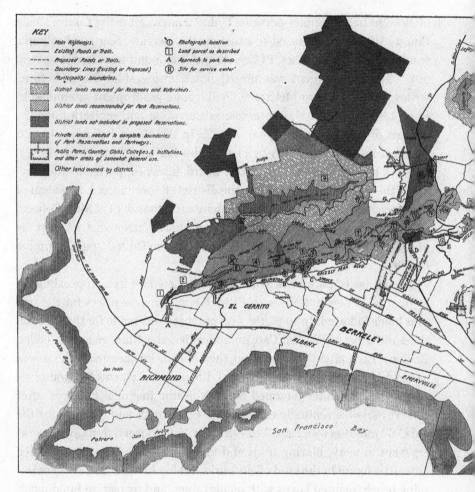

Map 4. Proposed East Bay Park Reservations. Surplus lands of the East Bay Municipal Utility District that formed the basis of the East Bay Regional Park District, 1930. Map courtesy of East Bay Regional Park District.

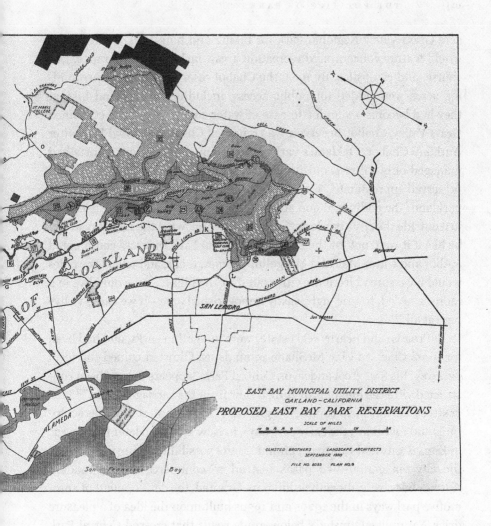

EAST BAY MUNICIPAL UTILITY DISTRICT
OAKLAND - CALIFORNIA
PROPOSED EAST BAY PARK RESERVATIONS

SCALE OF MILES

OLMSTED BROTHERS   LANDSCAPE ARCHITECTS
SEPTEMBER 1930

FILE NO. 6093   PLAN NO. 9

acre Grass Valley Regional Park for hiking and horseback riding; it too would feature concentrated recreation areas, including a gun range, golf course, and campsites. By 1964, the Chabot reservoir and 900 surrounding acres were added for public access, including boating and hiking; they had become a standby in case of water emergencies. The combined Grass Valley/Chabot Reservoir was renamed Chabot Regional Park after Anthony Chabot, Oakland's early water pioneer. Where city efforts had managed only paltry acquisitions, in less than 30 years the EBRPD had preserved approximately 6,000 acres of Oakland open space as permanent parkland; the additional 900 acres of Chabot Regional Park were located just outside the city's borders. "I shudder to think what the East Bay would be like if it were not for the East Bay Regional Park District," commented author and editor Malcolm Margolin. "Homes, roads, and telephone poles would have spread from the cities out over the hills... we would live in a more crowded, frantic, ugly, vastly impoverished area—if we cared to live here at all."[51]

But roads (and nearby real estate) were integral to parks, and had been for some time. As Clay McShane reminds us, Olmsted coined the term parkway; his first great endeavor, Central Park, "appears to have been constructed with the end of providing a view from the carriage drives."[52] Free of streetcars and strip commerce, graced with trees and sometimes sculptures and fountains, the early parkways, in New York, and later boulevards in Kansas City and Chicago, epitomized the possibility of moving through the city via garden-like paths instead of commerce-choked roads.[53] Automobiles were altogether different. Granted, the development of automotive parkways in the 1920s and 1930s built upon the idea of a pleasure drive. Yet unlike Olmsted's below-grade roads that crossed Central Park and did not interfere with its features, these vehicular parkways ruthlessly bisected existing parks, while their right-of-ways remained off-limits for safety reasons to pedestrians. The limited access highway may have emerged out of the parkway, but it brought to an end the parkway's benign and nonautomotive relationship with parks.[54]

From the start, as stated in *Proposed Park Reservations for the East Bay Cities*, it was maintained that parks must have easy automobile access and ample parking spaces.[55] How else would residents, dwelling miles below in the flatlands and lower hills, get to them? Some regional parks—Lake

Temescal, Roberts, and parts of Chabot—substituted for the city parks lacking in Oakland. Their swimming lakes, golf courses, picnic areas, sports fields, and other attractions demanded intricate and invasive internal road systems and parking lots. Others, like Redwood and Sibley, were provided with parking lots at trailhead entrances, but given their limited attractions aside from hiking, were spared too many internal roads and parking areas.[56]

The EBRPD's first master plan, issued in 1936, devoted considerable attention to automobiles and roads. It advocated for a continuous parkway from Claremont Canyon south to Lake Chabot, realizing that automobiles were necessary to access the ridges and their views of the bay and interior coastal ranges. To this end, parking lots and small picnic areas were planned. At the same time, park planners objected to residential development directly along the parkway—what became Skyline Boulevard. In fact, they recommended a 600-foot protective strip on either side of the roadway so that no adjacent structures would interrupt the view. They also favored slower roads that followed natural contours instead of high-speed roads built with long tangents and easy curves.[57] What they did not anticipate were the largely unavoidable consequences of road development. Roads not only brought Oakland's city dwellers to the new regional parks, they exposed them to undeveloped lands along the way, helping urbanites envision a new life in the upper hills. For several decades after the Second World War, Skyline Boulevard and the connecting arterials through the upper hills—Redwood Road, Keller Avenue, Golf Links Road—were consumed by residential subdivision activity; a Skyline Boulevard of linear parks offering splendid vistas of the bay was forsaken. The promotion of parkways (and regional parks) as recreational amenities suggested the appeal of not only getting out of the city on occasion but also of living permanently high above it.[58]

FANTASY PLAYLANDS

After the Second World War, William Penn Mott Jr., no relation to the mayor, ended up directing Oakland park planning toward a different kind of wonderland. A native of New York City, Mott Jr. had come in 1931 to study for a master's degree at UC Berkeley. After a 13-year career as a land-scape architect, he was appointed superintendent of Oakland parks in 1946; after leaving Oakland parks in 1962, he went on to head the EBRPD, the California State Parks, and finally the US National Park Service. From the get-go in Oakland, Mott Jr. crafted an ambitious 20-year plan envisioning automotive parkways to tie existing parks together as well as the acquisition of sizeable new lands beyond the approximately 950 existing acres of city parks. Plans were laid for a marine park on the south side of the Bay Bridge landing. A dam was proposed for Sausal Creek just above the Leimert Bridge in Dimond Canyon that would have created Inspiration Lake with beaches and boating facilities. Along Mountain Boulevard, near the site of the Chabot Observatory in Leona Heights Park, Mott Jr. came up with a vision for teenagers, replete with a miniature train track, model auto course, and other attractions like model airplanes and sailboats.[59]

These plans did not materialize, and by the late 1940s the Oakland Parks Department was running an annual deficit.[60] Procuring land for city parks in Oakland was still an uphill battle in a city run by anti-tax Republican mayors with meager civic ambitions. In response to this predicament, Mott Jr. changed course, embarking upon the creation of fantasy playlands on existing city parkland. He began at Lakeside Park. In 1948, Arthur Navlet, an Oakland nursery owner, had brought an idea to the Lake Merritt Breakfast Club, a group of prominent businessmen organized a little over a decade earlier to promote activities relating to Lake Merritt. Navlet had just returned from a trip east, where he had visited the children's zoo at Detroit's Belle Island Park.[61] Established the year before, it contained 20 enclosures for animals that eschewed drab cages and, instead, presented them in vivid colors and images taken from fairy tales and nursery rhymes. Navlet wanted to create something similar in Oakland and, with the support of the breakfast club, J. R. Knowland, Ingraham Reed, publisher of the *Oakland Post-Enquirer*, and Mott Jr. of Oakland Parks, that vision, Children's Fairyland, came together in a little over a year.

In September 1950, Children's Fairyland opened on a two-acre site in Lakeside Park. Right away the experience was unusual, as visitors—adults were admitted only accompanied by a child—entered through a door in

Mother Goose's shoe-house. Once inside, 17 thematic sets lay before them, financed by individuals, businesses, and institutions, and designed by Navlet, Mott Jr., and architect Russell Everitt, who had studied art at the Sorbonne in Paris.[62] They included curiously shaped abodes for the Merry Miller, Goosey Goosey Gander, the Old Woman in a Shoe, Peter Rabbit, the Little Red Hen, the Three Little Pigs, and the Little Red Schoolhouse.[63] Fairyland's innovation was to encourage children to play within those sets instead of looking at them from the outside as had been the case at the Detroit zoo. Going a step beyond books or movies, children could inhabit the spaces of fairy tales and incorporate their many textures and forms into their imaginative play.

A few years later, an acre of land was added. Sets were updated or replaced with new ones: a mushroom mailbox, Little Miss Muffet with an enormous black spider, Ten Little Indians, Alice in Wonderland, Robinson Crusoe, a Chinese Tree Tea House, a Chapel of Peace with stained-glass windows telling the story of creation, and the Jolly Trolley, little electric streetcars running around much of the site.[64] A memorable 1959 addition was the "Talking Book" for the various sets. A four-inch, golden key activated a small tape machine that played the standard nursery rhyme or a new version of it, asking the children to first listen closely and then riff off the respective story as they wished.[65] Within three years, one million paying visitors had sampled the magic and travelers from around the nation were adding Oakland to their itineraries.[66] Children's Fairyland's spawned many imitators, including Pixie Woodland in Stockton, Storyland in San Francisco, and Fairytale Town in Sacramento.[67] In 1954, Walt Disney visited, just at the time that Anaheim's Disneyland, costing $9,000,000 to Fairyland's $100,000, was under construction. A year later, the first director of Children's Fairyland, Dorothy Manes, resigned to take a much higher-paying job as public relations director for children at Disneyland.

While he was working on Children's Fairyland, Mott Jr. came up with another play place for slightly older children. It was called Peralta Playland and was situated between the Municipal Auditorium and the channel running from Lake Merritt to the Oakland Estuary. Inspired by the escalating range of transportation options at midcentury, epitomized by airplanes and automobiles, Mott Jr. crafted miniaturized sets where children could ride on older, now-nostalgic transport systems. Peralta Playland opened with the Oakland Acorn, a steam engine pulling five cars on 1,500 feet of track. A sort of "Oakland Yesterday," the fantasy park allowed children to bounce along on other imaginative play rides like the Overland Stage Coach, mount live ponies on a merry-go-round, or board a scaled-down paddle steamer named Lil Belle for a ride on the channel. Mott Jr. hadn't completely forgotten the contemporary transportation themes he had earlier proposed for Leona Heights Park, however. Two years after the launch of Sputnik in 1957, the Parks Department added the park's first futuristic exhibit—Star Flyer, a ride on a 60-foot-long aluminum rocket ship simulating for 32 passengers the sensations of a trip into space.[68]

Mott Jr. made a related mark on playground design. Manufactured appliances customarily made up playground structures: durable steel and wooden equipment used for climbers, slides, bars, and beams. Attitudes changed after the war. Landscape architects and artists now complemented industrial materials with recycled and more highly designed materials, aiming to challenge children's musculature and imagination.[69] During the 1950s, Oakland's parks department experimented with these types of playground equipment. At Peralta Playland, iron-pipe swings and slides gave way to landscape architect Amedee Sourdry's make-believe creations: a swing where kids sailed in a seahorse; another where they hung on ropes that were the tails of two "Soulful Lions" overhead; a slide where they skimmed down the back of a tiger.[70] Downtown, in Madison Square, an "Oriental type play area" was unveiled for Chinatown. Framed by twisting body of a concrete dragon, it boasted a giant abacus, "through the moon gate," and later a miniature Chinese Junk sailing ship. At Lakeside Park, on the beach in front of the Band Shell, Sourdry and sculptor Robert Winston's "fun tree" appeared. Also called "The Thing" and "Mid-Century Monster" and resembling a fallen 30-foot tree petrified miraculously into the age of plastic, its hand and food holds were an invitation to climbing, its tunnels a must for crawling. Frustrated by his inability to beef up Oakland's park acreage for everyone, Mott Jr. had reoriented his vision toward children, crafting intimate spaces that incorporated rich narrative and kinesthetic incentives. His playlands sought to transport young users out of their everyday lives and into inspirational realms of the mind/body structured around fairy tales, historical milestones, and recent technological achievements.

Going full circle back to the inspiration for Children's Fairyland, Detroit's Belle Island Zoo, Mott Jr. next took these ideas on themed environments to Oakland's woeful zoo. Around 1919, a zoo of sorts had been created by Henry Snow, a big-game hunter and collector, at his Snow Museum downtown at 19th and Harrison Streets. Seven years later, the Snow zoo was moved to Sequoia Park where the quarters consisted of windy, shade-less cages with cement floors, and a careless situating of animals, such as monkeys and bears, next to one another. In 1939, the zoo decamped once more to 15 acres on the Durant estate in southeasternmost Oakland, and was provided with a modest budget by the city. After multiple threats to close the zoo, Joseph R. Knowland, in yet another one of his many civic roles as chairman of the California State Park Commission, led an effort to purchase an additional 453 acres of the Durant property as a state park; in 1949, in honor of his efforts to add to Oakland's parkland in spite of municipal inaction, its name was changed to Knowland State Arboretum and Park.[71]

Mott Jr.'s first zoo proposal, in 1951, involved a "group living plan," an idea attempted earlier at the zoo in Fort Worth, Texas, where animals were taken from cages and allowed to roam among the plants, birds, and selected animals of their native habitats. For Oakland, he proposed an imitation Brazilian rainforest, with artificial rain every five minutes, tape-recorded jungle calls, and a collection of giant sloths, iguanas, turtles, frogs, and reptiles.[72] Instead of staring at animals through a cage, zoo visitors would take a journey around or above a habitat environment. They would have the feel of engaging animals in their natural surroundings—a living, wrap-around diorama. After the Oakland Parks Department assumed control of Knowland Park in 1956, he expanded these ideas into six display islands. Although some of the displays, such as the rainforest, were never realized, by 1970, the zoo had developed several new exhibits: most notably, a tower in which visitors spiraled up a ramp to view the gibbon habitat.[73]

In 1961, nearby the zoo, the park department added the 75-acre Dunsmuir/Hellmann Estate and its 16-room mansion. Inspired by Mott's playlands, City Manager Wayne Thompson came up with a concept for the adult imagination at the site: a retreat setting for scientific conferences. The Peralta Oaks Research Park was born, envisioned as a West Coast version of Princeton's Institute for Advanced Studies. In March of 1963, a conference, "Space, Science and Urban Life," was held, funded by NASA and the Ford Foundation.[74] Despite the ambitious launch, despite the progression from Mott's children's fairy tales to adult space exploration, the city couldn't keep the research park going. The estate lacked sufficient on-site dining and lodging and suffered from financing deficits the City of Oakland could not meet; in the coming years, the house and grounds turned into a venue for weddings and parties.[75]

FROM PEAKS TO SHORELINE

One of the City of Oakland's last significant park acquisitions took place on the channel between Lake Merritt and the estuary, where two linked parks were fashioned between 1972 and 1982. Designed by celebrated landscape architect Lawrence Halprin, Estuary Park emerged on the site of a former box factory, while Channel Park was built on former marshlands owned by Laney College. Together comprising 22 acres, the parks were graced with a sculpture garden of 12 large-scale works, including Michael Heizer's three-tiered steel "Platform," and works by Mark di Suvero, Dennis Oppenheim, Peter Forakis, Brian Wall, Steve Gillman, and Andrew Harader.[76] Like the Peralta Oaks Research Park, it was intended as an adult playland, a path past repurposed materials composed into unusual sculptural shapes that referred to the industrial structures of Oakland's waterfront. Administered by the Oakland Museum through the early 1990s, the art park was unceremoniously abandoned by the city-run museum, and many of its remaining works gradually fell apart. This important juncture between the estuary and Lake Merritt, what might have been the starting point for a great shoreline-to-peaks park, as envisioned by Charles Mulford Robinson, lay little used into the twenty-first century.

Channel Park had replaced Peralta Playland, which had earlier experienced a fall-off in attendance and attention from the city. Like Peralta Playland and the Peralta Oaks Research Park in the hills, the sad fate of the parks and sculpture garden illustrates a problem not unique to Oakland. Municipal interest in a new project is by far the greatest during planning and construction phases. Most time and money are channeled to those efforts. Once completed, there is rarely enough money in the general operating budget for adequate maintenance and hardly any funds for needed improvements. These park projects, like other city efforts with cultural venues and museums, were first energized by a vision, and then buried in bureaucracy or incompetence, famished of financing or simply allowed to wither on the vine. Other once promising yet now decaying parks litter the town: Grove Shafter Park, Central Reservoir Park, Union Point Park.

If parks stayed a low priority for the perennially cash-starved City of Oakland, they remained the reason for existence at the EBRPD. As it had during the 1930s and 1950s, the district continued to add hill parks within Oakland's boundaries. In 1973, the 240-acre Huckleberry Botanic Regional Preserve opened. The prior decade, alarmed at plans by a developer to bulldoze roads into the area, citizens formed a coalition, Citizens for Urban Wilderness Areas, led by Glenn Seaborg, a Nobel Prize–winning chemist at the University of California's Livermore Laboratory.[77] Huckleberry contained a collection of somewhat rare California plants, including wild huckleberries as well as Western leatherwood, silktassel bush, golden chinquapin, and two unusual manzanitas.[78] Its acquisition led to a reorientation of park planning around the conservation of valuable natural resources. From 1979 to 1986, a housing compromise resulted in the deeding of 289 hillside acres to the EBRPD; the Leona Heights Regional Open Space Preserve, described more fully in chapter 8, "Housing Injustice." Lastly, the Friends of Claremont Canyon fought ongoing subdivision activity above the Claremont Hotel. EBRPD board members Harlan Kessel and Mary Jefferds campaigned to have the land purchased by the district, despite the fact that the proposed park consisted of scores of individual lots that would have to be laboriously assembled. Their efforts prevailed and, in 1979, the 208-acre Claremont Canyon Regional Park was added to the EBRPD.[79]

The waterfront was the next target. The estuary and bay had long been polluted by urban wastes. Twenty-two large sewer outfalls emptied Oakland's wastes, and an additional eight outfalls dumped Alameda's sewage. As acknowledged in Oakland's *Shoreline Development* element of its Master Plan, published in 1951, "the sight of fecal matter floating in the water and noisome gases bubbling up out of the sludge banks surrounding the (sewage) outfalls is commonplace."[80] That year, EBMUD, another important regional agency, completed a sewage treatment plant alongside the Oakland entrance to the Bay Bridge, linked to a comprehensive system of 21 miles of interceptor sewers. By the 1960s, the bay and estuary's water quality was noticeably improved.

The first large shoreline park was created around San Leandro Bay near Oakland Airport. In 1940, the Port of Oakland had purchased its first 186 acres of marshland, and had steadily turned parts of it into industrial land. Aware of growing resistance to bay land reclamation by the late 1960s, in light of the creation of the Bay Conservation and Development Commission (BCDC), also discussed in chapter 7, "In the Wake of Deindustrialization," port planners acceded to the idea of a strip of parkland around the bay in its *Oakland Shoreline Plan* of 1968. Subsequently, in 1971, a citizen's group, the East Oakland Fruitvale Planning Center, assisted by Councilman John Sutter, former president of the Citizens for Regional Recreation and Parks (now Greenbelt Alliance), advocated for preserving the land in its natural state.[81] After five years of back-and-forth negotiations with the port, involving the EBRPD's general manager Richard Trudeau and sympathetic port commissioners like Chester Soda, the EBRPD received a long-term lease on 64 acres of land, nine miles of shoreline, and 675 acres of open water and degraded marshlands and tidal flats. Extensive restoration involved dredging to the original elevation in order to allow water to again flow into channels and allow a maze of cordgrass marshes to form. The park opened in 1979 as the San Leandro Shoreline Regional Park; in 1992, it was renamed after Dr. Martin Luther King Jr.[82]

The last major shoreline park debuted just after the millennium. In the early 1970s, a two-and-a-half-acre picnic area, observation tower, and fishing pier, Port View Park, had been established on Port of Oakland land alongside the 7th Street container terminal. Relocated and reconstructed to four acres in 1995, as a result of the 1989 Loma Prieta Earthquake, Port View Park was later joined, in 2004, to a much larger park occupying a piece of the former site of the Naval Supply Center at the juncture of the port's Middle and Outer Harbors—Middle Harbor Shoreline Park. Instigated by a 1992 report by the League of Women Voters, *The Waterfront: It Touches the World. How Does It Touch Oakland?*, the port began to conceive a waterfront initiative in conjunction with the city and the Bay Conservation and Development Commission. The port's *Vision 2000 Maritime Development Program* (2001) set the stage for transforming part of the Naval Supply Center into 38 acres of parkland ringing a restored lagoon and the preserved traces of the site of the former Western Pacific mole.[83]

TRIBUTARIES

By the twenty-first century, there were 2,500 acres of Oakland city parkland: 23 recreation centers, 53 athletic fields, and five public swimming pools. EBRPD lands within Oakland totaled close to 6,800 acres. And by this time, the EBRPD had expanded to all of Alameda and Contra Costa Counties, encompassing approximately 125,000 acres, over 12 times the size of the original zone of EBMUD surplus lands—the largest regional park agency in the United States.[84] There is a lesson to be learned. Through the EBMUD, the EBRPD, BART, AC Transit, bridge and highway districts, and many others, regional consortiums led to better public outcomes for Oakland than when the city went at it alone. While the city's attention was spread across many functions, and while its priorities were constantly shifting, regional consortiums, by their very nature, remained laser-focused on clear functional outcomes and enjoyed the advantages of (multi-city and county) economies of scale.

Overall, then, did the long view of Oakland's landscape change for the better over the course of the century? Earlier, in 1968, reprising aspects of Robinson's earlier critique, an assessment by the architectural firm of DeMars and Wells along with Jack Sidener had painted a glum picture of the city built up after 1906: "Oakland is still a sprawling, low-density city with centers that fail to look like centers, diffuse neighborhoods without strong physical identity, and a confusing, undifferentiated circulation system in which major streets are barely distinguished from minor ones."[85] The study, *Oakland's Form and Appearance*, assessed the role of borders and edges and topographic features as well as the rhythms between long-range vistas and spaces of intimacy. Singing the same tune as reports had throughout the century, it cited the city's deficiency in parks, arguing that parks were needed to break up the monotonous residential texture with areas of contrasting function, color, and texture. Indeed, Olmsted and Robinson's ideas for parks following canyons and their creeks to the bay reverberated throughout the text. Such parks could be crucial connectors of high and low lands as well as boundary markers between neighborhoods.

Before European settlement, from Claremont Creek in the north to San Leandro Creek in the south, 21 creeks and innumerable branches snaked down canyons from headwaters in the Redwood groves of the upper hills, meandering across the flats into the marshlands that made up much of the Oakland Estuary and San Leandro Bay. But wild creeks conflicted with city-making. From the 1860s onward, the larger creeks were dammed to create reservoirs and watershed lands. Their canyons were denuded of trees. Springs dried up and creeks diminished at their source. Streets, buildings, planted gardens, and weedy, disturbed borderlands replaced native vegetation. In wet years, floodwaters raged and residents petitioned to control the watery tributaries. The beautiful, if unruly creeks were diverted into concrete pipes, culverts, and channels that regulated drainage and replaced the creek environments with streets and buildings. Creeks went from a valuable resource into a nuisance and hazard and finally into a phenomenon hardly encountered. By the 1970s, only a few remained in anything resembling a natural state.[86]

Shortly afterward, a few East Bay residents became interested in their buried, practically forgotten treasures. Carole Schemmerling, chair of the Berkeley Parks Commission, advocated for creek restoration in her city. The first site encompassed a couple of blocks of abandoned railroad right-of-way in West Berkeley, underneath which ran a creek. Landscape architect Douglas Wolf dug up the culverted Strawberry Creek, restored its meanders and part of its flood plan; Strawberry Creek Park was born.[87]

Once again, Oakland followed Berkeley's environmental lead. In 1986, stonewalls replaced a 225-foot stretch of Glen Echo Creek's concrete embankments and native plants were arranged along the floodplain.[88] Subsequently, the Urban Creeks Council formed, dedicated to daylighting waterways, and groups like Oakland Heritage Alliance, Oakland Creeks Council, and the Sierra Club got on board with what was becoming another East Bay regional project. By the mid-1990s, public agencies like the City of Oakland and Alameda County Flood Control and Conservation District as well as private nonprofits like Friends of Sausal Creek and Friends of Temescal Creek commenced restoration efforts on many of Oakland's 15 creeks.[89] Some portions of creeks that still ran open, like Courtland Creek, were turned into linear parks. Gradually, sections of other creeks—Glen Echo, Sausal, Peralta, Lion, Horseshoe—were daylighted from their concrete culverts into more natural, open-air channels that support riparian environments.[90] Those environs, a framing of the city's landscape via the aquatic infrastructure that flows behind people's houses or underneath the city's streets, hold the best promise to thread handy green interludes across the town's grayscapes, paths from urban habitation into Oakland's natural place within the coastal ranges by San Francisco Bay.

5 Major League Venue

A wall of polished granite faces the south side of Lake Merritt, articulated by sculptural niches that celebrate "the wealth of the mind" and the "consolation of the arts," among other matters. Dedicated in 1915, the Oakland Municipal Auditorium (renamed the Henry J. Kaiser Convention Center in 1984) instantly became the city's premier civic monument. Outfitted with a 5,492-seat arena, a 1,900-seat theater, ballrooms, and a small art gallery, it hosted school graduations, circus troupes, and roller derby skaters; the Christmas pageant and New Year's concerts by the Grateful Dead; the Poultry, Pigeon, and Pet Stock and Cat Show as well as the Star Trek Space and Science Convention; concert seasons by the Oakland Symphony and performances by Elvis Presley, James Brown, and Public Enemy; speeches by President Woodrow Wilson, the Reverend Martin Luther King Jr., and the Dalai Lama.

After its construction, the auditorium was considered the centerpiece for a soon-to-be realized lakeside civic center. It would be flanked by a museum and library, testifying to Oakland's ascendant cultural standing.[1] The civic center did not turn out as planned. The library only relocated from 14th and Grove Streets in 1951, and then to a less prominent site a couple of blocks from the auditorium. The museum was eventually built alongside the auditorium, but not until 1969, and under circumstances where monumentality was consciously avoided. Over those many decades, the auditorium nonetheless functioned as a generator for dreams of a lakeside civic center and, even more importantly, an incubator for an array of cultural and sporting edifices that came about in the 1960s and early 1970s. The inadequate art gallery helped drive the museum's creation. The auditorium's arena, incapable of accommodating professional sports teams or large concerts, was augmented by the roomy Oakland–Alameda County Coliseum and Arena. The theater, judged insufficient for the needs of a modern symphony orchestra, sparked a renovation of the Paramount Theater for use as a concert hall.

These venues were the jewels in Oakland's campaign to crown urban life with beauty and spectacle. For a city that had earlier dropped the ball on a large central park, they helped Oakland rise above its hardheaded inclinations. For a second city perpetually in San Francisco's shadows, they established Oakland's reputation, akin to the regional parks, as a player on the national scene. Their locations pointed in divergent directions, however. The museum and theater aimed to solidify downtown as a destination for high culture. The sports complex promised the emergence of a populist subcenter in the vicinity of the airport in East Oakland.

Unlike earlier in the century, when civic structures could claim to represent and serve the majority of Oaklanders, the postwar edifices straddled the fault line of a racially bifurcated society.[2] Controversies over excessive government financing and marginal community participation dogged them. It got worse. The early 1970s relocation of Merritt College from black North Oakland to a new campus in the white, upper hills unleashed shock waves of resentment—the older campus had been the site of the birth of the East Bay black power movement. After 1977 and the downfall of the white establishment, the door opened for minority political leadership, but during times when government retrenchment tempered the ambition of civic venues.

A UNIFIED CIVIC CENTER

Oakland's efforts to create a civic center by Lake Merritt followed a well-trodden path. The City Beautiful Movement inspired cities across the country to create beaux-arts civic complexes as contrasts to the workaday downtown. Compared to the grid where buildings crowded their lot lines, civic center buildings were set back behind lawns and hedges and embellished with statues and fountains. There were no businesses. An atmosphere of repose was cultivated—a quality seen as critical to the advancement of culture, the arts, and government. In the western United States, two important civic centers preceded Oakland's efforts. Denver opened its Municipal Auditorium in 1908, stimulating the creation of a large civic center directly west of the State Capitol.[3] San Francisco had no State Capitol to work with, but assembled the essential pieces of its civic center in short order, in part because of the upcoming 1915 Panama-Pacific International Exposition. Between 1914 and 1916, Civic Center Plaza and several beaux-arts buildings around it, including City Hall, the Civic Auditorium, and the Main Library, were completed.

Lake Merritt offered Oakland a grand opportunity to frame monumental buildings against an expanse of water. But problems arose from the start. Real estate interests weren't in line with giving over much of the valuable lakefront property to civic structures. Any lakeside complex would have to proceed without the city's most prominent governmental building; in 1914, an elaborate City Hall had been finished far from the lake at 14th and Washington Streets, near the town's "100 percent corner," the downtown street crossroads with the highest land values and office rents. A year later, laissez-faire politician John Davie was elected mayor, replacing Frank Mott, instigator of both the Municipal Auditorium and City Hall. Nothing happened until the end of Davie's term, 1930, when the federal government's plans for a new post office, necessitated by the huge increase in mail caused by Oakland Airport's airmail service and Montgomery Ward's mail order business, forced his hand. He came up with an intentionally unrealistic idea of a 100-acre civic center between the auditorium and the estuary—including the post office as well as a museum, library, hall of records, courthouse and Union Station for the city's railroads.[4]

None of it was built and, in 1932, the central post office was completed at 13th and Jackson Streets, several blocks from the auditorium. Four years later, funded by a combination of a $1.7 million bond issue and Public Works Administration grants, the Alameda County Courthouse at

13th and Fallon Streets was dedicated. This time, it was located alongside the lake and nearby the Municipal Auditorium. At 12 stories, with a prominent spire, the wedding-cake structure designed by William Corlett was the first tall building erected outside Oakland's central business district.[5] By virtue of its size and grandeur, the courthouse kept the idea of a lakeside civic center alive.[6]

In 1947, city planners issued *The Civic Center and Lake Merritt Improvement* as part of the *Oakland Master Plan*. Citing the San Francisco Civic Center as well as newer ones in Los Angeles and Cleveland, the plan called for an ambitious two-part center at the lower end of the lake. The Municipal Auditorium would be framed by two groups of buildings: to the west, the existing courthouse and a new library; and, on the east side of the lake, a new opera house, art gallery and museum. Additionally, a governmental civic center would rise around a new three-block plaza between 11th and 12th Streets and Jackson and Fallon Streets; it would be framed by the existing courthouse and post office as well as a new city hall, justice building, state building, county building, and municipal building. The plan estimated the total site area required, 94.8 acres, and the amount of land in private ownership, 22.9 acres, that would have to be purchased for what it called "one of the greatest single opportunities afforded a community to manifest its appreciation of orderliness and beauty, as well as convenience and economy in rendering public service."[7]

In 1951, the new Main Library was built on the site recommended in the plan. Financed by a 1945 voter bond issue, it was Oakland's first large public building since the courthouse 15 years earlier. The greater plan languished. Purchasing at least eight blocks for the governmental center, clearing their buildings, and erecting public edifices (off the tax rolls) would have been extremely costly. Norman Ogilvie, president of the Oakland Real Estate Board, reprised Davie's argument against building on lakefront land valuable for residential property development.[8] Other programs like freeways and urban renewal pushed to the top of the city's agenda. In 1954, Planning Engineer Glenn Hall proposed a reappraisal of the civic center plan in light of the fact that it hadn't changed the commercial zoning in its boundaries, and thus was not preventing the intrusion of haphazard commercial developments.[9] The nail in the coffin of the lakeside civic center was driven toward the end of the decade when the City of Oakland changed its mind about locating the Hall of Justice there. In 1962, a new three-building complex (police headquarters, city jail, municipal courts) opened on lower Broadway, where land was cheaper.[10] Oakland henceforth operated with three dispersed civic complexes: one on lower Broadway and reaching west to Jefferson Street, one around City Hall, and one by the lake—a reflection of the fact that by this time, the earlier City Beautiful idea of uniting the town through a grandiose architectural complex was no longer feasible.

MUSEUM CONSOLIDATION

Completed in 1969 adjacent to the lakeside Municipal Auditorium, the publicly run Oakland Museum of California was the result of close to 50 years of efforts to provide improved public facilities for the city's private and separate history, art, and natural science museums. The oldest was the Oakland Public Museum, opened in 1910 in the Josiah Stanford Mansion, a two-story, wood-frame Victorian facing Lake Merritt and purchased by the city for that purpose. Its collection stemmed from Walter Bryant's ornithological specimens and Charles Wilcomb's archaeological, ethnological, and historical artifacts. Wilcomb, the Public Museum's first curator, assembled the basement rooms of Native American baskets and early American history: weavings, mechanical and farming implements, and, notably, two trend-setting period rooms re-creating a Colonial kitchen and bedroom.[11] Next came the Art Gallery, housed in a third-floor corner of the Municipal Auditorium, and containing the leftovers from the Chinese and Russian pavilions of the 1915 Panama-Pacific International Exposition as well as works from various East Bay artists and art clubs. Lastly, in 1922, the Snow Museum opened in the former Cutting Mansion at 19th and Harrison Streets, also purchased by the city for use as a museum. The adventurer Henry Adelbert Snow amalgamated rifles, animal pelts, bird eggs, and taxidermy from his expeditions to Africa and the Arctic; the city's first habitat diorama featured, in front of a painted backdrop of ice floes, a family of polar bears that Snow and his son had shot; his live specimens—lion cubs, an ostrich, and a bobcat—made up the core collection that would later become the Oakland Zoo.[12]

In 12 years, three museums had been established in Oakland, an accomplishment for a city that had not had any museums beforehand. But their buildings were inadequate with regard to industry standards of display and collections management. At the Public Museum, 14 exhibit rooms took up the bedrooms, kitchen, parlor, and dining room, and were lit by 400 lamps; every closet and cabinet was stuffed. The Art Gallery was considered a "temporary situation," almost closing in 1918 due to the influenza pandemic when the city needed more hospital space. Rescued by William Porter, president of the Art Association, the Art Gallery struggled on despite the fact that many traveling shows had to be turned down due to a lack of space. Despite the quality of the Snow Museum's taxidermy collection, one of the best of its kind in the United States during the 1920s, as museum historian Marjorie Schwarzer remarks, "it was stuffed in a mansion that was never designed to display it."[13]

Over the next four decades, what Oakland lacked in museum building was made up for in museum scheming. In 1916, a suggestion was floated to launch a museum complex in Lakeside Park, facing the Municipal Auditorium: an art gallery; a state building devoted to California county exhibits; a natural history building; an ethnological building combining the Oakland Public Museum's collections with the Egyptian collection of Phoebe Hearst; and a commercial museum.[14] In 1920, in another proposal, the museum returned once more to its place alongside the Municipal Auditorium, now flanked on the other side by a memorial hall for fallen soldiers of the East Bay cities; proposed by Mayor Davie, this iteration would have consisted of artworks, Snow's animal specimens, and curiosities from the National Guard.[15] By 1926, the museum plotting boomeranged back to Lakeside Park, as suggested by Edgar Sanborn, president of the park board, and Samuel Hubbard, former president of the Oakland Library Board. A horseshoe form, following the contours of the lake, was envisioned.[16] The most promising proposal was made a year earlier. Snow and a group of investors—George Jamieson, Norman deVaux, Arthur Breed—raised $1 million and offered it to the city for the erection of a natural history museum. They were willing to wait 50 years for any return on their investment. The idea, a leaseback-purchase that would later be commonly used for public projects, was ruled illegal by City Attorney Leon Gray.[17]

It was not until 1954 that the ball got rolling. That year, citizens led by socialite and restaurant owner Esther Torosian started the Oakland Museum Association. Within two years it had 1,200 members. Working with Paul Mills, director the Oakland Art Gallery, the association hatched a plan for an amalgamated museum that would cost around $6 million. Concurrently, *Oakland Tribune* reporter Bill Fiset penned a series of articles on the three makeshift museums, their cramped quarters, and bad displays for 100,000 objects owned by the taxpayers of the city. Complaining there was no room for acquisitions, concerned about the safety of objects and visitors, Fiset endorsed the association's plan for a single museum with three wings.[18]

Next, Mayor Clifford Rishell commissioned a survey for potential locations. Paid for by Edgar Kaiser and Stephen Bechtel Jr., it evaluated 18 sites. In 1957, the highest-ranked ones, in order, were a plot of land between Madison and Alice Streets and 17th and 19th Streets, Lakeside Park in Adams Point, and the area around the Municipal Boathouse on Lake Merritt. All had their complications. The first choice was pricey, requiring purchase of 3.47 acres of downtown property; the second was deemed too far from the city center; the third was opposed by Park Superintendent William Penn Mott Jr. because it would occupy park land. Snow Park, where the Snow Museum was situated, was also ruled out; there were plans for a hotel on that property. Despite opposition to using parkland for a private hotel, Mayor Rishell commented: "A hotel is a little cultural too, you know. If there's anything more important than a hotel, I'd like to know what it is."[19]

Finally, in 1961 a $6.6 million bond issue passed: 58,040 voted yes; 28,276 voted no; a margin of 497 over the two-thirds necessary for passage. Oakland voters also rejected a proposal to lease Snow Park for a 350-room Sheraton Hotel. But it no longer mattered to the museum plan. There were now just two potential sites: Joaquin Miller Park in the upper hills or a downtown block located between 10th and 11th Streets and Oak and Fallon Streets—adjacent to the Municipal Auditorium. The latter prevailed, favored by the business community and city planners for its central location, accessibility to the Nimitz Freeway and an anticipated BART station.[20]

In late 1961, an 11-member committee, headed by shopping center

Figure 15. Oakland Museum. Alameda County Courthouse in background. Photo by Mitchell Schwarzer, 2020.

developer Robert Nahas and advised by *San Francisco Chronicle* architectural critic Allan Temko and *New Yorker* architectural critic Lewis Mumford, was assembled to administer an international architectural competition.[21] Out of 37 entries, they chose Eero Saarinen; Philip Johnson and Paul Rudolph were the runners-up. Known for the TWA Terminal at New York's Idlewild Airport, under construction at the time, Saarinen died shortly before the decision was announced. The committee agreed that his partners Kevin Roche and John Dinkeloo should take over.[22] In June of 1962, reaction to Roche's design was glowing. Allan McNab, director of administration at the Art Institute of Chicago, and one of the consultants on the project, exclaimed: "This is the first American breakthrough in museum techniques in the 150 years that museums have been built here. All the previous structures follow the historical pattern of European palaces."[23]

An outgrowth of the European palace, museums had traditionally been set in parks and accessed up great flights of stairs. Their interior sequence began in a spacious entry hall and continued through rooms that functioned as both circulation corridors and rooms to view exhibitions. The modernist museum, beginning with Edward Durrell Stone's 1939 Museum of Modern Art in New York, challenged that formula, constructing the six-story steel-and-glass structure to lot lines on a busy midtown street and having patrons enter directly from the sidewalk through a revolving glass door, much as they would do when going to a department store. Roche took his design in yet another direction. Instead of a building block set in a park or on a street, Roche, working with landscape architect Dan Kiley and plant consultant Geraldine Knight Scott, crafted the museum as a landscape of superimposed buildings, terraces, and gardens. Concrete walls face the surrounding sidewalks, rising up to support a series of landscaped terraces. A partially covered central axis of stairs links three levels of galleries, café, store and gardens. As art critic Thomas Albright noted, "each of the three tiers overlaps and opens onto the one below, and all the galleries have access to an outside space."[24] Roche's museum brought people in and then walled them off from the surrounding city until they ascended to the upper terraces and experienced it once more as a vista akin to a painting.[25]

The site was cleared by 1963, ground was broken in early 1964, and completion scheduled for 1966. Yet building the four-block, 193,000-square-foot structure proved time consuming. Construction delays held up the project, some of them involving industry strikes, bad weather, and work order changes. The most serious concerned the construction of a parking garage and underpass connecting 11th Street to the 12th Street "highway dam."[26] The museum might resemble an independent cultural landscape, but as with other buildings of its time, it had to conform to the needs of motorists.

From three old museums emerged three new departments, setting the stage for the institution's later name, the Oakland Museum of California: Gallery of California Art; Cowell Hall of California History; and Hall of California Ecology. Initially, it was thought that the existing collections of the old museums would be integrated where appropriate, with natural history material from the Public Museum merging into the Hall of California Ecology. Yet because of the California focus, older collections ended up in permanent storage, on the auction block, or thrown away. In 1966, the

Oakland Museum Association announced a $2.5 million drive for new displays and exhibits. Upon opening, the large collection of California art made the museum a destination and helped to situate California within the history of art in the United States.[27] The Cowell Hall of California History, in part assembled by visionary curator Thomas Frye, featured a 1870s assay office from Nevada City where gold and silver diggings were evaluated as well as a World War II kitchen from the Hunter's Point Naval Base. The Hall of California Ecology reoriented the display of natural science collections from theatrical groupings of animals to meticulous depictions of the state's varied ecosystems.

Then racial controversy struck. About a month before the museum was to open in 1969, its director, J. S. Holiday, a white historian with a doctorate from the University of California at Berkeley, was fired. His dismissal by the Oakland Museum Commission after only a year and a half on the job exposed tensions between donor and community control—white and black Oakland. William Hayes led the commission, established after the 1962 bond issue to guide the museum project forward. It was composed of wealthy white donors, and was scheduled to cease operating once the museum opened. Yet leading up to the opening, the commission had come into conflict with another, different sort of group, the 59-member museum Community Relations Advisory Council.

The council was heavily composed of minorities who were appointed by Julia Hare, a black woman who had come to the Bay Area to pursue a dream of teaching and, frustrated by state requirements, ended up as coordinator of education at the new museum. Hare shared Holiday's vision of creating a people's museum that would participate in community activities, like meals on wheels, outside its doors.[28] But commission members felt that Hare had appointed troublemakers to the council, although according to Holiday the council functioned as a liaison to the minority community, working to address its grievances concerning the lack of African American presence in the opening schedule as well as the paucity of minorities employed as docents, staff, and senior-level administration.[29] For her part, Hare was outraged that the commission expected the council to content itself with "suggesting singing and dancing selections for black and brown portions of the September 20 opening."[30] After Holiday's firing, Hare resigned, as did Roger Olmsted, an art history curator. A compromise of sorts was achieved, as Hayes and the commission agreed to the council's demand that they have a voice in all museum activities in the future, and that no admission fee would be charged.

Months after the opening, Hare, no longer employed at the museum, continued to speak out about the power struggle between the white establishment who run museums, and often do not live in Oakland, and the city's large minority population, underrepresented at every level of the museum's content and control. She urged a system of decentralized neighborhood museums on the model of the public schools.[31] That did not happen, and through the remainder of the century, the museum became a national leader in collecting contemporary works and staging events in sync with local ethnic groups like the Mexican-themed Days of the Dead Community Celebration.

A SPORTING MEGALITH

An idea for what would become the Oakland–Alameda County Coliseum and Arena was floated as early as 1950, when Oakland city planning engineer John Marr explored the feasibility of a municipal stadium for baseball and football along the proposed route of the Eastshore Freeway, near where Hegenberger Road veered off toward the Oakland Municipal Air-port. It was one of the largest undeveloped tracts of land in the city. The East Bay Municipal Utility District (EBMUD) owned the bulk of it, while the Port of Oakland held the rest. The idea languished. Oakland had no major league teams.

Through the late 1950s, pitches were made to lure a team to Oakland that would require the construction of a stadium or, alternatively, to build a stadium that would serve as a magnet for a team. Suddenly, in January of 1960, it became known that Oakland had a shot to land the last of eight franchises in the new American Football League (AFL). While some league brass worried about a new Bay Area football team getting overshadowed by the National Football League San Francisco 49ers, Barron Hilton, the influential owner of the Los Angeles Chargers, loved the idea of a second AFL team in California and the likely north-south rivalry it would engender. Oakland became the logical choice.[32]

For a couple of years, until a facility was built, Oakland Raiders games were played in San Francisco and then on a small field near downtown Oakland. Meanwhile, the City of Oakland and the County of Alameda went about finding a site and financing a stadium. A number of locales were considered, tracts off Oakland Avenue, Seminary Avenue, and alongside the Bay Bridge. Attention narrowed to two properties, both partially owned by the Port of Oakland: the 104-acre Oakport site alongside the Nimitz Freeway that had been looked into a decade earlier; and 25-acre Peralta Park, adjacent to the Municipal Auditorium, which had been considered as early as 1945 for a sports and events palace. The Peralta site was close to downtown, but Oakport, near the airport, had the potential to stimulate development in what was seen as a growing area. In November 1961, a study by Tudor Engineering Company, financed by the Kaiser Corporation, settled the matter; the Coliseum could be constructed for $3.4 million less at Oakport.[33]

Robert Nahas, the same businessman who shepherded the Oakland Museum project, was chosen to head the Oakland–Alameda County Coliseum Inc., a nonprofit group that would guide its construction.[34] Instead of issuing a public bond needing voter approval, like the one secured by the museum, the stadium would be financed through sale-leaseback bonds. The Oakland–Alameda County Coliseum Authority bought the property and paid for the purchase by issuing revenue bonds to Coliseum Inc. equal to the purchase price. Coliseum Inc. then leased back the property from the authority, who used the lease payments (mostly from stadium revenues) to pay the principal and debt on the revenue bonds. As for the site, an agreement was reached between the Port of Oakland and EBMUD to trade parcels, which could then be purchased by the authority from the port.[35]

In 1961, Coliseum Inc. went about choosing a design firm. The choice came down to three: Praeger & Kavanagh, responsible for Dodger Stadium in Chavez Ravine and Shea Stadium in New York; Osborn Engineering, builders of District of Columbia (now RFK) Stadium in Washington, DC, Three Rivers Stadium in Pittsburgh, and Milwaukee County Stadium; and Skidmore, Owings and Merrill (SOM), who did not have a stadium to their credit. Unexpectedly, SOM got the job. Coliseum Inc. preferred a firm within the Bay Area—SOM had an active San Francisco office—

and was impressed by SOM's size and expertise with large jobs.[36] Myron Goldsmith of SOM's San Francisco office became lead designer.

By early 1963, the Coliseum project was approved by both the Oakland City Council and the Alameda County Board of Supervisors. The plan envisioned a 48,400-seat outdoor stadium and 13,500-seat indoor arena. Economically, the dual project was projected to have a ripple effect throughout East Oakland. Functionally, it could provide a venue for local high schools and colleges and special events like horse shows and track and field competitions. Strategically, it might be a magnet for securing an American League baseball franchise or a team of the Western Hockey League. Most of all, the Coliseum and Arena would project Oakland onto the big-league stage. The city would no longer be seen as just a "bedroom" of the Bay Area, a common complaint of city leaders. Instead, its team(s) and the city's name would be regularly read in the morning sports page and announced nightly on the radio waves and television broadcasts. Bill Rigney, manager of the Los Angeles Angels, remarked: "This would give Oakland a real identity, something that has been long in coming."[37] *Oakland Tribune* publisher William Knowland exposed Oakland's abiding sibling rivalry: "The success of the Raiders and the Coliseum complex is significant because of its shock value for San Francisco ... sometimes it's hard for older brother to realize that younger brother has grown up."[38] In a common refrain, the Coliseum was compared favorably to Candlestick Park. As one columnist concluded: "San Francisco got a lemon but Alameda County got a plum."[39]

Guy F. Atkinson, the contractor, broke ground in May of 1964. Despite significantly less fog than San Francisco, the fierce winds that often blew at Candlestick Park across the bay influenced SOM's site planning. The indoor Arena was situated to the west of the Coliseum, acting as a wind block. The playing field at the Coliseum was recessed 28 feet below ground level, half of its height hidden by an earthen berm that sheltered fans and players from winds; this arrangement also allowed spectators to enter at mid-level.

On September 18, 1966, an enlarged 53,000-seat Coliseum opened to the public when the Raiders played their first game against the Kansas City Chiefs. Oakland lost. But a little over a year later, Oakland got back at Kansas City—through baseball. Charles Finley, who had purchased the

Kansas City Athletics a few years back, wanted out of Missouri. He considered moves to Louisville and Milwaukee, yet other owners pressured for an American League team on the Pacific Coast. For a short time, Seattle became the favorite. In October 1967, Finley chose Oakland, his decision based most of all on the immediate availability of the Coliseum; Seattle's stadium was still in the planning stages. The Athletics began the 1968 season in Oakland; only four years later they won the first of three consecutive World Series titles.

More was to come for the Coliseum/Arena complex. Its backers had long coveted the San Francisco Seals of the Western Hockey League, who played in San Francisco's outmoded Cow Palace. In 1966, the 13 teams of the Western and American Hockey Leagues were invited to apply for membership in the National Hockey League; six were chosen, the Seals among them. That year, the Seals played their last season in the WHL, opening the 15,000-seat Arena in Oakland on November 1, 1966, as the California Seals in a game against the San Diego Gulls; the following year, 1967, the Seals entered the NHL.

That same season, 1967–68, the Oakland Oaks of the fledgling American Basketball Association began playing at the Arena. Though the franchise lasted two seasons, the San Francisco Warriors of the National Basketball Association (NBA) had been scheduling games at the Oakland Arena since November 1966. By 1971, Warriors owner Franklin Mieuli put sports-minded Californians on the edge of their seats with speculations that he would move the team to San Diego, or play half of its games in San Diego and the other half in Oakland, or simply relocate to Oakland. Once again, in part because of the problems with erecting the San Diego Sports Arena, Oakland won out and the Golden State Warriors, renamed during the San Diego–Oakland deliberations, took up residence at the Oakland Arena.

Remarkably, from 1966 to 1971, Oakland nabbed teams in all four major league sports—a fantastic coup. Some of it was due to alignments of the sporting gods. Some had to do with inaction in San Francisco, where the San Francisco Redevelopment Agency had proposed a downtown sports arena (for the Seals and Warriors) as early as 1963; to be called the Yerba Buena Center, it never progressed beyond the planning stage.[40]

From 1960 to 1971, 12 stadiums were built in the United States, from

Candlestick Park in San Francisco to Veterans Stadium in Philadelphia. Most were multipurpose venues, hosting baseball and football. Most were symmetrical, concrete buildings that blended more with freeways overpasses than old city fabric. "Standing alone amid acres of parking on the city's edge, the large, postwar stadiums are emblematic of an era committed to bigger-than-life civic symbols," commented historian Phil Gruen. "The postwar stadiums project the optimism and confidence that accompanied their construction, a confidence in the advances of their age."[41]

SOM's Oakland Coliseum and Arena was the most striking of these complexes. Before insensitive additions in the 1990s, two pristine forms rose from a 9,000-car parking lot. San Jose Mercury architectural critic Alan Hess praised the abstract duo as a civic monument for the modern age, echoing the ancient monuments of classical Greece and Rome. "The sinewy muscle of its (the Coliseum's) concrete structure has the classical proportions of an Olympic athlete," wrote Hess. "A ring of sculptured piers—each with one arm sticking straight out, one tapering upward at an angle—supports the upper tier of seats. The neatly etched stepped lines of the underside of the seat tiers cast deep shadows, the tapering line of the cantilevered piers give the stadium a light and even delicate feel. A crisp thin line caps off the top of the bowl."[42] Inside, spectators had only to feast their eyes on the playing field or, by looking up, a glorious view of the Oakland hills. Complementing the muscular exterior of the Coliseum was the cylindrical Arena, a 70-foot-high wall of 1,418 glass windows divided by 32 huge X-shaped columns. Inside, the structural complexity translated into a sequence of intricate transitions.[43] The X-columns supported a concrete compression ring from which sprung 96 steel cables—all supporting the saucer-shaped roof.[44] This time, watching the game and looking up treated a spectator to the marvel of apparently weightless concrete. At night, passersby saw an illuminated jewel box.

Still, as columnist Bill Boyarsky and writer Nancy Boyarsky pointed out a few years later, those same "passersby cannot help but wonder what these impressive structures are doing there among the vacant lots, factories, and housing projects in a dreary part of a city that looks as though it can little afford such luxuries."[45] Indeed, they aimed more at the suburbs than their immediate environs, more at southern Alameda County than East Oakland. And they were costly.

Figure 16. Oakland–Alameda County Arena. Seen across Interstate 880. Photo by Mitchell Schwarzer, 2020.

Construction costs of sports venues are typically underestimated, while revenues are overestimated. Here both maxims proved true. From 1962 to 1966, the cost of construction grew from $22.5 million to $30 million. The city and county were obligated for an annual payment of $1.5 million on the Coliseum's debt. In good years, with high revenues from packed events, profits covered those payments. In lean years, the city and county had to come up with the money. Between 1966 and 1991, there were nine profitable years. More often than not, then, the complex required an annual taxpayer subsidy.[46] When Bobby Seale ran for mayor in 1973, as kinesiology professor Maria Veri writes, "the Black Panthers framed Oakland's patronage of the Raiders as part of the political and economic dynamic that contributed to the oppression of urban black neighborhoods."[47] Yet aside from exceptional cases like Dodger Stadium, most sports stadiums have a hard time both improving the profitability of a team and paying back the costs of site preparation, construction, and operations.[48] In

Oakland's case, the issue of detrimental subsidies worsened in 1996, when a major renovation, demanded by Raiders owner Al Davis as a condition of moving the team back from Los Angeles, where they had relocated in 1982, led to a revenue shortfall of between $30 and $40 million that city and county taxpayers are still paying.[49]

The key to achieving real economic growth is measured by a sporting venue's ability to attract out-of-region dollars via new economic development: businesses that generate revenues that would not have occurred had the venue not been operating.[50] These might include hotels, bars and restaurants, and outlets for merchandise. Did the partially subsidized Coliseum complex make good economic sense or did it contribute, as a goodwill asset, more to externalities like regional pride and a positive image of the city? Aside from the construction jobs and sports fans' joys, did it help jump-start the depressed part of Oakland around it by attracting, as Coliseum Inc. promised, a wave of commercial investment?

The answers to these questions are mixed. The creation of the new airport in 1962, followed by the Oakland Coliseum and Arena in 1966, generated commercial development along Hegenberger Road—it briefly became known as "the golden corridor of economic development."[51] The trendsetter was the Edgewater Inn, which in 1961 opened a 174-room hotel nearby the Nimitz Freeway. Built around an Olympic-sized swimming pool and offering parking for 580 cars, it was "the first big new hotel in the Eastbay in more than 35 years."[52] Over the next several years, more hotels opened on the mile stretch of Hegenberger leading from the freeway to the airport: the Airport Inn, a Hilton Inn, a Holiday Inn, and the Royal Inn Hotel. As *Wall Street Journal* reporter John Lawrence noted at the time, "that's more new hotel rooms than Oakland has gotten at one time since the 1920s."[53] In the early 1970s, the port's nine-acre Oakland Airport Office Center, developed by Stolte Inc., led to office buildings occupied by both the Bank of America and Wells Fargo. Movie theaters too set up shop on Oakland's newest commercial strip: in 1968, the Century 21 theater adjacent to the Edgewater Inn, a domed theater where a 90-foot screen wrapped around the audience.[54]

The activity drawn to the airport stretch of Hegenberger Road was replicated only in the adjacent 500-acre industrial park across the Nimitz Freeway from the Arena. The name of the largest of the office buildings there, the 12-story Airport Corporate Center, finished in 1983 at 7677 Oakport Street, exposed the greater drawing power of the airport as opposed to the sporting complex. In 1963, a White Front store, a Southern California discount chain, introduced an Oakland branch at 663 Hegenberger—on the other, less desirable side of the Nimitz, and adjacent to the Coliseum parking lots; it closed within a decade and a later shopping center across Hegenberger struggled mightily. To the north of the Coliseum, the Coliseum Drive-In, at 5401 Coliseum Way, opened up shop in 1964; it was converted during the 1990s into a swap meet. Finally, when the $2.3 million overpass and exit for the Nimitz Freeway was finished at 66th Avenue in 1966, channeling traffic directly to the sports complex, it was assumed that motels, restaurants, and gas stations would materialize at the intersection. None did. Through the 1990s, the area's worsening reputation for crime, its proximity to the troubled Lockwood Gardens and San Antonio Villa housing projects, worked against retail development. On what had seemed to be prime retail land, warehouses, distribution centers, and storage facilities have long predominated.

SYMPHONIC DISSONANCE

In 1934, the Oakland Symphony Orchestra was founded as a community orchestra. A big change came 25 years later when Gerhard Samuel was hired as conductor. Professional musicians were increased to comprise 90 percent of the orchestra. Fundraising by Board Chairman Edgar Kaiser and President J. Allan doubled the number of annual performances. Samuel favored twentieth-century composers and hosted, over the course of a dozen years, 43 American and Pacific Coast premieres of new compositions.[55] As Mrs. George Havas, vice president of the orchestra association, bragged, since Samuel, our "comfortable little family orchestra has grown into a first-class metropolitan orchestra."[56]

By the early 1970s, backers of the newly vibrant Oakland orchestra clamored for a new home. They claimed the Municipal Auditorium Theater lacked sufficient parking, which was true, and that it was too far a walk from the Lake Merritt BART station, which was not—the distance was only three blocks. More likely, the recent completions of the

Oakland Museum and the Coliseum-Arena convinced orchestra backers that a new building would lift their institution in comparable ways.
The Oakland Symphony chose to place its future in a renovation of the
Paramount Theatre on upper Broadway. Even though the parking situation was worse, perhaps the shorter 96-step walk to the 19th Street BART
station would lure more concertgoers.

The Paramount was Oakland's art deco gem, debuting in 1931 as a
venue for variety shows and the silver screen. Architect Timothy Pflueger
announced its presence on Broadway through a 120-foot-high sign with
the word PARAMOUNT spelled out in neon letters. On the façade, two
huge and brilliant colored mosaic panels, separated by the sign, showed a
male and female figure manipulating four tiers of puppets. Inside, Robert
Boardman Howard and Ralph Stackpole were responsible the incised
glyphic decorations that covered the walls and ceiling of the grand lobby
and the auditorium, modulating the light and sound and providing a
material counterpart to what was happening on stage or on the screen.[57]
In 1970, the theater had gone dark because of declining patronage. Could
it work as a concert hall?

Between 1968 and 1973, as movie palaces were closing around the
country, five were converted to performing arts centers; most notably, the
transformation of the St. Louis Theatre in 1968 into Powell Symphony
Hall. Compared to the five years it would take to construct a new building, a conversion could be accomplished in less than two years and cost
much less than the $15 to $20 million required of new construction.[58] The
Paramount had cost $3 million to build in 1931. Forty-one years later, the
Oakland Symphony Association purchased the building from National
General Theatres for $500,000, donated by Edgar Kaiser and Stephen
Bechtel, Jr. Renovations cost another $1 million, and Harry Lange, pres-
ident of the Oakland Symphony Association, raised funds from donors
including Ben Swig, owner of the Fairmount Hotel; Milton Shoong, president of National Dollar Stores; Nils Eklund of Kaiser Industries; and
Joseph R. Knowland's grandson, Joseph. This would be the last time that
the old philanthropic elite contributed to Oakland's cultural enrichment.

By 1973, the renovations slightly reduced seating, replaced popcorn
machines and the candy counter with two bars, but retained the architectural grandeur. On September 22, the premiere, "The Paramount Plays

Figure 17. Paramount Theatre. Downtown on Broadway, ca. 1976. Photo by Robert Bernhardi. Courtesy of Library of Congress Prints and Photographs Division HABS, CAL 1-OAK, 9-2.

Again," included film clips, excerpts from the Italian opera *Pagliacci* and the American musical *Fiddler on the Roof*, and appearances by A-list celebrities Milton Berle, Rudy Vallee, and Henry Fonda. Not only was the Paramount home to the Oakland Symphony Orchestra, it hosted diverse entertainers and the Oakland Ballet, founded in 1965 by Ronn Guidi on the model of Serge Diaghilev's Ballet Russe.

Red ink soon surfaced. In late 1974, the Oakland Symphony Orchestra revealed that its $2.1 fundraising drive for an endowment was falling short. Operating costs for the theater and orchestra were rising and contributions were declining.[59] After Gerhard Samuel's departure in 1971, the orchestra under Harold Farberman had shifted to standard classical fare, losing its niche as a venue for contemporary and experimental music. That baton passed to Berkeley, when in 1978 Kent Nagano was hired as music director of the Berkeley Promenade Orchestra, changing its name to the Berkeley Symphony Orchestra, introducing a schedule heavy in experimental, twentieth-century music, and moving its venue from the First Congregational Church to 2,015-seat Zellerbach Hall (completed in 1968) on the University of California campus. The Oakland Symphony now had serious competition from both the avant-garde Berkeley ensemble and the prestigious San Francisco Symphony, which began performing at the new Davies Symphony Hall after 1980. Although the Oakland Symphony enjoyed a revival under popular, African American conductor Calvin Simmons from 1978 to 1982, his death in a canoeing accident left it adrift financially.

The orchestra couldn't fill the vast auditorium. To save money, it began playing concerts at Zellerbach, the Rheem Theater in Moraga, and once again in the renamed Calvin Simmons Theater in the Municipal Auditorium—which proved to be a much more intimate venue. Making matters worse, the board wasn't fundraising, either from the community or even enough from its own members.[60] Facing yet another deficit of three-quarters of a million dollars, the orchestra declared bankruptcy in 1986.[61] In the following decades, the Oakland Symphony was reborn several times in different guises and under different names, yet never again attained the status of a full-time, professional orchestra. The move to the Paramount Theatre proved unrealistic amid the decline of downtown, out-migration of potential audience, and retail collapse.

COLLEGE TRANSFERS

The locational geography of the town's colleges and universities has been no less volatile than that of its museum, sports, and concert venues. The sole stable institution of higher learning has been Mills College, which moved from Benicia to its current 135-acre campus in East Oakland in 1871. Across town, at Broadway above 51st Street, Frederick Meyer, founder of the School of the California Guild of Arts and Crafts (now the California College of the Arts), bought the four-acre Treadwell estate and relocated the school there from Berkeley in 1922; a second campus in San Francisco was established in the mid-1980s, and plans are underway to shutter the Oakland facility and consolidate operations there.

For some other colleges, demands for space and facilities amid the constraining development of neighboring land encouraged moves across town or out of town. The predecessor to the University of California started off in downtown Oakland in the 1850s and relocated in 1873 to a 160-acre campus outside city limits about five miles to the north—leading to the incorporation of the City of Berkeley a few years later.

St. Mary's College moved from San Francisco to Oakland in 1889, setting up a two-and-a-half-acre campus on the old Hamilton Estate at Broadway and Hawthorne Avenue, near today's Pill Hill medical complex. Although it was a mile north of the downtown, by the 1920s, Broadway had become the city's automobile row, filling up with repair shops and dealer showrooms. Hemmed in by the vehicular businesses around it and the hospitals above, the college announced in 1925 a plan to move to a spacious campus in East Oakland. The $3 million building fund campaign failed to raise even $1 million and the college shifted course; in 1927, it accepted a timely offer from a Moraga property owner to donate a 100-acre site gratis; the Moraga campus has since grown to 420 acres.[62]

In 1907, the College of Holy Names was established on a seven-acre site at 20th Street alongside Lake Merritt. Ultimately it too felt growth pressures that could not be accommodated on that small campus. In the mid-1950s, the property was sold to Kaiser Industries for their new office/shopping complex. In the meantime, the college had acquired a 33-acre tract on Mountain Boulevard in the Oakland hills, and a new campus was dedicated in 1958.[63]

Expansion and relocation fever next hit Oakland's community colleges. Armed with a budget surplus and responding to a fast-growing population, Governor Edmund Brown's 1960 Master Plan for Higher Education promised access to all high school students and called for a quadrupling of enrollment at California's public colleges. A gigantic building program ensued and changed the landscape of public, higher education in Oakland.[64] In 1964, the Peralta Community College District was established, covering Oakland, Alameda, Albany, Berkeley, Emeryville, and Piedmont. At the time, there were two community colleges in Oakland: Laney Trade and Technical Institute, located just east of the lake on E. 11th Street; and the Merritt School of Business, housed in the former University High School on 57th and Grove Streets; both had become junior colleges a decade earlier: Laney, specializing in vocational education; Merritt, in business and the liberal arts.

In 1965, Alameda County voters approved a $47 million bond issue to build new Peralta campuses. Initially, it had been thought that both Oakland junior colleges would be relocated to an undeveloped, 120-acre parcel of land in the upper hills off Redwood Road. But Oakland mayor John Houlihan preferred a campus near the downtown. A decision was made to erect two campuses: one in the East Oakland hills for Merritt College and one alongside the Municipal Auditorium for Laney College. The latter effort went smoothly. In 1971, Laney College opened on 46 acres of land that had been earlier acquired and cleared by the Oakland Redevelopment Authority as part of the Peralta Civic Center urban redevelopment project.

The transfer of Merritt College from Grove Street to the East Oakland hills proved to be anything but smooth. Merritt had become a cultural hub in the heart of predominantly black North Oakland. As historian Donna Jean Murch observed: "The boundary between Merritt and North Oakland was completely porous. People passed on and off the campus, and many residents from the surrounding area hung out in the cafeteria, a major hub for debate."[65] In 1962, an older student named Bobby Seale met a younger student named Huey Newton; both would go on to found the Black Panther Party, the most important black power movement in the country.[66] One day, as Seale recalls, there was a street rally in front of the school where Newton was "shooting everybody down," rapping off information and throwing facts. Seale asked him if the civil rights campaign was doing us some good and, as Seale remembers, "He shot me down too...He said, it's all a waste of money, black people don't have anything in this country that is for them...That's the kind of atmosphere I met Huey in...A lot of people were discussing with three or four cats in the Afro-American Association (AAA), which was developing the first black nationalist philosophy on the West Coast."[67] Indeed, the year before, a few black UC Berkeley graduate students—Donald Warden, Henry Ramsey, and Donald Hopkins—who were reading Pan-African nationalist Marcus Garvey and listening to recordings by Malcolm X—founded the AAA. Their reading group began to meet at Downs Memorial Methodist Church at 6026 Idaho Street, walking distance from Merritt.[68] They then set up an office at 5605 Grove Street, right across from the college, where the group acquired its largest following.

During the early 1960s, a quarter of Merritt's student body was black, many of them recent arrivals from the South and the first members of their family to attend college. Yet the standard college curriculum didn't take their interests and background into account. Borrowing books from UC Berkeley libraries, Bobby Seale (and his Black History Fact Group) set up courses on African and African American Studies and petitioned the Merritt College administration to incorporate them into the school curriculum. After the Merritt administration refused the demands of the Black History Fact Group, Seale and over 200 students threatened to shut down the campus; they were well aware of the protests engendered at UC Berkeley by the Free Speech Movement. Merritt relented, and in the fall of 1965, Rodney Carlisle, a white instructor, taught the college's first black studies class, one of the first of such classes in the country.[69] Next, the Soul Students Advisory Committee was formed, later renamed the Black Student Union. Their aims were to hire black faculty as well as a black president, create a full-fledged Afro-American Studies program where credits could be transferred to four-year colleges, and allow community college graduates to be hired as instructors after they graduate. At the end of the spring semester in 1968, Merritt acceded to all their demands.[70] By this time, close to a third of the 10,000 day and evening students were minorities as were a fifth of the faculty—the highest percentage in the state. Norvel Smith had been appointed president of the college that year, the first black to head an institution of higher education in California.

Figure 18. Black Panther protest. "Free Huey" demonstration, August 17, 1968, in front of Alameda County Courthouse. Photo by Keith Dennison. Courtesy of Oakland Tribune Archive, Oakland Museum of California.

The student activists continued to make demands: enhanced control over student government; textbook loans for needy students; hot meals for those who could not afford them. In 1969, tensions boiled over. Froben Lozada was hired as head of Merritt's Mexican Studies program without faculty involvement. The faculty complained. In response, 100 Mexican American students locked 30 faculty members in a room for almost four hours—a protest against their protest. The edgy atmosphere at Merritt led to other problems. There were frequent assaults, vandalisms, thefts of typewriters, and raids on the college bookstore, where books were stolen and resold.[71] With far more vehemence than at the Oakland Museum, black and brown outsiders were contesting and wresting control of a cultural institution set up by white insiders.

In March 1971, the impending opening of the new Merritt College in the hills fired up the volatile situation at Grove Street. Peralta College administrators advertised the move as an opportunity for students to study in a modern, spacious campus. Students and especially the Black Student Union viewed it as an attempt to destroy a vital resource in and of Oakland's black community, one of the incubators of the West Coast black power movement. The new campus was remote from their neighborhoods and hard to access without a car. Relocation would diffuse valuable political and pedagogical energy that had been built up over the past decade. That spring, 90 students occupied the office of the president and took over the campus switchboard, demanding that the Grove Street campus be kept in operation until a new campus for minorities was built nearby. A police raid ended the occupation a couple of days later. In a concession, after the hill campus opened, the Grove Street facility was kept going for a few years. Daniel Castro, a student who passed up the chance to transfer to the hill campus, explained that Grove Street was the only inner-city college in California and "produced people who are concerned about the community and will go back to work there."[72] It shut down in 1975.

BLACK AND WHITE POLITICS

Oakland's white power structure began to crumble in the epochal year of 1977. First, the Knowlands sold the *Oakland Tribune*, three years after

William Knowland committed suicide, and the once-powerful family disappeared from the Oakland elite; Robert Maynard was appointed its editor—the first African American editor of a major American newspaper. Second, Kaiser Industries—Sand and Gravel, Engineers, Broadcasting, Aerospace & Electronic, Aluminum, Steel, Cement—came apart; Kaiser Permanente, the nation's largest HMO, continued to be headquartered in Oakland. Last but not least, Oakland elected its first black mayor, Alameda Superior Court judge Lionel Wilson, as well as a black councilman, Carter Gilmore.[73] A couple of years later, Oakland elected Wilson Riles Jr. to the council, and in 1983, the city's first black city manager, Henry Gardner, was hired. Bobby Seale had run a surprising second to incumbent John Reading in the 1973 mayoral race,[74] but now black power finally ascended from the streets to the halls of government.

Did the streets benefit? New federal rules now required greater community participation and control for government programs.[75] Multiple organizations rose up—a newly neighborhood-focused Oakland Citizens Committee for Urban Renewal (OCCUR), the West Oakland Planning Council (WOPC), the Oakland Community Organizations (OCO), and Oakland Progressive Political Alliance (OPPA)—and politicked with the increasingly heterogeneous (black and white) structure at City Hall— some of these groups are discussed further in chapters 8 and 9, "Housing Injustice" and "Downtown Renewal and Ruin." Later, blacks gained a voice on the Board of Port Commissioners and the Oakland Redevelopment Agency. The city appeared poised to embark in a radically new political direction. Many in the African American community felt that the time had come for a radical shift to minority-dominated flatland neighborhood priorities. Yet such a shift would surely alienate the city's white, hill residents and downtown business community. Could Oakland reorient financial resources to more of its citizens without damaging the source of those resources?

Alas, the time needed for measured consideration of this question wasn't available. Toward the end of the decade and into the succeeding one, the city's budget took one hit after the other. In 1978, one year after Lionel Wilson's election as mayor, California voters passed Proposition 13, reducing commercial and residential property taxes by over 50 percent. City revenues plummeted. A nationwide recession followed and, by the early 1980s, the reactionary administration of President Ronald Reagan enacted severe cutbacks to federal employment, housing, and anti-poverty programs that impacted California and Oakland severely. From 1983 to 1999, Republicans, specializing in tax-cutting and slighting forward thinking, throttled California's cities. Oakland fell into a struggle to balance its budget and provide basic services like fire and police protection. Mayor Wilson aligned with downtown business interests. Progressive causes such as expanded rent control and minority job programs were set aside.[76] Hopes to coalesce a black-oriented political agenda went unfulfilled.[77] The tough times worsened amid the ensuing earthquake, hills fire, and crack epidemic. Oakland felt as if it had hit rock bottom.

By the middle of 1990s, during slightly improved economic times, Oakland voters passed Measure I, a $45 million General Obligation Bond for renovation and earthquake retrofitting and upgrading of parks and recreation centers, playgrounds, libraries, and cultural and education facilities. Part of the money from that measure went to two museum projects: the African American Museum and Library of Oakland (AAMLO) and the Chabot Space and Science Center. Together, they reflect the post-1977 political adjustments that redefined development of Oakland's cultural landscape.

In 1965, at the onset of the struggle for black seats at the tables of decision-making, seven individuals concerned about the lack of available information on black history and culture founded a grassroots museum in the East Bay flatlands. Their leader was a retired engineer, Eugene Lasartemay, who became president of the new East Bay Negro Historical Society. The society's first home was a Berkeley residence, followed by storefronts at 3651 and 4519 Grove Street in Oakland and, after 1982, a small space within the Golden Gate branch of the Oakland Public Library on San Pablo Avenue.[78] The society grew, and its aims evolved to demonstrating the importance of black history, providing a gathering space for the community, and nurturing black empowerment.[79]

In 1994, after a merger with the Oakland Public Library, the society became known as the African American Museum and Library at Oakland (AAMLO). A new permanent home, a former Carnegie library at 659 14th Street, opened in 2002 with a library on the first floor and museum on the second. Over the years, exhibitions of the wandering museum ranged from the historical roots of the California black community to the broader cultural and artistic contributions of African American society. The museum/library's origin, migrations, and merger with a city agency in a beaux-arts building, redolent of the City Beautiful era that inspired countless plans for a grand civic center, epitomized the trajectory that black Oakland had taken from the 1960s to the 1990s: from small, neighborhood-based, and seat of the pants to mid-sized, downtown, and structured within a durable, nonprofit/public framework.

A different museum project was launched in the upper hills. This time it involved a specialized activity, star gazing, and a venerable institution, the Chabot Observatory, founded in downtown Lafayette Square in 1882 by Anthony Chabot. In 1915, the observatory, staffed by personnel from the Oakland Unified School District, had moved uphill to Leona Heights, hoping to escape the light pollution of the electric age. Now, in 1989, seeking to expand access for the general public through the construction of a new building even higher in the hills, another partnership came into existence between the City of Oakland, the Oakland Unified School District, and the East Bay Regional Park District. The reconstituted Chabot Space and Science Center opened in 2000 after 13 years of planning and fundraising in an 86,000-square-foot, $76 million building on a 13-acre site off Skyline Boulevard. It hosts several public telescopes, a planetarium, and exhibit halls.

Tellingly, the Chabot Space and Science Center's principal buildings are named after Ron Dellums and Dick Spees. Dellums grew up in West Oakland. He represented the East Bay as a Democrat in the United States House of Representatives from 1971 to 1998, and for most of that time was one of Congress's most left-leaning voices. Dick Spees, a onetime chairman of the Alameda County Republican Party, was an executive at Kaiser Industries for 32 years and member of the Oakland City Council for 23 years. Dellums stood at the pinnacle of black progressive forces in the East Bay. Spees came out of the old Oakland white political elite. They now worked together. Dellums pulled in $20 million in federal funds for the Chabot Center, including construction grants through the US Air Force.[80] Besides being the major mover behind the project, Spees fundraised, most notably directing approximately $6 million of Measure I to the museum project.

Alongside the AAMLO, the Chabot Space and Science Center embodied the amalgamated black/white cultural politics of Oakland at the turn of the millennium: neither the white hegemony of the past nor the out-and-out progressivism that many blacks hoped would succeed it.[81] Each museum took its own approach. Chabot built upon the town's long-standing romance with the reaches of outer space. AAMLO zeroed in on its underrepresented black community. Both lacked the architectural verve and national ambition of earlier projects, like the Oakland Museum and Coliseum/Arena. Neither tried to stand for all of Oakland, as did civic center plans during the first half of the century. Modest, ground-up affairs, they responded to a time when the town was less driven to compete with San Francisco, when earlier ambitions for a major league venue modeled on others around the nation transitioned into homegrown showcases of Oakland's far-off visions and nearby recognitions.

Part III

6 The Promise and the Reality of Freeways and BART

By the 1970s, California's freeway system was nearly complete. *San Francisco Chronicle* columnist Jon Carroll described it in reverential terms: "an engineering event on the scale of the transcontinental railroad, over 15,000 miles long and fifty years in the making. By a long measure, it is the best highway system in the country, which means that it is the best highway system in the world."[1] Other observers weren't as enthusiastic. Essayist John Krich chided the eight-lane superhighway outside the drawn shades of his Lake Merritt apartment, the stereo turned loud to block the incessant rubberized gurgle: "Once before the freeway, there had been lovely houses here, curvaceous castles with high turrets and screened verandas. Now, there were three-story efficiency apartments on either side: no children, no pets, all-electric kitchen. Their concrete balconies and bunker windows were like arrows pointing the traffic on its way."[2] Freeways might inspire some people and sadden others, but nobody could ignore them.

Back in 1928, in *A Major Street Plan for Oakland*, urban planner Harland Bartholomew had called for a system of superhighways. If the idea stirred transportation futurists, it would take more than 20 years for just the first section of Oakland's first freeway to be built. Los Angeles beat Oakland to the punch. In 1940, the Arroyo-Seco Parkway, running between downtown and Pasadena, became the first limited-access road in the West.

Subsequent planning for California freeways was bound up with federal efforts.[3] In 1938, the United States Congress had authorized the Bureau of Public Roads to undertake a study on limited-access roads, *Toll Roads and Free Roads* (1939). It advocated a national system of highways, thousands of miles in length.[4] Planning continued during the Second World War, as evidenced by the 1944 report from the Roosevelt administration—*Interregional Highways*—envisioning a 33,920-mile highway network connecting all cities with populations over 300,000. To sell this idea to localities, the report identified an additional benefit: clearance of slums and blighted areas that would resect urban problems.[5] In 1947, the State of California got into the act, passing the Collier-Burns Act, which hiked the gasoline tax, in existence since 1923, earmarking it for highway construction.[6] Shortly afterward, the California Division of Highways authorized funds for right-of-way acquisitions leading to a planned 475 miles of freeway in metropolitan Los Angeles and San Francisco.[7]

From 1946 through 1985, the division engineered four freeways in Oakland: the Eastshore or State Road 17 (later the Nimitz or Interstate 880), which led from the Bay Bridge south through downtown Oakland, East Oakland, and on to San Jose; the Mountain Boulevard or State Road 13 (later the Warren), a spur in the hills of East Oakland; the MacArthur or Interstate 580, charging from the Bay Bridge through central and East Oakland to San Leandro, Livermore, and the Central Valley; the Grove Shafter or State Road 24, slicing through North Oakland to the Caldecott Tunnel and Contra Costa County. Other freeways were planned but never built. A heavy rail, rapid transit system accompanied the new highway infrastructure. During the 1960s and 1970s, BART extended tentacles through San Francisco, Alameda, and Contra Costa Counties, creating a hybrid means of locomotion—driving coupled with mass transit. Nothing of a comparable scope had been attempted before, or since.

Like steam rail transit and ferries a century earlier, freeways and BART converged in the East Bay metropolis. City leaders expected instant dividends in the form of new housing and commerce. It didn't turn out as intended. The infrastructural convergence in Oakland did not lead drivers and transit riders to alight in large numbers from the immaculate concrete corridors onto the gritty streets of the town. By cutting the time it took to traverse the Bay Area, the expanded regional transit net benefited San Francisco more than Oakland, the suburbs more than the inner city. The cards of metropolitan mobility reshuffled, Oakland turned into a player with a weak hand willing to go to showdown but unaware that the deck was stacked against it. Freeway and BART right-of-ways rode roughshod over cityscape that stood in their path, leading to thousands of buildings moved or demolished, scores of streets dead-ended or diverted, businesses disrupted, residents displaced. Commercial and industrial districts were bypassed, and their owners as well as many of the town's residents would look to the sparkling, fast corridors as a means of escape to the frontier beyond Oakland's borders.

AN EASTSHORE FREEWAY

Planning for Oakland freeways began in 1937, led by Oakland department store owner Irving Kahn, who had funded the earlier study that led to the creation of the East Bay Regional Park District. Chairman of the East Shore Highway Committee of the State Chamber of Commerce, Kahn advocated highways to alleviate congestion on the arterial avenues leading out of town, like San Pablo and E. 14th. His advice echoed the state's judgment that new through-roads, such as Berkeley's planned Eastshore Highway, were essential to Oakland's economic competitiveness.[8] A compelling model presented itself across the bay: the conversion of part of the 1920s-era Bayshore Highway linking San Francisco and San Jose into a four-lane, limited-access freeway. The effort was led in part by John Hunt Skeggs, state highway engineer, who had earlier worked on the Los Angeles Aqueduct and the Bay Bridge Distribution Structure.

By 1940, Skeggs was working with Oakland officials on a four-lane freeway, one that would provide improved transportation for agricultural and industrial needs, give residents an easier route to reach recreation areas, and eliminate bottlenecks to the city's new military bases.[9] Planning, interrupted by the war, resumed afterward and in 1947, the Oakland City Council published another report by Harland Bartholomew: *A Report on Freeways and Major Streets in Oakland, CA.*[10] Its analysis of the city's historical traffic patterns revealed a road infrastructure in the form of a flat V, following the sloping terrain, and directing routes to a congested downtown. Ten years after the opening of the Bay Bridge, Bartholomew spied an opportunity. The bridge and its Distribution Structure were mini-freeways, facilitating unimpeded movement. Why not use the three-pronged touchdown zone of the Distribution Structure as the starting point for an East Bay freeway network—instead of leading cars through downtown? The time had come, Bartholomew reasoned, to build freeways that extended bridge approaches across Oakland to the greater region.[11] Earlier, trains, streetcars, and interurbans had concentrated people, buildings, and resources downtown. Now, freeways would forge an auto crossing point for the East Bay, encouraging centrifugal movements in multiple directions. It would come to be known as the Maze.

Anticipating replacement of Key System interurbans using the bridge's lower deck, Bartholomew's report added that the new freeways might accommodate rapid rail lines in their median strips. Planning for the Eastshore did not, however, do so. Highway planners thought that improvements in motor vehicle corridors alone could alleviate automotive congestion. Those attitudes were bolstered by a 1954 study from the California Division of Highways claiming that a freeway would attract industries and residents to its adjacent lands and alleviate street congestion in built-up parts of Oakland by dispersing manufacturing plants to southern Alameda County.[12] Although no one knew the full ramifications at the time, the seeds for metropolitan decentralization and Oakland's decline were being laid out in wide ribbons of freshly poured concrete.

The Eastshore Freeway would proceed from San Jose to Oakland along the easterly shores of the bay and, after a juncture with the Bay Bridge, continue north as the Richmond-Carquinez Freeway, crossing a new cantilever bridge over the Carquinez Straits to reach Vallejo and eventually Sacramento. Unlike earlier limited-access highways in California, its route took it directly through Oakland's downtown. Sixteen entire blocks (between 5th and 6th Streets) from Oak to West Streets were leveled. A concrete barrier has henceforth run between the office/retail district and the warehouse/maritime district. Both the Asian and Mexican districts downtown lost scores of buildings. While Chinatown was reconstituted in the blocks to the north, the center of Mexican population and commerce relocated to the Fruitvale District.

Figure 19. Eastshore/Nimitz Freeway. Aerial view of construction through Jingletown, Montgomery Ward store in view, 1948.
Photo courtesy of Oakland Public Library, Oakland History Room.

South of downtown, the initial sections of the Eastshore passed through East Oakland's industrial waterfront. They too were destructive. Right-of-way clearance required the removal of businesses like California Wire Cloth, Marguart's Machine Shop, and E. K. Wood Lumber. Two other plants, National Auto Fibers and California Cotton Mills, were bisected, making efficient operations impractical—the plants later shut down.[13] Hundreds of private residences were moved or demolished.[14] Despite the fact that 15 grade separations (e.g., bridges, overheads, pedestrian overcrossings) were built, the Eastshore left behind a confusing traffic network, isolating some neighborhoods and subjecting others to the roar of its thunderous traffic.[15]

In 1948, after a major overpass was completed at 5th Avenue just south of downtown, the Eastshore's first section opened. Eleven years later, the entirety of the route in Oakland, from the San Leandro line to the Bay Bridge, was complete. The freeway was renamed for Admiral Chester Nimitz, commander in chief of the Pacific Fleet during the Second World War. He was on hand to cut the ribbon debuting its newest and most dramatic feature, the double-deck Cypress Structure—the first of its kind in California. Unlike in East Oakland, where the freeway cut though industrial or (further south) open land, older West Oakland was a dense patchwork of residences and industries. In order to insert as narrow a right-of-way as possible, highway engineers designed a 52-foot-high elevated highway. Yet similar to the freeway's impact downtown, the Cypress Viaduct functioned like a wall, cutting West Oakland in two.[16] Dwellings, businesses, a YMCA, and an orphanage were demolished or moved. Residents and activists of the largely black district claimed that the elevated freeway not only caused noise and air pollution but also increased cancer rates in its path past old Victorians and more recent housing projects.[17]

Freeway routes typically followed the path of least resistance: river-banks, parklands, industrial zones, and poor and minority neighbor-hoods.[18] Historian Brian Ladd reminds us of the geographic specificity of some superhighways: "To the delight of urban reformers eager to raze the slums, many routes also sliced through the lowest-value residential neigh-borhoods, which were typically where African Americans lived."[19] The goal of "slum" clearance, brought up earlier in *Interregional Highways* (1944), came to fruition in Oakland. The Eastshore Freeway first plowed through Oakland's Asian and Mexican downtown enclaves and then the Cypress Structure erected a wall in the midst of black West Oakland. Oakland's three principal minority districts were struck with one blow.

Even before the Cypress Structure was completed, plans were in motion to widen the Nimitz to eight lanes.[20] Oakland's first freeway was a great success—as measured by vehicle loads. But its safety was fatally exposed on October 17, 1989, when the magnitude 6.9 Loma Prieta Earthquake struck the Bay Area. Although centered over 60 miles to the south, Oakland suf-fered the quake's single greatest loss of life (which might have been greater if the Oakland Athletics were not playing the San Francisco Giants for the World Series at the time). The Nimitz's Cypress Structure had been built on precarious foundations, a mixture of bay mud and unconsolidated landfill that causes structures to vibrate wildly during an earthquake. A series of support columns on portions of a 1.25-mile section of the double-deck freeway failed. Forty-two people in vehicles were crushed to death as the upper deck crashed down onto the lower deck. Studies later found that the lateral bars that reinforced the freeway's columns against sudden

Figure 20. Collapsed section of Cypress Structure. Earthquake damage in West Oakland, 1989. Photo courtesy of African American Museum and Library at Oakland.

seismic movements were inadequate—double-deck structural construction was abandoned.

How would the collapsed freeway be rebuilt? Quickly, the City of Oakland and the Citizens Emergency Response Team, a coalition of environmentalists and neighborhood activists like Chappell Hayes, opposed a double-decker replacement or a wider freeway along the same route. In the transformed political environment of the late twentieth century, top-down planning gave way to community concerns. Elevated expressways should not ram through neighborhoods.[21] The lobbying effort convinced the state to shift the route to the periphery of West Oakland,[22] and by 1992, CalTrans came up with a ground-level design that cut through industrial areas and SP railroad yards.[23] Completed in 1998, the $933 million, five-mile Cypress Freeway Replacement Project contained just six lanes, two fewer than the demolished freeway.[24] Mandela Parkway was constructed along the path of the old Cypress Structure. It was envisioned by the Coalition for West Oakland Revitalization as an African-themed grand boulevard of small businesses, community centers, and parks.[25]

Only the parks were realized, for while there was money for highways, the state and federal largesse did not extend to other community aspirations.

HIGHWAY IN THE HILLS

In the 1940s, because of their spotty road network, Oakland's upper hills were lightly settled. Talk of improvements centered on a realigning and widening of Mountain Boulevard, the main through-route that followed the valley created by the Hayward Fault. Much of the boulevard ended up becoming Oakland's second freeway project when, in 1948, the State Highway Division designated a highway to run for 9.1 miles along the route of Mountain Boulevard, Tunnel Road, and Ashby Avenue, affording direct connection between the East Oakland hills and Berkeley waterfront.

In 1952, shortly after the first 1.1-mile section, from Broadway Terrace to Thornhill/Moraga Avenue, was completed,[26] Oakland's first freeway controversy took place. Eight property owners appeared before the city council with a petition of 800 signatures. They were not protesting the freeway, but were concerned about the inadequacy of the narrow, 52-foot-wide access road adjacent to the Montclair business district.[27] It was widened. In 1956, when the second section of the freeway reached east of Park Boulevard, the Montclair Methodist Church held a prayer vigil for the safety of drivers on the roadway and for the fact that the dirt and noise of the construction were now a thing of the past.[28]

Renamed after Earl Warren, then chief justice of the US Supreme Court, in 1957, the final southern sections of the Warren Freeway were delayed until the juncture with the MacArthur Freeway could be completed in 1966. Thereafter, the four-lane Warren Freeway would be a woodsy, bucolic ride, and a stimulus for residential development of the upper hills. That said, its northern section through Berkeley got stopped dead in its tracks. In 1961, the Berkeley City Council, aware that its portion of the freeway was routed through existing neighborhoods and alarmed at the impending scale of destruction, voted unanimously to cancel the 4.6-mile Ashby Freeway extension.

While more politically conscious Berkeley fought off a freeway, Oakland's highway planning would hardly miss a beat—Oakland lacked the students and political activists of Berkeley and the elites and alternative cultures of San Francisco, all of whom early on championed quality-of-life issues. Events at the national level were still supercharging the motor vehicle utopias. In 1956, Congress passed the Federal-Aid Highway Act, which resulted in the National System of Interstate and Defense Highways, a vast, interrelated array of limited, or controlled-access, highways—by the 2000s, over 47,000 miles of roadway from coast to coast.[29] The federal government henceforth picked up 90 percent of the tab for interstate highways. The California Division of Highways jumped on board with heightened ambitions, releasing *The California Freeway System* (1959), and calling for 12,500 miles of freeway across the state, about four times the length of the United States, with an intended completion date in the early 1970s.[30]

The engineers drew up grand plans for Oakland. They included the MacArthur Freeway (I-580); the Grove Shafter Freeway (SR 24); the Park Boulevard/Shepherd Canyon Freeway heading northeast from the Nimitz to Shepherd Canyon and a tunnel to Moraga; the Hegenberger Freeway beginning near the Oakland Airport and going north to link up with the intersection of the MacArthur and Warren Freeways; and the audacious Shoreline Freeway, built entirely on piles atop the bay and paralleling the Alameda shoreline on its route between the Bay Bridge and a proposed Southern Crossing Bridge to San Francisco. Most of these routes were incorporated into the *Oakland General Plan* (1959). With funding flowing from taxes levied by Sacramento and Washington, by the early 1960s over 150 miles of new California freeways were being finished each year.[31] Oakland and other California cities were poised for dramatic transformations and confrontations.

THE MIGHTY MADDENING MACARTHUR

In the early 1950s, B. W. Booker, assistant state highway engineer, argued that a freeway between the Eastshore and Mountain Boulevard (later Warren) was essential for Oakland's and the state's "adequate highway system."[32] The proposed MacArthur Freeway was seen as a crucial connector between the Bay Area and Central and Southern California, leading from the freeway nexus just east of the Bay Bridge to the head of Lake Merritt, at Grand Avenue and MacArthur Boulevard, and then further southeast along the base of the lower hills to Castro Valley and, ultimately, the Dublin/Livermore Valley and the Central Valley. There, it would join the most important north–south freeway project on the West Coast, Interstate 5, running from San Diego to Seattle. The MacArthur would therefore be a vital part of the fastest vehicular route between San Francisco and Los Angeles. Oakland was but a cog in a greater plan. The overall workings of the freeway system mattered more to politicians and highway planners than any adverse impacts it might have on a locality.

Highway planners promised that the MacArthur Freeway would improve local conditions in Oakland by taking through-traffic off an important cross-town avenue, MacArthur Boulevard—enhancing business and residential areas by reducing traffic congestion. What they learned the hard way was that vehicular traffic, especially after the demise of streetcars, was the lifeblood of commercial streets. Rerouting of traffic would hurt rather than help businesses. Highway planners also hoped the new freeway would provide an alternative route to the Eastshore Freeway, alleviating fears that a single freeway leading south and east from Oakland would be inundated with traffic. Confirming those qualms, in 1965, on the eve of the MacArthur Freeway's opening, traffic on the Eastshore (now called Nimitz) Freeway was deemed the worst in California. In comparison to Los Angeles, where freeways were arranged on four-mile grids, Thomas Whaley, urban planning chief for the Division of Highways, went on to lambast the Bay Area's smaller freeway network as completely inadequate—a "horse and buggy system."[33]

The route of the 12-mile, eight-lane superhighway was audacious. It would tear across the residential heartland of Oakland.[34] Thousands of residents and scores of businesses would be affected—mostly in white Oakland. Not coincidentally, for the first time, a freeway project provoked shock and anger. In 1954, shortly after the Division of Highways announced the $100 million highway, 700 people attended a protest meeting organized by the Lakeshore Homes Association at Crocker Highlands Elementary School, voicing fears that their properties would be condemned and property values would decline.[35] At a subsequent meeting organized by the State Highway Commission at the Municipal Auditorium, three groups came out in opposition: Lakeshore Homes Association, Lakeshore Business Association, and Grand Avenue Merchants Association. They contended that the freeway would leave a scar of blight across Oakland. Nonetheless, most of the 25 organizations invited to the meeting did not voice opposition, and some of them claimed that the freeway was the only means of relieving congestion for many of the business districts it would pass. Despite a static population and ongoing suburbanization, the mantra of "relieving traffic congestion" held sway. For its part, the Division of Highways kept repeating the mantra and insisting the chosen route was the least disruptive.[36]

In 1957, the Oakland City Council approved the plan. Despite protesters, organized in part by John Houghton, president of the MacArthur Freeway Citizens Opposition Committee, only a single council member, Glenn Hoover, voted against it.[37] A couple of changes were made. Mills College president Easton Rothwell had complained that the freeway followed too closely the 163-acre college campus's northern perimeter; its noise and unsightliness would interfere with the functioning of dormitories, the art gallery, and his residence.[38] In a compromise, an off-ramp was redesigned to eat up less space and a grove of trees were spared. The freeway was also bent around Knowland Park to preserve more open space. But the rest of the route was built as planned by the Division of Highways, according to criteria largely based on existing and proposed traffic volumes and origin-destination studies.[39] "Engineers," as Professor Tom Lewis describes, "knew they had the ability to put a highway anywhere, including places where automobiles had never been, and many reveled in the sheer joy of building without attention to the consequences."[40]

Starting in the late 1950s, affected property owners began receiving 60-day eviction notices. At Harrison Street and Oakland Avenue, a triangular block with eight businesses was demolished.[41] Along 36th Street, the California Center for the Blind and St. Andrews Church were razed. In East Oakland, EBMUD's Central Reservoir had to be cut and rebuilt. In all, 2,100 parcels were purchased, and more than half of the buildings demolished; the others were moved if they were in decent condition and vacant properties could be found to accommodate them. Some houses were moved via trucks and house-moving dollies down to the waterfront and others sent on barges up the bay and delta to Stockton.[42] Scores of

Figure 21. Bay Bridge approaches. Freeways merge before Bay Bridge. Port of Oakland terminals, *upper left*; EBMUD sewage treatment plant, *lower left*; 1998. Photo courtesy of Library of Congress Prints and Photographs Division HAER CAL, 38-SANFRA, 141-56.

Oakland streets were dead-ended and new frontage roads constructed. Residential subdivisions, like Lakeshore Highlands and Haddon Hill, suddenly found themselves on opposite sides of a concrete river. Most of the freeway was raised on an embankment in order to allow perpendicular streets to cross underneath. Many bridges were needed, the most significant being the construction of a 764-foot elevated causeway supported by round towers spanning Grand and Lakeshore Avenues in Eastshore (now Splash Pad) Park.

Construction began in 1960 and was finished six years later. As officials from the Oakland Chamber of Commerce, the Alameda County Supervisors, the California Department of Public Works, and California Highway Commission gathered to celebrate, Governor Pat Brown called the MacArthur "a vital link in the development of the thriving East Bay."[43] Business leaders praised the freeway for reducing street congestion and shortening trips for commuters and shoppers. The high-speed road was especially heralded for providing users a sequence of panoramas of Oakland and its landmarks.[44] E. D. Houde of the Highway Commission called the MacArthur a proving ground for many improvements that became standard practice: long sweeping curves, extensive landscaping. In 1969, the MacArthur Freeway won first prize in the US Department of Transportation's second annual Highway Beauty Awards Competition, and a year later it was added to the state's Scenic Highways System. The City of Oakland went a step further, in 1974, adding a new element to its Master Plan—*Scenic Highways*, as a means to protect roadways notable for the quality of their visual corridors. Enhanced mobility transformed a driver's encounter with the city from an immersive experience to one characterized by fleeting and distanced impressions. As such, Skyline Boulevard, the loping road at the ridge of the hills, was commended for its spectacular panoramas. The bulk of attention was reserved for the work-horse MacArthur Freeway, which by then was carrying between 87,000 and 138,000 automobile trips a day. City planners were impressed that its "dense clusters of pastel houses on irregularly platted streets create an appealing, almost Mediterranean pattern...The sequence of cut and fill necessitated by the rolling topography provides an interesting progression of expansive and enclosed spaces."[45] Reflecting the parkway orientation of highways reaching back to the nineteenth century, detracting factors were the quarry at Edwards Avenue and the intermittent presence of bill-boards, utility poles, and shopping center signs. More vegetative screening was recommended.[46]

The MacArthur did come about with a compromise that enhanced both its environment and that of its surroundings. Starting in 1951, because of a concern that trucks and associated businesses—like warehouses and industries—locating at key intersections were downgrading adjacent residential neighborhoods, trucks had been banned on MacArthur Boulevard. Those traveling through Oakland were diverted to E. 14th Street and later the Eastshore Freeway. By the early 1960s, while the MacArthur Freeway was under construction, residents, civic organizations like the Lakeshore Homes Association, churches, hospitals, and Mills College circulated a petition with over 20,000 signatures to extend the ban to the new roadway. In 1962, the Oakland City Council passed an ordinance to limit travel on the impending freeway to trucks weighing less than four-and-one-half tons.[47] Under significant pressure, in 1963, the State Highway Division agreed to extend the ban temporarily, until a review was completed by January 1, 1968. The MacArthur became the only freeway in California, other than a section of the Pasadena Freeway, to exclude truck travel. In 1967, aware of the impending review and aware that the California Trucking Association was arguing to lift the ban, John Sutter, a resident of the Grand Lake neighborhood, helped organize "Citizens Against Trucks on the Freeway." With overwhelming opposition to changing the status quo, the State Highway Division extended the ban indefinitely.[48] Trucks, one of the key users of highways, were banned in Oakland before they were similarly banned on Interstate 280 on the peninsula.

ONE LAST FREEWAY

An eastbound highway, the 16.4-mile Tunnel Road Freeway, was conceived in the late 1940s as a route between Oakland/Alameda and Walnut Creek. While the connection to Alameda never happened, plans went ahead for a six-and-a-half mile path through Oakland, from the Caldecott Tunnel to a juncture with the Nimitz Freeway. It would cut the driving time on the old Broadway/Tunnel Road route and, as an added benefit, incorporate a BART line (and two stations) for some of its length.

In the late 1950s, the state was supportive of a highway from Oakland to Contra Costa County. Assistant state highway engineer B. W. Booker stated that "approval of the Grove-Shafter route will lift a blight that has affected all of North Oakland."[49] Nevertheless, opposition by residents and businesses along the route of the 122-foot-wide freeway grew as planning progressed. By 1957, there was loose talk of North Oakland's secession from Oakland at a 500-person meeting at Ligure Hall in Temescal, a neighborhood that would be severely impacted by the chosen route. A year later, at a meeting at Oakland Technical High School, the College Avenue Merchants Association raised worries about the freeway's cutting their commercial district in half. Some of the objections were influential in rerouting the freeway to the north of the Temescal commercial district on Telegraph Avenue, although the slice across College Avenue remained and the diagonal cut across Claremont Avenue eliminated part of a commercial strip. In subsequent years, 33 streets crossing its route would be deadended. The Grove Street commercial district—now Martin Luther King Jr. Way—would be decimated and Telegraph Avenue businesses damaged as well.[50] The highway planners were wrong about what caused urban ills. Instead of alleviating a fictitious blight affecting North Oakland, the construction and presence of the Grove Shafter Freeway contributed to an exodus of businesses.

In 1959, a resident on Keith Avenue, adjacent to the proposed right-of-way, lambasted the possibility of losing 1,768 homes and 118 businesses.[51] Protests intensified as clearance and roadway preparation commenced. As was the case with the MacArthur Freeway protests, affluent neighborhoods, in this case in Rockridge, were best organized to fight the State Division of Highways. Groups—the Chabot Canyon Association and Save the Hills Association—formed in response to homes being moved and demolished, groves of trees cut down and, along Chabot Canyon, preparations for large changes in landforms.[52] In particular, a 150-foot-high, 160-foot-wide earth-fill embankment was fought, as was a freeway off-ramp that would have razed 13 houses.[53] When pile drivers, dump trucks, and derricks arrived, they stimulated more protests.[54] While small changes were made to the route to save a few houses and the embankment was reduced in scale, the Grove Shafter Freeway kept churning forward.

Part of what kept it going was its associated mass-transit project, the first of its kind in California. In 1960, a preliminary agreement had been reached between the State Department of Public Works and the proposed BART system. For three and a half miles, the eight-lane freeway would include a Bay Area Rapid Transit (BART) roadbed of the Concord Line in its center median; the transit joint venture encompassed both the MacArthur and Rockridge BART stations. By 1970, impelled in part by BART deadlines, the freeway was finished all the way from Walnut Creek to just north of downtown Oakland.

Up to that time, the California Division of Highways had built 370 miles of freeways in the Bay Area with 900 more miles on the docket.[55] Across the state, thousands of miles of freeway had been constructed, tens of thousands of acres of land acquired, more than 400,000 residents, 44,000 businesses, and 13,000 farmers evicted. For years, the sale and refurbishing of moved structures was a business in and of itself.[56] Using right-of-way agents to purchase properties and help relocate individuals, the majority of buildings were moved to vacant lots. But as freeway right-of-ways moved from corridors occupied by unbuilt land, railroads, or streetcar lines to crude slashes through established residential neighborhoods, the futuristic highways were losing their luster.[57] Not only were houses and businesses lost. The time span it took to design and construct a freeway was highly disruptive. Right-of-ways often sat vacant for years and became magnets for trash and vandalism. Once freeways were completed, the wasteland rarely disappeared. Piers, embankments, and walls attracted litter and vagrants.[58] Gas stations and automotive businesses replaced adjacent pedestrian-oriented commerce. Noise and air pollution worsened.

If Oakland's freeway protests had been modest in scale and accomplishment, an all-out revolt gripped San Francisco. Following the *Major Thoroughfare Plan* (1947) and *Trafficways Plan* (1955), the state's Division of Highways attempted to implement a system for 10 freeways that would have sliced across all parts of San Francisco: eight lanes underneath Russian Hill; a double-decker atop Mission Street; freeways through the Panhandle, Golden Gate Park, Marina Green. Starting in the mid-1950s, newspaper columnists, citizens, and neighborhood groups fought the freeway net and, in 1959, the board of supervisors canceled six of the ten projects.[59] By 1970, only a couple of freeways had been completed and a couple more under construction ended up as rumps to nowhere.[60] San Francisco's freeway revolt inspired opponents across California. Battles erupted in Marin County, Humboldt County, Chico, Monterey, Carmel, Ojai, Malibu, Beverly Hills, and Newport Beach.[61] Across the country, several prominent freeways were defeated: crosstown expressways in Manhattan; the Cambridge-Boston Inner Belt; the Riverfront Expressway through New Orleans's French Quarter. With nearly 16,000 miles of the Interstate Highway System completed, environmental and neighborhood associations were mobilizing and offering stiff resistance.[62]

In California, freeway work was further stymied by changes to the planning and financing formula. The Division of Highway's finance program, based on a stable gasoline tax, could no longer keep pace with escalating freeway costs. Dramatic increases in construction and maintenance costs had come about due to changes in freeway design: a trend toward uniform design standards such as consistent signage, lane striping, roadway geometry; an increase in the number of urban interchanges to integrate better freeways with local street systems; higher right-of-way acquisition costs; longer time frames for planning given heightened litigation and the process of public participation.[63] Yet politicians aware of the dislocations brought about by freeways had no desire for a battle to raise gas taxes.

Freeway fortunes in Oakland worsened. As Grove Shafter construction progressed downtown, the Legal Aid Society, Oakland Citizens Committee for Urban Renewal (OCCUR), Christian Action to Save West Oakland, and La Raza Unida filed a lawsuit demanding replacement housing for the hundreds of units estimated to be lost to further freeway construction.[64] In 1972, part of the freeway's rationale—its potential extension into Alameda—fell apart when voters nixed the Southern Crossing Bridge. Work ground to a halt, although only a little over a mile remained to push the Grove Shafter from 18th Street to the Nimitz (Interstate 880). It would take years and major lobbying efforts on the part of California governor Jerry Brown and Oakland mayor John Reading to put the project back on track. A diverse set of interest groups came to support it, from the Oakland Chamber of Commerce and Association of Bay Area Governments (ABAG) to OCCUR and even the Black Panther Party—who were brought in by promises of construction jobs for unemployed minorities. After federal funds were freed up, work began again in 1979, although the fact that minority jobs weren't materializing as anticipated generated new protests.

The freeway was completed in 1985. For the last time in Oakland history, hundreds of housing units were demolished or moved. In order to make the road less obtrusive, most of its corridor was depressed below grade level and numerous bridges were built for street crossings across this new barrier between downtown and West Oakland. A little-used roadway to this day, the final segment of the Grove Shafter is a case study in how freeway construction with overarching regional objectives trumped the local quality of life.

All told, the city's four completed freeways contributed to the loss of several thousand dwelling units and hundreds of businesses and institutions. Property values near the rapid roads declined. Businesses on adjacent or cut-off streets went belly up. Circulation patterns were disrupted. Thankfully, the other freeways planned by the Division of Highways in the later 1950s were stopped before they could cause extensive damage. In 1959, Corwin Mocine, Oakland city planning engineer, questioned the routes of both the Hegenberger/Shoreline and Park Boulevard/Shepherd Canyon Freeways because they would bisect residential neighborhoods.[65] The Park Boulevard/Shepherd Canyon project languished at the planning stage until 1972, when it was again condemned by State Assemblyman Ken Mende and City Councilman John Sutter, who warned that the physical fabric of Oakland was becoming a through-route serving people who lived in the suburbs, neighborhoods torn apart, divided from each other, and now threatened with decline.[66] Voted down by the Oakland City Council, it was subsequently deleted from the Division of Highways freeway program.[67] Around the same time, the Hegenberger and Shoreline freeways were scratched. Both had been inextricably linked to the Southern Crossing Bridge. When that project was cancelled, the idea of a freeway over the bay waters sank.

BART AND AC TRANSIT

Upon opening, the Bay Bridge was a smashing success—too much of one. It had been estimated that the bridge would carry six million vehicles in its first full year of operations, 1937. Nine million vehicles crossed that year. After a slowdown during the war, figures jumped to 33 million by 1955. The popularity of the automobile combined with a lowered 25-cent round-trip bridge toll lured mass transit riders away from the bridge's Key System rail lines, where a one-way charge was 30 cents per person. If bridge traffic kept increasing, insufficient capacity might strangle the region, choke off growth, and drive business elsewhere.[68]

Already in 1945, the California Bridge Toll Bridge Authority launched studies into a second bridge crossing between Oakland and San Francisco. Should it be a low-level bridge capable of handling freight and passenger trains or a high-level bridge solely for vehicles? Should it run parallel to the existing Bay Bridge, funneling traffic close to San Francisco's downtown or should it be situated several miles to the south, what became known as the Southern Crossing, running from Bay Farm Island in Oakland/Alameda to San Francisco's Hunter's Point, and requiring significant new freeway connections?[69] In 1947, a joint Army-Navy Board recommended a second bridge crossing as well as an underground tube between Oakland and San Francisco accommodating high-speed electric trains. Planning on each front proceeded over the next decade.

In 1949, Governor Earl Warren signed a bill making it possible to create a regional transit district, and two years later, the new Bay Area Rapid Transit Commission was empowered by the state legislature to study the creation of a 300-mile-long high-speed rail network through the nine Bay Area counties. In 1957, the state approved the Bay Area Rapid Transit District (BARTD, later simplified to BART). It was touted as a cure for the region's worsening traffic congestion and air pollution, but was reduced to a 120-mile system through five counties: Alameda, Contra Costa, San Francisco, Marin, and San Mateo. The centerpiece was the underground tube brought up earlier by the Army-Navy Board. The tube made the Key System lines on the lower deck of the Bay Bridge redundant; they were removed and, by 1960, vehicular lanes were increased to five on each deck. Most importantly, anticipation of the Bay Bridge's greater automotive capacity tipped the scales in BART's favor; the Southern Crossing Bridge lost momentum, although serious plans were floated as late as the early 1970s.[70]

BART was to be the future of transbay mass transit. In 1962, voters in Alameda, Contra Costa, and San Francisco Counties approved a $792 million construction bond for a further-reduced 75-mile system in those counties. Marin and San Mateo Counties had recently opted out of the system, and the lines to Palo Alto and San Rafael (including several stations along Geary Boulevard in San Francisco) were dropped. Was there a silver lining for Oakland? After all, the four spokes of the system—ending in Fremont, Concord, Richmond, and Daly City—now crossed at its downtown.

Construction began in 1964, and by 1972 the first trains ran from downtown Oakland to Fremont; two years after that, transbay service to San Francisco was launched. The engineering consortium of Parsons, Brinckerhoff, Tudor, Bechtel led design and construction, and their 1961 *Engineering Report to the San Francisco Bay Area Rapid Transit District* laid out the system's parameters. Aluminum and fiberglass electric trains would operate on their own grade-separated right-of-way. Seven-hundred-foot-long station platforms would accommodate 10-car trains. Thousands of cars would park in landscaped lots. The district's stated dual objectives were to "abate motor vehicle congestion on the regional highways and in the urban centers," and "compete with the automobile" with respect to fast speeds, frequent service, and comfort with respect to temperature control, noise level, and "pleasing internal and external appearance."[71] Engineers envisioning the BART system were well aware of the recent demise of the Key System and other electric rail systems across the country, and were eager to counter sentiments expressed earlier by Oakland planners who, in a 1950 report, *The Transit Problem in the East Bay*, lamented that mass transit "is regarded as the poor man's transportation, an inferior service to be avoided as soon as one can afford a car."[72]

That planning report also noted that, by midcentury, half of American cities had assumed public ownership over mass transit lines. Some had taken the regional approach; the Chicago Transit Authority was established in 1945 and the Metropolitan Boston Transit Authority in 1947. Along those lines, Oakland planners called for a detailed transit survey that could result in the formation of a regional East Bay Transit District. Since the takeover by National City Lines in 1947, the Key System had been subject to relentless service cuts and deteriorating rolling stock due to persistent deferred maintenance.[73] Electric streetcars and interurbans were not the only victims. Motor coach service was cut back several times.[74] Clamor for a regional public transit system for the East Bay only grew after a 76-day strike to the Key System in 1953, and accelerated in 1957 as the last days of Key System transbay service neared.[75]

At last, in 1959, a $16.5 million bond was approved to buy Key System properties—73 bus lines and 572 motor coaches—and establish a new transit district for 14 cities and numerous unincorporated areas in Alameda and Contra Costa Counties.[76] The new Alameda County Transit

(AC Transit) incorporated 170 miles of existing routes, and added 55 miles of new routes, mostly to growing suburban areas in eastern Contra Costa and southern Alameda counties.[77] By 1969, AC Transit was running 800 motor coaches.

From the start, lacking the subsidies supporting San Francisco's Muni and BART, red ink plagued the system. Growth was not necessarily a good thing; for the more passengers the buses carried, the more money AC lost.[78] An increase in annual ridership from 50 million passengers, in 1969, to 58.2 million, by 1975, could not alleviate the system's chronic deficits.[79] Through the 1970s and 1980s, most news about AC Transit was bad news. Riders were abandoning late night and early morning runs.[80] Robberies ended the practice of bus drivers carrying change.[81] In 1978, the passage of Proposition 13 produced drastic shortfalls in municipal property tax revenues and, the following year, service cutbacks up to 40 percent; there were discussions of ending evening service.

AC Transit did the best it could with limited resources, and pursued an incremental transportation strategy, where present resources were aimed at present requirements. By contrast, the better-endowed BART system was able to pursue a comprehensive strategy that anticipated future needs.[82] Since the debut of the full BART system in 1974, all lines except for the Richmond line have been extended. By contrast, AC Transit continued to rely exclusively on buses. From the 1980s to the 2010s, new light-rail lines were built across the nation and California: in San Diego, the Los Angeles area, Sacramento, San Jose, and San Francisco. Oakland and the East Bay—prior to the 1950s, home to one of the nation's largest urban rail systems—together hold the unenviable distinction of being the largest metropolitan region in the state not to add any light-rail lines.

The fragmented nature of Bay Area mass transit, with agencies largely based on counties and not the entirety of the region, did not help matters. BART was often unnecessarily competitive with AC Transit. After it opened, BART wanted AC Transit to discontinue its more lucrative transbay routes and increase feeder bus service to BART stations, arguing against the logic of overlapping service.[83] AC Transit largely won that battle, but in the decades that followed, East Bay transit users experienced two very different systems. Unlike the whiter, more affluent BART riders who drove their cars to BART lots, AC Transit ridership was heavily minority, lower-income, and more fully dependent on public transit. Yet BART received greater subsidies and was subject to fewer cutbacks.[84]

AC Transit took over a private transit company developed in the street-car era and attempted both to maintain its main routes and services and accommodate expansion within the rapidly growing suburbs. BART's mandate was to devise a regional system that could supplement the Bay Bridge and freeway network. Similar to automobiles, BART passengers sat on wide and soft seats. Long-distance journeys at peak hours were faster than by car. BART did everything in its power to "to provide a standard of service and comfort that would draw commuters out of their automobiles and off the region's crowded freeways and highways."[85] Two years after the system was fully operational, more than a third of riders were former automobile drivers.[86] The Bay Area built the first significant mass transit system after the war because BART aligned with the promise of the automobile instead of mass transit and its legacy of bad credit, shabby equipment, and disgruntled passengers.[87] BART was a supplement to automotive roads and freeways—not an alternative. As transportation journalist Harre DeMoro noted, in 1984, a decade after its debut, BART carried fewer transbay riders than the Key System did in 1925: 29 million passengers as compared to 39.7 million passengers.[88] In effectively trading the Key System for AC Transit and BART, did Oakland and the East Bay foolishly give up a more comprehensive mass transit operation?

Another outcome was clear. Because of BART's faster speeds and stations situated throughout the Alameda and Contra Costa suburbs, San Francisco benefited more than Oakland. The completion of BART's transbay tube contributed to a boom in office construction in San Francisco's financial district, funneling in workers who might not have been able to get there on the congested roadways.[89] Between 1968 and 1992, 40 million square feet of office space opened up in nearly 50 skyscrapers. These numbers affirm one of the system's original goals—to transport suburbanites to the region's core downtowns. In large part, the Bay Area Council (BAC) orchestrated this emphasis on white-collar, office employment.

Founded in 1945, the BAC was a regional version of a municipal chamber of commerce. Its membership included top officials from scores of businesses, among them: Bechtel Corporation, Bank of America, Standard Oil of California (later Chevron), Southern Pacific, U.S. Steel,

American Trust Company, Kaiser Industries, and Hewlett-Packard. The elite group conducted policy studies on industrial location, airports, and toll crossings, catalyzing the formation of the Association of Bay Area Governments (ABAG) in 1961 when more ambitious attempts at regional government failed.[90] In addition to its efforts to bolster corporate business activity, property values, and real estate activity, the BAC was also in large part responsible for BART's suburb-to–San Francisco focus.[91] It wielded great decision powers because no single public transit agency oversaw transportation in the inner Bay Area; indeed, BART, AC Transit, and San Francisco's Municipal Railway (Muni) would never be amalgamated into a single transit agency. That political failure on the part of Bay Area regional planning resulted in separate agendas for urban transit and regional transit, San Francisco and the East Bay, and BART's odd identity as a hybrid between an urban subway/elevated system and a commuter railroad.

Like urban mass transit, BART consists of different lines converging downtown yet never ending at a terminal station. Similar to commuter railroads, BART has a paucity of stations in Oakland or San Francisco—eight stations in each, about half of which are in the two downtowns. As a point of comparison, the Washington Metro, which opened two years after BART, has 39 stations in the District of Columbia, the majority of which are in the city's neighborhoods. The bulk of BART's stations and passengers were in the suburbs, and this condition would grow over time as BART expanded outward; all new stations added after 1974 have been located outside Oakland or San Francisco. By the early 2000s, the 46,000 free or inexpensive parking spaces at BART stations confirmed the system's suburban, vehicular focus.[92]

If BART fueled office development in downtown San Francisco, did it achieve another of its aims—a less decentralized region? The answer is no. Over three million residents were added to the Bay Area from the 1970s to the 2010s, and the population increases in the inner Bay Area—San Francisco, Oakland, Berkeley—account for only a small percentage of that gain. Decentralization was more pronounced in eastern Alameda and Contra Costa Counties, served by BART, than in Marin County, where BART did not penetrate. In those cases, county and city politics played a greater role in land-use development. It is even possible that residential sprawl may have been encouraged by later BART extensions to Antioch and Dublin/Pleasanton that offered alternative commuting options for home buyers worried about excessive traffic congestion on State Road 4 or Interstate 580.

LOCAL BENEFITS AND COSTS

BART was never designed to transport working-class residents lacking automobiles from the inner city to new suburban jobs, few of which were walking distance from BART stations.[93] Nor were buses routed from either minority neighborhoods in Oakland or from the suburban stations to job centers. Poorer blacks who couldn't afford a car, and were prevented from renting or buying homes in the exclusively white suburbs, had a hard time commuting to jobs in those expanding suburban locales. BART was planned to convey people from the suburbs to the region's downtown office centers, not the other way around. Consequently, BART disproportionately served white Bay Area residents. It contributed to increased land values in the suburbs and blight—due to construction disruption—around some of the Oakland stations in poorer neighborhoods like West Oakland.[94]

In the early 1950s, Oakland leaders had demanded that any rapid transit lines in the East Bay be centered on the city's downtown. That came to pass. As the juncture of the four completed lines, BART planners touted downtown Oakland as the most accessible point within the entire system, and its directors presumed that this accessibility would lead to a development boom.[95] Be that as it may, BART's positive impact on downtown Oakland development proved to be overstated; from Walnut Creek or Hayward or El Cerrito, it became easy to "rail-under" the Oakland downtown on the way to San Francisco's office or retail districts, just a few stops and 12–15 minutes further. As we shall relate in chapter 9, "Downtown Renewal and Ruin," office construction in downtown Oakland after BART was but a small fraction of what occurred in downtown San Francisco.

With minor exceptions, Oakland portions of BART were built as planned.[96] West of downtown, the heavy rail line rises onto an aerial structure—T-shaped concrete piers supporting pairs of concrete box girders upon which the tracks were laid—that parallels 7th Street and, after the station, briefly occupies a median strip before descending, near the loca-

Figure 22. BART train. Tracks beneath overpasses and ramps of MacArthur and Grove Shafter Freeways, 1973. Photo courtesy of California History Room, California State Library, Sacramento.

tion of the old Southern Pacific mole, to the 3.6-mile transbay tube that floats on soft alluvial deposits at the bottom of the bay. North of downtown, both the Concord (now Pittsburg–Bay Point) and Richmond lines rise up into a median of the Grove Shafter Freeway to a point slightly north of the MacArthur station. There, the Richmond line shifts onto an elevated median on Grove Street to the Berkeley line. The Concord line continues on the freeway median to twin 3.1 tunnels cut through the solid rock of the East Bay hills. South and east of downtown, the Fremont line rises up along 7th Street and then parallels, at grade, the tracks of the Western Pacific Railroad. After 19th Avenue, it rises further to an aerial structure within the median of E. 12th Street continuing to the San Leandro line.[97]

Other East Bay lines had been discussed, "particularly the densely populated MacArthur Boulevard and surrounding lower hill sectors of central and East Oakland."[98] It is possible that had BART planning taken place a few years earlier or, conversely, had planning for the MacArthur Freeway taken place a few years later, a serious attempt would have been made to accommodate another BART line in the median strip of the MacArthur Freeway. But when a BART line was briefly considered in the mid-1960s, it would have required complex switching facilities in downtown Oakland and extensive reconstruction of a freeway already under construction.[99] The matter was dropped. A couple of decades later, in 1997, BART opened a line on the median strip of Interstate 580, the continuation of the MacArthur into suburban Alameda County, with stations in Castro Valley and Dublin/Pleasanton.

At the center of the system, Oakland was affected most by right-of-way acquisitions and dislocations. One quarter of total BART land acquisition was in the town. Compared to 325 parcels taken by BART in San Francisco and Daly City, 775 parcels in Oakland, mostly single-family homes, were purchased by the district.[100] Downtown retail on Broadway suffered a major hit during the years of construction. Even worse, one side of the 7th Street commercial district in West Oakland and the Grove Street commercial district in North Oakland were decimated by BART's aerial structures.[101] It must be added, though, that when compared to freeway construction, BART was far less disruptive.[102]

Aside from downtown, did BART stimulate development around its neighborhood Oakland stations? When the system was approved in 1964, Stanley Scott, assistant director of the UC Institute for Governmental Studies, advised that the transit district acquire additional land near stations to recapture part of the anticipated increase in land values, and avoid excessive speculation.[103] That recommendation was not acted upon, largely due to the costs and added dislocations it would have incurred. Still, in 1969, Oakland's City Planning Department authored a study, *BART Impact: Five Oakland Stations*, raising the question: what kind of development should the five stations outside of downtown attract?

The West Oakland station received no recommendations in light of massive urban renewal activity then underway. Plans for Rockridge were different. It was the sole Oakland neighborhood station not located within a federally designated anti-poverty area. *BART Impact* recommended increasing residential density near the station, both on College Avenue and some nearby residential streets, and also advocated expanding the commercial area beyond College Avenue onto a few side streets.[104] These recommendations were not carried out. Strong sentiment to preserve the physical fabric of upper-middle-class Rockridge prevented any increases in density allowable by zoning; indeed, growing (NIMBY) sentiment in the area later led to downzoning.

Back in 1969, planners thought that the motel row on MacArthur Boulevard might benefit from the new MacArthur station, and should be strengthened with new restaurants and entertainment businesses. What they neglected to notice was the fact that the recently completed MacArthur Freeway took most tourist traffic off the boulevard. Many of the motels began to function as residential hotels for longer- (and sometimes much shorter-) term guests. At the time, planners felt there was no market in the vicinity of the station for privately developed apartments.[105] To this extent, they were right. The MacArthur transit village did not break ground until 2013.

Nor was dense housing envisioned in 1969 for Fruitvale station, given its lower-income demographics. At the time, planners recommended landscaping for the "formless area between the station and E. 14th Street." That stretch was not improved until 2005, when the initial phase of the Fruitvale transit village opened. In another misreading of urban trends, the eight-story Montgomery Ward's store, a third of a mile away from the station, was regarded by the writers of *BART Impact* as an anchor for neighborhood renewal; it closed in 1978.[106]

Lastly, San Leandro Street in front of Coliseum station, and nearby the new sports complex, was envisioned as a site for retail strip development. The planners realized that public action would have to be taken to acquire the low-intensity industrial uses in order to launch retail businesses, steps that were never taken.[107] It is striking to note how planning ideas on development around BART stations during the period leading up to the launch of the system were so far off the mark; urban analysts

were unable to predict the extent to which enhanced vehicular infrastructure, freeways, and other socioeconomic phenomena were affecting urban
development in Oakland.

The reason for the minimal development around the five neighborhood
BART stations in Oakland had to do with a transportation mindset that
promoted stations surrounded by parking facilities. The West Oakland,
Fruitvale, Rockridge, and MacArthur stations were treated more like
the suburban Orinda and Hayward stations than those at 16th and 24th
Streets in San Francisco's Mission District, where trains ran underground
and demolition around them was minimal. In San Francisco, the four
neighborhood stations had no parking lots: the exception being a couple
score of stalls at Glen Park. In Oakland, parking lots isolated each neighborhood station from surrounding commerce. The number of parking
spots ranged from 400 at West Oakland to 943 at Coliseum. Even at the
Lake Merritt station, on the eastern edge of downtown Oakland, a 240-car
lot was included (with a 25-cent fee), partially to serve the new six-story
BART headquarters building.[108] The Oakland stations, despite robust residential densities in their surroundings, were conceived from a commuter,
not a neighborhood, orientation, and with a regional, not a city, focus.

Oakland's neighborhood stations were regarded as transfer points—
from car to rapid rail—for hills residents commuting to San Francisco.
This assessment is borne out by the fact that distances between these stations are greater than the advertised two-mile separation of the system
as a whole. In all of East Oakland there are but two stations: Fruitvale
and Coliseum. Lake Merritt and Fruitvale stations are 2.9 miles apart;
it takes another 2.2 miles to reach Coliseum station, and then 3.1 miles
to San Leandro station. From downtown, West Oakland station is 1.6
miles distant, while MacArthur station is two miles distant. Only the 1.3
miles separating the MacArthur and Rockridge stations compares to the
commonplace distances between stations in San Francisco: between 0.9
mile and 1.2 miles. Planning for the nine-county BART system in 1956
had forecast four more neighborhood stations in Oakland: one north
of MacArthur on the Richmond line; and three interspersed along the
Fremont line between Lake Merritt Station and San Leandro. Possibly,
between that time and the mid-1960s, a large increase in black population in both East and North Oakland, and the anticipated neglect and

decay due to unacknowledged racist practices, led BART to reconsider those additional stations.

HYBRID INFRASTRUCTURE

The freeway system and BART recast the way people got around Oakland and interacted with each other and the town. Earlier, Key System interurbans had included many Oakland stops. Neighborhood housing and commerce had grown up in conjunction with those stops and those of the more numerous streetcar lines. Getting around Oakland meant using transit vehicles in conjunction with foot traffic past houses, stores, and restaurants. Afterward, sights shifted to the greater region. Freeway and BART travel took place in high-speed corridors physically separated from neighborhoods. Akin to the large parking lots and access roads around BART stations, freeways catalyzed vehicular environments around their on- and off-ramps, this time consisting of gas stations, automotive businesses, or cheap apartments, all of which stood in sharp distinction to the surrounding residential fabric and commercial corridors and often contributed to their decline. Approaches to freeway intersections were similarly widened into higher-speed vehicular environments that discouraged walking alongside them and made crossing difficult and unpleasant.

Building design changed as well. Earlier commercial and residential buildings were planned with respect to how one accessed them on foot. Reliance on vehicles now ramped up the scale of access routes from narrow paths to wide driveways and the character of entry portals from narrow doors to wide garage bays—especially with respect to trucks. New development incorporated greater numbers of parking spaces, both within and around buildings. If older buildings emphasized relationships to the natural landscape and human scale, newer buildings functioned increasingly as nodes within expansive vehicular (and rapid rail) networks of parking lots/garages, access roads, and accompanying arterials.

The highways and heavy rail lines allowed Oaklanders to extend the distance of their commutes as well as their shopping, recreational, or other excursions. Individuals with a car or using car and BART could travel almost anywhere in the region on their own initiative and schedule. The intensification of mobility could be liberating and exhilarating. One could work in suburban Pleasanton, hike at a regional park on Richmond's shoreline, and shop in San Francisco's Union Square. A Bay Area perspective augmented their Oakland identity. Within Oakland, though, not everyone enjoyed automobile access and a sense of ease in traveling throughout the metropolitan area and beyond. White residents could easily drive or BART past poorer, minority neighborhoods, endowing them with greater control over the social environments of their excursions and destinations. They could similarly enjoy the options of the suburbs and outlying rural areas without worries about being singled out. The same ease of movement was not true of the city's poorer black and brown residents, confined, if they lacked access to a car, to BART lines and more commonly AC Transit routes. Nor was it true of minority residents who ventured by car into the suburbs, regional parks, or further semi-rural reaches infrequently and with an understandable sense of caution. Even more than the earlier Key System, the new freeway/BART transportation infrastructure was a platform for extending racial divisions over a sprawling geography.

A comparison with Los Angeles is apt. In *Los Angeles: The Architecture of Four Ecologies* (1971), the architectural historian Reyner Banham hit upon an experiential way to capture the Southland metropolis's jumble of multiple cores and sprawling, seemingly vacuous urban form. Banham characterized LA as consisting of three topographically distinct elements—its beach communities, flatlands, and foothills—linked together by a monumental freeway network, or Autopia. As in Oakland, well-off residents populated the hill districts while industries, the poor, and minorities constituted the flatlands. In both cities, streetcars followed by roads and highways fed a real estate industry ravenous for undeveloped lands to be urbanized. Of courses, LA's beach communities were unique, glamorous, distinct from anything in Northern California; Oakland's waterfront was filled by industry and later the port—allowing scant space for recreation. But like Los Angeles, Oakland's appeal to migrants was long advertised on the basis of its superior, Mediterranean climate. And to this day the East Bay city is defined less by architectural masterworks than by its topographic zones, downtown marking the character of the city no more than the forest of cranes at the port, the expanses of flatland housing and industry, the Mediterranean terraces of hills housing, and the freeway corridors from which that total urban form is best perceived.

Ultimately, this NorCal version of Autopia has been less separate and less utopian than its counterpart 370 miles to the south. Within the considerably smaller East Bay city, freeways quickly lead one into a tunnel, a bridge, another city. The freeway linkage to BART, to a hybrid automobile/railcar journey toward San Francisco, means that the joyride at high speeds or the slog in traffic mixes with rapid transit stations, railcars, and the dense streets of the walking city. To a greater extent than the Southland, then, where so much of the region was remade in the car's image, Oakland's development via rapid road and rail evidences more interactions with older grids and streetcar-influenced urbanity. Likewise, unlike East Bay suburbanites in Fremont or Lafayette, whose built landscape emerged directly out of the characteristics of freeways and BART commutes, Oaklanders contended with a split city, one part older and more intimate and pedestrian and the other newer, dispersed, and premised on high-speed movement. Many of Oakland's desirable urban qualities were lost in the rush toward automotive bliss, while other regional qualities, led by speedy access to the California hinterland and suburbs, were gained. From the point of view of high-speed transportation, Oakland is part LA and part SF, part suburb and part city, for some observers not enough of either and to others just the right mix.

7 In the Wake of Deindustrialization

"You're Lucky When Your Office is in Oakland!" So proclaimed a pamphlet issued by the chamber of commerce in 1959. It touted the city's fine homes and mild climate, first-rank schools, universities, and hospitals, opportunities for boating, golf, and an easy parking space. Founded in 1905 by 21 businessmen, the chamber had long advocated for Oakland through its weekly *Oakland Outlook*, and earlier pamphlets like "Thrive with Oakland" from the 1930s, a pitch for new industries, tourists, and the completion of the harbor, port, and airport. Once again, the 1959 pamphlet emphasized the city's crucial transportation connections to other places and, in a nod to the future, heaped praise upon the new Pacific Telephone and Telegraph Company Building, which included a direct dialing center linking the nation to Hawaii and the Pacific Ocean area. The chamber of commerce message: the city's fortunes depend on connections forged with more remote places through novel technologies.

Only seven years later, Warren Hinckle penned an altogether different appraisal in *Ramparts*, a onetime liberal, Catholic magazine that now, with Hinckle as editor, had become a voice of the New Left. "Oakland was doomed by its own geography," he lamented. "Its flatlands provide a natural base for industrial expansion of hilly San Francisco, an expansion that assumed forest-fire proportions as the 20th century pressed on."[1] Piers, factories, warehouses, storage tanks, and worker cottages crowded those working districts. As time went on, however, those precincts were both losing their industrial edge and becoming a place of last resort for white residents. "Race begins at sea level in Oakland," Hinckle continued. "Some 90,000 Oakland Negroes, constituting almost one quarter of the city's total population, are jammed into restricted and blighted flatland areas on both the east and west sides of the city. As the height above sea level increases, the population becomes paler. The attractive, sylvan hill areas are reserved for expensive homes for whites."[2] His message: Oakland's geographic, race-based divisions were dragging it down.

What a difference a few years makes. Beginning around 1960 and continuing through the end of the century, plant closures led to thousands of job losses. Black migrants arrived in a city with escalating unemployment and racist barriers to their fair share of the shrinking pie. They were understandably confused. And as time went on, that confusion turned to rage. Instead of a rising industrial powerhouse, Oakland was turning into a racial powder keg. Government leaders came to fear a riot akin to the conflagration that occurred in 1965 in the Watts section of Los Angeles and responded with programs aimed at increasing minority employment.

Soon after the completion of the transcontinental railroad in 1869, the long-distance transportation of people and transshipment of goods became Oakland's calling cards. That's what brought industry to town in the first place. The collapse of the manufacturing sector challenged that equation. Following San Francisco's lead, the political and commercial elite came up with a revised business model for Oakland: a command and control center of an expanding East Bay region anchored by a larger office downtown as well as a cutting-edge seaport and airport, ideas that, surprisingly, encouraged industrial decentralization to suburban Alameda County. From the 1950s through the 1980s, the city positioned itself as the East Bay switchboard of industrial research, development, and production. That vision was unrealistic, unfair, and unsustainable.

In a region with an increasing number of competing (and often suburban) subcenters, it soon became clear that not enough business operations would gravitate toward downtown Oakland. Nor did the model address the town's unemployed and underemployed black residents and the job discrimination they faced. Finally, creating regional networks, as we saw with automobiles and highways, came at great cost to the town's land and waterscapes. The Port of Oakland's requirement for vast acreages of land-fill—its filling of San Francisco Bay—would only be tolerated for so long.

METROPOLITAN OAKLAND

During the 1920s, after attempts to forge a Greater Oakland out of the inner East Bay had failed, a phrase cropped up—Metropolitan Oakland. Joseph R. Knowland, the chamber of commerce, the Downtown Property Owners Association, and the Real Estate Association envisioned an East Bay economy with Oakland at its center, a "city" larger than its legal boundaries, economically cemented to Alameda County.[3] In the ensuing Depression years, the Metropolitan Oakland Area Program (MOAP) called for industrial development of rural lands outside the city's boundaries. It made some sense. The town's fortunes were better than those in most of the nation, and the program sought to convince national corporations to locate branch plants on vast stretches of farmland or wild land, industries that would be tied by fast highways to Oakland's seaport, airport, and downtown.

Interrupted by the war, the program was revived in the 1950s, at a time when the industrial base started to erode. The first two casualties were shipbuilding and cotton products. As they had in 1919, maritime military contracts dried up after 1945. Three years later, the Alameda Works of Bethlehem Shipbuilding closed shop. Moore Drydock Company, last of the great shipbuilders, limped along until 1961.[4] Meanwhile, in 1954, the California Cotton Mills ceased operations in Jingletown after 80 years.[5] This time, freeway infrastructure was the culprit. A year earlier, construction for the Eastshore Freeway severed the plant in half, eliminating buildings and disrupting operations. The plant may have soon shut down anyway. By this time, National Automotive Fibres had acquired the company, and products had been downscaled to wrapping and agricultural twine; synthetic fibers had eaten into the market share of cotton products.[6]

Oakland's other industrial plants appeared to be in fine shape. Manufacturing plants churned out dried and canned food, iron and steel, plastic and wood products, paper products, machines, pumps and valves, tractors and farm machinery, trucks and automobiles, furniture and household goods, electric motors and transformers, stoves and washing machines.[7] Nonetheless, it was impossible not to notice that industrial growth was heading elsewhere. In 1950, Columbia-Geneva Steel, a subsidiary of U.S. Steel, built the Bay Area's largest steel plant in Pittsburg, 32 miles to the east of Oakland.[8] To the south, in San Leandro, Hayward, and the small towns that would become Fremont, thousands of acres of dairies, fruit orchards, and truck farms specializing in cucumbers and tomatoes were repurposed into subdivisions, industrial parks, and shopping centers. Escalating land values forced out approximately half of the county's farmland, and as reporter George Ross lamented, the farmer was now "in the way of a rubber-tired migration turning California towns into cities and cities into super-cities surrounded by suburban sleeping quarters trimmed with lanais, patios, barbeque pits, kidney-shaped swimming pools and double garages filled with station wagons and power tillers."[9]

Demographic decentralization doubled the population of Alameda County, but mainly outside Oakland. The city grew during the 1940s, largely on account of wartime industrial expansion. But during the next decade the upward trend reversed for the first time—population declined by 18,000 residents. Younger whites were leaving and blacks were arriving. In 1940, Oakland had 8,462 black residents (2.8% of the total). By 1950, the black population quadrupled to 47,610 (12.4%). In 1960, it almost doubled to 83,104 (22.8%). Conversely, by that time, there were 58,000 fewer white residents. These demographic trends continued through 1980, when 47 percent of Oakland's population was black, with the white population dwindling to 38.6 percent.[10] Where did the whites go?

Many moved east along the Highway 24 corridor to the suburbs of Contra Costa County. Walnut Creek's orchards were leveled for subdivisions, and population grew from 3,000 in 1950 to 37,500 in 1970. Even more moved to southern Alameda County. Between 1940 and 1970, Hayward's population leapt from 6,736 to 93,058, San Leandro's from 14,601 to 68,698. Housing discrimination kept populations upward of 99 percent Caucasian. In the 1950s, while Oakland added 38,000 black residents, San Leandro's total number of blacks declined from 20 to 17.[11]

San Leandro appealed because it embraced a civic model that brought in industry in order to levy taxes on it, and thus keep residential property taxes low.[12] Along the Eastshore Freeway, greenhouses and farm fields gave way to manufacturing plants: Republic Supply (marine and oil well materials); Crown Zellerbach (paper products); Pioneer Flintkote (building materials); and Caterpillar Tractors (agricultural machines). The Caterpillar plant was locally grown, the successor firm to Holt Manufacturing, whose founder, Benjamin Holt, had devised a better tractor to negotiate the clay soil of the Central Valley by replacing its back drive wheels with a pair of tracks, two feet wide and nine feet long—the crawler-type tractor, or Caterpillar.[13] Most promising for San Leandro was the decision, in 1948, on the part of the Chrysler Corporation to build a Dodge and Plymouth plant on these alluvial plains. Four years later, the Davis Street factory expanded. Then, in 1955, after a disastrous sales period, it suddenly shut down. Chrysler consolidated West Coast car production in Los Angeles, and over 1,600 East Bay autoworkers lost their jobs. It was a harbinger of disruptions to come.

The quick demise of Chrysler highlighted the instability inherent within corporate business culture. Companies opened, closed, or relocated their branch plants with alarming rapidity. Their multistate and often multinational character transcended allegiance to any locale. And when local expansion was called for, new plants rose in the nearby suburbs. Those would be the major reasons, alongside automation, anti-unionization, and global competition, for the succession of plant closings across Oakland in the coming decades.[14] Geographer Richard Walker makes a case for the fact that industrial suburbanization was as important, if not more so, than residential suburbanization in pushing urban growth outward. Bay Area industry largely started in San Francisco, then in the decades after the 1906 calamity, much of it moved to Oakland and the inner East Bay and some to South San Francisco. Now, in the 1950s, industry was moving once more. As Walker describes the saga, the key to decentralization of manufacturing in the Bay Area was industrialization itself, "i.e., the force of technical and market change unleashed by capitalist accumulation. Swiftly growing sectors can erupt in quite unexpected venues, while stagnant sectors and established sectors fade away."[15]

Centrifugal forces began to hollow Oakland manufacturing. In 1954, *Oakland Tribune* reporter Bill Stokes concluded that "decentralization is a threat to Oakland's status as a central city."[16] As he and many others diagnosed the problem, the issue was space, or a lack thereof. Industries coveted huge parcels of flat, undeveloped land where they could build one-story plants with plentiful parking and trucking bays, buildings whose horizontal floor-plates were easily negotiable by vehicles and mechanical forklifts. No such tracts of land remained in Oakland. Either submerged lands would be claimed from the bay or businesses would head down the freeway to undeveloped south county.

The chamber of commerce's revival of the MOAP responded to this predicament.[17] Working with the Bay Area Council to guide regional planning for transportation and industry, it effectively embraced suburban decentralization.[18] According to historian Robert Self, "The chamber envisioned an acceleration of the regional dispersal that had begun before World War II. But boosters believed that as long as development occurred 'with Oakland as the center,' the city itself would continue to prosper even as outlying suburbs grew and became investment magnets in their own right."[19] With the hindsight of history, MOAP's vision appears foolhardy. Earlier, transportation networks attracted industry and plentiful jobs to Oakland. Now, MOAP was predicting that the city would somehow benefit from industries locating outside its borders and taxing jurisdiction. Belief in the MOAP only makes sense when one considers the fact that Oakland had prospered first through trade, with manufacturing coming later. If new linkages, like freeways and, as we will see, a container port and jet airport, were developed, the city's status as a crossroads of industrial production and trade might persevere.

Some of Oakland's most influential business families crafted a model for running far-flung operations from the town. In 1902, Warren Bechtel had moved to Oakland and made a fortune building power plants, laying pipeline, and in conjunction with a consortium, the Six Companies, constructing dams across the American West. Stephen Bechtel Sr. (and later his son Stephen Jr.) continued his father's enterprises, expanding to shipbuilding, oil refineries, and nuclear reactors—and doing so on a global scale.[20] While Bechtel's company headquarters were in San Francisco, Warren, Stephen, and other family members lived in Oakland or Piedmont and played important roles in the city's business and philanthropic community.

Oakland's greatest industrialist, Henry J. Kaiser, arrived in Oakland in the early 1920s, and lived close to Lake Merritt on Haddon Hill through the 1940s. Along with his son and successor Edgar, Henry J. played an even more outsized role in Oakland politics and culture. Kaiser's company too had been part of the Six Companies construction consortium. It similarly profited from developing the resources of the American West. Over time, Kaiser diversified its operations to include pipelines, dams, steel and aluminum, real estate development, automobile assembly, and health care management, becoming one of the greatest builders in the world. Even though almost all of these ventures occurred outside the town—including, during the Second World War, the massive Richmond shipyards—they were run from the Oakland headquarters.[21]

In the 1950s, Kaiser, a Democrat, along with Bechtel and other members of the city's Republican elite, sought to plant these center-periphery, Oakland–East Bay workings at the core of the city's business model. Who was to stop them? Oakland had long been controlled by a business oligarchy. There had been a general strike in 1946 over unfair hiring practices at department stores, and a brief glimmer of progressive power a couple of years later. But an old boys' club of business leaders continued to monopolize the city's resources, maintaining low taxes and minimal government involvement in urban development.[22] To political scientist Edward Hayes, midcentury Oakland displayed "a pattern of political elitism and class rule, rather than pluralism, in that the election of public officials is controlled from the top, the social basis of recruitment of both elected and administrative officials is limited to the middle class or business."[23]

Given the success and influence of the Bechtel and Kaiser companies and the media reach of the *Tribune*, the Oakland Chamber of Commerce signed onto an outgrowth of the quixotic MOAP scheme. It involved several pieces. Freeways, BART, a container port, and airport would provide Oakland with the best intraregional and international transportation networks in Northern California. Urban renewal programs would remake the poorly performing parts of the downtown and its periphery. In their place, offices, hotels, shopping centers, and higher-income residences would rise up. Office buildings would predominate over factories and white-collar workers over unionized, blue-collar occupations. The technologies and economies of scale that created the office building and the beginnings of a bureaucratic, managerial class decades earlier, would now complete that transformation in working environments. What wasn't advertised was the worsening socioeconomic hierarchy, where highly compensated white managers and professionals would be supported by low-paid service workers, largely people of color.

From the 1950s through the 1980s, San Francisco undertook the shift described above, and established itself as a tourist mecca as well. It would fail in Oakland. The town fell far short of its aim to be a center for finance and management. The transition to a largely office-driven economy would be long and hard. After all, it drew a trifling tourist trade. Few higher-income residents chose to live downtown. Oakland shared these characteristics with many other previously successful and now downtrodden industrial cities, from Buffalo to St. Louis. Interestingly, Oakland was closer than most to making that transition, to mimicking San Francisco. The coming of Safeway, Kaiser, and Clorox had been good omens. Several barriers arose, however. They included the buyout of Oakland banks by San Francisco banks; the collapse of Kaiser in the 1970s; the larger scale of East Bay deindustrialization; and a rapidly growing black population denied fair participation in the workplace.[24]

MANUFACTURING MELTDOWN

After the war, General Motors plants in Oakland were humming. In 1957, they assembled 95,286 Chevrolet cars and trucks, and employed 3,460 workers.[25] From 1916 through 1963, four million Chevrolet cars rolled off its assembly lines.[26] None made that journey afterward. The collapse of Oakland's auto industry began in 1960, when Peterbilt Motors, the successor firm to Fageol Motors Company, shuttered its Oakland truck factory on MacArthur Boulevard and 106th Avenue, moving operations and 400 workers down the Nimitz Freeway to suburban Newark. A year later, GM announced it too was heading south on that freeway, building a 2.5-million-square-foot plant on 392 acres in Fremont. In 1963, when the new factory opened, all three GM plants in Oakland closed. This exodus was part of the nationwide movement of auto-making from cities to suburbs; in the mid-1950s, Ford had relocated from the city of Richmond to suburban Milpitas.

Greater disruptive forces were at work. In 1960, California accounted for a substantial part of nationwide production—658,000 automobiles annually, as compared to 2,113,000 cars produced in Michigan. Outside Detroit, St. Louis, and the Baltimore to New York corridor, the East Bay was one of only four urban centers in possession of assembly plants of two of the big three carmakers.[27] Now, as the Big Three renewed their focus on eastern manufacturing, the era of automobile branch plants was winding down. One reason was that the situational costs of Midwest production, the transportation of raw materials to the factory and shipping of finished products to market, improved. Another factor was the introduction, in 1960, of tri-level rack cars on trains, permitting long-distance shipping of automobiles at a relatively low cost. Product diversification and the huge increase in number of models—from 216 in 1955 to 370 in 1967—also played a role. The conversion of regional assembly plants to specialized factories that produced one or two models for nationwide sale made West Coast production unprofitable.[28]

From 1963 to 1986, California production of fabricated metals and transportation equipment—primarily cars and trucks—fell off a cliff.[29] In fact, the suburban Ford and GM plants in Milpitas and Fremont themselves ceased operations by the early 1980s.

Oakland's biggest job losses were in automobile and truck assembly (from 5,320 to 310 jobs), railroads (from 4,600 to 3,240), and food products and canning (from 11,780 to 10,010).[30] Passenger railroads, the transportation sector that had been chipped away by the automobile, succumbed to changing technologies. Now, the conversion of main-line locomotives to diesel engines, the closure of redundant lines, largely completed by the mid-1950s, made the Southern Pacific Railroad's large yards in West Oakland obsolete.[31] Meanwhile, the frozen food wave of the 1950s, microwave cooking of the 1970s, and later consumer preferences for fresh fruit and vegetables eroded California's canning industry.[32] But Oakland's problems ran deeper. Nearby cannery operations began to cease operations during the 1950s as farms in southern Alameda County converted to housing tracts. Canneries consolidated in the Central Valley to be closer to their product. Between 1977 and 1989, every CalPak/Del Monte plant in Oakland, Emeryville, and Alameda stopped their assembly lines.[33]

While the semiconductor and computer industry was lighting up the corridor between San Jose and Palo Alto into what has come to be known as Silicon Valley, older electrical industries in the East Bay were burning out. Like automakers, like high tech companies, these industries craved huge, unbuilt tracts of land—the kind only available in the as-yet-undeveloped suburban lands. In 1963, Smith Corona Marchant moved its calculator production from Oakland to South Carolina. From 1961 to 1981, General Electric pulled the plug on its three facilities in West and East Oakland. A string of other plant closures decimated Oakland's once-thriving manufacturing sector: in 1988, the Carnation Company; in 1991, Shredded Wheat; in 1992, Clorox;[34] and in 1995, Granny Goose.[35] Losses occurred across the board: resource-based industries and advanced industrial products; locally grown companies and branch plants.

A new word entered the vocabulary of urban places—deindustrialization. It involved, as Barry Bluestone and Bennett Harrison described in *The Deindustrialization of America* (1982), the widespread and systematic disinvestment in the nation's basic productive capacity, as capital was diverted into speculation, mergers and acquisitions, and foreign investment.[36] Deindustrialization first affected New England in the 1920s. By the 1950s, manufacturing employment was falling sharply in cities like Philadelphia and the Midwest, what has subsequently become known as the Rust Belt. The falloff of well-paying factory jobs soon afflicted California. By the late 1950s, the formerly paternal model of business, involving a strong connection to local community, was eroding into a more mobile and detached stance. California's high (living) wages, extensive union participation, and frequent labor disputes convinced many boards of directors that manufacturing could be better (i.e., more cheaply) accomplished elsewhere.[37] A couple of decades later, corporate raiders responsive to stockholder calls for greater efficiency and productivity instituted programs aimed at reducing labor costs via automation, relocation, and sell-offs.[38]

Deindustrialization hit Oakland hard. Instead of announcements in the newspaper that a new plant was coming, stories detailed plant closures, numbers of laid-off workers, and rising unemployment rates. Instead of a cityscape humming with workers shuttling between home and factory, weighty brick and concrete buildings went empty. "The workplace culture," as historian Steven High writes, "that had sustained and legitimated

Figure 23. Naval Supply Center. Former 3rd and G Streets, looking south along Warehouse Row, 1941. Photo courtesy of Library of Congress Prints and Photographs Division HABS CAL, 1-OAK, 16–21.

individual pride and dignity was replaced by a post-industrial culture that measured hard work by education credentials rather than seniority and physical prowess."[39] Oakland had indeed changed, as the MOAP predicted. Only the aftermath wasn't smooth or seamless for the working classes.

In a 30-year period from 1954 to 1985, Oakland lost over 20,000 industrial jobs, as the number of manufacturing plants decreased from 1,405 to 475.[40] Similarly, by 1990, most industrial plants in neighboring Emeryville (Paraffin Paint and Judson Steel) and Berkeley (Colgate Palmolive and Heinz) shut down.[41] The losses resounded throughout the Bay Area's aging industrial corridors. In 1970, 23 percent of the regional workforce in San Francisco and the East Bay was employed in manufacturing; after 2000, less than 10 percent had manufacturing jobs.[42]

The final affront to workplace culture was the rapid-fire closure of military bases and installations during the 1990s. One of the nation's largest concentrations of military installations was hollowed out. In 1993, the Base Closures and Realignment Commission recommended closing facilities across the country, including one in Alameda and two in Oakland: the Naval Air Station, the Naval Supply Center, and the Naval Hospital.[43] All were huge operations: the latter had dedicated a nine-story, 650-bed hospital in 1968; the Naval Air Station had recently served as the home base for the aircraft carriers *Coral Sea*, *Ranger*, *Hancock*, and *Midway*. All shut down between 1995 and 1998, along with thousands of naval postings and civilian jobs. Another round of the commission, this time in 1995, finished off the inner East Bay's military presence, as the Oakland Army Base appeared on the list. It closed in 1999. By 2000, the town's major employers were the city, the county, the school system, the post office, the community college district, BART, AC Transit, PG&E, and the Kaiser and Summit healthcare systems. Oakland had gone postindustrial.

HIRING BIAS

Deindustrialization was especially damning to blacks who had long been denied the kind of job opportunities that whites took for granted. In 1923, "when he arrived in Oakland," the future lawyer and activist "C. L. Dellums learned the axiom that there were only three types of employment for Negroes there: you could go down to the sea in ships, work on the railroads, or do something illegal."[44] Oakland blacks actually worked mostly in domestic service and secondarily in manufacturing.[45] But discriminatory hiring practices were the norm, except for one significant respite. The military-industrial colossus built up between 1939 and 1945 drew huge numbers of southern blacks to Oakland. In what has become known as the Great Compression, a shortage of factory workers increased hiring for blacks, other minorities, and women, and decreased wage differentials between the races. The word went out and blacks flocked to the West Coast. Amid demobilization, however, blacks, the last hired, were usually the first fired; their unemployment rate skyrocketed to 20 percent in the late 1940s. Conditions improved somewhat during the industrial revival of the early to mid-1950s, but worsened after 1960 amid deindustrialization.[46] By 1990, the city's three military bases employed roughly one-third of the black workforce in Oakland, and their subsequent closures capped off what had been a decades-long employment bloodbath.[47]

After the war, Oakland's Republican political establishment derived its appeal not just from its stances on low taxes and laissez-faire government. In a rapidly diversifying city, white residents and workers favored policies that would maintain their favored employment status. Historian Thomas J. Sugrue studied like phenomena in 1950s Detroit—systemic forms of racial discrimination responding to the "Negro invasions" taking place in northern and western cities. Like Oakland, Detroit was a city that grew on the basis of the automotive industry as well as enthusiasm for driving; outside California, Detroit constructed one of the nation's most extensive freeway networks. Like Oakland as well, the lot of blacks in Detroit had improved amid the military buildup of the war years and then regressed during the peacetime scale-back. To an extent, the United Automobile Workers heeded the grievances of black workers about workplace discrimination in Detroit's automotive manufacturing plants, but by and large, as Sugrue tells us: "Campaigns to educate and persuade white workers of the necessity of racial equality fell on deaf ears... whole sections of plants and whole job classifications remained racially segregated."[48] Hundreds of manufacturing firms also fled the city of Detroit for its overwhelmingly white and segregated suburbs, another foreshadowing of the location-based job discrimination that would afflict Oakland's black workers less than 10 years later.

Fair employment policies and affirmative action programs emerging out of these postwar conflicts centered around race in the workplace, and expressed growing awareness among liberals that racist practices were keeping blacks out of most (and certainly the best) jobs in the economy.[49] In 1959, the State of California passed the Fair Employment and Housing Act (FEHA), mandating investigations and remedies for discrimination. A few years later, a study of the Negro male participation in a range of skilled and semiskilled occupations in the San Francisco–Oakland metropolitan area revealed the extent to which they were excluded from most occupations. The problem, racism, was deep rooted. In 1960, blacks constituted 22.8 percent of Oakland's population, 19.6 percent of Berkeley's, and 10 percent of San Francisco's—a total of 180,000 in the three largest cities of the metropolitan area. Yet among 254,066 total employees counted by the survey, only 2,500 were blacks—one percent. The study found no black artists or art teachers, no black firemen. In a host of job categories, blacks numbered under one percent: engineers, reporters, accountants, dentists, architects, meat-cutters, and salesmen. Those with the highest black employment, between 2.1 and 2.3 percent, were blacksmiths, printers, and social scientists.[50] Across the work spectrum, in white-collar and blue-collar jobs, in the professions and skilled trades, in manufacturing and services, blacks were shut out. In 1962, out of 1,158 teachers in the Oakland public schools, 164 were black; out of 139 principals, five were black.[51] In 1965, there were a mere 13 blacks among the 1,255 employees at the *Oakland Tribune*.[52]

A 1963 study, *Negro Californians*, found that black unemployment was double that of whites, and that those who worked were concentrated in low-income, low-skilled jobs: maids, janitors, and secretarial positions in government agencies.[53] As they had in wartime shipyards and postwar industries, blacks were much more likely than whites to hold low-status occupations.[54] Because of the endemic poverty afflicting the community, they made up a large percentage of General Assistance cases, AFDC (Aid to Families with Dependent Children, or welfare) cases, and tuberculosis cases.[55] Through the 1960s and beyond, the dream of a good job, and with it the promise of a better life, faded for the recent migrants. In a region with a long history of worker organizing, and in a time where protests were taking over college campuses, Oakland blacks took to the streets.

Civil rights organizations, church groups, neighborhood associations, and students protested the plight of their community. Among them were national organizations like the NAACP and CORE as well as local churches and groups like the East Bay Civil Rights Congress, the West Oakland Planning Council (which grew out of the Model Cities program), and the Black Panther Party. In 1963, CORE picketed the Montgomery Ward store on E. 14th Street, claiming Ward's, whose workforce was only two percent black, was making only token efforts at hiring black workers.[56] A landmark agreement was reached for Ward's to institute new recruitment drives and projections of goals.

In 1964, the Ad Hoc Committee to End Racial Discrimination protested

Two East Oakland Residents   See article on minority employment, page 1   photo by Lynn Phipps

THE FLATLANDS

"TELL IT LIKE IT IS AND DO WHAT IS NEEDED"

Volume 1, Number 14   OAKLAND, CALIFORNIA September 11 to September 24, 1966   10¢ a copy

HIRE THE JOBLESS!

City Hall Urges Businessmen To Change Hiring Procedures

EDITOR'S NOTE: Joblessness among Negroes and unskilled workers throughout the country has just reached the highest level of the year. But the economy booms and the nation prospers as it has never prospered before. Why are the hard core unemployed excluded from this?

Lack of training and the vanishing number of unskilled jobs, explain business and government; and perhaps even deeper than these reasons, though rarely mentioned, the ever popular image of the unemployed as shiftless bums.

To break this vicious cycle in Oakland, vocational training programs like the Skills Center are now in operation, and federal funds to help expand or start businesses and thereby create jobs are pouring in. The total number of minority unemployed these programs affect, however, remains small.

The biggest hope for a breakthrough, judging from the thrust of Mayor Reading's new Job Program, lies in changing the attitudes of the business world. To do this, he has committed the City government to the plight of the unemployed.

Relying in part on his own personal prestige, Mayor Reading has begun a campaign to sell the business and industrial community in Oakland on the idea of hiring the hard core of the jobless. To begin with, he says, unrealistic employment requirements.

The highlights of the Mayor's campaign are a series of seminars and a Job Fair through which businessmen can come to grips with the unemployment picture.

"We can't force them but we can educate them," the Mayor told the Oakland Economic Development Council last week when he asked for their endorsement of the program. And this is the basis of his compromise approach.

To many civil rights leaders and groups working with the unemployed, however, the Mayor is letting business off far too easily. Making business the prime target of the program is all right because, as one member of a seminar panel told his audience, "businessmen are the only ones who can get these people off welfare." But to see the hard core unemployed into the mainstream of the labor market, business has to "bend a little." It has to be willing to fill a job opening with the ones who've had the least experience, not necessarily the one who's best qualified.

The Job Program planners and its civil rights critics both know that business is not yet ready, on its own, to make this move. Nor has the Job Program demanded it. The Mayor, standing awkwardly in the middle, coaxes business the idea of federal funds for training and expansion in exchange for lowering hiring requirements and hiring minority unemployed. Meanwhile, Senator Knowland pressures the businessmen at the seminar, "We're not asking you to hire a stenographer who doesn't know how to type or spell." And so goes another is asked of Job Fair participants that they will make a certain number of job openings available for the unemployed who come.

In contrast to the skepticism and restraint showed by some civil rights leaders and employment groups to the Job Program, the business community has understandably responded with enthusiasm. The Mayor points with pride to the fact that in the short weeks over 90 firms have agreed to participate in the Job Fair, whereas in the San Francisco Job Fair only 75 firms turned out after nine months of preparation. Participation, he has been warned by his critics, however, is costing business little more

Continued on Page Five

Photos: Lynn Phipps

Flatlands youth. The highest rate of unemployment is among 16 to 21 year olds

Figure 24. The Flatlands, "Hire the Jobless," vol. 1, no. 14, September 11–24, 1966. Courtesy of African American Museum and Library at Oakland.

unfair hiring practices outside the *Oakland Tribune* building. The following year, following protests at a Mel's drive-in restaurant in Berkeley, CORE organized pickets on three consecutive weekends of restaurants in Jack London Square, protesting racial discrimination in hiring; William Knowland, editor and assistant publisher of the *Oakland Tribune*, happened to be dining at the Sea Wolf Restaurant at the time.[57] Nor was the employment situation at the new BART system any better. In 1965, only four out of 160 BART workers were black. The Reverends J. Russell Brown of the First African Methodist Episcopal Church and Alexander Jackson of the Church by the Side of the Road led a series of marches and protests under the banner JOBART—Justice and Jobs on BART. They demanded more hiring of minorities to construction jobs and staff positions. While BART negotiated with JOBART, job goals were slow in coming.[58]

The City of Oakland made feeble progress hiring minority police officers.[59] In 1966, with more than 600 police officers in Oakland, only 19 were black.[60] By 1970, the department had grown to 711 officers, 36 of whom were black—5 percent of the force despite the fact that blacks made up 34.5 percent of the population that year. What's worse, relations between black community and the white police were deteriorating as the community was growing and poverty increasing. One of the first significant actions of the Black Panther Party was to follow Oakland police cars in order to monitor their treatment of black citizens and prevent harassment.[61] Many in the black community saw the police as an occupying army, yet crime was also worsening year by year. Chronic high unemployment and underemployment had led to widespread participation within underground economies and fostered the formation of gangs: Felix Mitchell's 69 Mob, Mickey Moore's The Family, and Harvey Whisenton's Funktown USA.[62] The number of annual murders in the city soared from 20 in 1960 to 69 in 1970, 106 in 1975, and from that point on, a tally that usually topped 100 homicides per year through the early twenty-first century. From strong-arm robberies to house break-ins to the drug trade, crime sustained many of Oakland's long-term unemployed and, at the same time, filled prisons and funeral homes. It smeared the town's reputation and drove away business and residents.

Programs for ameliorating black unemployment largely failed to deliver. In 1958, Kaiser Industries and local realtors launched the Oakland

Adult Minority Employment Program. Lacking funds for job creation, only 123 persons out of 2,300 applicants were hired. In 1966, the State Department of Employment set up the Skill Center, yet the short-term training program proved insufficient for the 1,500 hard-core unemployed participants.[63] In *Implementation* (1973), sociologists Jeffrey Pressman and Aaron Wildavsky examined one the most ambitious attempts of the 1960s to couple the funding of public infrastructure with the hiring of unemployed minorities. Instead of spreading the funds in projects around the country, and potentially diluting their effects, almost $23 million was targeted to one city, Oakland.[64] The funds were directed to four construction projects, three run by the Port of Oakland and one by the city: a hangar to handle World Airways fleet of 747 aircraft; the 7th Street Terminal at the container port; an industrial park; and an interchange on the Eastshore Freeway to the Oakland–Alameda County Coliseum and Arena.

What went wrong? It turned out that coordination of the stakeholders—federal agencies, city departments, the Port of Oakland, World Airways, black leaders, construction firms—led to lengthy negotiations and major construction delays. "In the Oakland ghetto, there was a strong feeling that previous Federal activity there had resulted in much study, but no action," wrote newspaper executive Amory Bradford at the time.[65] After much criticism, the delays were followed by a dash to construction. The rush to complete the projects led to the abandonment of the complicated, lengthy training programs and thus one of the program's two key goals. Likely, the federal subsidy should have gone directly to wages for minority workers and not capital projects, whose hiring practices depended on third actors like the Port of Oakland.[66] Such problems with employment initiatives extended to most forms of domestic aid. During the same years, a Model Cities employment program forecast to create 475 Oakland jobs ended up creating but 43 jobs.[67]

The priority placed on projects for the airport and seaport revealed Oakland's larger goal of developing infrastructure for regional and, in these cases, global communications and trade. A realignment was taking place, a shift from an economy where a majority of citizens were employed in its industries and held realistic hopes to ascend the economic ladder to one where almost half the population, especially the black community, suffered persistently high unemployment, substandard housing, segregated and underfunded schools, exclusion from the political arena, and low family income.[68] The entry-level jobs that were available were mostly in the support or service sectors, paying low wages and offering limited security and few benefits. During the closing decades of the century, blacks looking for work also had to compete with a large and growing number of immigrants coming primarily from East Asia and Latin America. Those new Oaklanders, willing to work long hours for low wages, filled service and manual labor positions—cashiers, stockers, dishwashers, cooks, roofers, painters, plumbers, construction workers, house cleaners, gardeners—that kept the town running for its more affluent inhabitants.

A PIONEERING CONTAINER PORT

On August 31, 1958, the *Hawaiian Merchant*, a C-3 cargo ship of the Matson Navigation Company, sailed from Alameda to Honolulu with 20 steel containers on board. It was the pioneering passage across the Pacific Ocean.[69] Only two years earlier, the first such venture had taken place, when Malcolm McLean's *Ideal X* sailed with a load of trailers from Newark to Houston. McLean, owner of McLean Trucking, had come up with the idea of putting truck trailers (their wheels detached) onto an old oil tanker.[70] Once the ship reached its destination, the trailers wheels could be easily reattached and pulled by a tractor truck. A transportation revolution was at hand.

For millennia, ships had carried their cargo as either bulk or break bulk. Bulk items included liquids, grains, or other granular items that could be shoveled or poured into the cavernous holds within a ship's hull. Break bulk—consisting of food items, machines, and consumer goods—was transported in crates, bags, or barrels, and then lifted by cranes, one by one, from the ship to pallets on the quay. There, they were again loaded, individually, onto drays or other vehicles and taken to a warehouse where they were stored on other pallets. From the warehouse other drays took the break-bulk goods to a railcar or truck, where they were transferred yet again for their journey to a wholesaler or, eventually, retailer. Each loading or unloading took a great deal of time and labor. Containerization changed everything. At a factory or warehouse, a batch of goods was packed into a uniform steel box—eight feet in height, eight feet in depth, and in standard lengths of 20, 30, and 40 feet. The goods stayed together in the container through numerous trips and transfers, on both sea and land—reducing theft or damage. Epitomizing the concept of intermodal transport, containers could be rapidly handed off from ships to trucks and trains. Once, it took 160 longshoremen to unload a ship in a week. With containers, 50 workers could do the same job in less than 20 hours.[71] Container ships stayed in port for shorter periods and container ports employed fewer longshoremen, generating substantial cost savings for shipping companies.

Instead of being job intensive, instead of providing a substantial, alternative source of employment to the city's working classes during a time of deindustrialization, container shipping would prove to be capital intensive. It required lightweight yet strong containers, more sophisticated cranes that could handle their weight and accurately set them on truck trailers, and complex logistic operations to coordinate the marshaling of containers.[72] It was also land intensive. At a time when industries were abandoning plants up and down Oakland's waterfront, the viability of the container port depended upon the conversion of bay waters into landfills, vast concrete aprons behind the quays that could support thousands of containers and their related equipment as well as land-based cranes.

In the mid-1950s, the *Ideal X* and other early ships run by McLean had been equipped with onboard cranes; ports did not yet possess the larger gantry cranes that were required to lift the larger and heavier containers, weighing up to 35 tons. In 1958, Matson took a different approach. At the Encinal Terminal in Alameda, the shipping company built the world's first onshore facility for handling container traffic. Pacific Coast Engineering Company (PACECO) was commissioned to build the landside crane. Founded in 1923 in Oakland, PACECO had moved to Alameda in 1941.[73] Operational in 1959, the initial A-frame container crane reached 113 feet in height, and could handle 400 tons of containers per hour—or 40 times the capacity of longshoremen using shipboard cranes for break-bulk cargo.[74]

The Port of Oakland soon got in on the game. In 1960, McLean changed the name of his company from the Pan Atlantic Steamship Corporation to Sea-Land Service. Two years later, Sea-land's *S.S. Elizabethport* made its first call at Oakland. At the time, there were no land-based cranes at Oakland's port, and only six acres of backup space, just resurfaced, fenced, and lighted for container storage. This was about to change. By 1964, the port strengthened docks and installed rails to accommodate two gantry cranes servicing the ships on a Sea-Land route from Oakland to Newark and Rotterdam.[75] In response to increased port traffic caused in part by the escalation of military operations in Vietnam, the company was operating 15 ships of its own out of its 44-acre Outer Harbor Terminal. Harry Gilbertson, manager of Pacific Operations for Sea-Land, pioneered a system to link container ships with trucks and railroads on regular schedules, speeding loading to five times as fast as that required earlier for break-bulk cargo.[76]

Sea-Land Service was just the beginning of the Port of Oakland's transformation. In 1962, Ben Earl Nutter was promoted from chief engineer to executive director. Born in Kansas and educated in civil engineering at Oregon State University, Nutter had been working at the port for five years, observing developments in containerization. Up to this point, Oakland had been a mid-sized general cargo port, specializing in outbound cargo, while San Francisco handled most inbound traffic. Seeing containers as a way to capture a larger share of the bay's shipping, Nutter took a gamble on a new container terminal. Absent firm commitments from shipping lines, in an era when many shipping executives regarded containers as a passing fad, Nutter engaged Kaiser Industries to come up with a Master Plan for a 140-acre, $30 million container facility on landfill in the bay— the 7th Street Terminal. Like subsequent port expansions, it was paid for by revenue bonds to be generated from the completed project, instead of general obligation bonds that require voter approval. Financing also came from coordination with BART's transbay tunnel project as well as a federal grant for job training and placement.

In 1965, construction, in conjunction with preparatory work for the eastern terminus of the BART tube, began on a peninsula jutting 3,000 feet westward, from the site of the Oakland Ferry Terminal (Oakland mole) to the San Francisco County Line.[77] As work was proceeding on the terminal, Nutter recruited Shoichi Kuwata, a retired Japanese shipping executive, to serve as the port's representative to Japan. In 1967, after two years of negotiations, they persuaded six Japanese steamship companies to base their

US operations in Oakland.[78] Other steamship lines—American President Lines, K Lines, Matson Navigation, NYK Line, Pacific Australian Direct, Maersk—subsequently left San Francisco for Oakland.[79] The Port of San Francisco's old piers could not support the weight of stacked containers, nor could its cramped finger piers accommodate vessels that had grown from around 17,000 tons in the 1950s to well over 500,000 tons in the 1970s. Oakland held other important advantages: rail and freeway connections essential for intermodal connectivity; newly available landfill for the required backup space to store stacked containers, trucks, and other vehicular equipment.[80]

The 7th Street Terminal boasted onshore gantry cranes, ample space for the storage of containers, and, given the newness of container shipping, a few traditional break-bulk-loading facilities and warehouses. The gamble paid off. "With container traffic," Nutter bragged, "we got the inbound and the outbound because of the lines' need for centralization of this kind of operation."[81] By 1968, the terminal vaulted Oakland to the status of the largest port on the West Coast, with 3.3 million tons of freight, 1.5 million tons of which traveled in containers. Oakland's was suddenly the second-largest container operation in the world in size. Its 180 acres fell right behind New York's 192 acres and ahead of Rotterdam's 164 acres.[82]

By 1977, when work was completed on converting the old Moore Shipyard into a container terminal, the port featured almost 300 acres of container shipping berths: 85 at the Middle Harbor; 60 at Sea-Land in the Outer Harbor; and 140 at the 7th Street Terminal. The tonnage of containerized traffic had risen from 375,000 in 1965 to over 6 million, in just 12 years. The newest A-frame cranes were 230-feet tall when the boom was raised.[83] From afar, the port's appearance matched the vivacity of its business activity, a city of robotic towers.

Oakland's new container port in no way resembled its general cargo predecessor. Where narrow finger piers had been largely taken up with enclosed warehouses, the container port was an enormous asphalt and concrete field on whose edges were located ship's berths and gantry cranes. The deep interiors were taken up with stacks of colorful containers.[84] The port functioned as an infrastructural interface between shipping lanes on the seaside, and railways and highways leading to landside warehouses and distribution centers, often many miles away: along the bay south of

Figure 25. Container Port. View of port cranes; Dellums Federal Building downtown, *right*; ca. 1998. Photo by David DeVries. Courtesy of Library of Congress Prints and Photographs Division, HAER CAL, 1-ALAM, 4Q–3.

Oakland, and on the western edge of the Central Valley. Indeed, alongside the growth of trucking on the nation's highways, container ports contributed to deindustrialization in the United States, including Oakland. Highways and trucks had earlier freed industrial plants to relocate away from their customary urban sites along railroad tracks. Now, by dramatically reducing shipping costs, containerization facilitated the shift of manufacturing to countries with lower wages and costs of production, especially East Asia. Their intermodal nature of transport meant that a port was not their true destination. It was just a step in the shipment of goods from producer to consumer.

The port's upsurge paralleled manufacturing's decline. Container shipping's reason for existence lay in eliminating jobs and union salaries; by definition, it could not be a foundation for broad, citywide employment. Through the 1980s, as Oakland's manufacturing plants retrenched and unemployment increased, the port continued to expand its physical footprint and scale of operations. And in a distressing omen, the Port of Oakland was falling behind other West Coast ports.[85] In the early 1970s, at its peak, it handled a little under 40 percent of the West Coast's cargo business. By the mid-1980s, although the port had grown to handle 12.5 million tons, it had fallen behind the Port of Los Angeles/Long Beach, at 19.5 million tons. The Southern California ports benefited from the region's larger population. Smaller Seattle's port too had become larger than Oakland's, in part because it was located a day and a half closer to Asia.[86] In addition, an innovation in rail transport, long an advantage for the Port of Oakland, leveled the shipping field. In 1984, the advent of double-stacked railcars made it possible to ship cargo more cheaply over land. But the tall cars could not pass through the low mountain tunnels of the Sierra Nevada, the direct route from Oakland to points east.[87] Los Angeles/Long Beach and Seattle benefited. By the end of the millennium, the Port of Oakland was the nation's fifth busiest container port, with 33 different shipping lines.[88] Its maritime facilities grew to 550 acres, yet that increased acreage was less than half of the size of Los Angeles/Long Beach. Ships kept getting heavier and longer, requiring deeper channels, longer berth lengths, and greater backup areas.[89] The port dredged the shipping channels; converting the Naval Supply Center to a park and container facility, and modernizing and expanding whenever it could.[90]

THE DISAPPOINTING JETPORT

During the Second World War, great improvements were made to aircraft, playing a leading role in expanding civilian aviation. The invention of pressurized cabins for the B-29 Superfortress made transcontinental civilian flights viable. The shift from two- to four-engine planes increased capacity. "The introduction of a cabin-class ticket in 1948, 30 percent lower than the previously standard first-class fare," historian James Goode tells us, "revolutionized air travel almost overnight."[91] Airports were poised for rapid growth.

In anticipation of civilian needs, the Oakland Post-War Planning Committee commissioned a Master Plan in 1944 that recommended a thorough expansion of the airport's aging facilities: a new terminal, runways on bay fill.[92] As reporter Bill Eaton later warned, Oakland Municipal Airport was becoming "a mere roost for a conglomerate flock of nonscheduled airlines."[93] By contrast, San Francisco International Airport had become the primary airport for the bay region. In the early 1950s, when Oakland Municipal Airport's annual passenger total reached half a million, San Francisco International Airport's hovered around two million. The disparity would only grow, since San Francisco was greatly expanding its facility on a 2,100-acre tract of land claimed from the bay.[94]

Awakened by the accelerating progress across the bay, Oakland voters passed a $10 million bond issue in 1953 for a new airport terminal and runways.[95] A year later, a New York engineering firm was hired by the port to assess improvements to the airport's facilities. Its "Development Plan for the Oakland Metropolitan Airport" recommended starting over, envisioning a 10,000-foot runway and new buildings on an expanded 1,400-acre bay-fill site—to be located one mile to the south of the main field on 600 acres of filled tidelands.[96] Yet even though diking and ground preparations soon began, the onset of construction was delayed until 1960. The reason: Should the Port of Oakland plan for an airport serving the needs of the mid-1960s or the mid-1980s? Airport planners and officials realized that they had to estimate the growth of air travel and account for the introduction of jet aircraft in the near future. As it turned out, the Boeing 707 began operating in 1958 and the DC-8 two years later. Jet propulsion presented opportunities and challenges. On the one hand, jet aircraft were the first commercial aircraft to carry more than a hundred passengers, and were suited for higher speeds than propeller planes, reducing flying times between distant locations. On the other hand, their higher takeoff speed required longer runways, and their noise levels caused problems for nearby residents. Relocating from North Field, as the old airport would henceforth be called, made sense;[97] a longer runway could be erected further south on bay fill and situate aircraft approaches and departures further away from residential development. Yet the City of Alameda wanted to develop Bay Farm Island for thousands of residences, a highly questionable regional planning objective whose eventual realization came to haunt the development and operations at the expanded Oakland airport.

Finally, in 1962, architect John Carl Warnecke's 160,000-square-foot terminal debuted, noticeable for its hyperbolic-paraboloid concrete shell covering at the curbside drop-off as well as its 10-story steel-and-glass air traffic control tower. Yet despite the 10 new gates and 3,000 parking spots, by this point Oakland Metropolitan Airport had fallen off the aviation industry's radar. In 1953, Oakland's annual passenger numbers had represented 14 percent of the Bay Area total. By 1960, that figure fell below 7 percent.[98] When the new airport opened, just six carriers offered 25 flights a day at South Field, mostly "milk runs," calls at smaller cities on route to final destinations. That year, there were only 312,000 passengers, compared with more than four million at San Francisco International Airport. Worst of all, all flights at the advertised jetport were propeller aircraft.[99] The city and port responded by organizing a "Fly Oakland Jets" campaign, and residents wrote letters to the Civil Aeronautics Board asking for more Oakland flights. In 1963, jet service began with a TWA Convair 880 flight and, in 1964, with Boeing 707 service on American Airlines. Still, for the next couple of decades Oakland Metropolitan Airport was kept alive by cargo traffic, supplemental airlines (principally military traffic connected to nearby Travis Air Force Base), and nonscheduled, or charter, airlines. There was a track record for this sort of aviation business dating to the late 1940s: Orvis Nelson's Transocean Airlines, offering low-cost charters to Europe and Hawaii; Edward Daly's World Airways, the world's leading charter airline by the mid-1960s; Kirk Kerkorian's Trans International Airlines.[100] These charter airlines, and not regularly scheduled flights, introduced wide-bodied Boeing 747s and DC 10s to the airport and improved its fortunes.[101]

Annual passengers reached the one million mark in 1966. The port anticipated an increase in passenger counts from 2.35 million, as of 1973, to an eventual 24 million; after all, OAK was a closer drive for 40 percent of Bay Area residents.[102] Expansion plans were afoot. A second runway, 12,500 feet long, would be added. The terminal would be enlarged and the number of gates and parking spots increased.[103] After 18 months of planning for the 400-acre landfill operation, the plan was dropped. By the end of the century, South Field consisted of its original, single runway along with two terminals and 22 gates (in a total of 432,000 square feet), serving slightly over 10 million passengers.

The container seaport and jet airport could not make up for the job losses incurred during decades of deindustrialization. Since the early 1970s, black activists complained that the Port of Oakland, a key part of the city's white power structure, did not offer enough employment opportunities for minorities.[104] After the mayoral election of Lionel Wilson in 1977, the situation improved, to the point by the late 1980s when blacks achieved employment parity with whites. As Robert Stanley Oden noted: "The port was no longer an entity controlled by a white bureaucracy and businessmen operating without a clear relationship to the City of Oakland. The economic independence of the past had been transformed into economic interdependence."[105] Yet if the port appeared to be Oakland's new economic engine, its revenue stream funding many projects and helping stabilize the city's finances, its low job numbers had only limited economic spillover with respect to Oakland's long-term, minority unemployed.

Earlier, the MOAP proposed a realignment of the city's economy from manufacturing to office/transport jobs, from making things to moving things and connecting places. Aspects of that mentality persisted almost to the end of the century: links stretching across land, sky, and sea; strings of packages and messages moving intermodally and electronically; people taking to the highways and airways. One rationale was grounded on predictions of the increasingly globalized character of international manufacturing and Oakland's historic ability to function as a transshipment node. Another rationale took into account the virtual absence of flat, undeveloped land in the city, as compared to the suburbs. Oakland's answer was to expand its shoreline out into the bay. The 7th Street Terminal was emblematic of this approach, a huge slab of new land jutting into the bay and facilitating oceanic commerce. By the early 1970s, however, the failure of the airport to add a second landfilled runway and the inability of the container port to expand blue-water frontage brought up a flaw at the core of this equation of transport infrastructural growth through landfilling— residents would no longer tolerate a shrinking bay.

SAVE THE BAY

South Field's second runway was not built because Oakland's longtime habit of expanding onto the wetlands of the bay hit an immovable obstacle, the newly established Bay Conservation and Development Commission (BCDC).[106] It was a watershed moment.[107] For 120 years, from the first pier jutting into the estuary, the first marsh solidified by dikes and earthen fill, the first slough dredged and walled, San Francisco Bay had been treated as a resource to be plundered, processed, profited from, and gobbled up. Much of the bay was shallow and the zone between low tide and high tide changed not only daily but also seasonally. As there was no clear line between land and water, the intermediate zone took on a host of names—salt marshes, swamplands, mudflats, tidelands, overflowed lands, water lots—that could be bought and sold, filled and built upon. By the late 1950s, approximately 242 square miles of the originally 680-square-mile bay had been reclaimed, to use the favored, if clearly biased, terminology of the times. Residents were increasingly cut off from the waters by a thick swath of factories, warehouses, piers, and runways. Recreation was an afterthought. In the early 1960s, public parks occupied only four miles of the 276-mile perimeter of the bay.[108]

In 1942, a plan had actually been proposed to eliminate most of the bay. John Reber, a producer and director of amateur theatrical musicals, proposed construction of two, wide earthen dikes (containing highways and rail lines) that would create two freshwater lakes in the upper and lower arms of the bay. In between, fronting the remaining bay, 20,000 acres of industrial and port land would spring up along the East Bay shore.[109] While the Reber Plan was never acted upon, fill operations accelerated in the postwar decades. In the late 1950s, 375 acres off the south shore of Alameda were filled for housing, a shopping center, and parklands. More audacious plans were floated, such as 880 acres of Bay Farm Island filled by the Utah Construction Company for between 5,000 and 21,000 residential units.[110] Over in Berkeley, in 1963, the Santa Fe Railroad proposed the Tidelands project, a gargantuan fill operation for 100,000 residents—4,700 acres of mudflats and 9,600 acres of open bay—between the Bay Bridge and Richmond that would have inserted a massive shopping mall, 20-story apartment buildings, and island hills formed not by earth but five-story parking garages. Not to be outdone, two years later, the Port of Oakland proposed adding to the 7th Street Terminal, then underway, developing a harbor atop most of San Leandro Bay, and restarting the 1,400-acre North Harbor, just north of the Bay Bridge, which would have cut the distance between the Oakland shoreline and Treasure Island from

21,000 feet to 3,200 feet.[111] Mayor Houlihan and the port anticipated a few landfill parks on the San Leandro side of the airport, but Oakland's vision for the waterfront was overwhelmingly given over to port infrastructure.

While Santa Fe's Tidelands and the Port of Oakland's North Harbor were dropped, other fill operations continued through the 1960s: at Oakland's airport and container port; in the creation of new peninsulas for housing, hotels, offices, and recreation off Emeryville and Berkeley. The East Bay appeared to face a stark choice: either sprawl inland or fill more of the bay. As Mel Scott wrote in his 1963 study, *The Future of San Francisco Bay*: "As land close to the centers of metropolitan activity is built upon, as orchards and vegetable fields all of fifty miles from San Francisco or Oakland give way to tract houses, space near the geographical center, especially, becomes ever more desirable and even scarcer."[112] The compulsion to use the bay for urban development appeared irreversible.

Or was it? In January of 1961, a dozen people met in a Berkeley house to devise a response to the City of Berkeley's role in fill projects in the bay. Findings published in a 1959 study prepared for the Army Corps of Engineers, *Future Development of the San Francisco Bay Area, 1960–2020*, had them especially alarmed. Seventy percent of the bay was less than 18-feet deep at low tide. Approximately 248 square miles of tidal and submerged lands were susceptible for land reclamation. That would leave only 186 square miles of the bay as a deepwater channel for shipping.[113] Since most marshlands had already been filled, leaving only 77.6 square miles left, the bulk of the potential filled lands, or 250 square miles, would come from open waters—tidal and permanently submerged lands.[114] The group became the Save San Francisco Bay Association, later shortened to "Save the Bay," and was led by three women: Esther Gulick, Kay Kerr, and Sylvia McLaughlin. They financed Scott's 1963 study and used its detailed information to advocate at the state level in Sacramento for a plan to protect the bay.[115]

Environmental concerns had spawned several regional agencies over the past decade: in 1949, the Regional Water Quality Control Board; in 1955, the Bay Area Air Quality Management District.[116] In 1965, after pressure from "Save the Bay" and other regional officials, the state legislature passed the McAteer-Petris Act, adding the Bay Area Conservation and Development Commission (BCDC) to that roster. Made permanent in 1969 by Governor Ronald Reagan's signature, BCDC was given control over a 100-foot-wide strip around the bay. From now on, all proposals for bay filling would have to receive a permit the commission based on two criteria: Is the project necessary to the health, safety, and welfare of the Bay Area? Will the project not adversely affect the comprehensive plan to protect the bay?[117] Whereas tidelands or mudflats were once seen as "land" awaiting eventual development, they were now appraised for their importance in fostering communities of plant and animal life, in oxygenating the bay's waters, and in cleansing sewage. The long era of indiscriminate conversion of the bay into urbanity ended. One of Oakland's last frontiers for new development closed. From the 1970s onward, the city's industries and its port were forced to operate within existing boundaries.

In 1968, a report by the Oakland City Planning Department, *Oakland's Housing Supply*, evaluated the red-hot residential sector. From 1960 to 1966, 18,000 market-rate housing units came on line: apartments around Lake Merritt; single-family houses and cluster complexes in the upper hills. In the same period, 11,800 units were demolished, mostly in the poor and minority-dominated flatlands—leveled by freeway and BART projects, new public housing, and, most of all, urban renewal. As the authors summarized: "While much of the housing in the poorer parts of the city was being eliminated, the higher-income areas were rapidly being built up."[1]

This skewed portrait of housing stemmed from plans hatched the previous decade, and cannot be separated from the Metropolitan Oakland Area Program (MOAP). In 1954, Corwin Mocine, the new city planning engineer, called for a great wave of market-rate development aimed at the white-collar workers the city hoped to attract; homes in what he termed the vacant hills; hotels and luxury apartments around the lake and overlooking the estuary; apartments dotting single-family neighborhoods.[2] A couple of years later, Mocine's department published the *Oakland Residential Area Analysis*, which set forth a different path for West

Oakland and inner East Oakland.[3] These impoverished districts would be remade into a middle-class, mixed-race city serving the downtown and port. This brushing aside of the minority poor was cruel, but not unique to Oakland. Geographers John Jakle and David Wilson, referring largely to the 1940s through the 1960s, wrote: "Prejudice against blacks and other minorities on the part of whites has torn the traditional city apart through the mechanism of an exaggerated dual housing market."[4]

The first market built upon private real estate development going back to the early twentieth century. It encompassed housing sold to the white upper classes, professionals and businesspeople, and to a lesser extent the white working and middle classes, from factory workers to small shopkeepers to civil servants. Especially in Oakland's affluent and restricted areas, the American Dream was in full bloom—the intentional mobility required to seek out homes that featured space, privacy, gardens, panoramas, and good schools.

The second market serving poor and minority residents could hardly be called a market. Prevented from moving to restricted newer neighborhoods, filtered-down older housing remained their main option. Yet packed with people on the lower economic rungs denied housing opportunities elsewhere, built stock deteriorated. Evictions, rising rents, and substandard and crowded living conditions forced people into perpetual transience, a foreshadowing of the contemporary crisis in housing affordability and homelessness.

Federal New Deal programs both bettered and worsened the housing situation for people of color. On the one hand, the United States Housing Act of 1937 brought about low-rent projects built and maintained by the government for the working (and later nonworking) poor. On the other hand, the creation of the Home Owners Loan Corporation (HOLC) in 1933 stimulated a massive migration, for whites alone, to the newly built hill neighborhoods and suburbs. Finally, urban redevelopment plans hatched in the 1950s, led by local agencies but increasingly financed by federal dollars, resulted in the clearance of some older slums in poor parts of town—those redlined by the HOLC as ineligible for bank loans. There were massive displacements, and replacement housing did not come close to making up the difference.

Oakland always had rich and poor areas, yet postwar a racially biased housing system forged an even more unjust geography of residential opportunity.[5] With respect to segregation, what had been done informally neighborhood by neighborhood in the past was enshrined, from the 1930s through the 1960s, into municipal plans and federal laws. The consequences are still with us.

THE RISE AND FALL OF PUBLIC HOUSING

Oakland's housing production peaked in 1925, slid to a low in 1934, and begun to rebound a few years later. Because of the overall decline in construction during the Great Depression, supply contracted, rents rose, evictions mounted, and quality worsened. By 1937, Oakland had 35,637 single-family houses and 52,025 rental units—the latter the result of apartment construction as well as the breaking up of single-family houses into multiple units and rooming housing.[6] A survey of real property undertaken by the Works Project Administration a year later revealed that 14 percent of Oakland's total units were in need of major repairs or unfit to use.[7] In California, one didn't see slum areas akin to those back east, characterized by block after block of crumbling, masonry tenements. But the sunnier visual impressions concealed a harsher reality. The working or unemployed poor crowded into worn wooden homes broken up into rooming houses or apartments and plagued by deferred maintenance.

In 1937, the US Congress passed the Wagner-Steagall Housing Act, creating the United States Housing Authority. For first time in history, the federal government became involved in the construction and administration of low-rent housing. Some cities had already taken the lead. The nation's first public housing projects opened in 1935 in New York, Atlanta, and St. Louis. The first housing authority was founded a couple of years earlier in Cleveland, and by the time Wagner-Steagall was signed into law the Ohio city had built two public housing estates; by 1943, Cleveland had seven segregated residential projects.[8]

The Oakland Housing Authority (OHA) was formed in 1938 as the city's lead agency to construct housing for struggling families living in substandard conditions. Under its first administrator, Nathan Strauss, the OHA joined the US Housing Authority's public housing program.[9] Given West

Oakland's deteriorating housing stock and proximity to industrial jobs, it was chosen for two of the first three projects; the third would be built in East Oakland.[10] As in other cities, admission standards were initially high. The target audience for public housing was not the long-term poor, but the down-on-its-luck working class who needed a break on its rent until the economy improved.[11]

The first permanent public housing, Campbell Village, opened at 8th and Campbell Streets in 1941; 67 houses were demolished to make way for 18 two-story buildings containing 154 units. Not only was Campbell Village's government financing and management novel, its site planning stood out.[12] Traditionally, houses were situated on separate lots that were deeper than they were wide. Here, following modernist urban planning approaches, the new concrete buildings were horizontal slabs grouped around common open spaces that extended over much of their block. The three blocks were joined into a superblock, and a new street, Campbell Village Court, ran through the complex. Roughly half had individual walk-up entrances, while the others had central entrances and interior access corridors. Two years later, Peralta Villa was built nearby between Union and Cypress Streets, 8th and 12th Streets: 256 houses on close to 10 city blocks were demolished to fit 396 units in 35 slab buildings. Once again, superblocks with interior streets and wide, horizontal buildings were fashioned. This time, though, construction was plaster atop a wood-frame, a cheaper approach that would be followed for the third permanent housing project, 1942's Lockwood Gardens at E. 14th Street and 66th Avenue in East Oakland: 372 units in 53 two-story buildings; their entrances were reached via exterior stairways and breezeways.[13]

All three Oakland housing projects were smaller than the huge complexes built in Cleveland and other eastern cities. Not all were segregated. The project built in East Oakland, Lockwood Gardens, was designated for white residents, but the other two projects, in mixed-race West Oakland, called for a balance between whites and blacks. There were no protests in overcrowded West Oakland. But Lockwood Gardens was near a restricted subdivision. The Havenscourt District Pride Club claimed theirs was a nonslum area that didn't need government-assisted projects.[14]

The Second World War interrupted any gradual evolution of public

Figure 26. Lockwood Gardens. Low-rent housing near Havenscourt District of East Oakland, 1942. Photo courtesy of Oakland Public Library, Oakland History Room.

housing. As war workers streamed to the Bay Area's shipyards and other military industries, Oakland's vacancy rate plunged from 2 percent in April of 1941 to 0.06 percent in September of 1942. More single-family houses were converted into boardinghouses.[15] All of Oakland's recently completed permanent public housing units were reassigned as temporary war worker housing. Additionally, 3,000 units in 14 temporary projects were constructed from 1942 to 1945, accommodating war workers and their families.[16] Most of the temporary housing was located on leased, vacant land, usually landfill sites zoned for industrial expansion and adjacent to railroad tracks and industries: sites subject to mud, flooding, refuse, noise, and pollution. The two-story buildings were insubstantial, their wood-frames covered with inexpensive plasterboard or gypsum board siding, and topped with tar and gravel roofs.[17]

The racial dynamic worsened at the temporary projects. Southern white migrants demanded segregation. The government gave in to reduce inter-racial conflicts. In East Oakland, the High Street Homes and Auditorium Village admitted only whites. In West Oakland, Bayview Villa, Cypress Village, Magnolia Manor, and Willow Manor were targeted to blacks.[18] After the war ended, the temporary housing projects were scheduled for demolition. But since the housing shortage persisted, they didn't begin to close until the 1950s, when enough war workers and veterans were able to find private housing. A few decaying complexes hung on until the early 1960s.

During these times, the Oakland NAACP and a few unions and politicians supported the building of additional low-rent, public housing. Opposed was the private housing industry: realtors, builders, apartment house owners who feared competition. The city council, dominated by those business interests, took a dim view of acquiring non-tax-producing properties if they were public housing—and not freeways. In 1950, they scaled back the OHA's request to build new units and required that they be situated on vacant land or sites occupied by wartime temporary housing.[19]

The onset of highrises worsened receptivity for public housing. In the wake of the federal Housing Act of 1949, cities around the nation began to construct taller projects, whose greater densities could accommodate more poor residents. One of Oakland's more controversial proposals began in 1950, when the OHA, using federal funds, purchased eight acres of land at 103rd Avenue and E Street in the Stonehurst neighborhood for three 11-story buildings containing 336 units. They would replace many of the temporary public housing units that were being phased out. Then, dissuaded by business interests, the OHA changed its tune that more low-rent housing was needed. In 1953, even though the project would cost nothing to the city or OHA, it was dropped by the city council.[20] Public housing was becoming identified as Negro housing, and that didn't help garner advocates among the exclusively white political and business class. By the early 1950s, 43 percent of the 15,000 residents in Oakland's permanent and temporary projects were black; one out of every eight black residents in the city.[21] Ten years later, hardly any whites lived in the cheaply built and poorly maintained projects.

Finally, between 1962 and 1966, the OHA erected four more permanent family projects, containing almost 500 low-rise units: Westwood Gardens and Chestnut Court in West Oakland; San Antonio Villa and Tassafaronga Village, replacing the last of the temporary war housing projects, in East Oakland.[22] Compared to most cities in the country with comparable socio-economic demographics, however, Oakland built very little public housing; in 1966, the total 1,422 permanent units represented approximately 8 percent of the low-rent supply in the city and only 1 percent of the total 144,000 residential units in the city.[23] Poor Oaklanders continued to rely on a tight supply of filtered housing.

Those family housing projects would be the last of that type ever built by the OHA. The city's sole highrises, MOR Housing in West Oakland, were shepherded by the nonprofit More Oakland Residential Housing Inc. and completed in 1975. The nonprofit intended to sell the 300-plus units in three 12-story towers and accompanying townhouses as condominiums to tenants in the future.[24] These sales never took place. By this time, a couple of decades after the federal government lowered admission standards, the clientele of public housing had changed from the working poor to the dependent poor. The most desperate families on relief streamed into what eventually became known as welfare housing, many of them, as in the case of MOR Housing, relocated from urban renewal slum clearance.[25] Years of cost-cutting design, shoddy construction, inadequate funding, poor maintenance, and chronic mismanagement took their toll.[26] In the MOR complex, the open space around buildings, intended once to promote a feeling of spaciousness, became anonymous, indefensible wastelands.[27] Murders, thefts, broken facilities, and stolen supplies were soon commonplace.[28]

Similar problems afflicted Oakland's older low-rise projects, most notoriously Lockwood Gardens and San Antonio Villa. Residents there faced inadequate garbage pickup and pest control, poor building maintenance and landscaping, a lack of recreational facilities, and rampant drug trafficking.[29] San Antonio Villa became home to Felix Mitchell and his heroin operation. As journalist Gary Rivlin wrote in *Drive-By* (1985), Mitchell's 69th Avenue mob "turned this complex of three-story, bunker-like buildings into an assembly line plant for selling heroin. Paid sentries patrolled the rooftops with walkie-talkies, watching for cops along the only two roads in or out of the complex."

As large complexes fell out of favor, the OHA continued to build senior housing as well as experiment with scattered-site public housing for families—small complexes with between 4 and 12 units. In 1966, voters approved 2,500 units of scattered-site public housing, also known as Turnkey Housing because private developers constructed the buildings and then sold them, turning over their keys, to the OHA. The Turnkeys had the advantage of not isolating public housing residents in racially stratified areas.[30] By 1973, 255 Turnkeys were built, containing 1,621 family units. They were predominantly located in areas of the flatlands where large public housing complexes had not been built. Still, problems arose. Because private contractors knew the housing units would be purchased by the OHA, they frequently cut corners on landscaping and construction quality and located unsightly parking lots in front of the buildings. Many neighboring households complained that the poor Turnkey residents wrecked their quality of life with rising crime and noise at all hours. In light of mounting neighborhood opposition, the remaining 879 units were never built.[31] A dual housing market for the minority poor, on the one hand, and the white middle class, on the other, worked for the latter as long as the two were geographically separated.

From the 1980s through the turn of the millennium, the lead stories of public housing in Oakland turned first to rental subsidies for market-rate housing, the Section 8 program,[32] and then to refurbishment of public housing stock. Beginning in 1995, the three original 1940s projects were renovated and superficially redesigned, gables inserted to vary the flat roof profiles, fences put in to subdivide the unruly open space, paint and wood added to the barren concrete or stucco surfaces. Despite these efforts, they remained places of concentrated poverty.

After 2000, the OHA leveraged federal Hope VI grants with private funds to replace the troubled 1960s family projects. The program intended to break the isolation of the poor by replacing distressed family housing projects with new complexes that featured mixed incomes, some townhomes for sale, and far better landscaping and architectural design.[33] This time, the results were better. The new complexes—Chestnut Linden Court, Lion Creek Crossings, Mandela Gateway, and yet another version of Tassafaronga Village—provided a "sense of home" more akin to privately built housing; they featured units oriented to the street,[34] improved maintenance, and residents from a range of races and incomes. Still, the

Hope VI initiatives decreased the overall number of rent-subsidized units. In a city that had never built enough public housing in the first place, in a region notorious for not building enough market-rate housing that could eventually filter down to the poor, astounding increases in rents and house prices would become the norm during the twenty-first century. Low- and even middle-income Oaklanders would face bleak odds in their efforts to secure a home. While public housing was widely blamed as a failure, it was not. A laissez-faire and racist climate in Oakland and elsewhere sabotaged its execution in matters from design to construction to maintenance to services to demography—thwarting shelter for poor and minority peoples despite the fact that the marketplace had long failed in that regard.

THE CALAMITY OF URBAN RENEWAL

Alongside public housing, urban renewal—or urban redevelopment, for the terms were often used interchangeably—of areas deemed blighted had a disproportionate impact on Oakland's minority poor.[35] In 1930, economist C. Louis Knight defined a blighted area as "one of economic retardation, physical deterioration, and economic decay."[36] The definition grew to include old age, dilapidation, overcrowding, faulty planning, and lack of ventilation, light, or sanitation facilities.[37] Some blighted buildings were built irregularly or shoddily from the start. Others fell into decay through a lack of maintenance. In any case, a designation of blight pointed to reduced property values and harm to the quality of life.[38] To combat blight, the California Community Redevelopment Act of 1945 enabled cities or counties to form redevelopment authorities. At the national level, Title I of the Federal Housing Act of 1949 authorized redevelopment loans to cities.[39] Under a local redevelopment agency and its plan, the feds would fund land assembly, surveying, building clearance, and landscape and infrastructural improvements leading to new construction.[40]

Oakland's Republican leaders signed on to urban renewal. Instead of building housing for the poor, urban renewal promised to turn poor neighborhoods into middle-class ones, remaking downtown and its environs into a white-collar business and residential precinct. Already in 1949, the City Planning Commission issued a study, *Urban Redevelopment in Oakland*, declaring West Oakland, by then becoming majority black, as blighted.[41] Five years later, top business executives, led by Kaiser Industries, formed Oakland Citizens Committee for Urban Renewal (OCCUR), which functioned for the next decade or more as a business advocacy group. In 1955, Oakland was the first western city to seek federal aid under the 1954 Urban Renewal Act, money that would cover two-thirds of the cost of a project,[42] and one year afterward, the Oakland Redevelopment Agency (ORA) was founded.[43]

A group of government and business officials instrumental in its creation—US senator William Knowland, Oakland mayor Clifford Rishell, several councilmen and members of the chamber of commerce and real estate board—took a study tour of recent urban renewal zones in Baltimore, St. Louis, Philadelphia, Cleveland, and Kansas City. Baltimore had enacted a program of strict code enforcement in a 300-block area, mandating improvements to substandard housing units. St. Louis had cleared 127 acres of slum housing for a huge public housing project, the 2,868-unit Pruitt and Igoe Homes. The delegation came home impressed with the scale of efforts back east. That said, they concluded that code enforcement coupled with building rehabilitation might be preferable to slum clearance in Oakland.[44]

The city's first redevelopment effort, the *Clinton Park Urban Renewal Plan*, approved in 1957, took that route. Coordinated by Jack Taylor, building and housing administrator, and Enrico LaBarbera, urban renewal chief, a heightened inspection program aimed to put slumlords out of business and eliminate substandard housing. The plan encompassed a 78-block area just east of Lake Merritt: from Park Boulevard to 14th Avenue, E. 12th/E. 14th Streets to E. 21st Street.[45] Many of the buildings had been converted into boardinghouses or apartments during the Great Depression and subsequent wartime housing crisis. Now, each building in the mixed-race residential zone was subject to intensive scrutiny. Higher standards prohibited baths and kitchens that served more than one unit or dirt floors in basements or garages.[46] If structures were found to be deficient or substandard, they were required to be brought up to minimum standards of respective Oakland codes.[47] If owners did not conduct repairs and receive a certificate of occupancy after back-and-forth rounds with inspection teams, the city was authorized to condemn and raze the building.[48]

Of 1,330 buildings evaluated, 1,253 were required to undertake some repair work with a licensed contractor. Only 5 percent met code. In 1957, demolitions began on structures that were in the worst condition. Eight blighted houses along 10th Avenue, between Foothill Boulevard and E. 15th Street, were torn down to make way for a playground and community center.[49] Five years later, 1,081 structures had been repaired and 117 demolished.

The *Clinton Park Urban Renewal Plan* instituted new zoning, encouraging apartment construction in the largely single-family district—similar to a practice occurring across the lake in Adams Point.[50] It was hoped that their construction would increase the city's supply of rental units and lessen crowding. In 1958, an entire block of houses at the intersection of 12th Avenue and E. 19th Street, some dating to the 1890s, were torn down. Replacing the rhythm of individual lots—houses and their rear yards— were four slab buildings taking up the perimeter of the block—the 144-unit Clinton Park Manor; the interior of the block was entirely devoted to parking.[51] Across Clinton Park, three-story slab apartment buildings, often containing 10 or more units, were slotted onto what had been one-or two-house lots. The gain in housing units was impressive, although the economy-driven effort to cram units onto small lots led to minimal outdoor space and open-air parking underneath structures supported by thin piers, a dangerous practice in earthquake country. Fifty-seven such apartment buildings (with 1,108 units) were built.[52] In retrospect, the *Clinton Park Urban Renewal Plan* did not raise the district back to middle-class status. In the coming decades, the presence of flimsy apartment buildings on most blocks slowed efforts at revitalization of the single-family housing stock.[53] Yet compared to the disaster that was about to come to West Oakland, Clinton Park was a success story.

In 1958, the ORA put out the *West Oakland General Neighborhood Plan*, which despite its stated preference against slum clearance still included it as an option. Oakland's historic black neighborhood, home to a thriving commercial corridor on 7th Street, was divided into several geographic zones, each of which was assessed as to its level of blight. The clearance options then ranged from none to partial to total.[54] By 1961, when the

Figure 27. Clinton Park. Modern apartment building alongside Victorian house on 10th Avenue; encouraged by Urban Renewal Plan. Photo by Mitchell Schwarzer, 2020.

Acorn Redevelopment Plan received its final approval, total clearance was mandated for a vast 50-block area between the Southern Pacific Railroad tracks and 10th Street, and Adeline and Brush Streets.

The idea was to raze obsolete industrial buildings and blighted houses and apartments, 1,790 structures in all, and construct in their place a new industrial zone and middle-income residential neighborhood. Industrial development proceeded smoothly, as more than 20 firms—Mack Trucks, United States Plywood—were attracted.[55] The residential plan was another matter.

Even though the 6,000 residents of the district were poor and mostly minority, the projected mix of new residents was to be half white and all moderate income. Middle-class whites, the ORA planners claimed, would be attracted by the low rents, high design quality, and proximity to office jobs in a growing downtown.[56] The ORA needed them to create an income and racial transition between the city's poorest minority slums in West

Oakland and a planned community of semi-luxury apartments down-town, as envisioned in the *Corridor Redevelopment Plan*. This empha-sis on partially white, moderate-income replacement housing explains why Oakland leaders readily signed on to urban renewal, when earlier they had showed reluctance with public housing directed largely at low-income blacks. It accorded with chamber of commerce (and MOAP) goals to transform downtown into a white, middle-class bastion.

By 1970, private developers had erected Acorn I & II, containing 672 units. The two-story structures followed the cluster pattern of develop-ment that was earlier used for public housing. At first, Acorn adhered to the desired 50-50 black-white ratio, but within a few years it became largely black. Whites, as we shall discuss below, had better options else-where. By 1976, lacking enough moderate-income tenants, Section 8 sub-sidies were approved, making most units available to low-income house-holds. The government did not build Acorn as public housing; its builder was a private company, Filbert Ltd. Be that as it may, Acorn appeared to be yet one more troubled public housing project. In 1992, due to mainte-nance and crime problems, the federal government's Housing and Urban Development Department took over its management.[57] Reporter Rick DelVecchio reflected on its legacy: "Acorn was a 1960s vision of suburbia in the central city with plans for tenants from all income levels facing one another over grassy courtyards. But the middle class did not respond, and eventually Acorn's population became made up almost exclusively of ten-ants receiving federal rental assistance."[58]

The dislocations caused by the Acorn urban renewal were compounded by demolitions for the construction of the BART line and its West Oakland station, and another colossal government project that expressed Oakland's objective to become an infrastructural hub. In the early 1960s, a 20-acre site on 7th Street, between Peralta and Wood Streets, was chosen to be the US Post Office's regional distribution center for Northern California and the Pacific Ocean area. At nearly one million square feet, it would be the largest postal facility west of the Mississippi, employing 3,500 work-ers. In 1965, in order to prepare the ground, a Sherman tank of World War II vintage was employed to clear away houses and commercial build-ings; in all, 187 properties were torn down.[59] Designed by architects Stone, Marraccini & Patterson in a style that could be best called "concrete fortress," the windowless building was surrounded by loading docks, parking lots, and spaces to maneuver trucks.[60]

The other urban redevelopment project in West Oakland was Oak Center. This time, 56 blocks, due north of the Acorn site, were targeted: from 10th to 18th, and Cypress to Brush Streets. Encompassing less-blighted housing stock, the plan was launched in 1961, but ran into opposition a few years later when it became apparent that ORA director Thomas Bell intended to raze 80 percent of the houses. The Oak Center Neighborhood Association mobilized and forced Bell out of his position; John B. Williams, the city's first black ORA director, replaced him. Born in Georgia, Williams studied art before being hired as a planner in Cleveland—eventually heading that city's Division of Urban Renewal.[61] In 1965, after much negotiation, Williams took a different route than that attempted at Acorn, scheduling up to 75 percent rehabilitation for Oak Center.[62] Through the late 1960s, 465 buildings were restored and almost as many new units added in several new apartment complexes.[63] Like the older stock, replacement buildings were typically two stories in height, but were both of wooden and pre-cast concrete construction and set back further on wider lots. Some 300 wooden buildings deemed beyond salvation were demolished, displacing, alongside the renovations, almost 1,300 individuals and 149 businesses.[64]

In the 1960s, urban renewal had been justified on the basis of outside observations like those of urban critic James Bailey, who described West Oakland as "as a cheerless swath of flatland where 50,000 people, 70% of them Negro, live in conditions as oppressive, stultifying, and potentially explosive as any in the country."[65] Yet urban renewal did not solve the shortage of decent housing for low-income renters. To the contrary, because the program resulted in net housing losses, it made it more difficult for poor Oaklanders to obtain housing.[66] During the 1960s, depending upon the estimates, between 5,100 and 9,700 housing units were lost in West Oakland alone.[67] Most of the displaced were poor blacks, who were forced to leave the neighborhood and search for housing elsewhere, paying higher rents and contending with white discrimination.[68] In the process, the cohesive black community of West Oakland and its commercial spine, 7th Street, was torn asunder.

At the height of the demolitions and displacements, in 1967, the West

Oakland Planning Council (WOPC), an umbrella group encompassing over 150 local organizations, was formed—a response to the federal Model Cities program mandate to increase community participation in all federally assisted programs. Led by Ralph Williams, WOPC extracted concessions from the city and redirected urban planning, from the 1970s onward, toward the existing community and away from detrimental and unrealistic makeovers. West Oakland's days of storm and stress were over, but not without serious, lingering effects.

GEOGRAPHIES OF RACIAL CHANGE

In 1940, the E. B. Field Corporation built the 315-home Sheffield Village at the far end of East Oakland. At the time, it was the largest single housing development in the West financed by the new Federal Housing Administration (FHA) loan program, which revolutionized housing finance by providing insurance for mortgages.[69] Four years later, another builder, David D. Bohannon, who went on to build residential and commercial developments across Northern California, embarked on a far larger project, San Lorenzo Village, a speculative venture of 3,000 dwellings on 350 acres south of Oakland and adjacent to the anticipated route of the Eastshore Freeway. Within two years, half the homes, nearly identical one-story, three-bedroom dwellings, had been erected in an industrialized building process, anticipating New York's Levittown, where specialized work crews moved from house site to house site adding to construction already underway.[70] The compact houses in Sheffield Village and San Lorenzo Village were intended for returning veterans and workers in wartime industries, but unlike the temporary public housing in Oakland, FHA-insured loans and the GI Bill, a 1944 federal program offering low-cost mortgages (and other services) to returning veterans, facilitated the home-buying process. That meant that neither development allowed minorities. The FHA forbid loans to racially integrated developments, and subdivision covenants restricted ownership and occupancy to persons wholly of the Caucasian race.

Postwar black suburban growth was miniscule, confined to towns with existing black populations.[71] In southern Alameda County, there was only one such place. Less than two miles from San Lorenzo Village, on the bayside of the Southern Pacific railroad tracks, Russell City had been since the 1940s south county's nonwhite town, populated mainly by Mexicans and African Americans prevented from living in other parts of San Leandro, San Lorenzo, and Hayward. Filled with churches, nightclubs, and substandard dwellings, and lacking most modern infrastructure, it was referred to as Alameda County's "shack town," a slum at the edge of shiny, new suburbia.[72] Any chance for it to be modernized into a suburb accommodating minorities went by the wayside in 1963 when the county began the forced eviction of its 1,200 residents and later bulldozed the entire town for an industrial park.

From 1949 to 1951, aided by federal loan guarantees, 75,000 building permits were issued for new private dwellings in Bay Area suburbs, yet only 600 of these were located in neighborhoods open to black buyers.[73] In the early 1960s, a study found that of 350,000 new homes built in Northern California after the war, minorities had purchased fewer than 100 of them.[74] Even in Oakland, with its large minority populations, lending practices discouraged housing investment in parts of the city where minorities lived alongside whites.

Federal housing policy under FDR's New Deal established a generous housing market for whites and a callous one for minorities. In 1933, the HOLC attempted to salvage homeownership during the worst years of the Great Depression, replacing home-buying norms where buyers had to put up at least half of the cost of a home and repay the bank loan in a dozen years or less. The government now guaranteed lower down payments and longer 30-year mortgages. The HOLC also instituted standards for predicting how housing value might fare in the future, ratings that would determine a bank's approval of a mortgage loan. This systematization of housing appraisal went beyond the structural integrity of houses. Appraisers evaluated the quality of their inhabitants and neighborhoods. The resulting 1938 Federal Housing manual, color-coding maps for 239 cities, downgraded neighborhoods on the basis of older buildings, the degree to which housing was mixed with other uses such as commerce or industry, and the extent to which races were mixed together.[75] Highlighted by Kenneth Jackson in his history of American suburbia, *Crabgrass Frontier* (1985), the maps show that the presence of black or brown inhabitants was a key criterion for denying a loan.

Redlining, or the withholding of credit by lenders from downgraded neighborhoods, had existed prior to the HOLC and FHA maps.[76] Instigated by the National Association of Real Estate Boards in the 1920s, it had long been practiced informally by lenders in higher-risk housing cases, where borrowers were required to pay higher interest rates, put down larger down payments, and accept lower loan-to-value rates and shorter loan maturity terms.[77] But now it was the law of the land.

The 1938 Oakland HOLC map shows four neighborhood grades: green for the highest value; blue for second; yellow for third; and red for the most questionable. Loans would be routine in green and blue zones and routinely denied in red ones. Almost the entirety of Montclair, Piedmont, and many of their surrounding neighborhoods were colored green. Red areas included West Oakland; North Oakland roughly west of Telegraph Avenue; Chinatown; industrial East Oakland between E. 14th Street and the waterfront; small parts of Fruitvale, Melrose, and Elmhurst uphill of E. 14th; much of the San Antonio neighborhood; and the northern half of Millsmont in the foothills. According to the criteria, the red areas contained either deteriorating housing stock, an interspersing of housing with industry and commerce, or the presence of significant numbers of minorities. There was no winning for Oakland's minority residents. If they were black and lived, say, in a neighborhood that was mostly black, and thus largely poor, their loan would be downgraded for the low quality of the area's housing stock or its proximity to nonresidential uses. If they resided in a neighborhood alongside whites, that mixture was reason enough for downgrading. And if they lived in a well-off, all-residential, and all-black neighborhood, well . . . there were none of those until the end of the century. The great migration of southern blacks had not yet begun, and the playing field was already rigged.

Sociologist Eric Brown tells us that the characteristics of the migration to Oakland differed from cities in the East and Midwest for three reasons: a smaller number of blacks moved to Oakland; the trek took place later, during and after the Second World War, a time when eastern and midwestern cities were experiencing their second wave; and the large numbers of black migrants moved into a city that already had appreciable numbers of other minorities.[78] In the period from 1940 to 1970, encompassing the key moments of public housing as well as urban renewal, the black percentage

Map 5. HOLC Zones. Green, blue, yellow, and red zones (shown in grayscale),
corresponding to federal government's graded risks for banks and mortgage

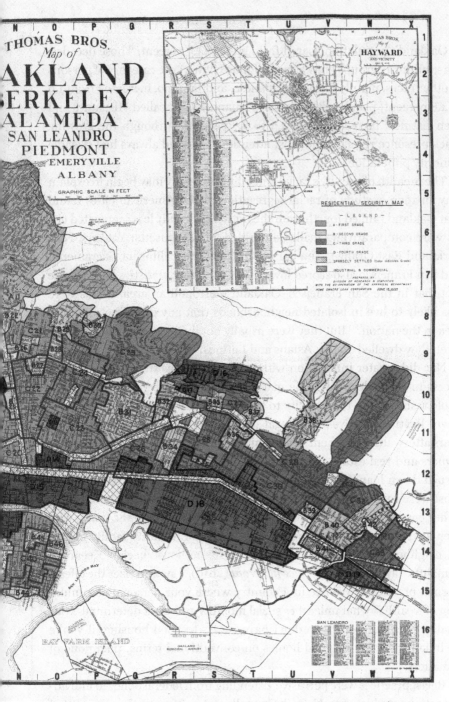

lenders, 1938. SOURCE: Wikimedia Commons. Creative Commons Attribution
Non Commercial Share Alike 4.0 International License.

of Oakland's population soared from 2.8 to 34.5 percent. Those decades, other minority groups grew as well, if more slowly: the category of persons of other races, mainly Chinese, Japanese, and Filipino, increased from 1.9 to 4.8 percent; people with Spanish surnames, later called Hispanics and then Latinos, increased from 4.3 to 6.7 percent. Although the growing black presence received the most attention, Oakland always had sizeable minority populations.

The breadth of the city's racial and ethnic diversity may begin to explain why, in 1970, a study of racial segregation in 109 American cities found that Oakland ranked fourth from the bottom; the only less segregated cities were comparatively small: Cambridge, Massachusetts; Yonkers, New York; and East Orange, New Jersey; in Northern California, Sacramento and San Francisco also scored low.[79] Ten years later, statistics bore out the fact that in the San Francisco–Oakland metropolitan area, blacks were less likely to live in isolated neighborhoods that any other metropolitan area in the nation.[80] But they were usually not living among whites; more often they dwelled among Asians and Latinos.

Nor did greater integration with other minorities translate to greater access to the wider real estate market. All minority groups faced formidable resistance to their ability to buy or rent property in white parts of town. Restrictive covenants (legal up to 1948, and used informally for years afterward) kept them out of white neighborhoods. Individual homeowners and real estate agents refused to sell.[81] Banks and other lenders turned down loans outright or scrutinized minorities so stringently that most were turned down eventually.[82] Often, the first nonwhite residents either passed for white or used a white proxy to purchase the house who then sold it back to them. Sometimes, once the minority family moved in, neighborhood associations tried to buy the house back.[83] Keeanga-Yamahtta Taylor, author of *Race for Profit* (2019),[84] summarizes the effects of such practices: "We live in a country where your personal accumulation of wealth is what unleashes social mobility and what determines your quality of life...But if you don't have access to good housing, if you're excluded from buying good homes on conventional terms, then none of it matters."[85]

Racist practices were pervasive, extending from federal policy to individual actions. As historian N. D. B. Connolly states: "As a system—or a set of historical relationships—white supremacy was and is more than the overtly and occasionally racist act. It includes laws and the setting of commercial and institutional priorities. White supremacy also includes the everyday deals that political operators and common people strike in observing white privilege or, more accurately, white power."[86] Many Oakland whites, as elsewhere in the country, believed that Negro morals and standards were below those of whites. They admitted as much in questionnaires, saying they were prejudiced and inclined to practice housing discrimination.[87] Others, aware of the systemic racism inherent in the housing system, might not have approved of it, but since they believed that the arrival of minorities coincided with white flight and a perceived lowering of property values, they were opposed to minority buyers on their block.[88]

In 1963, the Rumsford Fair Housing Act, instigated by African Americans to combat discrimination by property owners who refused to sell or rent to minorities, was passed by the California legislature. A year later, state voters passed Proposition 14, nullifying it. In 1966, that nullification was overturned by the State Supreme Court, and two years later the Fair Housing Act was signed into law by President Lyndon Johnson, prohibiting discrimination in the sale, rental, and financing of housing.

Even before the legal walls of segregation began to tumble down, blacks pushed out of the West Oakland ghetto. The reason: whites were moving out of town or up to the hills and blacks were often the only ones willing to buy or rent the vacated flatland units. During the 1950s and 1960s, tens of thousands moved from West Oakland to North and East Oakland.[89] By the 1970s, Telegraph Avenue in North Oakland and MacArthur in East Oakland had become de facto dividing lines. Whites lived uphill and blacks toward the bay. Part of the rapidity of the black push across North and East Oakland had to do with blockbusting.[90] As historian W. Edward Orser describes: "Blockbusting was the intentional action of a real estate operative to settle an African American household in an all-white neighborhood for the purpose of provoking white flight in order to make excessive profits by buying low from those who fled and selling high to those who sought access to new housing opportunities."[91] From the mid-1950s to the 1970s, blockbusting abetted the new dynamics of racial change, as marginal ghetto expansion was replaced by the racial transformation of entire neighborhoods in a matter of years.

Working-class neighborhoods that had been built up quickly due to their proximity to wartime industries turned fastest from white to black. Near Oakland Airport, Columbia Gardens was erected between 1943 and 1944: 350 modest, three-bedroom ranch-type homes. Upon completion, it was a completely white community, mostly defense worker families. Within five years, many of these families had moved on as the shipyards cut back operations. Yet demand by white buyers was lacking. Whites in older parts of Oakland who were seeking to buy a first home or larger home were deciding to move to the suburbs. Their flight was motivated in part by central city decline and racial animus; more importantly, they were drawn out of Oakland by favorable loan conditions, the American dream of a new life in more spacious surroundings, and the decentralization of jobs.[92] Given these circumstances, "non-white entry was accepted by realtors and some property owners, who saw it as the only feasible way to clear the listings coming on the market in the area," explained economist Luigi Laurenti.[93] In 1951, 15 black families arrived. The next year, 100 black families purchased homes. Soon, most sales in Columbia Gardens were made to black families and by 1955 Columbia Gardens was 60 percent black. Prices did not tumble. They remained stable because of black demand.

The same scenario played out in other East Oakland defense-worker communities. Shortly after the start of World War II, Albert Bernhardt, E. L. Stoneson, and E. B. Field developed Brookfield Village, across the freeway from Columbia Gardens, with 1,500 single-family homes, a small shopping center, and a park. Intended for war workers, houses could be purchased for as little as $100 down. The houses were advertised as having all modern conveniences and within close driving distance to the shipyards along the estuary. Yet because of their low prices, the homes came without sidewalks or garages and with minimal landscaping.[94] There were no blacks in 1950, yet half the community was black five years later. An analogous, rapid demographic transition occurred a few years later in the adjacent 550-home Sobrante Park subdivision.[95] And like Columbia Gardens and Brookfield Village, it suffered a decline in resident quality of life as whites moved out en masse. By 1957, complaints already arose of problems with undesirable business encroachments; there were too many junkyards, bars, and liquor stores nearby.[96]

In Elmhurst, the easternmost section of Oakland where these neighborhoods are located, the percentage of black residents jumped from 16.4 percent in 1950 to 61.2 percent in 1960.[97] Black churches, formerly concentrated in West Oakland, followed the residents and set up in storefronts, houses, and churches vacated by white congregations. Shortly after the First World War, Allen Temple Baptist Church had become the first black church in East Oakland, locating on 85th Avenue off East 14th Street. After 1960, other churches arrived: Paradise Missionary Baptist Church in Columbia Gardens; Center of Hope Community Church, at the foot of the lower hills on MacArthur Boulevard and 84th Avenue.[98] The churches provided the new residents with a crucial support network, especially given the fact that by the 1970s, one-fifth of Elmhurst's residents lived below the poverty line; per capita income was half of the Bay Area mean.[99] The district became Oakland's poorest. Reporters described streets filled with free-roaming dogs, corners without proper stop signs, derelict buildings, blight in public housing, and criminal acts.[100] In a city that had experienced a perpetual housing shortage, over a thousand housing units were abandoned or allowed to deteriorate in Elmhurst and across greater East Oakland—in Fruitvale, Seminary, and Melrose—many of them emptied by redlining loan denials, foreclosures, or HUD repossessions.[101] The filtering of housing was working too well; because of the enormous construction of houses in the suburbs and upper hills of Oakland, because of white flight, for a time supply exceeded demand. The black exodus from crowded West Oakland to the subdivision expanses of East Oakland could not fill the large number of vacated, rundown properties.

Oakland's growing black middle class strove for better options.[102] Their first destination had been North Oakland, followed by southwest Berkeley. But as they arrived, whites departed. Because of the small numbers of the black middle class, working-class African Americans poured in. As these neighborhoods transitioned from white to black, and middle to working class, the institutions and actors that sustained their housing either withdrew or participated at reduced levels. Banks withheld loans. Landlords were less committed to maintenance. Public services were reduced. Property values held but did not increase as much as nearby white neighborhoods where services were better. In a few cases the new black homeowners fought back. Until 1973, a neighborhood of 70 acres in the Golden Gate District, west of San Pablo Avenue and between 53rd and 69th Streets, had been zoned industrial, even though single-family houses occupied 90 percent of the land. Homeowners petitioned to change the zoning to medium-density residential. While the Oakland Chamber of Commerce and several industries in the area fought the rezoning, claiming that there was very little industrial land left for development, it was approved by the city council.

How were upwardly mobile blacks to find neighborhoods that appreciated in value and provided access to good schools for their children, that gave them the kind of "privileged access to insider information and personal networks," as American Studies scholar George Lipsitz notes, which were enjoyed by their white counterparts and a key to securing good jobs?[103] In an essay from 1983, the writer Ishmael Reed recounted living in chiefly white neighborhoods in various California cities. His experience was sobering. He was harassed by the Los Angeles police, faced unfriendly attention in Berkeley, and witnessed white drivers in El Cerrito regard him with suspicion when he walked past children. Reed finally bought a house on 53rd Street in North Oakland, a block near Children's Hospital that had become mostly black. Here he came to know his neighbors by name and observed "teenagers moving through the neighborhood carrying radios blasting music by Grandmaster Flash and Prince, men hovering over cars with tools and rags in hand, decked-out female church delegations visiting the sick."[104] He describes a sense of belonging among the black working and lower middle class, something lacking in white neighborhoods of more affluent and well-educated folks.

For many other members of the black middle class, white neighborhoods in the hills were still the promised land. In a 1964 study, *Filtering and Neighborhood Change*, real estate economist Wallace Smith found that suburban housing construction was opening quality older housing to buyers with middle-class incomes and minority racial characteristics.[105] Racial transition began in neighborhoods like Maxwell Park and the Seminary district near Mills College. Aside from higher price points, an explanation for why the transition proceeded much more slowly and smoothly than in the flatlands was the fact that 1920s-era communities had stable white populations, not dominated by highly mobile defense workers aiming for the American Dream in the suburbs.

Many black professionals found homes in East Piedmont Heights, a 450-home section off Lakeshore Avenue, encompassing Balfour, Santa Ray, and Calmar Avenues. Doctors, lawyers, and businessmen moved there from West Oakland, North Oakland, and Berkeley. Like their white counterparts, they were seeking larger homes to accommodate growing families, a more pleasing physical environment, more stable property values, and better schools. By 1969, black children made up 40 percent of the enrollment at the nearby Crocker Highlands Elementary School. At the time, many neighborhood residents wondered if East Piedmont Heights would become an all-black neighborhood, the pattern established in poor, working-class, and even some middle-class districts of the city. But like Maxwell Park, it did not. Home values held. The neighborhood remained integrated. Here at least, black professionals did not unduly unnerve their white counterparts; many commuted together to similar kinds of jobs in San Francisco.[106]

The black middle class gravitated later to the developing East Oakland upper hill districts. The small residential area around the Sequoyah Country Club had once been all white and restricted. From the 1950s through the 1980s, numerous subdivisions like Sequoyah Crest and Sequoyah Hills were built. Over time, they became more open to upper-end black buyers; for instance, Joseph Eichler, developer of a 50-unit subdivision adjacent to Sequoyah Hills completed between 1965 and 1966, was known for selling to minorities before open housing was required by state law. By the 1990s, the Sequoyah District had become predominantly black and upper middle class—a first for Oakland.[107]

LAKESIDE APARTMENTS

By the end of the 1950s, while urban renewal plans were underway, Oakland planners and developers expanded their sights to the market-oriented city. Aware of the remarkable growth of the suburbs and the city's relative stagnation, they came up with plans to jump-start housing production. There were two tactics: the introduction of greater density by way of apartments, and the construction of more single-family houses across the unbuilt parts of the upper hills.

Figure 28. Lake Merritt Apartments. Park Bellevue, *left*; Bellevue Staten, *right*. Photo by Mitchell Schwarzer, 2020.

The *Oakland General Plan* (1959) outlined a scale of newly allowable densities: a *Very High Density* for downtown abutting on Lake Merritt; *High Density*, highrises and midrises in West Oakland and the area north and east of Lake Merritt; *Medium Density*, lowrise apartment buildings and duplexes for most of the city's flatlands; and *Low Density*, or single-family houses for the upper hills. In 1963, the city planners built upon these recommendations in *Modern Zoning for Oakland*, implemented in 1965. As compared to the 1935 zoning code, 12 categories were added; there were now nine residential zones; nine commercial zones; four industrial zones; and six special zones. There were higher-density apartment districts, requiring both off-street parking and some outdoor space, and a townhouse and garden apartment district. In the upper hills, there were new super-low-density districts, going beyond the standard 40- to 50-foot frontage and 5,000 square-foot lot: for the A1, a 90-foot frontage and 12,000-square-foot lot; and the AA Estate, a 25,000-square-foot minimum.[108] Through these plans Oakland sought to mimic the sprawling suburbs in its hill areas and copy the development patterns of compact cities like San Francisco in the central districts around the lake.

Aided by zoning changes, developers built over 4,000 market-rate apartment units between 1960 and 1965.[109] Two types of structures predominated: midrise complexes set as close to the lake as possible and geared toward the middle class; and a dozen or so lakeside highrise towers at higher price points. The apartment boom satisfied a need for dwelling units for several growing populations: single adults, students, retirees.

Starting things off in 1959 were the Lake Royal Apartments, designed by George Meu and Walter Harada. Located at 19th and Jackson Streets, the building was set back from its street perimeter by landscaping, imitating its nearby, venerable predecessors from the 1920s. But in a nod to the automobile-oriented times, the Lake Royal Apartments featured a two-level parking podium. Views had become a must-have feature, and the 12-story L-shaped tower was angled so that each unit offered a panorama of the lake from floor-to-ceiling picture windows, sliding glass doors and balconies. Stacked atop one another, the 55 apartment units were an interpretation of the suburban ranch house for a downtown site. In 1968, architect Michel Marx's Meritian Apartments, at 1555 Lakeside Drive, reprised the concept on a tighter lot. Rising 20 stories behind a small landscaped setback, all 81 units faced the lake through large plate-glass windows and bow-shaped balconies. Converted to condominiums in 1973, marketed as "Lakedominiums," it was renamed the Lakeside Regency Plaza.

In 1960, the Jackson Lake Apartments at 1537 Jackson Street set the trend for the midrise apartment model. On a large site, the four-story, atop-parking building fit 192 units—the largest apartment building up until then in Oakland's history.[110] Similarly scaled buildings popped up in the Gold Coast—the residential portion of downtown facing the lake—and on the lake's other sides, blanketing the slopes of Adams Point and the bluffs above the east side of the lake and below Haddon Hill. Far more noticeable was 1200 Lakeshore Avenue, opened in 1967. The 26-story building was almost as wide as it was tall, its 173 rental units topped by a roof garden. Designed by John Sardis with a five-level parking podium (and pool on top) alongside the tower, 1200 Lakeshore Avenue illustrated the area's evolution. In 1902, William Dargie, publisher of the *Oakland Tribune*, had built a mansion on the site. Near the eastern side of the 12th Street dam, it was demolished in 1927 for a gas station, and in 1949 a street widening reduced the size of the lot.[111] During the 1960s, developers gained renewed faith in the area's apartment potential. Indeed, they even thought that construction would not only follow the lake perimeter but also extend south along the channel, reaching the estuary and replacing the warehouse and produce district.[112] That prognosis only began to be actualized during the Jack London Square condominium boom of the late 1990s.

Across the lake on the Adams Point side, controversy dogged the Park Bellevue at 565 Bellevue Avenue. Proposed in 1963 by Perma-Bilt Enterprises, the 26-story tower was not finished until 1968. Designed by Fisher Friedman, it consisted of a five-story parking garage, an open recreational level with swimming pool, and 152 condominium units possessed with panoramic views. These were the kind of amenities, the building's marketing claimed, that were required of those executives of industry Oakland hoped to attract.[113] Neighbors saw the sleek gray tower differently. The city's second tallest building, after the Kaiser Center, would be located in a residential area. It would block lake views. It would worsen the shortage of curbside parking in the area. Although Park Bellevue was built, it would be 34 years before another highrise, luxury residential building, the Essex, rose along the lake.

SUBURBS IN THE UPPER HILLS

At midcentury, the principal supply of vacant land for housing lay in Oakland's upper hills, referred to as wildflower land for their annual bouquets of poppies and mustard. Only parts of Montclair had been subdivided. A 1942 study estimated that 6,000 acres in the hills remained available. Out of that total, a quarter of the land was too precipitous or inaccessible to be put to economic use, leaving 4,500 acres that could potentially accommodate, at five houses per acre, 25,000 building sites; that meant adding a population of 78,750, accounting for the average family size at the time of 3.5 persons.[114] Local builders and realtors could stay in business for decades.

In 1947, a large development was proposed near the Chabot Golf Course at the southeastern end of the city, estate-type lots with 150-foot frontages, bay views, and proximity to bridle trails off Skyline Boulevard.[115] Over the next five years, Chabot Park Estates and Chabot Park Highlands were built with 275 ranch houses and split-levels. Similar subdivisions of view homes were launched across the breadth of the Oakland hills: Hillcrest Acres, Rancho San Antonio, Glen Manor, Sequoyah Highlands.

Residential development increased population and overloaded school enrollments. In response, city voters in 1956 approved the largest school construction bond issue in history: $40 million for 46 new and replacement buildings. The majority of the new schools were built in the hills, including Joaquin Miller (later renamed Montera) Junior High School and Skyline High School.[116] In 1962, the high school opened on a 35-acre site on Skyline Boulevard. Yet before classes began, controversy broke out concerning its demographics.

Until this point, four out of Oakland's five high schools—Oakland Technical, Oakland, Fremont, and Castlemont—had boundaries that reached from the waterfront to the top of the hills, thereby including students from poorer as well as wealthier families, minorities and whites; only McClymonds High School, located in West Oakland, was almost totally black (97 percent). By contrast, as reporter Dick Ricca remarked: "In drawing up the attendance area for the new school, the Oakland Board of Education chopped off the top of each of the other schools' attendance areas and gave them to Skyline."[117] Its boundaries (and those of its feeder elementary and junior high schools) encompassed solely the Oakland hills. The NAACP claimed that these boundaries would keep out low-income and minority students, and that Skyline would function as a "private prep school" supported by public funds. In 1965, after numerous protests, the school district compromised, and opened Skyline to three more junior high schools; the percentage of black students at Skyline quickly rose from less than 1 percent to 8 percent.[118] By the mid-1980s, nonwhites comprised 57 percent of Skyline's students.

Related to this attempt to craft a white, public school zone within the Oakland Unified School District was the growth of private schools. Head Royce, a Berkeley school for girls, established a new Oakland campus on Lincoln Avenue in 1964, later adding boys. In 1970, the Bentley School similarly moved from Berkeley to an Oakland hills campus in Hiller

Highlands. Five years later, the K–8 Redwood Day School relocated to a former Lutheran Church on Redwood Road, and eventually settled on a campus on Sheffield Avenue. In 1983, College Preparatory School moved from Claremont Avenue to a campus on upper Broadway. Each of the schools benefited from hill sites much larger than those available in the older parts of Oakland. All were conveniently located along the Grove Shafter, MacArthur, or Warren Freeways. All drew from affluent families, leading to student populations that skewed far whiter than Oakland Unified. All showed the importance of superior schools for high housing values and buyer satisfaction.

From the Berkeley border above the Hotel Claremont to the edge of San Leandro near the Oakland Zoo, and beneath the austere spires of the Oakland Latter-Day Saints Temple, erected in 1964, builders brought the suburbs to the hills. Like nearby Castro Valley or Orinda, they put out variations on the midcentury California dream home—the ranch house.[119] Unlike earlier houses, they had blank facades dominated by garage doors; given few bus lines and long distances to retail areas and other services, automobiles were omnipresent. Beyond their property, a homeowner's focus shifted from the neighborhood to the region: the road network that accessed the home; the panorama from the rear of their home toward San Francisco, the bridges, and the bay. In 1942, an ad for a hills home on a three-quarter-acre lot touted both its level lawn and fruit trees and its location above the fog affording commanding marine and mountain views. By 1973, level lots with views were long gone, and an ad by Mason-McDuffie for an executive home exposed the new residential equation: "Enjoy trees, BAY VIEWS and deer in your garden?" The ranch house's ground-hugging silhouette was modified. Garages were situated at the top level, and a set of stairs led down to the entrance and a house volume that stepped further down, sometimes three or four stories, with the topography and available vistas.

When there were problems in the upper hills, they were far less elemental than those confronting the flatlands. If most homes advertised sightlines, their occupants often also coveted seclusion. Those values could come into conflict with each other. Trees provided a house with privacy from its neighbors and a sense of living in the wilderness. Yet those tall Monterey pines, redwoods, and eucalyptus could block a neighbor's precious views and detract from a home's financial value. In 1980, an Oakland View Ordinance (amended in 2006) tried to ameliorate both camps by ensuring property owners "a reasonable amount of the view that they had when they purchased the property."[120]

Apartments were a bigger flashpoint. In 1961, a partnership of the U.S. Plywood Champion Papers, Bothin Real Estate, and the Moana Development Corporation proposed 667 luxury condominium units for the former 62-acre Stanley Hiller Estate—exemplifying the vastly larger scale of postwar development. New citizen groups, Save the Hills Committee and the Federation of Hill Area Homeowners Associations, took the project to court, claiming the permit was inconsistent with the General Plan, constituting an illegal rezoning in a single-family residential area; an apartment complex would worsen traffic congestion and overburden city services. Courts overruled the objections and the Hiller Highlands project was approved in 1965 but at a reduced scale: 480 rental and condominium units. What upper hills neighborhoods wanted with respect to new housing construction and what developers and the city wanted were drifting further apart. In 1969, a study by the Oakland City Planning Department recommended huge increases in both single- and multiple-family housing for the upper hills.[121]

A related matter involved site planning. Should units be spread out on individual lots, the traditional practice, or clustered together as a Planned Unit Development (PUD)? PUDs offered a larger range of dwelling types: detached houses, attached townhouses, and apartments. They featured common areas: from community rooms to swimming pools. By waiving individual yard requirements around units, they grouped buildings more tightly together, preserving contiguous areas of open space; in 1972, a 274-unit PUD off Redwood Road on Sereno Circle devoted 22.4 out of 31 acres to open space.[122] From afar, the clusters of multiple-unit buildings prevented the visual scarring of hillsides that came from the development of broad swaths of single-family homes. When such complexes included townhouses or apartments, they offered a dwelling option for more than families with kids: singles, empty nesters, retired folks. As with apartments in the flatlands, supporters of PUD housing argued that such growth was essential to accommodate both California's natural attributes and rapid population growth.[123]

Figure 29. Sereno Circle. Planned Unit Development of townhouses off Redwood Road in Upper Hills. Photo by Mitchell Schwarzer, 2020.

PUDs had their detractors, especially when they were large. In 1971, Challenge Developments, the real estate subsidiary of Alcoa Aluminum, proposed Mountain Village on a 685-acre site between Merritt College and the Oakland Naval Hospital—the largest undeveloped parcel of land in Oakland. The concept envisioned between 1,800 and 2,200 units in both single-family houses and apartments. Challenge proposed setting aside 70 percent of the land as open space. Nonetheless, several groups— Save the Hills Committee, Redwood Heights Improvement Association, Hillcrest Homeowners Association, Crestmont Homeowners Association and, most notably, the Sierra Club—rose in opposition, aided by Marian Reeves, a professor of botany at Merritt College. They claimed the development would crowd local schools, destroy the single-family character of the area, and cost taxpayers money for improvements.[124] They objected to the development plan to build a road along (or atop) Leona Creek and create a lake as a centerpiece for the subdivision. The review process—reports followed by meetings among project sponsors, planners, and community groups—dragged on for years. Finally, in 1979, approval was granted for little more than 200 units on a ridge overlooking the creek. The latter area, consisting of 289 acres, would be preserved and given to the East Bay Regional Park District—it became Leona Canyon Regional Park in 1986. To this day the contrast between the sylvan trails in the canyon and the boxy, suburban homes atop Campus Drive is jarring.

Park advocates and neighborhood groups opposed to hillside development were satisfied by the resolution. But as professor of urban planning Bernard Frieden pointed out, the massive reduction in units resulted in houses that sold for 50 percent more: "From the point of view of the housing consumer, the end result was a deep cut in the amount of housing available ... combined with a drastic increase in price. What started out as middle-income housing came out instead as luxury homes."[125] Mountain Village was a case study of how California's lengthy review process, especially after the adoption of the California Environmental Quality Act in 1970 and its requirement for environmental review in large projects, public or private, could lead to smaller projects at higher price points.[126] By lowering the quantity of housing production, fewer new units were available to middle- or upper-middle-class homebuyers. Consequently, fewer older units were available elsewhere in the city to be filtered down to working- or lower-middle-class renters or buyers. Given the low levels of public housing construction and the practically nonexistent production of new rental housing for the lower classes, the cumbersome review process is in part to blame for the dramatic rises in housing costs in the Oakland (and the greater Bay Area) ever since the 1970s. In one prosperous neighborhood after the other, citizen groups fought new projects, using a bevy of arguments: construction noise, traffic congestion, the loss of trees and open space, as well as the aesthetic impacts associated with replacing views of greenery with views of building. As Oakland City Council member Mary Moore stated in 1986 with regard to a proposed development in Montclair: "What goes on in the hill area concerns me because that's my vista and I don't want it garbaged up."[127]

On October 20, 1991, a cataclysm struck the Oakland hills. A fire that had begun on a rubbish pile at a construction site the day before wasn't completely extinguished by the next morning. Hot Diablo winds from the interior blew furiously by morning, lowering humidity and stirring a firestorm that fed on wooden houses and their shake roofs and redwood decks, consuming the dense tree canopy and even leaping over the eight-lane Highway 24. In what turned out to be one of the largest urban fires in American history, 25 people lost their lives, 150 were seriously injured, and 2,843 homes were completely destroyed. The fire perimeter reached over five miles, from the Berkeley border to the edge of Montclair, from the high hills down to Rockridge.[128] The very homeowners who had craved a suburban-style sanctum high above Oakland's urban malaise, who had voted overwhelmingly for 1978's low-tax Proposition 13, were impacted by chronic shortages now affecting city agencies, including the fire department.[129]

Rebuilding hinged on whether streets and blocks would be reconstituted as is or if up-to-date planning and environmental considerations would govern re-platting. Alas, as had been the case in San Francisco after the 1906 Earthquake and Fire, a desire to rebuild quickly doomed sensible plans, among them, a goal to widen streets so that fire trucks could navigate them more successfully. Some off-street parking bays were added. Regulations were instituted to establish larger vegetation-free perimeters around houses. Regrettably, redwood decks and wooden roofs were still permitted on the replacement buildings. Nor were eucalyptus trees, known to create copious amounts of flammable litter at their bases, banned.[130] Approximately 60 percent of the residents chose to rebuild. The postmodern replacements were showy and bulky, causing them to appear to be stacked one atop the other.[131] Speculative developers and homeowners leapt at the chance for an extra bathroom and bedroom, a larger great room, more closets; houses grew greatly in volume. Toward the turn of the millennium, Oakland real estate aligned one more time with long-standing traditions—the building of sumptuous residences for the affluent and little for everyone else. True, restrictive covenants were a thing of the past. But high price points continued to tilt the complexion of hill residents to the paler side. In a city reeling from crime, tax revolts, and environmental disasters, municipal government was all too happy to expedite this exercise in material ambition, anxious to retain the upscale population and its tax base—less concerned this time with a view "garbaged up."[132]

It is important to add that in the years of rebuilding that followed the fire, Oakland's stark black/white neighborhood divisions had become a thing of the past. The great influx of Asian and Latino immigrants had by now reshuffled the composition of most of the town's neighborhoods: wealthier Asian Americans (and smaller numbers of blacks) moved to previously all-white hill districts, including the newly built fire zone; working-class Asian Americans, Latinos, and East Africans settled the flatland hoods that had been largely African American for several decades. Artists, hipsters, and educated professionals, mostly white but including many Asians and some Latinos and blacks, and also large numbers of LGBTQ+ households, settled across the breadth of Oakland—from waterfront industrial districts like Jingletown to swanky Rockridge. Spatially speaking, by the year 2000, the town was far more diverse with respect to race and ethnicity than ever before. But as we shall discuss in the following chapters, a worsening shortage of affordable housing, amid growing economic inequalities, has threatened to undermine that splendid intermingling.

9   Downtown Renewal and Ruin

Bernard Maybeck was one of the most original architects in East Bay history, influencing the careers of subsequent architects from Julia Morgan
to William Wurster. In Oakland, his Earle C. Anthony Packard Showroom
was completed in 1928 on Lakeside Drive and 21st Street. By this time,
automobile dealerships were learning to cultivate a fantasy atmosphere,
one where buyers would be transported out of the here and now, perhaps
with open pocketbooks. Maybeck employed a mélange of Persian arches
and other Middle Eastern ornamental references to tower over a room
filled with the latest Packard luxury cars. He further linked the cars in
the showroom to the street traffic outside, showcasing them on stage with
"the hard white line of automobile headlights gliding past the base" of the
building.[1] Decades later, in 1972, a citizen's committee chaired by Marie
Converse initiated a campaign to establish Oakland's initial Landmarks
Preservation Advisory Board so that esteemed buildings like the Packard
Showroom could stand for all time.[2] It came too late. On October 1, 1973,
the very day the Oakland City Council was meeting for the first time to
deliberate how to implement the new Landmarks Preservation Ordinance,
the showroom fell to the wrecking ball, to be replaced by a parking lot.[3]
    In 1974, when another historic building, the downtown Western Pacific

Railroad station, was threatened by yet another parking lot, demolition was halted and the old station became the Oakland's first landmark. Hundreds of individual building and historic district designations followed.[4] In 1993, the new *Historic Preservation Element* of the *Oakland General Plan* cited the Packard Showroom as one of many significant buildings razed after World War II: "Oakland has lost large numbers of historically or architecturally significant properties, either through demolition or insensitive alteration. These include hundreds of Victorian houses, most of downtown's pre-1900 commercial buildings and several large churches and civic buildings."[5]

Historic preservation was spurred by the damage done to the town's architectural heritage between the 1950s and 1970s. Lakeside, apartment construction practically eliminated the stock of nineteenth-century mansions. In West Oakland and Clinton Park, urban renewal took out thousands of residences. Downtown, *Operation Padlock* tore through the residential hotel district around lower Broadway. Freeway construction erected a wall between the waterfront and the core and, later, erected a canyon between downtown and West Oakland.[6] Finally, radical surgery was performed on the old retail core just south of 14th Street, an operation that resected 18 entire blocks in the hopes of building a new skyscraper/shopping mall complex—City Center.[7]

The city's business elite, along with several mayors, city planning heads, and the Oakland Redevelopment Agency, believed that sweeping urban renewal was a necessity if the central business district was to keep up with the vehicular-inclined suburbs. In fact, the private sector had already shown the way nearby. After 1960, at the edge of Lake Merritt, an automotive-oriented office district sprang up in the vicinity of the new Kaiser Center. Along those lines, City Center urban renewal promised a newly competitive core, served by both BART and adjacent freeways.

Alas, key elements were never built. Most cleared blocks sat unoccupied for years. Like urban redevelopment analyzed earlier—especially Acorn in West Oakland—the total remake led to manifold business and residential displacements and architectural devastation. In the wake of disappointing effects and outcomes, Oakland planners rethought the equation of progress with building clearance, block consolidation, and auto-oriented, suburban-style complexes. They looked back to downtown in the streetcar era, an epoch that took a decided commercial turn, but also one where a mix of commerce and residence still nurtured a productive feedback loop. Toward the end of the century, a new mayor, Jerry Brown, redirected downtown redevelopment away from mega-projects and toward infill, market-rate housing. Downtown's identity was once again changing. Would Oakland's center emphasize its built heritage or the need for ongoing modernization, its pedestrian legacy or the demands of vehicular circulation, its relationship to surrounding urban neighborhoods or larger regional ties, its historic role as Oakland's commercial center or its potential status as nexus of the greater East Bay?

COMMERCE ON THE MOVE

Downtown Oakland never stood still. Originating on the waterfront in the early 1850s, its center of business gravity moved steadily inland along the Broadway corridor for a century. But there was a downside to the restless movement. Investors sought opportunities on the frontier of expansion, neglecting the older areas that lay behind. By 1930, as port activities relocated to newer wharves, as stores relocated to upper Broadway, the waterfront warehouse and factory district faded and lower Washington Street's retail zone began to stagnate.

In 1932, the Downtown Property Owners Association came up with a program to revitalize retail buildings along Washington, a modernization of store interiors and especially building facades. Architectural tastes had changed. Sleek lines were ascendant and buildings were remade to look as if they were new. Irving Kahn, owner of the eponymous department store—and involved with the East Bay Regional Parks and freeway planning—described the approach: "Cupolas, bay windows, and gingerbread have been replaced by tile, glass and chromium in simple, modern designs."[8] The J. C. Penney department store tripled in size, adding wider aisles and, on the exterior, a sleek surface of tile and show windows.[9] Hale Brothers, a low-cost department store founded in Sacramento, enlarged its windows to provide compelling street-side displays. Mass merchandiser W. T. Grant similarly added a 90-foot sweep of glazed, sidewalk spectacles.[10] By 1944, 39 Washington Street facades had been modernized.

Coupled with the wartime boom, the program stemmed Washington Street's decline. But by the 1950s, commercial investment was leapfrogging to Oakland's outlying districts and the former agricultural lands of Alameda and Contra Costa Counties. Fourteenth and Broadway remained the city's epicenter, yet that status was waning. A technologically impelled disruption of unparalleled scale and speed was at hand. Along with the long-standing volatility of people and capital, along with traditions of flexible techniques of land valuation, regulation, and taxation, the gas combustion engine accelerated urban sprawl and decentralization beyond all bounds.[11] Stores and offices voted with their feet, and began to forsake the old core.

In 1959, a mixed-use complex debuted along the northwestern arm of Lake Merritt. Designed by Welton Becket, the Kaiser Center was a different sort of office building with respect to design, function, and location.[12] At 390 feet, the thin curving slab of aluminum-framed glass curtain walls crowned the skyline of Oakland, announcing an end to a 30-year drought in office construction. The seven-acre super-block development featured an office tower for the various aluminum, steel, and construction businesses of the Henry J. Kaiser empire, and additionally, a shopping center including a Grodin's menswear outlet that had moved from 12th Street and Broadway and a branch of the San Francisco–based White House department store. The complex also included a massive, five-story, 2,500-space parking garage, and a modernist, landscaped garden atop its roof. Its covered entrance was set back from the street, reached by a curving driveway that emphasized entry by car and not by foot.[13]

That same year, First Interstate Bank erected a glass and steel skyscraper, a 297-foot tower rising from a podium and clearly distinguishing its office floors from its elevator bank. Notably, it was the first tower built at 14th and Broadway, the historic 100 percent corner commanding the highest rents in town, since the early years of the Great Depression. It was also the last until 1975. Indeed, from 1960 to 1990, only two more private office towers rose in the vicinity. Much of the reason may be attributed to Kaiser Center's formula—the key elements of suburban commerce squeezed onto an extra-large city block. Its location was crucial, more than seven blocks from the nearest large office building—on the city's wealth axis leading toward high-end neighborhoods. Kaiser Center catalyzed a lakeside office

Figure 30. Kaiser Center. Office tower seen from modernist landscape garden, ca.
2000. Photo by Brian Grogan. Courtesy of Historic American Landscape Survey
(Library of Congress) HALS CA-3.

district where the bulk of the town's privately financed office construction took place. In 1970, the aluminum-clad Ordway Building was erected next door and, at 404 feet, became the tallest building in the city.[14] Between 1982 and 1992, seven more skyscrapers were completed in the vicinity— many occupied by the nation's largest HMO, Kaiser Permanente. They constituted a competing city-within-a-city, a zone where most employees drove to work and had less to do with older parts of the downtown. Instead of cohering downtown, the office towers by Lake Merritt pulled it apart, resulting, as reporter Gerald Adams remarked, in a "disconnected series of developments separated by rather desolate blocks."[15]

At the onset of the twentieth century, bank/office buildings had inaugurated the development of the 14th and Broadway core. Their locational geography changed as well. Between 1961 and 1969, several banks either relocated from the old core or launched branches in the vicinity of the Kaiser Center: Central Valley National, Wells Fargo, First National of Oakland, Sumitomo of California, and Security Savings and Loan. Unlike the earlier structures, where banks occupied the lower floors of an office tower, these banks were single-purpose, one-story, suburban-style structures with drive-up tellers and parking lots. Constructed for the most part of reinforced concrete with large plate-glass windows, the sculptural edifices were oriented to automotive perception and mobility. The perspectives of a driver or rider, not a walker, now determined building orientation, scale, and appearance.

THE CENTER LEFT BEHIND

In 1960, *San Francisco Chronicle* architectural critic Allan Temko lamented downtown's emptiness: "Aside from its magnificent lake, and a few recent embellishments such as the Kaiser Center, downtown Oakland is an inchoate assemblage of aging commercial structures, ramshackle dwellings, hotels varying in quality from mediocre to poor, block-busting parking lots, and street advertising of almost incredible vulgarity...in this environmental desert it is difficult to find a civilized amenity such as a first-class restaurant."[16] True enough, decades of parking promotion had ripped out many buildings. Replacements related more to cars than to people. Remaining residents were poorer and more likely to be minorities, as residential segregation prevented the growing black population from moving, as whites were doing, to the suburbs.[17] Why would anyone expect to find a first-class restaurant in such circumstances?

Municipal officials agreed with Temko's bleak assessment and envisioned revitalization that would make the downtown more attractive to wealthier people and suburbanites. On the model of the Clinton Park code enforcement program, the City of Oakland first took aim against residential hotels—Operation Padlock. In conjunction with the construction of a new Hall of Justice on lower Broadway, from 1960 to 1962 inspectors scrutinized approximately 100 aging residential hotels—from 6th to 10th Streets and from Webster to Jefferson Streets—and cited owners for code violations. They had 90 days to undertake repairs before the city initiated procedures to condemn and demolish the substandard structures. As Jack Taylor, building and housing administrator, described the padlocking of newly vacant residential hotels: "These are just some of the fruits of one of the toughest code enforcement programs in the United States."[18] Thirty-six owners undertook repairs, while 18 hotels were immediately closed and replaced by service stations or parking lots. Over time, 35 others were torn down. The physical and social environment was sanitized—poor and indigent people, old and decrepit buildings removed from a city intent on upping its status.[19]

Tenants who occupied rooms in residential hotels were mostly low-income, single men, many of them elderly. They rented by the week or month, occupying small rooms usually lacking a kitchen and served by a bathroom down the hall. Hotels had their clienteles: merchant seamen at the Travelers Hotel; divorced men at Hotel Harrison; the elderly at the Woodrow and Alice Club; students at the Jackson Residence Club.[20] In *Living Downtown* (1994), Paul Groth argued that residential hotels, or single-room occupancies (SROs), offered a crucial dwelling option in a city, serving the needs of people who were not well adapted to permanent residence, or the ownership or rental of property, and yet were not in a state of true transience, moving between tourist or business hotels. Compared to houses or apartments, residential hotels fit the unstable lifestyle of unattached people with few possessions, those who worked intermittently and changed locations frequently. They provided access to transit, workplace, stores, bars, and cheap eateries[21]—but not for much longer. This dwelling style would no longer be tolerated in the new Oakland. By the 1980s, after a couple decades of downtown revitalization and urban renewal, only around 25 residential hotels with around 2,000 rooms remained. Some of their former residents had no option but to turn to living on the streets. Alongside the draconian cuts to social and psychiatric services of the Reagan era, the steady eradication of residential hotels in cities across the country, once one of the largest reservoirs of low-rent housing, was a prime cause for the now ubiquitous phenomenon of urban homelessness.

Through the 1960s, even as residential hotels were being reduced in number, middle-class shoppers were continuing to turn away from downtown Oakland. The retail vacancy rate soared to 21 percent by 1965.[22] Department stores were losing their traditional backbone—white middle-class customers who didn't want to shop alongside the poor.[23] As Oakland's once vital retail sector tailed off, Washington Street south of 14th Street, the locus of the earlier façade modernization, suffered the most. Its remaining department stores, like J. C. Penney's, and its smaller stores selling shoes, luggage, jewelry, linens, and rugs, experienced drops in sales. Some larger stores were in full flight. In 1959, Smith's, a men's and boy's store, relocated from 12th and Washington to the bottom floors of the recently completed First Interstate Building on 14th and Broadway. Three years later, W. T. Grant moved across the street from Smith's. In 1963, Hale Brothers simply closed.

The chamber of commerce and Downtown Merchants Association came up with yet another solution to address Washington Street's malaise. In the mid-1950s, inspired paradoxically by the very shopping malls that were attracting retail trade away from downtowns, several older cities placed their hopes on pedestrianized shopping streets.[24] In 1961, Oakland followed examples from Kalamazoo, Michigan, to Springfield, Oregon, and jumped on the mall bandwagon. The five-block-long Washington Street Mall was finished in 1963 through a consortium of municipal and retail interests. Whereas the City of Oakland had spent the past several decades widening streets for additional vehicular lanes, traffic lanes on Washington between 9th and 14th Streets were henceforth reduced from five to two. Sidewalks were widened, and trees, fountains, kiosks, and

Figure 31. Washington Street retail district. City Hall in background, ca. 1958. Photo courtesy of Oakland Public Library, Oakland History Room.

benches shielded the stores from the cars.[25] Surely, shoppers and private investment dollars would follow. Within a short while, however, it became apparent that the refurbished Washington Street was not attracting large stores to replace the vacancies caused by Hale's closure and the earlier relocations of Smith's and W. T. Grant's to Broadway.[26] The downhill retail slog continued.

The abortive renaissance on Washington Street stemmed in part from its halfhearted remake. Unlike Victor Gruen's 1964 Fulton Street Mall in Fresno, eight downtown blocks lavishly landscaped by Garrett Eckbo with sculptures and fountains,[27] Oakland landscape architects Ralph Jones and John Vogley made relatively minor changes to Washington Street's appearance. More problematically, in comparison to Gruen's 1962 Midtown Plaza in Rochester, which introduced interiorized, climate-controlled shopping, the deteriorating social climate attendant to the older parts of Oakland's downtown plagued outdoor Washington Street. In California, the issue wasn't weather. Oakland's pedestrianized street couldn't attract chain stores and compete with an indoor shopping mall's coordinated management and shop hours, careful maintenance, and reputation for safety.[28] Nor could it generate pedestrian traffic sufficient to maintain high levels of retail activity.[29] Finally, the Washington Street Mall lacked ample parking and, given the proximity of its benches to soup kitchens and remaining residential hotels, became a magnet for transients. In 1965, only a couple of years after it debuted, Mayor John Houlihan lambasted the Washington Street Mall as a "skid row festering in the center of our city."[30]

The office success of Kaiser Center and the retail failure of the Washington Street Mall led to two decades of planning that placed a priority on slum clearance—land and block consolidation, building demolition, and large-scale new construction—and ultimately urban futility. Instead of seeing the city's historic architecture and established small businesses as resources, Oakland's leaders embarked on a series of plans to remake the old core in ways that recalled the modernist city of skyscrapers in a park, on the one hand, and the isolated suburban shopping mall, on the other; "insurance," as ORA planners would call it, "against threats of changing urban trends, economic insecurity, obsolescence and decay."[31]

CLEARING OUT THE CORE

The role of urban redevelopment in city redesign was catalyzed nationwide by John F. Kennedy's 1961 Housing bill and Lyndon Johnson's subsequent infusion of funding for anti-poverty efforts, such as the Model Cities program. Rebuilding in that manner meant replacing much of the old city with a new one, and scaling that replacement to compete with the corporate economics of the burgeoning suburbs. Through the 1970s, urban redevelopment projects premised on slum clearance and modernist superblock-and-tower construction recast the form and function of downtowns from coast to coast.[32] During the late 1950s, redevelopment chief Ed Logue's Church Street Project in New Haven, Connecticut, bulldozed the city's retail core of mostly independent small stores and service establishments.[33] Automotive-friendly arteries, parking garages, and a high-end shopping center replaced the "blighted" small-scale buildings; opened in 1967, the fully enclosed Chapel Square Mall limped along until its closure in the early 1990s. In aiming toward high-end stores like Macy's, New Haven planners, following the suburban shopping mall prototype, over-reached the capacity of their city's largely poor and minority base of retail shoppers.[34]

Businessmen and government officials in Oakland similarly focused on eradicating downtown blight and similarly overestimated their city's magnetism for suburban-style projects. Planning for what would be even-tually be called City Center began in the late 1950s as part of a General Neighborhood Renewal Program encompassing West Oakland and downtown. At the end of 1964, efforts accelerated when John B. Williams took over the ORA.[35] Over the next 12 years, Williams was the face of downtown urban renewal, and worked closely with mayors Houlihan and his successor John H. Reading; ORA staff and its seven commissioners, who included officials from leading corporations, civic clubs, neighbor-hood improvement associations, labor, and Alameda county government; the City Planning Department and its director Norman Lind; and other institutions like the chamber of commerce, whose members included for-mer senator William Knowland, publisher of the Oakland Tribune, Elmo Mazzera, vice president of the Bank of America, and Edward Ryan, chair-man of the board of Transamerica Corporation.[36] Collectively, these indi-viduals embraced Williams's blunt charge: "A brutally ugly and economi-cally wasteful downtown in one of the most beautiful cities in America."[37]

By 1965, the area under study for downtown renewal was gigantic, encompassing 70 blocks (160 acres).[38] Four redevelopment projects were established: Corridor, several blocks that paralleled the proposed route of the Grove Shafter Freeway on the western edge of downtown and intended for high-rise luxury housing; Telegraph Square, four blocks west of Telegraph Avenue from 17th and 20th Streets, a proposed trans-portation center and commercial complex aimed at connecting the old core to the new Kaiser Center; Chinese Community, 27 blocks across Chinatown; and Civic-Center Peralta, an even larger area encompassing much of what was to have been Oakland's grand, lakeside civic center.[39] Thankfully, some of the outrageous plans did not proceed. By the early 1970s, Chinese Community project was scaled back to four blocks, while the Peralta project went ahead on just part of its site with the construc-tion of Laney College. The Corridor and Telegraph Square projects were dropped because of a lack of interest from private residential and commercial builders. In their stead, a new redevelopment project was born— City Center, located just south of 14th Street and west of Broadway and with an emphasis on mixed-use commercial development.[40]

The *Oakland Central District Plan*, issued in 1966, provided theoretical justification for the City Center makeover.[41] Inspired by urban theorist Kevin Lynch, who asserted that the character of cities derives from visually strong boundaries, clear gateways, and emphatic focal points, planners proposed countering over a century of haphazard, scattered development by concentrating commercial energy.[42] To create a sense of place and economic vitality, they encouraged development of dense, single-use subdistricts. Unregulated retail and office development on a homogenous street grid had dispersed downtown's concentrations of density so that no sufficient and compelling focal points existed. To the planners, the city's nodes of density—the lakefront civic buildings, the 14th and Broadway skyscraper core, the new Kaiser Center, the linear retail district—were unproductively separated by block after block of low-intensity uses.[43] Many of these were turning into pockets of blight. The retail zone, stretching over nine blocks, had to shrink in order for there to be mutually reinforcing effects between Washington Street stores and those Uptown.[44] The *Oakland Central District Plan* aimed to head off these defects of private-sector commercial decentralization by luring back white, middle-class shoppers and office workers to a new publicly planned downtown focal point.[45]

Soon afterward, the renamed City Center Redevelopment Project began to take shape around the goal of replacing "an obsolescent portion of the central city" with a marquee hotel, convention facilities, office skyscrapers, and major department stores.[46] Approved by the city council in early 1968, the project quickly received encouraging news.[47] In September of that year, Oceanic Properties, a Hawaiian development company, proposed a grandiose 18-block urban renewal plan near the focal point of City Hall, consisting of office towers, a galleria of stores, and a hotel-convention center, all tied to the anticipated construction of two downtown BART stations and the Grove Shafter Freeway.[48] Ten months later, the developer backed away.[49] ORA director Williams and Mayor Reading claimed they were not discouraged by this sign of marketplace trepidation

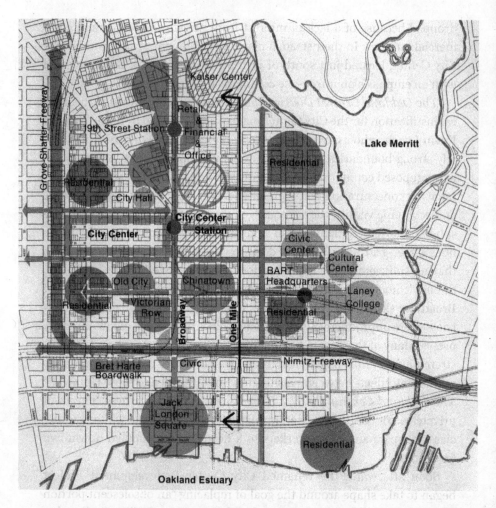

Map 6. City Center Context. Central District Plan, 1966. Map courtesy of Oakland Public Library, Oakland History Room.

at the experimental partnership between public and private sector interests to remake a deteriorating downtown. Planning efforts continued, and in early 1969, the ORA approved a $50 million City Center, albeit reducing its scale to six blocks.[50] That fall, a second Hawaiian developer, Dillingham Land Corporation,[51] supported by the local firm Grubb & Ellis, enhanced the project's scale to $90 million and 15 blocks. ORA commissioner Nate

Frankel expressed the agency's desire for swift and decisive action, commenting: "A 'vast wasteland' of blight is spreading over Oakland faster than urban renewal can wipe it out."[52]

Subsequent plans—foremost among them the *Central District Urban Renewal Plan* of 1969—kept dreaming big, giving up on mutually reinforcing retail effects and signing Washington Street's death warrant. In order to counter sluggish office development in the old skyscraper core and weakening department store performance on both Washington Street and upper Broadway, efforts would be concentrated at the City Center. Rather than taking a critical stance toward the cycle of urban/suburban advance and abandonment, the plan replaced gradual abandonment with coordinated, mass destruction.[53] In 1970, with federal financial backing in place, the ORA embraced a six-block slum clearance plan, extending to 11th Street.[54] Demolition began that year on both sides of Washington Street. By 1972, additional federal funds allowed the ORA to expand the clearance zone to 15 blocks (or almost 40 acres): from Broadway to Castro Street, from 11th to 14th Street.[55] Only a few structures were spared—the old main library, a church, and a few Victorian houses.[56] Over a hundred businesses, largely on Washington Street, were evicted, alongside hundreds of lower-income residents, most of whom were minorities.[57]

Oakland City Center followed on the heels of an avalanche of downtown slum clearance projects, such as Hartford's Constitution Plaza (1962–64), Baltimore's Charles Center (1962–76), and Cleveland's Erieview (1964–73), modernist projects graced by broad plazas and gleaming glass and steel skyscrapers. Each castigated downtown development as it had unfolded over a long span through unregulated private sector forces and promoted, instead, a government-directed design blitzkrieg against blight. In scope, the Oakland effort neither preserved as many significant older buildings as Charles Center nor employed the total tabula rasa approach taken at Erieview.[58] In ambition, though, the Oakland plan faced the same questions as these and other American redevelopment plans. Could federal/municipal makeovers invigorate a downtown's office and retail sectors? Or would they draw remaining businesses from older buildings and merely disguise the larger problem of downtown's competitive disadvantage with the suburbs?[59]

ONE STEP FORWARD, TWO STEPS BACK

The ORA had good reason to be optimistic of a government-launched reversal of downtown Oakland's fortunes; in those years the city was largely kept afloat by close to 140 nonmilitary federal programs spending $100 million a year.[60] The scope of the City Center urban renewal plan was nonetheless unprecedented. Historically, retail and office development had been instigated by private interests and accommodated to workable sites within the grid. Now, planners aimed to redirect growth to the City Center superblock, eliminating a great many streets and a far larger number of small businesses, and separating vehicles, underneath, from pedestrians on the raised plazas. Historically, transportation planning had not been part of a developer's commercial equation. Now, car traffic was to flow into a new City Center garage from the proposed Grove Shafter Freeway extension, while two new BART stations placed close together (at 12th and 19th Streets) were to bring in other office workers and shoppers.

City Center was not aimed at the needs of most Oakland residents, and a small chorus of voices raised objections to the scope and character of the urban redevelopment plan. Gary Reber, president of the Institute for the Pursuit of Economic Justice, based in Berkeley, argued that a public project of this scale should not be owned by a privileged few.[61] At an ORA community meeting, Elaine Brown of the Black Panther Party raised the issue of housing for displaced persons while Michael Bledsoe, director of Oakland Citizens Committee for Urban Renewal (OCCUR), brought up the lack of jobs for minorities and inadequate citizen participation.[62] By this point, OCCUR, pressured by activists like Paul Cobb who in 1968 founded the Oakland Black Caucus, was on its way to becoming a community-based voice for minorities, quite a change from its incarnation in 1954 on the part of the city's leading businesses.[63] Later, Norman Spaulding's analysis for the American Investment Management Company of Oakland pointed out that the project was elitist and that the claims made by Grubb & Ellis and the Office of Community Development with regard to increased jobs and minority participation were inflated.[64] Minority participation was, indeed, a question mark at all levels of the project. Even though the black population of Oakland was rapidly growing, ORA director Williams, himself an African American, usually found himself working in rooms of white businessmen and government officials.

Figure 32. Wells Fargo Building. Aerial view of first completed office building of City Center project, 1973. City Hall, *left*; Kahn's Department Store dome, First National Bank Building, and Federal Realty Building, *right*. Photo courtesy of Oakland Public Library, Oakland History Room.

Community doubts were paralleled by different worries on the part of City Center's corporate players. In 1970, Dillingham dropped out, leaving Grubb & Ellis as the primary developer. A year later they unveiled a grand, 15-block vision that called for a 55-story skyscraper surrounded by three 35-story and three 20-story buildings as well as three or four department stores surrounding an enclosed shopping mall.[65] In May 1972, Mayor Reading presided over the groundbreaking for City Center. But Oakland's small commercial real estate sector could not absorb an increase in office space that would have more than doubled its entire office supply. PG&E canceled its office building. By 1975, the seven towers were scaled back to five smaller buildings.[66] For many years, even that ambition proved too much.[67] The sole structures completed in the plan's original time frame were the 10-story Wells Fargo Building (1973), the 24-story Clorox Building (1975), and a 1,080-car, two-level parking garage (1977).[68] Clorox was City Center's greatest coup. The Oakland-based company moved

475 workers to the new downtown headquarters from offices out by the airport.

By 1980, empty blocks were the main visual attribute of the vast City Center site. Two years later, yet another developer team, the Oakland City Center Development Company, led by the Canadian Bramalea Limited with Grubb & Ellis playing a secondary role, proposed yet another version for the empty blocks: more office buildings, a scaled-back shopping center, and a hotel/convention center.[69] Final commitments from Bechtel Corporation and other anticipated private companies fell through. City Center redevelopment, whose site had been assembled and cleared with government money, turned to the government for building construction and tenants: in 1984, a pair of small government buildings went up across from City Hall; and in 1993, the twin-towered Federal Building opened.[70] The only private towers to open in City Center after 1975 were the American President Company Building at 1111 Broadway (1991), the 555 Twelfth Street Building (2002), and the Blue Shield of California Building at 601 12th Street (2018). Still, compared to the retail fiasco, office development at City Center was a relative success.

Across the country, more than a hundred downtown retail centers—regional shopping centers, festival marketplaces—opened between 1970 and 1988.[71] In the one of the greatest planning failures in Oakland history, the ORA failed to deliver on a regional shopping center. In Grubb & Ellis's 1972 version of the plan, some of the city's four remaining department stores—Capwell's, White House, Rhodes, and J. C. Penney's—were to relocate to the City Center superblock alongside another prestige anchor store and over a hundred smaller shops and services. Gobbling up more than nine city blocks and streets, the enclosed mall would have been an indoor magic castle, containing stores, movie theaters, and a skating rink. This fortress would also have been walled off from the surroundings. Minimal spillover would have benefited the city's other retailers, for pedestrian sidewalk density no longer counted in this redevelopment equation. The principal means of access was to have been a set of ramps leading between the new Grove Shafter Freeway and a multistory parking garage holding approximately 3,300 cars. A park, now occupied partially by the Preservation Park Victorian simulacrum, was intended to take up the residual land at the western edge, underneath ramps connecting to the freeway.

City Center's suburban-style mall was not only antithetical to Oakland's streetscape, it proved to be out of step with the city's economy and society. Instead of the working-class and African American women who had become the principal shoppers downtown, it hoped to draw on white middle-class shoppers driving in from the city's hillside neighborhoods and outlying suburbs.[72] This was a chimera. Those shoppers had ample opportunities elsewhere.

Downtown acquired a bad reputation. Journalist Mark Blackburn asked: "Why does downtown look as though somebody dropped a bomb on it? Why are there so few shoppers and so little merchandise in Liberty House? Who is that man reaching for my handbag?"[73] No wonder final commitments from financiers and department stores like Macy's or Bullock's remained elusive. At the time, much of the blame was placed on delays (and even a brief cancellation) of the Grove Shafter Freeway, the shopping center's lifeline.[74] Despite considerable planning and journalistic boosters, the kinds of retailers and commercial real estate interests accustomed to doing business in suburbia or nearby San Francisco remained skeptical of City Center's bold, yet dicey frontier—what was being "branded," negatively, as a black city.[75]

In 1985, the Grove Shafter Freeway was finally completed on what now became downtown's sharp western edge, eliminating more streets and buildings. The same year, the city announced that the long-delayed regional shopping mall, now called the Oakland Eastbay Galleria, would be relocated to a smaller, six-block site Uptown—between 17th and 20th Streets, San Pablo Avenue and Broadway. James Rouse, America's famed builder of suburban malls and urban festival marketplaces, was the developer.[76] But in 1992, what had looked like a coup turned into defeat. Federal urban development area grants, crucial for site acquisition and preparation, had dried up. Rouse couldn't come up with financing. Not enough stores would commit. Seeking to explain what happened this time, Julia Brown, Oakland's economic development director, remarked: "It (the site) looks like you're in downtown Beirut (during the Lebanese Civil War). That's a major detractor when you're trying to bring retailers in, no matter what incentives you have to offer."[77]

Most of downtown's large stores had closed by now. Breuner's shuttered its flagship Oakland store in 1975. William Breuner, great grandson of the founder, remarked: "People were moving to the suburbs. So we moved out of downtowns too. There we remained open on weekends, and we opened large stores."[78] Earlier, in 1960, Kahn's had been recast as Rhodes Department Store, and later still, in the early 1970s, it became a branch of San Francisco's Liberty House, only to close in 1984. Finally, in 1995, a shakeup occurred at Oakland's two remaining department stores on upper Broadway. I. Magnin's shuttered its doors and the Emporium-Capwell was replaced by a Sears, itself relocated from a longtime building at Telegraph and 27th Street.[79]

By the mid-1990s, rather than worrying about restoring vitality to one of the historical linchpins of downtown development, Oakland faced a future with hardly any retail trade at all. In demolishing most of Washington Street and its close to 300,000 square feet of space, urban redevelopment drove out those businesses serving the working class while not being able to lure profit-making department stores serving the middle and upper classes.[80] In pinning hopes and dollars on gigantic suburban-style malls that stayed permanently on hold, the city neglected the resources it had. In 2014, Sears too ceased operations.

REGIONAL COMPETITION

Would Oakland have been better off without the City Center urban redevelopment project? Could those buildings and streetscapes lost to the bulldozer have served as the historic/architectural foundation for a revitalization of downtown? Or would the absence of major governmental actions have allowed the central business district to continue deteriorating, bleeding stores, scaring off new office buildings, and ultimately leaving downtown with even fewer sources of tax revenue and employment?

In approving City Center in 1968, the ORA lamented that automobile dispersal had toppled Oakland from its status as a total city providing a complete range of services to its surroundings. Planners hoped to counter that trend by repositioning Oakland, via BART and the Grove Shafter extension, at the pivot point of the Bay Area.[81] The ORA accordingly vowed "to establish a new urban center in the deteriorating southern portion of the downtown core as a firm anchor point for new development, permitting a progressive restructuring of the existing low intensity land use to a high intensity land use, consistent with the new transportation facilities now being constructed."[82] Developers shared this vision of a high-intensity, multi-use City Center built upon transportation advances. Oceanic's 1968 report cited downtown's supportive context of freeways, port facilities, the jetport, a new art museum, Jack London Square, and the Coliseum-Arena complex: "These, combined with Oakland's central posture in the Bay Area Rapid Transit System, provide a context for a regeneration that few other cities in the United States can claim."[83]

If City Center shared these advantages of land availability and transportation access, the product it was offering—office, retail, and hotel space—could come about only through the multifaceted actions of private-sector interests. The ORA might assemble the land and facilitate the planning process, but buy-in was needed from numerous companies (as the lessees of office or retail space) for developers to proceed with construction. Yet City Center's product necessarily contended with manifold commercial real estate projects across the Bay Area that, as it turns out, were equally buttressed by recent transportation projects.

In 1974, the completion of the transbay BART tube stimulated the development of 34 office towers in San Francisco, and far fewer in Oakland; by 1990, Oakland counted a mere 7 million square feet of space versus over 60 million square feet across the bay. San Francisco had maintained enough corporate headquarters, financial firms, and business services to revitalize their downtown. Oakland did not have anything close to those assets. Moreover, if suburban office commuters could drive-by and train-by Oakland, so too could shoppers. As historian Robert Self summarizes: "BART did less for downtown Oakland, which now suffered from even greater comparative disadvantage: high-end shoppers could by-pass the city altogether in favor of San Francisco, an eight-minute train ride away."[84]

ORA, civic leaders, and developers repeatedly touted downtown's seminal transportation centrality. But Oakland's location at the nexus of the Bay Area freeway and BART networks led to naive assumptions. Unlike streetcars, whose lines ended downtown at transfer points encouraging commercial development, drivers on freeways and passengers on BART system lines could change lines, underneath or in the vicinity of downtown Oakland, without ever setting foot on its streets. Other BART system stops—those in downtown San Francisco and in Concord, Walnut Creek, Bay Fair/San Leandro, and later Dublin/Pleasanton—successfully competed with downtown Oakland for office and retail development. What's more, the region's freeways facilitated commercial growth at suburban intersections blessed with large tracts of undeveloped or underdeveloped land, lower taxes, and fewer urban issues. Transportation centrality alone would not lure businesses to downtown Oakland. The socioeconomic context of downtown and its surroundings was the other key factor underlying any potential renaissance.

Here another contrast with San Francisco is telling. As mentioned in the previous chapter, during the same postwar decades, San Francisco remade its downtown by redeveloping the surrounding mix of maritime uses, wholesaling, manufacturing, and working-class housing into a postindustrial center of tourism, corporate administration, cultural attractions, and upper-end housing.[85] Urban renewal strategies worked in sync with this goal. At the Yerba Buena and Embarcadero Center/Golden Gateway redevelopment projects, working-class/skid row housing and light-industrial/ wholesale warehousing were cleared for the kind of upscale developments that provided an attractive context for luring office buildings, hotels, and department stores to downtown San Francisco.[86] To the contrary, Oakland was incapable of attracting middle-class renters to its urban redevelopment projects in West Oakland. The failure to create mixed-income residential communities to the west of City Center, or for that matter elsewhere in downtown, doomed for many years the preservation-oriented development to its south, a collection of old buildings spared the bulldozers and considered to be the among the most outstanding concentrations of commercial Victorian structures in the western United States.[87]

Beginning in 1975, these blocks had been added to the Central District Redevelopment Area, and architects Glenn and Richard Storek began to restore 11 buildings along 9th Street between Broadway and Washington— what has since become known as Old Oakland.[88] Proponents of historic preservation tell us that the frequent entrances and architectural diversity of older buildings lead to a richer pedestrian experience.[89] Yet for all its Victorian scale and finery, ground floors in the Old Oakland redevelopment project were long filled with offices and nonprofit agencies instead of stores and restaurants.[90] Tourists were a tough draw. Nor would enough city residents go there when they had services aplenty in their own neighborhood shopping streets.[91] Views of cast-iron columns couldn't counter the atmosphere of desolation and menace that wafted through downtown after dark.

City Center may have been hindered by its very goal: to remake the downtown's former 100 percent corner. The clearance of over 20 blocks (if one counts the adjacent Chinatown urban renewal project) resulted in incalculable losses in social and architectural terms and created a void at the heart of the city. In San Francisco, redevelopment focused on the two zones bordering on downtown that were least harmonious with the business community's upscale commercial and residential vision for the city; the financial and retail core was undisturbed and, at the same time, fortified on its edges.

In Oakland, such intervention at the edges was deemed insufficient. Market failure in Oakland's retail and (to a lesser extent) office sectors encouraged the ORA and city leaders to embrace a drastic remaking of the city's old retail core. Since the stakes were higher, the prospects for failure were greater. When downtown's transportation centrality proved to be less of a catalyst than hoped, when nearby residential redevelopment projects proved incapable of buttressing downtown with stable, middle-class neighborhoods, when slum clearance left Oakland with far less retail activity (and pedestrian vibrancy) than before, the ORA found itself with few means through which to attract department stores and corporate office tenants. National chain stores especially were put off by downtown's racial and economic demographics, and lacked confidence that Oakland's central business district could attract the kind of shoppers they coveted—middle-class white women. As had been the case with mortgage redlining and other racially informed means of disinvestment in communities of color, prominent retailers regarded such areas as places not to conduct business.

In 1983, Oakland did score on one redevelopment ambition.[92] A 21-story Hyatt Regency Hotel opened at Broadway and 10th, and, next door, a mid-sized convention center—measuring slightly under 100,000 square feet—provided a smaller, lower-cost alternative to the Moscone Center in San Francisco. The two-block hotel/convention center was to be, however, the last superblock assembled from the historic downtown grid. Throughout the nation, the focus on highways and ring roads, and large-scale land assembly and clearance for urban renewal, was yielding to new strategies emphasizing historic preservation, specialized shopping, and expanded open spaces.[93]

All in all, City Center failed in its attempt to function as a quasi-suburban shopping node. It succeeded in attracting a hotel/convention center and close to a dozen office buildings: although a great many of them are government office buildings—not the largely corporate tenants originally intended. That nucleus provided thousands of jobs, generated secondary businesses, and fed tax revenues into the city coffers. The ORA's marshalling of business forces played a vital role in preventing what could have been an utter collapse of the commercial real estate market and the ensuing abandonment of much of the downtown. At the same time, urban renewal was antagonistic to downtown's historic architecture and cadastral grid. Its regional focus shifted attention away from long-standing urban adjacencies—downtown's role as a commercial center for surrounding neighborhoods. Its top-down planning approach limited meaningful input from community stakeholders, preventing the emergence of ideas that may have embedded the project more firmly within its urban socio-economic milieu.

RELYING ON RESIDENTS

In 1992, Jerry Brown, a two-time governor of the state who had just failed in his third presidential bid, moved to Oakland, creating a visionary live-work commune nearby Jack London Square and devoting his energies, for a time, to local matters. Between 1998 and 2006, as Oakland mayor, Brown steered the ORA away from slum clearance and toward the urban strategy that saw drawing new residents as essential to any downtown revitalization. He envisioned downtown as a mid-sized place that could, like the town's better neighborhoods, reap the Bay Area overflow of persons and businesses interested in an urban setting, yet unable to afford San Francisco. His 10K Initiative—ten thousand residents—proposed scattered market-rate housing across the downtown, and led to a boom in eating, drinking, and entertainment establishments.[94]

Brown's vision for the town could not have succeeded much earlier. Home ownership in multiple-unit buildings—condominiums—only became widespread in the United States after 1980. Likewise, conversion of industrial or commercial buildings for residential use—loft living— spread from New York City to the rest of the country in roughly the same time frame. Still, he is to be credited for acting upon this emergent paradigm of residential development: the possibility of luring upper-middle-class home buyers to new projects in the midst of commercial (or formerly industrial) properties; and, correspondingly, the creation of a residential real estate frontier across the extent of downtown. Instead of a downtown, as recommended in the 1966 *Oakland Central District Plan*, of geographically distinct functions, instead of a regionally focused City Center paralleling other mega-projects like the port and sports complex, the twenty-first-century downtown would generate its commercial activity from its own residents and those in nearby neighborhoods.

The 10K Initiative included no skyscrapers or shopping malls; it was not limited to one or two redevelopment zones; it would not demolish any architecturally or historically significant buildings. At the same time, the only significant architectural addition of the era did not come in the form of Brown's housing plan but rather at the lakeside Cathedral of Christ the Light (2008)—a sloping glass cylinder articulated by an Early Christian symbol of Jesus, the *Vesica Pisces*, which takes the shape of a fish or that created by the intersection of two disks with the same radius—designed by Craig Hartman of Skidmore Owings and Merrill.

Brown proposed housing for artists, professionals, singles, yuppies, retirees, and empty nesters, downtown residents who would support enhanced retailing, dining, the arts, and even tourism.[95] "I already have affordable housing in Oakland," he proclaimed, "I want unaffordable housing."[96] New buildings were constructed on empty lots or replaced one-story structures. Over 60 such development sites were identified, room enough for more than 10,000 newcomers.[97] A century earlier, downtown growth had been premised on commercial buildings succeeding single-family houses. Now, multifamily dwellings took the place of marginal or defunct commercial enterprises.

One of the first residential projects predated the plan by a couple of years and was located in Old Oakland: 98 market-rate condominiums in a faux Victorian building that replaced a weed-filled lot at 10th and Clay Streets.[98] Stimulated by Brown's vision and ORA's support, many others followed. While losses during the Great Recession were brutal,[99] while the 4,400 units completed or under construction by 2008 did not initially match the advertised 10,000 residents,[100] the real estate recovery that began in 2012 filled all of the units. Most importantly, Brown's 10K Initiative capitalized on Oakland's unique strengths, such as its transit links, pedestrian-friendly grid and collection of architecturally significant buildings. The plan began a process of repairing Oakland's many missing, broken, or unsuitable pieces. The housing diagram scattered units: by the warehouses at Jack London Square; amid the Victorian commercial structures of Old Oakland; on the edges of the long-standing residential area by Lake Merritt; in the heart of the office-civic core by City Hall; across Uptown, the city's geographical frontier during the early 1930s; and in Chinatown, what had long been Oakland's sole 24-hour subdistrict.

Effectively, the 10K Initiative extended Chinatown's formula throughout the downtown and amid other population groups, starting a process for enhanced retailing and services by first attracting a resident population that would support them. It's not enough to say, as city plans had long been doing—if we build it, they will come. Discussed in the next chapter, the Chinatown example showed that *they*—customers from elsewhere—would come only if someone was there first. In the three subdistricts where most housing was added, Old Oakland, Uptown, and Jack London Square, a substantial number of retail and service businesses opened. Old Oakland attracted restaurants and bars. In Uptown, the Fox Theater reopened for concerts in 2008, while the intersection of Broadway and Grand became a hub for eating and drinking establishments as well as additional residential developments.[101] Nearby Jack London Square, warehouse conversions, and condominiums on the adjacent streets attracted a movie theater, music clubs, and more restaurants.

Downtown's reemergence did not come about without concerns. After the recovery from the Great Recession, worries about gentrification and displacement replaced those about decentralization and decline.[102] In a positive sense, gentrification was credited with drawing affluent people, investment capital, and development projects back to the inner city.[103] Without such forces Oakland would continue to decline. On the other side of the ledger, economists like Neil Smith noticed early on that the back-to-the-city movement was characterized by the ever uneven movements of capital: "Many downtowns are being converted into bourgeois playgrounds replete with quaint markets, restored townhouses, boutique rows, yachting marinas, and Hyatt Regencies."[104]

An analysis of gentrification in Oakland between 1990 and 2011 divided its effects by severity: the most extreme were in North Oakland; next were parts of West Oakland and San Antonio; after that came downtown.[105] A nationwide study, looking at the period 2013–17, found San Francisco-Oakland to be the top metropolitan area for gentrification. Oakland had the largest number of gentrifying tracts, including most of West and North Oakland, downtown, and about a quarter of East Oakland—a sizeable portion of the city's historically low-income, minority flatlands.[106]

Beginning in the 1980s, artists had begun to occupy and reuse empty warehouses and factories along Oakland's industrial waterfront for housing, workspaces, and intermittent entertainment venues. Favoring large and cheap spaces, adopting a low profile due to their frequent skirting of building permits, they neither displaced any residents nor interfered with neighboring industrial businesses. Yet, in a nationwide trend going back to the transformation of New York's Soho district, artists endowed parts of the city with a cachet that would later draw the interest of real estate developers and young professionals, persons who would have escalating conflicts with remaining industries regarding noise, garbage, and parking.

Mayor Brown's encouragement of residential construction downtown, similarly, led to few direct displacements of poorer residents. Most had been displaced earlier by urban renewal and actions like Operation Padlock. Nevertheless, rapid appreciation of real property in a revitalizing downtown resulted in displacement through rent increases amid renovations and rebuilding projects. Gentrification was a two-edged sword, crucial for urban vitality but decidedly disruptive to poorer residents. One can understand how it could be seen negatively within the context of Oakland's history of housing inequity. In the postwar decades, as middle-class whites left the city, the poor and minorities were left behind in deteriorating downtown. In the twenty-first century, as the upper middle class returned, the poor, minorities, and even many in the middle class found it difficult to afford the higher standard of living in a rebuilding district.

Earlier, white flight from Oakland to suburbia was voluntary, impelled by greener pastures and facilitated by government loan programs. Later, displacement of the poor and minority communities was involuntary, the result of pressure exerted by the Silicon Valley technology boom and the waves of migration it sent from the West Bay to the East Bay.

10 Shopping Centers and Storefront Streets

In 1956, a study entitled *New Shopping Areas: San Francisco Bay Area Market* examined how shopping centers were revolutionizing the daily routines of Bay Area residents.[1] Three types of emporia were emerging. The neighborhood center was structured around a supermarket and a few other stores; it provided parking for between 40 and 250 cars. The community center added a junior department store or large variety store and parking for up to 500 cars; it took in a trading area reaching five miles. At the top of the scale, a regional center was anchored by a major department store and incorporated a smaller department store, a supermarket, and other stores and services; with far more parking, it catered to people from different cities. Alameda County already had 10 neighborhood centers, five community centers, and two regional centers. Oakland trailed. There were but three fledgling, neighborhood centers: a supermarket and drug store in the Dimond District; a drug store and restaurant along E. 18th Street by Lake Merritt;[2] a big supermarket at Broadway and MacArthur Boulevard.

Shopping centers were a principal arena for capital investment, and groundbreaking with respect to scale as well as centralized ownership, planning, and spatial organization. In the streetcar era, commercial strips of separately owned buildings had come about over many years through the efforts of diverse builders. By contrast, shopping centers were typically planned and owned by a single company working with a team of engineers, architects, landscape architects, and retail marketers. They opened their outlets in a carefully planned rollout. They took in large tracts of land and coordinated buildings and businesses. Their operations were harmonized around signage that guided shoppers through access roads, free parking lots, and then store aisles.[3] From outside the complex, tall pylons showcased major retailers, while dedicated traffic signals led motorists to entrance drives. In such isolated and highly controlled settings, shopping was promoted—and nothing else.[4]

While the attributes of shopping centers, one-stop choice, and convenience, as well national franchises, were popular with consumers, they had adverse impacts on older cities like Oakland. Through the 1950s, it had been the hub of East Bay shopping, home to most of its department stores. Fifty years later, it was one of the largest underserved retail trade areas in the United States.[5] Losses extended from downtown to streetcar commercial strips and were injurious to lower-income, minority communities as well as the city budget. If much of the blame can be placed on suburban shopping centers, the town's own shopping centers also displaced nearby commercial businesses; and several failed within a couple of decades of their opening. Why did Oakland shopping in all its manifestations take a turn for the worse in the age of the automobile? To answer this question, it is necessary to examine shopping centers within the East Bay suburbs outside Oakland, those within Oakland itself, and their cumulative impact on the town's older shopping streets.

Beginning in the 1970s many of those older storefront streets began to revive, unevenly but undeniably. A few bohemians seeded a few faded strips with alternative businesses. By the 1980s, immigrants from across the globe were settling across North and East Oakland, making their presence felt by opening ethnic foods stores, restaurants, and other services. Finally, around the turn of the millennium, yuppies and then hipsters brought upmarket retail and food offerings to the town. Once again, older built paradigms, seemingly consigned to the dustbin of history by urban progress, roared back—but with altered appeal and function. Cities always change, yet they don't do so in a strictly linear or cyclical way.

SUPERMARKETS AND NEIGHBORHOOD CENTERS

By the 1920s, consumers were deviating from their habits of strolling to the dry cleaners or taking the streetcar to the hardware store. They got into their car and drove to a street filled with commercial storefronts. As more of them shopped this way, a problem emerged. Buildings occupied almost the entirety of their lots, right up to where the lot lines met the street. Only curbside parking was available. Pressure for off-street parking catalyzed a set of experiments that resulted in the birth of the shopping center between the 1930s and 1950s. Department stores and supermarkets took the lead. They were larger than other retail outlets and already had integrated smaller units into a systemic operation—the foundation of a shopping center. As importantly, their scale of operations afforded them the capital and space to include parking lots.

Department stores emerged in the nineteenth century, long before supermarkets. As with any retail type, their innovators sought out competitive advantages: engaging in frequent remodeling to keep up with their style-conscious merchandising; improving internal circulation and sightlines to provide a better customer experience; adding display windows to captivate sidewalk shoppers. Eventually, their attention turned to accommodating vehicles.[6] In 1929, when Sears Roebuck opened its first Oakland store, the giant retailer looked just outside downtown, to a parcel at 27th Street and Broadway that had space for an adjacent, structured garage. A transitional type resulted. While the building was constructed to lot lines and featured display windows oriented to pedestrians on the sidewalk, Sears was proud to claim that "there is free parking for customers in the store, parking from which the menace of tags and time limits is eliminated."[7]

Supermarkets burst forth in the 1930s.[8] Smaller and more ubiquitous than department stores, they took gambles that were crucial for the development of shopping centers. While the Bay Bridge was under construction, supermarket-magnate Andrew Williams made a shrewd calculation. He assumed that once it opened—the late fall of 1936—traffic would increase exponentially on Moss Avenue, the arterial that led from the bridge to the recently completed Broadway Low-Elevation Tunnel. He was correct. Overnight, the corner of Moss and Broadway became the East

Bay's most congested intersection. Here, in 1937, Williams opened a new Andrew Williams Store. He had been in the grocery store business since 1919, having built a chain of food outlets running up and down the Pacific Coast and in the Hawaiian Islands. Now, for his largest effort, Williams erected a 60-foot-tall neon sign calling out to passing cars. Vehicular entrances on both streets led to parking lots. Henceforth, practically every Oakland shopping center would be located on a heavily trafficked arterial and provide free parking.

Inside, the Andrew Williams Store was novel as well. Unlike a central food market, with its stalls rented to individual purveyors, Williams's supermarket offered 10,000 food items in 14 separate departments under a single management.[9] Upon opening, it was the largest food store in Northern California. Ten years after the store debuted, architects Douglas Stone and Lou Mulloy enlarged the building to 45,000 square feet and the count of departments to 25. There were now not only numerous self-service food and meat departments but also a jewelry and watch stand, home appliance department, beauty salon, drug store, coffee shop, restaurant, cocktail lounge, and even a kiddie park.[10] The Andrew Williams Store was a nearly complete shopping experience under just one business license. Following its example, new neighborhood centers—with multiple business licenses—would build on a supermarket's advertising dollars and parking availability, adding subsidiary stores and services that would bring in additional dollars in rent. In Oakland, often enough that supermarket was a Safeway Store, the giant chain that maintained its national headquarters in the town for over half a century.

In 1915, Marion Barton Skaggs opened a grocery store in American Falls, Idaho, and came upon an innovation crucial to the future of American grocery shopping. He instituted a system of cash and carry, eliminating store credit and allowing his customers to select their own purchases from accessible display cases and shelves; they then carried the goods to the cash register themselves and brought them home themselves in lieu of delivery. Within ten years, Skaggs United Stores had 300 stores and had relocated its headquarters to Oakland. In 1926, he merged his chain with the 150-store Safeway Stores of Southern California, and adopted the Safeway name.[11] Three years later, Safeway Stores added Piggly Wiggly Western States as well as Mutual Stores to its growing food empire.

Safeway was now the largest grocery chain in the West, and one of the largest and most innovative supermarket chains in the nation, a status it would hold for much of the remainder of the century. After 1931, Safeway established its main offices at 5726 E. 14th Street in East Oakland, a brick and terra-cotta warehouse building built a few years earlier for Mutual Stores and distinguished by a 150-foot tower.

By this time, the supermarket was coming into its own, identified by several features: the selling of produce as well as baked goods, meat, and fish; larger sales volumes because of small profit margins; more nationally advertised merchandise, packaged, bottled, or canned to lengthen shelf life at home; and consumer-friendly innovations like "cash and carry" and self-service.[12] Supermarkets were relatively small at first, occupying existing storefronts on commercial strips. Not long after World War II, in a change reflecting heightened automobile usage and economies of scale, Safeway Stores committed to running fewer, larger stores; a prewar Safeway measured 6,000–7,500 square feet with parking for 20 cars; the new stores would be 15,000–30,000 square feet and come with 250-car parking lots.[13] No longer would Safeway rent space in existing streetcar commercial strips. The new scale demanded either stand-alone stores or ones integrated into a planned shopping center.

Safeway continued to grow alongside the frozen-food craze of the 1950s. Larger, more diverse inventories raised the volume of sales and net profits, and stimulated store redesign.[14] What distinguished Safeway most after 1955, when Robert Magowan took over the helm, was its attention to the coordination of signage, circulation, and display. How could signage, beginning with the street-side Safeway sign, lead shoppers through the parking lot and, once in the store, wend them efficiently through the aisles to products strategically exhibited on shelves or cases? In 1959, architects Wurster, Bernardi, and Emmons came up with one of the more influential supermarket prototypes. In San Francisco's Marina District, Safeway unveiled a spacious and light-filled store, its interior height raised on wooden arches and its front consisting of a gigantic wall of glass windows. Together, the curved arch roof profile and giant SAFEWAY letters marching across the glass provided instant recognition.[15] Most likely, the glass front had little to do with displaying interior products or even lighting them, as the view from the parking lot was too distant and fluorescent

Figure 33. Safeway store. Interior view of Marina-type version on two levels, Montclair, ca. 1960. Photo courtesy of Oakland Public Library, Oakland History Room.

tubes provided plentiful illumination.[16] Rather, the modernist supermarket design symbolized the mobility and optimism of the postwar automobile age. A shopper directing their cart through the supermarket wasn't all that different from a driver in the city; both spent their time cruising past an endless series of enticements.

The first Marina-type Safeway in Oakland opened in 1963 at Broadway and 29th Street; like the San Francisco model, the Oakland store was huge, 33,295 square feet, and redolent in amenities: a snack bar, a courtesy counter. Other Marina-style Safeway stores were soon built at College and Claremont Avenues, and at Foothill Boulevard and Fruitvale Avenue.[17] Each was set back a considerable distance from the street, in order to show passing automobiles its dynamic curving lines and illuminated glass as well as the fact that there was ample and convenient parking. In Montclair, a compressed, sloping site led Safeway to deviate from the usual approach. For this Safeway, also finished in 1963, Wurster, Bernardi, and Emmons adapted the store and lot to its irregular site by placing some of the parking atop the building's roof, and redesigning the façade, now facing a small ground-level lot, with concrete piers and shallow arches.[18]

As historian Richard Longstreth tells us, the neighborhood shopping center transformed the supermarket from a lone-wolf operation to the anchor of a larger enterprise, an integrated structure whose businesses shared a parking lot and reciprocal shopping effects.[19] In 1963, a Safeway store was chosen to anchor its first Oakland neighborhood shopping center, a 10-acre site located at the intersection of Redwood Road and Mountain Boulevard. Redwood Road had recently been widened as a major connector to new subdivisions in the hills. Ramps for the Warren Freeway, then under construction, sat a few hundred feet from the center. The John M. Grubb Company developed the Lincoln Square Shopping Center as a 44,000-square-foot complex with parking for 300 cars. Here Safeway used their alternate modernist design, an interior raised on a set of wooden gables and expressed on the front as a great glass pediment. Unlike the overtly vehicular focus of single Safeway stores, a supermarket set back behind a sea of parking, architects Goetz & Hansen planned Lincoln Square's Safeway and three other buildings to relate to both cars and pedestrians. Safeway and most of the stores faced the parking lot at ground level. Additional stores, at a second level, opened onto an outdoor mall shaded by olive and Monterey cypress trees.[20] Like a small-scale mall, Lincoln Square catered to shoppers arriving by car and, once there, offered them a pleasant pedestrian environment.

COMMUNITY AND REGIONAL CENTERS

In 1951, developer Graeme MacDonald, head of the MacDonald's Products Company, convinced financiers to lend him money on what must have appeared a wild hunch. He wanted to build a regional shopping center alongside the intersection of State Road 24 (Mount Diablo Boulevard) and State Road 22 (Main Street) in Walnut Creek. At the time, hardly anyone lived in Walnut Creek. In spite of that, atop two creeks, MacDonald succeeded in constructing two streets, buildings housing 38 stores and, between them, parking lots that could accommodate 1,500 cars. The 200,000-square-foot Broadway Shopping Center featured several major department stores: J. C. Penney, Sears, Joseph Magnin, and a Lucky Supermarket; in 1954, the first suburban branch of Oakland's Capwell's Department Store joined the retail mix.[21] In the following decades, residential subdivisions fanned out from the merchandising hub of Contra Costa County. It was one of the first times in history that a shopping center generated the residential development of a whole suburban region.[22]

After the Second World War, the car-dependent suburbs were growing much faster than Oakland and department stores sought out their promising geographies. In 1957, Capwell's launched its second branch in downtown Hayward. A year later, it opened its third branch in conjunction with smaller stores at a small regional mall, El Cerrito Plaza. Malls were the latest shopping trend and that same year, 1958, a larger and more architecturally daring regional shopping mall opened in San Leandro—on the site of the Oakland Speedway, half a mile from the new Eastshore Freeway and about four miles south of the Oakland border.

Its designer was Victor Gruen, known for the innovatory Northland Center outside of Detroit, completed in 1954. There he had crafted an inward-focused, open-air pedestrian shopping complex surrounded by a ring of vehicular access roads and several thousand parking spaces. Gruen reprised the formula for the 48-acre Bay Fair Center in San Leandro. A large landscaped plaza was surrounded by a Macy's department store, a supermarket, and eventually some 80 other stores as well as an outer ring of 3,600 parking spaces. It was the fourth Bay Area branch of Macy's, but the first to be located in a shopping center.[23] Compact shopping lanes minimized walking distances. Landscaped terraces and courtyards maximized the festive atmosphere.[24] Stores were located on both a mall and a terrace level, and ingeniously each opened directly onto the parking lots; the originally flat site was graded to make this possible. On the exterior, Gruen designed with characteristic minimalism. Part of his legacy to later shopping center design was an emphasis on signage, profile, and mass, basic geometric elements that could be easily perceived from a long distance by shoppers arriving in cars.[25]

From 1948 through 1961, suburban shopping centers and branch department stores grew their share of retail trade from 31 to 60 percent.[26] Aware of these advances, the 1959 *Oakland General Plan* recommended a transformation of existing commercial streets into shopping centers by pruning their far ends and adding parking lots. While lots were added alongside many streetcar commercial strips, these actions in and of themselves could not create shopping centers. The shopping center was a more complex organism than a set of stores with parking. Oakland's planners knew that a genuine community or regional shopping center hadn't yet been built in the city. In response, the *General Plan* called for the construction of several: one at 51st and Broadway; two in West Oakland; and five on the widened arteries bisecting the East Oakland hills.

The first community shopping center opened in 1962, Foothill Square at 10700 MacArthur Boulevard, hard by the San Leandro line. On the 13-acre site of the former Fageol/Peterbilt automotive assembly plant, Draper Companies erected a 142,000-square-foot complex with 850 parking spots. They hired one of the best design teams ever to work on a shopping center in the city. Welton Becket was the architect and Lawrence Halprin designed the outdoor landscaped mall, reflecting pools, and fountains. The 29 stores were mostly mid-range: S. S. Kresge, Thrifty Drugs, Lucky Stores, Roos Atkins, and Bank of America.[27] But Draper Companies also sought to capitalize on their location near to new middle-class subdivisions rising in San Leandro and along Oakland hills streets like Golf Links Road and Malcolm Avenue, attracting a branch of Liebes, a stylish women's clothing store. They also included an indoor food court that sold items from around the world—calling it the first of its kind west of the Mississippi.

Across town, the Albert-Lovett Corporation had proposed a retail complex at the corner of Broadway and 51st Street in 1961.[28] Unlike either Foothill Square or Lincoln Square, both erected in developing areas, the Rockridge Shopping Center was slotted into a part of the city that had been built up decades earlier; the land was acquired by purchasing the 18-acre site of the Bilger quarry, closed in 1945. It was regarded by planners as the sole, large tract in affluent north Oakland on which to erect a community shopping center. Between 1965 and 1967, the shopping center opened with a Pay Less Drug Store, a Safeway store, and a freestanding bank. Surprisingly, given its upscale location, the Rockridge Shopping Center was built as a no-frills effort without any outdoor pedestrian spaces. Stores were aligned on a zigzagging frontage behind a 900-car lot, far from both the corner and surrounding streets.

An altogether different community shopping center was built on the site of the Mayfair Supermarket (formerly the Andrew Williams Store). Already by the early 1950s, the six-acre site at Broadway and MacArthur Boulevard was considered too valuable for just a single supermarket surrounded by surface parking lots. Developer Edmund Herrscher proposed replacing it with a 28-story glass-sided office building, housing a department store at the ground level.[29] South of the site, the Sheraton chain announced a related eight-story, 350-room hotel. Neither plan came to fruition, but by 1963, aware of the 150,000 automobiles passing the site every day, Herrscher was at work again, demolishing the supermarket and erecting, the next year, the MacArthur Broadway Center (MB Center).[30]

Herrscher had just finished the large Century City complex of office towers, hotels, and shopping in Los Angeles, and now offered a scaled-down "city within a city" for Oakland. Architect Irving Shapiro maxed-out the site with a two-story shopping complex, above which rose a seven-story office building, striking for its expression of concrete beams and floor slabs framing a glass curtain wall. Although there was a sidewalk and some store entrances facing it, the focus of the MB Center was on the interior—the essence of a mall that works to lose its customers in the bliss of consumption. On the ground level, the 26 stores (among them Woolworth's and Drug King) and 10 restaurants also included a 600-seat International Food Bazaar offering Japanese, Swiss, and Hofbrau delicacies.[31] An angled moving walkway, an idea borrowed from the New York World's Fair, streamed shoppers and their carts to 650 rooftop parking spots.[32] Alas, the MB Center had but a short reign of success. The opening of the MacArthur Freeway in 1966 took much of the Bay Bridge traffic off MacArthur Boulevard and with it the MB Center's principal clientele.[33]

The only regional shopping center ever built in Oakland began to rise in 1965 on the site of the former Chevrolet plant at Foothill Boulevard and 73rd Avenue. By now, downtown interests understood the impact a new regional center could have on their business, and they fought the plans. Oakland's flagship department store, H. C. Capwell, had already birthed numerous branch stores that were draining dollars from its downtown flagship. Nevertheless, the city's hunger for new business and taxes prevailed, and over the next decade or so the pieces of the 33-acre Eastmont Mall came into alignment. The Hahn Companies, the larg-

Figure 34. MacArthur Broadway Center. Community shopping center at the corner of Broadway and MacArthur Boulevard, 1965. Photo by Julius Shulman. Courtesy of J. Paul Getty Trust, Getty Research Institute, Los Angeles (2004.R.10).

est mall developer on the West Coast, built much of the center and, in 1966, a Safeway Supermarket, Pay n' Save Drug store, Super S Store, and a dozen smaller stores debuted. The main mall opened in 1970, designed by William Pereira: two, enclosed levels featured terrazzo tile floors, carpeted staircases, and light wells; alongside it, a four-story office building. It was anchored by a three-story J. C. Penney department store and 85 smaller outlets, including Grodin's, Roos Atkins, and Woolworth's; the Penney store came at a cost, as the downtown outlet closed. Eastmont again expanded in 1974, adding a Mervyn's junior department store. By now, it totaled 800,000 square feet and featured over 100 stores, a four-screen movie theater, and parking for 2,500 cars.[34]

The regional center was the culmination of integrated management and merchandising techniques that had begun with the neighborhood center.[35] Like others around the country, Eastmont Mall appeared to constitute a separate environment from its surroundings, both residences and commercial strips. Despite its distance from a freeway, a study by Burke Marketing in 1977 found the mall's fortunes bright; thousands of upper- and middle-income Oakland women were frequenting it, drawn by Penney's and the free parking; it was briefly ahead in sales of the larger

Bay-Fair, Sun Valley, and Southland malls.[36] But Eastmont had also been hailed as the first of its kind to be built in a working-class, minority neighborhood suffering the effects of both redlining and deindustrialization. Other reports from the time pointed out problems stemming from its location.[37] The mall was poorly maintained and tenants were often moving out. There were thefts of automobiles, purse snatchings, muggings, and gang activity.[38] Eastmont's fate could not be separated from the poverty and ills of the East Oakland flatlands around it and the racial biases of national realtors who had little interest in ongoing investment in the black inner city.

DECLINE OF THE NEIGHBORHOOD COMMERCIAL STREET

The combination of discontinued streetcar service, freeway bypass routes, and shopping centers with free parking took its toll on the town's neighborhood shopping streets. By the early 1960s, failing businesses and vacancies plagued even upscale strips catering mostly to whites like College Avenue in Rockridge and Lakeshore Avenue in Grand Lake.[39] Black retail corridors suffered far worse outcomes. By the early 1970s, the once-vital shopping strip along 7th Street in West Oakland had practically disappeared. During and after the Second World War, it had been supercharged by the influx of black migrants and the bustle generated by military contracts, offering essential stores and services for the city's African American community as well as famed nightclubs like Slim Jenkins Club and Esther's Orbit Room. BART construction, urban renewal, and the regional post office subsequently tore it apart. Seventh Street lost not just its businesses, but also most of its buildings.[40] Whereas the more affluent residents of Rockridge and Grand Lake took to their cars to patronize far-flung shopping centers across the East Bay, West Oakland residents, due to poverty and racist barriers, had far less mobility. For many black Oaklanders, the age of living in a city with meagre shopping options had begun.

East 14th Street in East Oakland illustrates this predicament. The opening of the Eastshore (and then Nimitz) Freeway in 1958 had two detrimental impacts on the venerable commercial strip. First, the freeway provided easy access for Oaklanders to shop at suburban shopping centers. Second, the Nimitz caused nonlocal traffic, as state engineers had planned, to bypass the once congested arterial. It turned out that in the automotive age, stores on old commercial arteries needed the heavy car traffic for business. In 1964, in response to this situation, the largest store on the strip, Montgomery Wards, undertook a modernization, building a 1,500-car parking garage for customers (and its 1,000 workers). All the while, though, reduced customer traffic led Bank of America, Wells Fargo, and Sanwa to close their branches.[41] Fewer banks resulted in fewer commercial loans and investments in the neighborhood. By the mid-1970s, one-third of the money East Oakland residents spent on consumer goods left East Oakland.[42] A 1977 business façade improvement plan, using $528,000 in federal community block grant funds, did little to arrest the escalating decay. In 1978, a decade and a half after the modernization, the Montgomery Ward store shut its doors.[43] Through the 1980s, E. 14th Street businesses experienced high failure rates and its buildings fell into disrepair. Mile after mile, auto-related enterprises, small personal service and repair shops, fast food chains, storefront churches, check cashing services, liquor stores, boarded-up stores, and vacant lots pockmarked the arterial.[44]

Across its snaking length, MacArthur Boulevard too suffered the effects of reduced traffic. A major commercial thoroughfare leading into the city from the 1930s through the 1960s, it had consolidated Oakland's largest collection of motels. Afterward, the completion of the MacArthur Freeway and the replacement of the Bay Bridge Distribution Structure led most through-traffic to bypass MacArthur Boulevard, robbing not only the MB Center of passing travelers but also harming the arterial's numerous motels, many of them turning into low-cost housing and, occasionally, hosting a clientele renting rooms by the hour.[45]

Other flatland streetcar strips saw their fortunes plummet. In North Oakland, one of the larger retail districts along San Pablo Avenue had been built up around its intersection with Stanford Avenue—the Golden Gate District. The location benefited from a richness of rail-based transit: steam railroads, streetcars, and interurbans. Then, from 1941 through the early 1950s, that infrastructural equation disintegrated. Rail lines were disbanded and a parallel automobile network arose to the west; the Eastshore Highway from the Bay Bridge to Berkeley and Richmond had

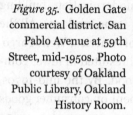

Figure 35. Golden Gate commercial district. San Pablo Avenue at 59th Street, mid-1950s. Photo courtesy of Oakland Public Library, Oakland History Room.

debuted in 1936 and was reengineered two decades later into the limited-access Eastshore Freeway, Interstate 80. Traffic leaving downtown Oakland toward Berkeley and the Carquinez Bridge no longer had to slog up San Pablo Avenue.

The hotels closed first, among them the Stanford, Hansen, and Golden Gate. Through the 1960s and 1970s, their closures were followed by many other businesses: Golden Gate Hardware, Al's Mens Shop, The Fair (furniture and appliances), Strom's Clothing Store, Gordon Drugs, Gateway Music Company, Barney's Photo, San Pablo Tailors and Cleaners, a Safeway store.[46] Hagstrom Food Store turned first into a pool hall, and then a used furniture store before being razed to the ground. Spellman Clothiers went from a pawnshop to a beauty salon to a vacant storefront. The Siddha Meditation Ashram eventually moved into what had been the Stanford Hotel. Star Bethel Missionary Baptist Church took over the Bank of America building. The Gateway Theater was demolished for a parking lot.[47] In 1972, the original location of Hinky Dinks—what became Trader Vic's—at 6500 San Pablo closed; the site declined into a weedy lot. In a 1979 report, the *North Oakland Neighborhood Commercial Revitalization Project Market Analysis,* the street was described as a "generally deteriorated strip commercial" with "not well-kept small stores."[48]

The continuing saga of Safeway epitomizes Oakland's neighborhood commercial decline. In 1943, there were 82 Safeway stores in the city, all of them small, all situated on neighborhood commercial streets. Like a drug store, movie theater, and hardware store, Safeway stores were mainstays of their shopping districts. By 1969, the number of stores had dwindled to 21, many of them the large type premiered in the late 1950s and early 1960s, and set in isolated shopping centers. Those years, the supermarket share of the retail food market jumped from 35 to 70 percent, powered by a trend toward fewer and bigger stores. The large supermarket had seceded from the streetcar commercial street, taken some retail types with it, and left the remaining businesses with greatly reduced traffic and sales volume.

As time went on, it became apparent that Safeway's mid-sized flatland stores were not valued by the company. In January of 1978, a protest was held at the Safeway store at 807 27th Street in West Oakland. Shoppers claimed it was small and unclean, that the poorly stocked shelves sold inferior products to those found in larger stores in the hills or suburbs. J. Terese Burton, of the Neighbors United for Action, commented: "We feel that since this Safeway is in a black neighborhood, that should not have any bearing on the quality of merchandise or service."[49] Remarkably, only two months later, black activists were fighting not for the improvement of another older Safeway store but for its very survival. The 15,000-square-foot Safeway at 490 40th Street, just off Telegraph Avenue, was slated to close. Paul Cobb, director of OCCUR, bemoaned the terrible impact the closing would have on the area: "They used us until they used us up, and now they're leaving."[50] Safeway countered that there were 12 remaining stores in Oakland and a large Marina-style store nearby at 2900 Broadway. To make matters worse, not long afterward, the poorly stocked store on 27th Street in West Oakland was terminated.

Between 1978 and 1984, amid a turn to even larger stores with higher profit margins, Safeway shut down more than 600 stores in inner-city neighborhoods across the country.[51] Average store size rose to 36,000 square feet. Safeway explained its actions for leaving the inner city: the lower purchasing power of the poor, a fear of crime and store shrinkage, the unavailability of large sites, and lack of financing. Across the Oakland flatlands, every Safeway closed, the buildings turning into auto parts stores, Walgreens Drug Stores, a bank, a print and supply warehouse, a Grocery Outlet, and some vacant buildings and empty lots. In an era of black political rule at the mayor and city manager's offices, Oakland's black neighborhoods were abandoned by a business headquartered in Oakland.

Poor flatland residents without a car were forced to shop at mom-and-pop stores where they paid prices much higher than in suburban super-markets and had limited access to healthy food.[52] "It's a vicious cycle come full turn," remarked Lois Salisbury of Public Advocates. "Decades ago the supermarkets moved into these neighborhoods and ran the smaller markets out by underselling them. Now they're pulling out."[53] The num-ber of grocery stores in West Oakland declined from 137 in 1960 to 22 in 1980, alongside a concurrent rise in the number of liquor stores.[54] There were no longer any supermarkets.[55] The term food desert became a part of the urban lingo. It was defined as a situation where the transportation constraints of carless residents combine with a dearth of supermarkets to force residents to pay inflated prices for inferior and unhealthy foods at small markets and convenience stores.[56]

The trend at Safeway and other larger supermarket chains to aban-don minority neighborhoods did not let up.[57] By 1996, the average new Safeway store size shot up to 55,000 square feet and the giant retailer was moving its corporate offices to the Centrepoint Office Park in suburban Pleasanton, a location chosen because Safeway claimed that most of its employees lived out there. A year later, asserting it was losing $1 million a year on the Oakland flagship store, Safeway shuttered the Marina-style Safeway at 29th and Broadway. Into the 2000s, Oakland was left with but six Safeway supermarkets, all of them in the whiter and more affluent hill sections of town. Besides the store closures and headquarters reloca-tion, Safeway did not serve Oakland well. Compared to department stores, newspapers, or some large corporations, the massive corporation played a minor role in either philanthropy or planning for urban development.

OVERREACH AT JACK LONDON SQUARE

The first piece of East Bay waterfront to be abandoned and reconceived for commercial purposes was the original stretch alongside downtown. By midcentury, it consisted of several decrepit wharves and warehouses, some struggling lumberyards, and a few recent restaurants: the Oakland Sea Grotto, the Bow and Bell, and the Sea Wolf. On May 1, 1951, the Oakland Board of Port Commissioners christened the four blocks at the foot of Broadway where the restaurants were located "Jack London Square," in honor of the writer who had sowed his wild oats in that exact area half a century earlier.[58] Across the bay, San Francisco's Fisherman's Wharf had grown from a few fish and seafood stalls to a budding tourist zone. Couldn't dining by the sea launch a similar commercial marvel for Oakland?[59]

Over the next couple of decades, more restaurants set up shop, as did the world's first boat motel, The Boatel Motor Lodge. Jack London Village, a 60,000-square-foot shopping center in the guise of a weathered fishing hamlet, joined the mix in 1975; it was developed by Signature Restaurants Corporation and designed by architect Ted Cushman. The Village specialized in the kinds of tourist goods unavailable elsewhere in the East Bay: soaps, candles, and trinkets; Philippine, Polish, and Latin American imports.

The 1980s brought forth ambitious plans to expand commerce at Jack London Square, and toward the end of the decade the Port of Oakland came up with Jack London's Waterfront. Largely completed in 1989, it consisted of several new retail buildings forming a pedestrian street; an office building that became the new home to the Port of Oakland; an expanded hotel; parking structures; a marketplace intended as a food court; and a comprehensive landscaping plan by Satoru Nishita of Lawrence Halprin & Associates. Jack London's Waterfront was envisioned as a regional shopping center. By this point, Oakland City Center had failed. A city of approximately 400,000 residents had almost none of the national, franchise stores that had located in surrounding suburban shopping centers and were draining Oakland's retail dollars out of the city. These were the kinds of stores that the new Jack London Square project was intended to attract: Williams-Sonoma, Pottery Barn, The Gap, Sharper Image, Eddie Bauer and Ann Taylor.

National retailers never signed on and the regional shopping center was a bust. It failed for several reasons. Parking in its structured garages wasn't free. Although Interstate 880 ran nearby, off-ramps didn't provide easy access. Meanwhile, other recently built shopping centers in the town were not performing. Both the Foothill Square Shopping Center and

Eastmont Mall contended with shoplifting, vandalism, and other crimes. In 1991, Eastmont's primary anchor, J. C. Penney's, departed. Two years later, Mervyn's and Woolworth's closed up shop. The mall went into bankruptcy and foreclosure.[60] As Oakland city councilman Nate Miley noted: "It had built up a reputation of being dangerous."[61] As had been the case with City Center, corporate retailers being courted for Jack London Square were put off by Oakland's crime, souring economics, and minority demographics. Like Safeway, they invested where affluent, white residents resided.

EMERYVILLE 2.0

Another industrial waterfront, just north of Oakland, provided a more successful approach to developing shopping centers. By the mid-1960s, the small city of Emeryville had also fallen on hard times. Its ballpark, amusement park, and racetrack were but memories, the commercial strip on San Pablo Avenue was deteriorating, and industrial plants were closing. Its crime and poverty rates were similar to adjacent areas of Oakland. Ten years later, however, the results of an ambitious 1966 *General Plan* began to bear fruit.

Like Oakland and Berkeley, Emeryville possessed many large, vacant parcels. Unlike those larger cities, Emeryville underwent a remarkable transition from industry to retailing. To lure business, the small city highlighted its low-tax and pro-development posture, and added automobile-friendly zoning.[62] Shortly after 1970, the last of the East Bay's large bay fill operations, agreed upon before BCDC regulations went into effect, resulted in the construction of a hook-shaped peninsula that was soon home to the city's first substantial park, a highrise Holiday Inn Hotel, a couple of office buildings, and 1,250 apartments, which doubled the city's population.[63] Other housing towers and office parks followed: in 1983, the 30-story Pacific Park Plaza marketed condominium units to single adults, working couples without children, and retirees. Later, empty industrial buildings attracted information-age businesses: among them, Cetus, Chiron, and Pixar Animation.

Shopping centers would epitomize resurgent Emeryville, and over 30 years the small city became a laboratory for their post-mall evolution. In 1975, architect Robert Clark, working for Consolidated Equity Company of Beverly Hills, converted the Paraffine warehouses (once producing paint products and roofing materials) into the Emery Bay Public Market. Consolidated Equity's model was the Farmer's Market in Los Angeles: historic buildings featuring stalls selling fresh food and mom-and-pop eateries, and yet providing plenty of parking. At Emery Bay, the formula was altered to focus on ethnic self-service restaurants—Italian, Indian, Creole, German, and English—and shops selling produce, seafood, wine, bread, and pastries. The market stands as a link between the short-lived 1960s attempts, at Foothill Square and the MB Center, to offer East Bay residents an array of international foods and the post-1990 epoch where scores of storefront streets and shopping centers alike offer foods from around the globe.

Soon after the Emery Bay Public Market's founding, its manager, Joseph D'Alessio, made a prescient statement about the city's potential: "Emeryville is still geographically a manageable piece of property—it can be transformed in a way that larger places can't...because of its size, its problems can be realistically dealt with."[64] He neglected to add that there were few people and neighborhood groups to object to bold plans.

The next step came in 1988, when developer David Martin carved out a 160,000-square-foot center with 25 stores—Powell Street Plaza. It was the first regional shopping center built between Hayward and Richmond since Oakland's Eastmont Mall debuted two decades earlier. Furthermore, it was a regional shopping center of a different flavor. Instead of the enclosed mall model, anchored by a couple of department stores and scores of small outlets, Powell Street Plaza featured an open-air lineup of mid- and large-sized stores, a few of which were of the new category killer variety, like Circuit City Electronic Goods and Rainbow Records. Category killer stores featured, at competitive prices, a large selection within a focused line of merchandise, and because such stores required a large population base to generate customers, they sought out urban locations.[65]

Emeryville was a perfect site, close to the Maze, the East Bay's busiest freeway juncture: indeed, the eighth busiest in the nation, with more than 250,000 cars per day passing by the city.[66] Other commercial developers took notice. In 1992, south of Powell Street Plaza, on the Oakland border, the Catellus Development Corporation unveiled the East Bay Bridge Center—a 50-acre parcel once occupied by the Santa Fe Railroad and the Judson Iron Works. For this larger, 480,000-square-foot enterprise, Catellus attracted more category killer stores (Home Depot, BizMart, and SportMart) as well as other big box stores selling food or general merchandise (K-Mart, Pak n' Save). This lineup introduced another innovation, the power center, where a grouping of three or more category killer or big box stores promised to attract more customers. Likely, this power center was inspired by one of the innovators of the type, the 280 Metro Center in Colma, south of San Francisco, which debuted in 1986.

While the East Bay Bridge Center included 360 loft dwellings, signaling a turn toward mixed-use projects, the residences bore minimal connection to the retail boxes across the asphalt. Powell Street Plaza, the East Bay Bridge Center, and an Ikea store (2000) were isolated from each other and wholly oriented to automobile transportation. Lacking adequate streets or sidewalks connecting the stores, customers either walked through asphalt parking lots past boxy blank walls and underneath metal-halide lighting or drove the short distances between them.[67]

In 2002, yet one more major shopping center, Bay Street, opened in Emeryville, and rectified some of the anti-pedestrian qualities of the city's retailing projects. Built on the 20-acre site of a former Sherwin-Williams plant, developer Madison Marquette aimed at a tonier array of shops and an upscale design aesthetic. To do so, they hired shopping center maven and architect Jon Jerde to come up with yet another prototype—the shopping center as mixed-use urban street. An outgrowth of the lifestyle center, where the absence of an anchor department store was made up through enhanced design, landscaping, and store quality, Bay Street was built at the same time as San Jose's Santana Row. Similar to that project, Bay Street's 65 stores (totaling 400,000 square feet) were lined up on a narrow walking street that culminated in a 16-screen movie theater. Behind the stores (which included venerable brands such as Banana Republic, H & M, Talbot's, Ann Taylor, and an Apple store) were structured parking garages accommodating 1,900 cars. Atop them were 400 condominiums; an adjacent 230-room hotel rounded out the huge complex.[68] Despite its name, Bay Street didn't resemble older urban shopping streets. Given its attention to crafting an isolated pedestrian environment, Bay Street harkened back to the shopping centers of the 1950s, like Gruen's Bay-Fair. Granted, the project added residences and a hotel to the mix. But although Bay Street, atop a former Ohlone shellmound, was wedged in a narrow corridor between rail yards and the freeway, no real attempt was made to link it to older shopping centers. Customers drove in, did their business, and drove out—what amounts to a fling with urbanity.

Emeryville remains the inner East Bay's shopping hub. Whereas Oakland generated less than one-sixth of its budget from sales taxes, Emeryville's sales taxes made up a third of its budget. The tiny city was far less dependent upon property tax revenues than its large neighbor.[69] Seeking to imitate Emeryville's success, Oakland developed a few shopping centers along Interstate 880. In 1995, a Super Kmart was built at 4000 Alameda Avenue. It closed in 2003, and was replaced a year later by a Home Depot. At the site of the boarded-up CalPak cannery #37 at 1071 29th Avenue, the Fruitvale Station Shopping Center debuted in 1997, containing a supermarket and 16 smaller businesses. Finally, the 23-acre Hegenberger Gateway Shopping Center opened in 2005. It included Oakland's first In-N-Out Burger and WalMart store.[70] If Emeryville shopping embraced the automobile age, warts and all, Oakland's decidedly mixed shopping center experience reflected the city's reluctance to transition to the vast, isolated, and parking-filled commercial footprints of the suburban age. Ironically, this seemingly backward stance prepared it well for another shopping trend—the revival of the streetcar retail strip.

IMMIGRANTS TO THE RESCUE

In 1965, the Immigration and Nationality Act phased out the quota system on national origins that had been in place since 1921, and affirmed family connections as the basis for permanent admission to the United States. It stimulated the greatest immigration wave in the nation's history, with over 60 million arrivals by the 2010s. The majority came from Asia and Latin America. In Oakland, from 1970 to 2010, the Asian-origin population rose from 4.8 to 16.8 percent of the whole and the Latino population grew from 6.7 to 25.4 percent. Not since the earlier black migration had Oakland's demography changed so conclusively.

The immigrants landed in a postindustrial economy where unionized, blue-collar work was giving way to low-paying manual labor or service employment: cleaning, gardening, and construction; restaurants and fast food outlets; delivery; garment sweatshops. Many opened businesses, often targeted to people from their country of origin. Chinatown was one of the first beneficiaries.

Chinatown had formed after the 1906 Earthquake and Fire when a large number of Chinese Americans relocated from San Francisco to the area east of Broadway reaching from 8th Street to the waterfront. At the time, some white residents were incensed at the changes, one evicted man saying: "I have nothing against Chinamen as a race, but I believe that it is a great injustice for white people to be made to vacate their homes for them."[71] Like other minorities, Chinese Americans suffered from rampant discrimination in housing and employment. Job discrimination was prevalent in mechanical trades: boilermakers, electrical workers, ironworkers, sheet-metal workers, plumbers.[72] It took until the postwar years for residential clusters to develop outside Chinatown: one, just east of Lake Merritt, became known as China Hill.

Throughout, Chinatown remained the heart and soul of the community. In the 1920s, there were 43 Chinese-owned businesses there. By the late 1940s, as a result of the wartime boom, that number had jumped to over 200 enterprises: grocery stores, restaurants, herbalists, barber shops, and stores selling lottery tickets. The population had risen to 5,500, making it the third largest Chinatown in the state: following San Francisco and Los Angeles; and ahead of Sacramento and Stockton.[73] Those gains were followed by setbacks. Business wasn't what it had been during the war. Then, in the mid-1950s, the residential part of Chinatown below 7th Street was demolished by construction for the Eastshore Freeway. More dwellings were lost to 1960s construction projects for BART's Lake Merritt Station, the Oakland Museum, and Laney College; and four blocks adjacent to Broadway were cleared for urban renewal.[74] By 1970, the population of Chinatown had shrunk to less than 2,000.[75]

Fueled by immigration, Chinatown grew once more. The first significant addition to the district was the 14-story Sun Yat Sen House, built in 1974 and extending Chinatown's western boundary to Broadway. Situated on the site of the defunct Simon's Store between 8th and 9th Streets, the tower included three underground floors of parking, plentiful commercial space, and 320 condominiums. Nearby, the Silver Dragon Restaurant, founded in 1956, expanded to a much larger site at 835 Webster Street, a three-story building with Chinese ornamental features designed by architect Henry Chang, and including a banquet hall for 700 persons.[76] By the mid-1980s, the number of restaurants and shops had doubled from the prior decade, and Trans-Pacific Centre, a six-story mixed use building, opened on one of the redevelopment blocks at 10th Street and Broadway.[77] In 1993, the even larger Pacific Renaissance Plaza added 200 condominiums and 50 retail spaces. By this time, Chinatown boasted hundreds of businesses, encompassed more than 12 square blocks, and had become one of Oakland's most energetic commercial areas.

Chinatown was never wholly Chinese. A Manilatown once existed within it along 11th Street. The Japanese-Buddhist Nishi Hongwanji Church was built at 825 Jackson Street, and anchored the city's small *Nihonmachi* (Japantown) until the Second World War. Nearby, the Wanto Grocery at 401 8th Street was made famous by a photograph taken by Dorothea Lange. It showed the façade of the store where the words "Fruits and Vegetables" and "Wanto Co." were inscribed in the glass. Two new and larger signs were plastered atop: I AM AN AMERICAN, put up by the owner, Tatsuro Masuda, following the attack on Pearl Harbor; and SOLD, White & Pollard, placed atop the façade after the Masudas were forced to sell. Lange took the photograph on March 13, 1942. On April 30, all of Oakland's Japanese Americans were ordered to report for removal, and were given a week to comply. Most were taken to the Tanforan Assembly Center in San Mateo County, before relocation to internment camps for the duration of the war. The Japanese Americans lost their homes, businesses, and, for several years, their freedom. After the war, few traces, besides the Buddhist Temple, remained of the old Japanese subdistrict.

By the late 1980s, Southeast Asians were crowding into Chinatown and, following Chinese geographic trajectories, many moved east of the lake to China Hill, Clinton Park, and San Antonio. Mexicans had traditionally had a small business district downtown, along 6th, 7th, and 8th Streets, east of Broadway. Displaced by the Eastshore Freeway and the Acorn urban redevelopment, they too relocated east across the breadth of the Fruitvale and Melrose Districts. Salvadoreans, Guatemalans, and Puerto Ricans moved to emerging Mexican neighborhoods in East Oakland, while Koreans, Arabs, Eritreans, and Ethiopians settled across North Oakland. Wherever they ended up, immigrants revitalized neighborhoods, renting apartments, buying and fixing up homes, and establishing commercial enterprises that provided work to their communities.[78] Sometimes, ethnic groups specialized in commercial lines: Japanese import stores; Korean bars and barbeque joints; Yemeni and Palestinian liquor stores and produce markets; Chinese laundries and dry cleaners; Vietnamese nail salons; Cambodian donut shops.[79]

East 14th Street transformed in character and changed its name. In 1996, the City of Oakland christened it International Boulevard, reflecting the multicultural qualities of a street where the Saigon Market was located nearby the Tijuana Restaurant. The 2000 US Census revealed that 26.6 percent of all Oaklanders were foreign-born, and their presence was most evident along the 100-block artery. Oakland reflected California's role as a primary port of entry for post-1975 immigration. While still a corridor passing through poor neighborhoods, stretches of International boasted scores of small shops and restaurants, offering foods, media, music, and other products from the homeland. Most employed recent immigrants. It was characteristic of such businesses to have more self-employed workers than employees, a phenomenon that accelerated their economic mobility beyond the opportunities they may have found in the general labor market.[80]

Over 20,000 people of East Asian origin settled in the vicinity of Clinton Park.[81] Commerce followed. On streets long stricken with boarded-up storefronts, immigrant businesses set up shop to serve growing residential communities. In 1994, responding to crowding in Chinatown and the opportunities beckoning east of the lake, Paul Wong opened the Sun Hop Fat grocery store on E. 12th Street. He even went as far as to put up a sign reading "New Chinatown," banking on the association with the thriving Chinatown downtown. Similar to the linkage between San Francisco's Chinatown and its Clement Street offshoot, Clinton Park became a colony of Oakland Chinatown due to its cheaper rents and bus route along E. 14th Street linking the two districts.[82] Shortly after, assisted by Councilman John Russo, a Merchants Association was organized; the area's name was now advertised as "Eastlake" in order to ameliorate complaints on the part of Mexican, Vietnamese, and Cambodian merchants that the name "New Chinatown" wasn't inclusive enough. A regional Vietnamese magazine, *MO*, relocated to the district, and the Sun Sang Market, that had earlier burned, reopened.[83] Other Asian markets and a dense mix of Chinese and mainly Vietnamese restaurants endowed the neighborhood with a distinctive character. By 2004, a $2 million streetscape redesign, consisting of enhanced sidewalks, bulb-outs, and date palm plantings, was led by the East Bay Asian Local Development Corporation and the Eastlake Merchants Association.[84]

Further out along E. 14th Street, Mexican immigrants poured into the Fruitvale District, which along with San Antonio was the fastest-growing part of the Oakland in the 1980s.[85] The neighborhood had a Latino presence going back to the 1960s, when restaurants like the Chichen at 4719 E. 14th Street were gathering spots into the late night. As the community grew, racist practices paralleled what had been happening to blacks, and Mexican Americans, with the aid of the Black Panthers, founded groups like Chicano Revolutionary Party to combat police brutality and provide food and education programs to poorer residents.

Ongoing immigration from Mexico spawned a host of spontaneous food-vending practices new to Oakland. In 1984, the first taco truck—Mi Grullense—opened on E. 14th near Fruitvale, followed a year later by the El Guadalajara truck.[86] By 1986, as more Mexican-oriented businesses were just getting established, Jesus and Socorro Campos opened a small market, and a couple of years later the Otaez Restaurant, soon a fixture in the Fruitvale. The first Mexican American representative to the Oakland City Council, Ignacio De La Fuente, was elected in 1992, and worked to bring more businesses to it—helping broker deals for the Fruitvale Station shopping center and the Fruitvale Transit Village. In fact, the latter effort transformed the city's understanding of the land surrounding its BART stations.

Responding to overcrowding at its parking lots, in 1991 BART was planning to erect a large parking structure. Arabella Martinez and the Spanish-Speaking Unity Council objected to the utilitarian structure, fearing it would further isolate BART from the neighborhood. With help of architectural interns from the University of California at Berkeley, the Unity Council came up with an idea for a parking structure alongside

Figure 36. Mi Grullense taco truck. International Boulevard and 30th Avenue; Fruitvale Medical Building in background. Photo by Mitchell Schwarzer, 2020.

other services and housing—the genesis of the Transit Village, a mixed-use complex organized around a mass transit hub. Within a year, the plan had evolved to include a shopping/eating plaza, and had won the backing of Mayor Elihu Harris, BART director Michael Bernick, and a $470,000 grant from US transportation secretary Federico Pena. Completed in 2004, the $100 million Fruitvale Transit Village offered BART riders a choice upon leaving the station. They could walk to a parking garage or they could peruse the Village's plaza, where a walkway led to the dense commerce of International Boulevard. The first phase consisted of a four-story building with 47 affordable housing units, a senior center, a day care center, medical clinic, branch library, and a mix of stores and restaurants.[87] It was one of the first transit villages built in the United States.

By the turn of the millennium, over a hundred taco trucks peppered the arteries of the Fruitvale and greater East Oakland, taking up under-utilized lots along International and Foothill Boulevards, giving energy to avenues long afflicted with commercial blight. Brick-and-mortar operations thrived as well. As a case in point, Juvenal Chavez, who immigrated to America when he was 24 years old, came up with a strategy of opening Mexican-oriented supermarkets in Northern California where large grocery stores were few and far between and where the Mexican population was at least a third of the whole. In 2007, in recognition of those factors in the Fruitvale, he opened a 32,000-square-foot Mi Pueblo Food Center at 1630 High Street, a former Albertson's/Lucky store. Amid bold Fiestaware colors, Mi Pueblo specialized in the kinds of products one couldn't find at Safeway: handmade tortillas, Nopal con Espinas, chile amarillo fresco.[88]

Koreatown, along Telegraph Avenue north of downtown, grew differently. A large population of nearby Korean residents did not exist, as Korean Americans had dispersed across the Bay Area. Instead, the Korean-oriented strip emerged out of business decisions reflecting social needs. Drawn by the cheap rents, the Korean Community Center of the East Bay bought a defunct mini-mall at 44th Street in 1977, brought in several Korean businesses, and in 1989, renamed it Koryo Village Center.[89] Koreans from outlying areas flocked to the new center. In 1995, on the other end of the arising Koreatown, Alex Hahn got several Korean businesses off the ground on the 2600 block of the avenue, which blossomed further in 1997 when Pusan Plaza, a Korean supermarket, opened.[90] Hahn, journalist Kathleen Richards writes, "set his sights on Oakland as the perfect location for a Koreatown. Using Los Angeles's thriving Koreatown as a model, he decided San Jose was too big and San Francisco didn't have a large enough Korean population. Telegraph, he reasoned, was centrally located, close to transportation, and had ample parking."[91] In a metropolis knitted together by freeway travel, an ethnic shopping district could draw customers from across the Bay Area.

FROM ALTERNATIVE TO UPMARKET

From the late 1950s through the 1970s, Berkeley (alongside districts in San Francisco like the Haight-Ashbury) pioneered businesses catering to an alternative set of patrons—intellectuals, artists, beatniks, political radicals, hippies, and proto-foodies. A European-inspired assemblage of stores first coalesced on Telegraph Avenue a few blocks south of the University of California campus: Cody's, Shakespeare's, and Moe's bookstores; Caffe Mediterraneum; the Print Mint. Next, a challenge was made to the supermarket paradigm of cans, packages, and freezer cases. In 1968, Mary and Tom Fujimoto, whose Southern California farm was lost during the Japanese Internment, changed their Monterey Market on Hopkins Street to an all-produce store, offering East Bay residents a wide and healthy array of fresh fruits and vegetables; nine years later, the Berkeley Bowl reprised that recipe in a converted bowling alley south of downtown.

Food-obsessed Berkeley soon germinated a district. In 1966, north of downtown, Alfred Peet set up his eponymous store at 2124 Vine Street, selling fresh, dark-roasted beans and serving drip coffee in distinctly un-American fashion—strong. Peet's was followed a year later by the Cheeseboard, which went on to become one of the finest emporia of coagulated dairy proteins in the world. The year 1972 brought Chez Panisse, complete with mismatched silverware and chairs, red-and-white-checked oilcloth tablecloths, and handwritten menus.[92] Helmed by Alice Waters, the restaurant cooked French recipes with California ingredients. Over time the emphasis on local fixings wove into the diverse demographics of Bay Area residents and took Chez Panisse in an inventive, hybrid direction that would become identified as "California Cuisine."[93] Based on its small-batch coffee, sliced sashimi, chocolate truffles, and Tomales Bay bluepoint oysters, the stretch of North Shattuck became known as the Gourmet Ghetto.

Reporter Liza Bercovici noticed something different about the new haute cuisine coming out of Berkeley: "These restaurants and food stores are being manned by former graduate students and professionals who are finding 'la cuisine' more satisfying than white-collar work."[94] To take her idea further, it appears that a holistic culture around food and drink, book knowledge and manual skill, international exposure and local appreciation, was coming about. Growing, preparing, shopping, and eating and drinking became the diverse yet interrelated elements of new way of approaching life, career, and community. In one respect, folks in Berkeley were discovering something that had long been part of French, Italian, and other world regions. Yet in California this encounter with old world traditions was a rejoinder to America's industrialized food and eating sys-

Figure 37. Rockridge Café. College Avenue at Lawton Street. Photo by Mitchell Schwarzer, 2020.

tem. The dialectic would proceed amid the rediscovery of cities as a place of lifestyle reinvention.

As in political and environmental matters, Oakland followed Berkeley's lead. The year 1973 marked a beginning. On Grand Avenue, Marshall Curatolo founded Walden Pond Books, while the Coffee Mill opened across the street the following year. On College Avenue, Bill Chung opened the Rockridge Café with 13 seats, trailed by the Edible Complex, a couple of blocks north and a couple of years later. In 1974, Mama's Royal Café debuted at 4012 Broadway in a former Chinese restaurant. The new establishments challenged Oakland's timeworn commercial culture, increasing both quality and selection. In 1976, Michael Wild opened Bay Wolf at 3853 Piedmont Avenue in a former brown-shingle house, while Peet's launched its third outlet up the street. Restaurant reviewer R. B. Read wrote: "The Bay Wolf brings to Oakland—and to us all—a bright example of the Now genre of young-people place...of which Chez Panisse has emerged as

Numero Uno...a serious and inventive intelligence focused where it matters—on the kitchen."[95] Later, reporter Gerald Nachman penned a requiem: "Oakland, the last refuge of meat-and-potatoes cuisine, is being threatened on every front by Berkeley's gourmet mafia and would-be San Franciscans who feel uneasy out of arm's reach of a kiwi."[96]

In Rockridge, resistance to fast-food outlets converged with neighborhood planning. In 1974, the Rockridge Community Council blocked a Taco Bell from opening on College Avenue.[97] They later fought to downzone the district, imposing a three-story height limit on College Avenue (or 45 feet) and requiring, in residential areas, conditional use permits for two units on a lot, and an outright prohibition of more than two units. Their aim was to preserve and protect the residential area from the kind of change that came with apartment development by the lake and keep the commercial district full of unique, specialty shops and free of auto-related uses.[98] The Rockridge rebellion would spread to other parts of the city, as neighborhoods were downzoned closer to their existing scale, and industrial zones and overlays were eliminated in flatland areas like West Oakland. As parcels were no longer viewed as potential development sites, speculation decreased. Neighborhood stability and investment in the existing building stock increased.

By 1987, Nimby (not in my back yard) sentiments had mushroomed in Rockridge and come into conflict with yuppie (young urban professional) lifestyle improvements. Developer Tom Wilson and architect Peter Wilson proposed Market Hall for the corner of College and Keith Avenues, the former site of the Chimes Theater and vacant for 15 years.[99] While there was little opposition to the European-style food market, residents worried that the three-story building, though allowed by zoning, would be out of character with the neighborhood, and opposed 40 apartment units proposed above the market.[100] The three-story Market Hall was built without the apartments.

Between the late 1970s and 2000, relatively inexpensive alternative businesses transitioned into pricier upmarket enterprises across Berkeley. But aside from College and Piedmont Avenues, Oakland didn't go upscale until the twenty-first century, when trend-setters were launched across town: Thai and vegan restaurants, East Coast pizza and bagels, bicycles and vinyl records, yoga studios and tattoo parlors, cannabis dispensaries and farmers' markets. In 1994, Farmer Joe's had opened a small produce store in the Laurel District and, in 2006, launched a second, larger branch at the Dimond District site that had been one of Oakland's inaugural neighborhood shopping centers. Demonstrating the heightened importance of upmarket food businesses in revitalizing a shopping district, Farmer Joe's Dimond arrival attracted a cluster of bakeries, cafes, restaurants, and boutiques like Oaklandish, once a public arts project focused on Oakland history that had transitioned into a retail operation specializing in Oakland-centric goods.

Temescal soared to destination-neighborhood stardom. It had long been an Italian neighborhood, yet by 1987, most of its standby businesses—Buon Gusto Bakery, the Union Meat Market, Lucca Deli—had closed.[101] Describing Temescal, a reporter predicted changes: "Along Telegraph you won't see many chic new yuppie businesses that tend to dominate the gentrified neighboring Rockridge area. Eventually more of that will come."[102] A little over a decade later, more of that did come—Doña Tomás, Blue Bottle Coffee, Pizzaiolo, Bakesale Betty—with yuppies yielding to hipsters. Temescal was dubbed by the *Wall Street Journal* in 2007 as the new Gourmet Ghetto, "one with a funkier edge than the idealistic epicurean enclave in North Berkeley."[103] Chefs, sommeliers, fromagers, bakers, and coffee roasters became celebrities, rock stars of a new urban scene preoccupied with the artisanal aspects of food and drink. Restaurants "can anchor a neighborhood and turn blight into bright," noted food writer Sarah Henry.[104] They were agents of revitalization or, depending on one's view of their small portions and big prices, gentrification. In affluent communities, households ate out all the time, and a restaurant meal was often an evening's main event. No wonder streets peppered with farm-to-table restaurants, third-wave coffee shops, or bakeries featuring Heuft ovens and grains milled on-site became the stuff of real estate fliers. "Good restaurants," real estate professor Hugh Kelly tells us, "bring in people from outside of the neighborhood. And this creates an identity that increases the value of property—you don't see that with drugstores, banks and nail salons."[105]

Suburban sprawl and its freeways and shopping centers had once sounded the death knell for many older streetcar strips, the kind that provided basic goods and services to nearby residents. Major arterials along with smaller strips lost their drugstores, banks, and most everything else. Several local shopping centers failed, for many of the same reasons. Customers could drive to safer, larger, better stocked, and more up-to-date stores elsewhere. Poorer black districts suffered the most.

The storefront strips that came back were those in neighborhoods repopulated by alternatives, immigrants, and later yuppies and hipsters, those that augmented basic offerings with specialty goods—either ethnic-specific or geared to the shifting tastes of the town's more privileged residents. In wealthier parts of town, they operated as catalysts for dramatically appreciating home values. In transitioning neighborhoods, they facilitated gentrification. There's a lesson here. The forces impacting neighborhood appeal had contracted. Once a large set of urban functions—employment opportunities, schools, recreational and civic attractions, transportation linkages as well as commerce—played key roles; once basic goods and services were all required of a commercial area. Now, upmarket food businesses and trendy retail/services assumed heightened importance with respect to neighborhood desirability. Public spaces were yielding to privatized ones, and the consumption patterns of a growing class of affluent residents were raising the stakes for Oakland's commercial corridors and their environs.

Coda

From 1900 to 1975, ambition, disruption, and homogeneity marked Oakland's urban development. A couple dozen years of decline with hardly any development at all followed. Toward the turn of the millennium, a different type of building revival began, a scaling back of the size of projects and their unsettling impacts alongside a promotion of heterogeneity in the form of both mixed uses and populations.

Earlier, government planners and private builders alike strove for single-use districts: monumental, if sterile, civic complexes; automobile-only roads; single-family residential districts and shopping centers unencumbered by uses other than commerce. That emphasis produced some architectural successes but more urbanistic failures. Mixed-use then became a development mantra, the notion that an assemblage of functions would better ensure vital municipal spaces. Likewise, the town started to value its polyglot population; in 2017, 27 percent of Oaklanders were foreign born. From being dominated by a conservative, white elite, from fostering racist policies across the range of urban affairs, Oakland shifted leftward politically, adopting policies for social justice, inclusive employment, restrained policing, and housing equity.

A similar, dialectical arc is apparent in most of the functions and typologies analyzed in this book. A century ago, streetcars gave way to automobiles and overassertive road networks, only to provoke an eventual reaction led by pedestrians and bicyclists. Streets were widened and historic buildings routinely demolished, before catalyzing movements to preserve significant buildings and districts. After decades of headlong industrialization and then crippling deindustrialization, an artisanal boom in coffee, beer, and other culinary delights recalled a onetime abundance of food-based businesses. Latter-day commercial successes have taken place less in suburban-style shopping centers, many of which failed, and more on the town's older storefront streets. Most housing production once occurred, suburban style, on huge tracts of unbuilt land, but has been succeeded by dense infill within commercial and industrial districts. Earlier, parks were seen through the lens of human recreation; subsequently, environmentalists put energy toward daylighting creeks, nurturing native plant communities, and safeguarding the bay from landfill operations. Oakland had long swung for the fences, pioneering a container port, helping assemble the West's largest heavy rail transit system, acquiring major league franchises, creating architecturally noted cultural venues, but then failing to launch a downtown shopping mall or initiate an airport or tourist waterfront on the scale of San Francisco's. The town subsequently learned to content itself with fewer home runs, and that meant fewer strikeouts.

Oakland is no longer the region's second city, and no longer sees itself in perpetual competition with San Francisco. San Jose now holds the largest population, and the territory between it and Palo Alto, Silicon Valley, is not just the economic engine of Northern California but the nation's center for information age research and development. Sometime after the new millennium, the Bay Area transitioned into a *Weltstadt*, a world city, premised on high technology and featuring astounding capital accumulation and global dominance on the part of its large corporations.

The boom following the Great Recession was more convulsive than in any other part of the country. Silicon Valley had less room for new office parks and subdivisions. It enveloped its surroundings, including San Francisco.[1] And when San Francisco gets rocked, some of the loosened pieces inevitably roll toward Oakland. After April 1906, a tsunami of San Franciscans had rolled eastward. A little over a century later, a tidal wave of migrants priced out of San Francisco hit Oakland's shores.

Architectural offices (Gensler), tech firms (Square, Kapor Capital), non-profits (the Sierra Club), and media companies (*Sunset Magazine*) moved their offices to downtown in order to take advantage of its comparatively lower commercial rents. Larger outfits like Blue Shield of California and Pacific Gas & Electric followed. Office towers were planned, financed, and built. Renters and homebuyers, frustrated by San Francisco prices, scoured Oakland streets, appreciative of lower numbers. The city eased zoning requirements and removed parking requirements.[2] Developers took notice. Downtown, residential skyscrapers—reaching 40 stories—rose along Broadway and its surrounding streets. Midrise projects sprouted along the former auto district on upper Broadway, across North Oakland, and in formerly depressed West Oakland.

The crime rate dropped. Budget deficits eased. Streets began to bustle. The town was on the upswing. But almost as quickly, the good news was interpreted by some activists as bad news. There were too many projects. Too many affluent newcomers. The sweet spot most cities crave, an influx of dollars and people that betters most aspects of urban life, that lifts up longtime poorer residents alongside the wealthy, was souring. How long would less prosperous folks be around to appreciate the improvements? Rising rents and housing prices were blowing them out of town.[3]

While almost all of the new housing was built on vacant or underutilized commercial land, the boom had a ripple effect on most residential districts. They became more desirable and less affordable. Not only increased demand was to blame for escalating price points. Oakland was paying for the sins of the Bay Area and coastal California that had been accumulating for decades. Appreciative of their quality of life and seeking to minimize threats to it, well-off cities and neighborhoods had reduced residential densities and limited new development. The California Environmental Quality Act became a tool to delay, litigate, and, ultimately, defeat or shrink the scope of new projects. The housing deficit kept on growing—estimated by the state's Department of Housing and Community Development at 3.5 million units in 2019.

Unlike earlier booms, new supply was targeted just to the upper end of the market—for reasons that include higher land and construction costs, longer project timelines, and increased impact fees. In the 1920s, single-family homes had been built for the working, middle, and upper classes.

Postwar, private builders narrowed their scope to the middle classes, but the government built low-rent housing for the poor. In the 2010s, aside from a varying fraction of units mandated as affordable, generally 5 to 12 percent, new housing was out of reach even for the middle class.[4] By 2020, the average rent for an apartment (old or new) was over $2,700, while the median value for a home was well over $700,000—a surge of over 250 percent during the first two decades of the century. Oakland was now one of the most expensive cities in the nation.

Millennials, driven by lower prices, as compared to the west side of the bay, flooded in. Lower- and middle-class Oaklanders, who for years had suffered from the disinvestment attendant to decentralization and suburbanization, experienced an influx of higher-wage earners that loosened their grip on their home and city. Black Oakland was hardest hit. Its populace had been grievously affected by Oakland's late twentieth-century downturn. Yet aside from homeowners who were able to cash out and move elsewhere, the twenty-first-century upturn wasn't turning out all that much better. On average, significantly lower incomes and wealth made black Oaklanders who wanted to remain in their city more vulnerable to escalating housing costs than whites, and most black neighborhoods were now experiencing a white influx.[5] While the city's black population had been decreasing for decades, a product of reduced in-migration and increased out-migration to suburbs and other cities and states, the housing crisis sped demographic falloff.

Some poorer Oaklanders became Nimbys. A condo project, bicycle lanes, a yoga studio, signaled improvement, but not for them. They began opposing new development. At least one individual took to arson, burning five market-rate buildings under construction: downtown, in West Oakland, and in Emeryville. Others occupied empty units—held out of the market for speculation—or held rent strikes where escalating rents were out of line with substandard dwelling conditions. Those with the least means ended up on the streets, panhandling in front of stores and at stoplights on major avenues, erecting tent clusters under freeway overpasses, along industrial corridors, and atop city parks. From 2017 to 2019, the homeless population in the city grew by an astonishing 47 percent.

Development was lopsided, highly privatized, and weak on public projects, heavy on market-rate commercial and residential construction, light on parks, schools, civic buildings, transportation infrastructure, and affordable housing. Two sports teams left town: in 2019, the Golden State Warriors to San Francisco; in 2020, the Oakland Raiders to Las Vegas. If Oakland was getting wealthier, it was still finding it hard to compete with locales that were home to the superrich.

In early 2020, the Covid-19 pandemic struck. Shelter-in-place orders were implemented. Hospitalizations and death counts rose, especially among essential workers of color. Offices, schools, and mass transit emptied. Those who could worked online from home. Outdoor space was used more than ever. Some restaurants built parklets; others closed for good. Early amid the viral tragedy, George Floyd's murder by Minneapolis cops provoked uprisings across America. Oakland, home to the nation's most convulsive Occupy Movement, from 2011 to 2012, as well as the site of large protests over the police murders of Oscar Grant and so many others, was once more rocked by outrage against police brutality. Violent crime also rose alarmingly in the epochal year.

Urban development is an optimistic endeavor and some real estate projects were postponed or cancelled. Overall, the economic picture has been uneven. Rents have plunged. Bidding wars are still the norm for home purchases. Unemployment numbers have shot upward. So too has the stock market. Given the dynamic and unpredictable nature of urban change, it is uncertain where the town's roller coaster ride of city formation will lead next. Still, there are some clues. Oakland was charting new paths before the pandemic, managing a development boom while attempting to come to terms with its highly disruptive legacy of outsized ambition amid appalling inequality. These paths indicate a turn from short-sighted action toward long-range reflection. In California, in Oakland, where promise of a better future has birthed so many dreams, yet so much folly, we all benefit from digging hella deeper into the place we call home.

Acknowledgments

I am grateful to the libraries and archives that made my research possible: the Alameda Free Library; the Association for Bay Area Governments Library, San Francisco; the Berkeley Public Library; the California State Library, Sacramento; the Caltrans Transportation Library, Sacramento; the City of Oakland's Housing Authority, Parks & Recreation Department, and Planning and Building Department; the East Bay Regional Park District Archives; the Hayward Public Library; the Lakeshore Homeowners Association Archives; the Mechanics Institute Library, San Francisco; the Metropolitan Transportation Commission Library, San Francisco; the Oakland Museum; the San Francisco Public Library; the San Leandro Community Library; the University of California, Berkeley libraries—Bancroft, Business, Doe, Environmental Design, Institute for Governmental Studies, Institute for Transportation Studies, Northern Regional Library Facility. Most of all, I want to thank the Oakland Public Library and its various sites, from the African American Museum and Library to the branch libraries, and especially Dorothy Lazard and the Oakland History Center.

My ideas have been augmented and sharpened through conversations and exchanges with many individuals, among them: Andrew Alden,

Samantha Bempong, Kevin Blackburn, Daniel Brownstein, Robert Bruegmann, Christopher Buckley, Michael Corbett, Ignacio De La Fuente, Dennis Evanosky, Deborah Frieden, Morten Jensen, Jerry Kent, Betty Marvin, Brenda Montano, Woodruff Minor, Robert Ogilvie, Eric Porter, John Raeside, Chris Rhomberg, John Russo, Libby Schaaf, Naomi Schiff, Fred Setterberg, John Sutter, Joe Tuman, John Wilkins, and Bill Wong. Mabel Wilson and Richard Walker were extremely generous with their time reading the manuscript and more than helpful with their critiques and insights.

The California College of the Arts helped make this book possible through granting me a recent year-long sabbatical. And needless to say, this book would not be possible if not for the University of California Press, without Editorial Director Kim Robinson's support and stewardship, and without the contributions of other project managers, designers, and copyeditors at the press (and associated consultants) like Summer Farah, Teresa Iafolla, Jessica Moll, David Peattie, and Paul Tyler.

I lastly want to thank my wife, Marjorie Schwarzer, who walked most of the streets, stairwalks, and trails of Oakland with me, listened to my evolving theories, and gave me invaluable feedback on the manuscript.

Notes

INTRODUCTION

1. See the discussion of Stein's Oakland visit in Matt Werner, *Oakland in Popular Memory: Interviews with Twelve Cutting-Edge Artists from Oakland and Beyond* (Berkeley: Thought, 2012), 122–24; and Roy Morris Jr., *Gertrude Stein Has Arrived: The Homecoming of a Legend* (Baltimore: Johns Hopkins University Press, 2019), 199–220.

2. My first encounter with Oakland's historiography was Beth Bagwell's *Oakland: The Story of a City* (Novato, CA: Presidio Press, 1982). A few academic histories stand out to me for their depth of analysis on the town's economic and social matters: Marilynn Johnson, *The Second Gold Rush: Oakland and the East Bay in World War II* (Berkeley: University of California Press, 1993); Robert Self, *American Babylon: Race and the Struggle for Postwar Oakland* (Princeton, NJ: Princeton University Press, 1993); and Chris Rhomberg, *No There There: Race, Class and Political Community in Oakland* (Berkeley: University of California Press, 2004). A select bibliography of books on Oakland follows the text.

3. Since the publication of my *Zoomscape: Architecture in Motion and Media* (New York: Princeton Architectural Press, 2004), transportation infrastructure has been central to my urban understanding. My earliest inspiration for writing this book may have been Mel Scott's *The San Francisco Bay Area: A Metropolis in Perspective* (Berkeley: University of California Press, 1985), which offered a wide-angled lens on the transport-led evolution of the Bay Area.

4. On the issue of race and urbanism I have benefited from a growing literature, from Thomas Sugrue's *The Origins of the Urban Crisis: Race and Inequality in Postwar Detroit* (Princeton, NJ: Princeton University Press, 2005) to Keeanga-Yamahtta Taylor's *Race for Profit: How Banks and the Real Estate Industry Undermined Black Homeownership* (Chapel Hill: University of North Carolina Press, 2019).

CHAPTER 1. STREETCAR STRATIFICATION

1. Greg Hise, "Homebuilding and Industrial Decentralization in Los Angeles and the Roots of the Postwar Urban Region," *Journal of Urban History* 19.2 (February 1995): 97.

2. John Beatty Dykstra, "A History of the Physical Development of the City of Oakland: The Formative Years, 1850–1930" (master's thesis, University of California, 1967), 146.

3. For a discussion of these phenomena in a larger city like Chicago, see Ann Durkin Keating, *Chicagoland: City and Suburbs in the Railroad Age* (Chicago: University of Chicago Press, 2005).

4. On the invention of the streetcar, see William Middleton, *Frank Julian Sprague: Electrical Inventor & Engineer* (Bloomington: Indiana University Press, 2009).

5. Peter Muller, "Stages in the Spatial Evolution of the American Metropolis," in *The Geography of Urban Transportation*, ed. Susan Hanson and Genevieve Giuliano, 3rd ed. (New York: Guilford Press, 2004), 67–69. For a description of the impact of streetcars on urban land, see Scott Bottles, *Los Angeles and the Automobile: The Making of the Modern City* (Berkeley: University of California Press, 1991), 6–12.

6. James Vance Jr., *Geography and Urban Evolution in the San Francisco Bay Area* (Berkeley: Institute of Governmental Studies, 1964), 50.

7. William Middleton, *The Time of the Trolley* (Milwaukee: Kalmbach Books, 1967), 66–77.

8. Mark S. Foster, *From Streetcar to Superhighway: American City Planning and Urban Transportation 1900–1940* (Philadelphia: Temple University Press, 1981), 14.

9. *The Independent* 54.1, January 2, 1902, 1498–99.

10. Sam Bass Warner, *Streetcar Suburbs: The Process of Growth in Boston 1870–1900*, 2nd ed. (Cambridge, MA: Harvard University Press, 1979), 153, 159.

11. Zane Miller and Patricia Melvin, *The Urbanization of Modern America: A Brief History*, 2nd ed. (New York: Harcourt Brace Jovanovich, 1987), 72.

12. Bill Stokes, "Eight Miles an Hour," *Oakland Tribune*, May 1, 1952.

13. Ruth Woodman, *The Story of Pacific Coast Borax Co.* (Los Angeles: Ward Ritchie Press, 1951), 25, 44.

14. Peter Collins, *Concrete: The Vision of a New Architecture* (New York: Horizon Press, 1959), 62.

15. Amelia Sue Marshall, *East Bay Hills: A Brief History* (Charleston, SC: History Press, 2017), 112.

16. George Hildebrand, *Borax Pioneer: Francis Marion Smith* (San Diego: Howell-North Books, 1982), 154–55.

17. On the early history of interurbans, see George Hilton and John Due, *The Electric Interurban Railways in America* (Stanford: Stanford University Press, 1960), 8–44.

18. Stephen Goddard, *Getting There: The Epic Struggle between Road and Rail in the American Century* (Chicago: University of Chicago Press, 1994), 75–77.

19. Hildebrand, *Borax Pioneer*, 170.

20. Judith Goldsmith, "Losing Track," *East Bay Express*, July 22, 1983, 5–7.

21. "Interurban Car Service Urged," *Oakland Post Enquirer*, August 30, 1920.

22. Ray Raineri, "The Interurban Electric Railway—Southern Pacific's Spectacular Red Trains," *Piedmonter/Oakland Bulletin*, February 11, 1987.

23. Brian Cronk, "The Sacramento Northern Railway," *The Montclarion*, May 15, 1984. On the train's impact in North Oakland, see Jeff Norman, *Temescal Legacies: Narratives of Change from a North Oakland Neighborhood* (Oakland: Shared Ground, 2006), 37–61.

24. Mel Scott, *The San Francisco Bay Area: A Metropolis in Perspective* (Berkeley: University of California Press, 1959), 123.

25. Russell Lowry, *History of the First National Bank of Oakland, California* (Oakland: First National Bank, 1908).

26. The 1850 grid ended at 14th Street; above that line, streets were platted somewhat haphazardly with reference to the two diagonal avenues, San Pablo and Telegraph.

27. Fred Reichman, "A Salute to the Broadway Building," *Oakland Heritage Alliance News* 16 (Summer 1996): 6–7.

28. Betsy Yost and Phil Bellman, "Oakland's Remarkable Flatirons," *Oakland Heritage Alliance News* 13 (Summer 1993): 1–4.

29. "The Oakland City Hall," *The Brickbuilder* 23 (July 1914): 159–62.

30. Gary Knecht, "Oakland's Wholesale Produce Market," *Oakland Heritage Alliance News* 7 (Spring 1987): 2, 6.

31. On the history of wholesale and retail market halls in the United States, see Helen Tangires, *Public Markets* (New York: W. W. Norton, 2008), 25–29.

32. Periodically, a new building and site were essential to increasing a store's scale of operations, freshening its marketing allure, and keeping it within proximity of downtown's changing center of gravity.

33. "Special Rites Today Mark Kahn's 75th Anniversary," *Oakland Tribune*, March 3, 1954.

34. An addition in 1923 brought the square footage to 385,000.

35. N. A. Lafler, "Trend of Growth of Oakland's Business Center," *Oakland Tribune*, May 20, 1917.

36. "Store Marks City Progress," *San Francisco Chronicle*, August 8, 1929.

37. Acquired by the Army in 1942, the hotel served as a hospital until 1962. Sold to the city, it was converted into senior housing 14 years later.

38. In 1981, the hotel closed after going into bankruptcy; the building was converted into offices.

39. On annexation efforts of the period, see Charles Wollenberg, *Golden Gate Metropolis: Perspectives on Bay Area History* (Berkeley: Institute of Governmental Studies, 1985), 276–77; and Gray Brechin, *Imperial San Francisco: Urban Power, Earthly Ruin* (Berkeley: University of California Press, 1999), 270.

40. Homer Hoyt, *The Structure and Growth of Residential Areas in American Cities* (Washington, DC: US Government Printing Office, 1939), 116–18.

41. On this phenomenon, see Robert E. Dickinson, *City Region and Regionalism: A Geographical Contribution to Human Ecology* (London: Trubner, 1947), 96–97.

42. J. F. Dunn, "Apartment Houses," *Architect & Engineer* 58.3 (September 1919): 43, 81.

43. Oakland Cultural Heritage Survey, *Lakeside Apartment District*, vol. 12 (Oakland: Oakland City Planning Department, 1985), 6.

44. Beth Bagwell, *Oakland: The Story of a City*, 2nd ed. (Oakland: Oakland Heritage Alliance, 2012), 208.

45. Sam Whiting, "Gold Coast Redux," *San Francisco Chronicle*, June 23, 2002.

46. John Gothberg, "The Local Influence of J. R. Knowland's Oakland Tribune," *Journalism Quarterly* 45 (September 1968): 492.

47. Paris Williams, "The California Hotel History Project," *Oakland Heritage Alliance News* 12 (Summer 1992): 1, 3.

48. "Dimond Has a Well-Developed Business Center," *Oakland Tribune*, October 28, 1921.

49. Zura Bells, "Grand-Lake Seen as Second Michigan Avenue," *Oakland Tribune*, January 24, 1930.

50. Dallas Walker Smythe, "An Economic History of Local and Interurban Transportation in the East Bay Cities with Particular Reference to the Properties Developed by F. M. Smith" (PhD diss., University of California, 1937), 69–86.

51. Dykstra, "History of the Physical Development of the City of Oakland," 172.

52. Smythe, "Economic History of Local and Interurban Transportation," 130–31.

53. Bill Stokes, "Eight Miles an Hour," *Oakland Tribune*, May 1, 1952.

54. Albert Norman, "One Hundred Years of Subdivisions," *Oakland Tribune*, May 1, 1952.

55. John Reps, *The Making of Urban America: A History of City Planning in the United States* (Princeton, NJ: Princeton University Press, 1965), 361.

56. Vernon Sappers, *Key System Streetcars: Transit, Real Estate and the Growth of the East Bay* (Wilton, CA: Signature Press, 2007), 39, 52–53.

57. "Key Route Inn, Finest Hostelry in Oakland Opened This Afternoon," *Oakland Herald*, May 7, 1907.

58. Ralph Craib, "Key Trains Halt, Rail Era Ends Here," *Oakland Tribune*, April 20, 1958.

59. Stanley Mallach, "The Origins of the Decline of Urban Mass Transportation in the United States, 1890–1930," *Urbanism Past and Present* 8 (Summer 1979): 1–2.

60. Smythe, "Economic History of Local and Interurban Transportation," 70, 146, 600, 605; Hildebrand, *Borax Pioneer*, 166.

61. Robert Peter Giles, "Oakland Leads Nation in Percentage of House Owners," *San Francisco Chronicle*, November 13, 1920. On nationwide trends in this period, see Robert Barrows, "Beyond the Tenement: Patterns of American Urban Housing, 1870–1930," *Journal of Urban History* 9.4 (August 1983): 402.

62. Michael Doucet and John Weaver, "Material Culture and the North American House: The Era of the Common Man, 1870–1920," *Journal of American History* 12.3 (December 1985): 566.

63. Marta Gutman, *A City for Children: Women, Architecture, and the Charitable Landscapes of Oakland, 1850–1950* (Chicago: University of Chicago Press, 2014), 18.

64. Paul Groth, "Workers'-Cottage and Minimal-Bungalow Districts in Oakland and Berkeley, 1870–1945," *Urban Morphology* 8.1 (2004): 15–19.

65. Groth, "Workers'-Cottage and Minimal-Bungalow Districts," 20–23.

66. Henry Lafler, "Oakland Makes New Record in Building Boom," *San Francisco Chronicle*, June 2, 1922.

67. Clay Lancaster, *The American Bungalow, 1880–1930* (New York: Abbeville, 1985), 119–21.

68. "Desirable Section Shows Heavy Growth," *Oakland Enquirer*, September 2, 1911; "Big Building Program at 64th Avenue and E. 14th St.," *Oakland Tribune*, November 30, 1924.

69. Ann Keating, *Building Chicago: Suburban Developers and the Creation of a Divided Metropolis* (Columbus: Ohio State University Press, 1988), 68–70.

70. Advertisement, *San Francisco Chronicle*, May 11, 1912.

71. Carolyn Loeb, *Entrepreneurial Vernacular: Developer Subdivisions in the 1920s* (Baltimore: Johns Hopkins University Press, 2001), 112.

72. "Rockridge Tract to Be Open Today," *San Francisco Chronicle*, May 26, 1912.

73. Robert Fishman, *Bourgeois Utopias: The Rise and Fall of Suburbia* (New York: Basic Books, 1987), 141–42.

74. Mary Corbin Sies, "Paradise Retained: An Analysis of Persistence in Planned, Exclusive Suburbs, 1880–1980," *Planning Perspectives* 12 (April 1997): 163.

75. On the practice in California, see Scott Kurashige, *The Shifting Grounds of Race: Black and Japanese Americans in the Making of Multiethnic Los Angeles* (Princeton, NJ: Princeton University Press, 2008), 13–90.

76. Michael Jones-Correa, "The Origin and Diffusion of Racial Restrictive Covenants," *Political Science Quarterly* 115.4 (Winter 2000–2001): 559.

77. Chris Rhomberg, *No There There: Race, Class and Political Community in Oakland* (Berkeley: University of California Press, 2004), 81–82.

78. Robert Self, *American Babylon: Race and the Struggle for Postwar Oakland* (Princeton, NJ: Princeton University Press, 2003), 164–65.

79. Dean Yabuki, "Trestle Glen Transformed: Lakeshore Highlands Marks 75 Years," *Oakland Heritage Alliance News* 11.4 (Spring 1992): 2–4.

80. Mansel Blackford, *The Lost Dream: Businessmen & City Planning on the Pacific Coast, 1890–1920* (Columbus: Ohio State University Press, 1993), 1–2.

81. Adam Rome, "Building on the Land: Toward an Environmental History of Residential Development in American Cities and Suburbs, 1870–1990," *Journal of Urban History* 20.3 (May 1994): 414.

82. Carl Kramer, "The Evolution of the Residential Land Subdivision Process in Louisville, 1772–2008," *Register of the Kentucky Historical Society* 107.1 (Winter 2009): 47–54.

83. Marc Weiss, *The Rise of the Community Builders: The American Real Estate Industry and Urban Land Planning* (New York: Columbia University Press, 1987), 109–10.

84. Richard Yearwood, "Land Subdivision and Development: American Attitudes on Land Subdivision and Its Controls," *American Journal of Economics and Sociology* 29.2 (April 1970): 122–23.

85. Mel Scott, *American City Planning since 1890* (Berkeley: University of California Press, 1969), 168–69.

86. Weiss, *Rise of the Community Builders*, 86, 150.

87. City Planning Commission, *Twelve Years of Zoning Administration, Oakland, California* (Oakland, 1947), 4, 33–34.

88. "New Zoning and Map Laws Are Passed," *Oakland Tribune*, February 6, 1935.

89. On the concept of filtering, see Stuart Rosenthal, "Are Private Markets and Filtering a Viable Source of Low-Income Housing?" *American Economic Review* 104 (February 2014): 687–706.

CHAPTER 2. INDUSTRIAL POWERHOUSE

1. Christiane Craseman Collins, *Werner Hegemann and the Search for Universal Urbanism* (New York: W. W. Norton, 2005), 110.

2. Werner Hegemann, *Report on a City Plan for the Municipalities of Oakland and Berkeley* (Oakland and Berkeley: Municipal Governments, 1915), 25–41.

3. Hegemann, *Report on a City Plan*, 75–76.

4. Oakland Chamber of Commerce, *Oakland, California: The Coming Commercial City of the Pacific Coast, the City in Which Three Transcontinental Railroads Terminate* (Oakland, 1908), n.p.

5. Hegemann, *Report on a City Plan*, 72.

6. John Borchert, "American Metropolitan Evolution," *Geographical Review* 57.3 (July 1967): 303.

7. Ralph Fisher, "Development of the Port of Oakland and the Oakland Municipal Airport—The Intelligent Capitalization of Natural Advantages," *Oakland Tribune Yearbook* (1929): 191.

8. *The San Francisco–Oakland Metropolitan Area: An Industrial Study* (1932), 30.

9. *Information Concerning the Terminus of the Railroad System of the Pacific Coast* (Oakland: Daily Transcript Book, 1871), 1–7; *Southern Pacific's First Century* (San Francisco: Southern Pacific Company, 1955), 17.

10. On the impact of the railroad on Oakland, see William Deverell, *Railroad Crossing: Californians and the Railroad, 1850–1910* (Berkeley: University of California Press, 1994), 23–27.

11. The Oakland mole ceased operations in 1958 with the disappearance of the last ferries and was demolished in 1966. "Progress Claims the Mole," *San Francisco Chronicle*, May 5, 1965.

12. While originally on the waterfront, the station found itself a mile inland by the 1930s due to bay fill. Amtrak abandoned it in 1994. Jeff Swenerton, "Will the Town Save One of the Most Beautiful (and Neglected) Landmarks?," *Alameda Magazine* 12 (January–February 2013): 53.

13. Paul Groth, "A Profile of West Oakland in 1952," in *Sights and Sounds: Essays in Celebration of West Oakland*, ed. Suzanne Stewart and Mary Praetzellis (Oakland: CalTrans, 1997), 213–17.

14. Joel Snyder, *History Property Survey Report, Volume 4, Part 7C: Southern Pacific Railroad Property* (Sacramento: CalTrans, August 1990), 1–4.

15. Oakland tended to handle cheaper bulk cargoes of grain, lumber, and other agricultural products. Tim Reagan, "The Restless Shore," *East Bay Express*, April 25, 1986, 8.

16. Matthew Morse Booker, *Down by the Bay: San Francisco's History between the Tides* (Berkeley: University of California Press, 2013), 40–41.

17. The opening of the Posey Tube in 1928 allowed for the demolition of the swinging drawbridges at Webster and Harrison Streets. Board of Port Commissioners, *Port Progress: 125 Years of Oakland Waterfront Growth* (Oakland, 1977), 9–12.

18. Board of Port Commissioners, *The Port of Oakland: Sixty Years: A Chronicle of Progress* (Oakland Public Affairs Department, Port of Oakland, 1987), 3. In 1906, the California Supreme Court settled the waterfront dispute in favor of the

city and against the Southern Pacific railroad; the stranglehold ended by 1910. See Andrew Rolle, *California: A History*, 2nd ed. (New York: Crowell, 1969), 337–46.

19. Woodruff Minor, *Pacific Gateway: An Illustrated History of the Port of Oakland* (Oakland: Port of Oakland, 2000), 14.

20. On the shifting fortunes of ports, see Guido Weigend, "Some Elements in the Study of Port Geography," *Geographical Review* 48 (April 1958): 185–200; Hans Harms, *Changes on the Waterfront—Transforming Harbor Areas* (Berkeley: Institute of Urban and Regional Development, 2008), 9.

21. Paul Sorensen, *Development of Containerization at the Port of Oakland, 1962–1974* (Oakland: Port of Oakland, 1975), 2.

22. "Tonnage Tripled Here since '27," *Oakland Tribune*, February 12, 1937; Board of Port Commissioners, *Port of Oakland: Sea-Air-Rail-Truck Center on San Francisco Bay* (Oakland, 1954), 14–16; "Port Activity Boosted Here," *Oakland Tribune*, July 5, 1951.

23. Paul Rhode, *The Evolution of California Manufacturing* (San Francisco: Public Policy Institute of California, 2001), 11–13.

24. On the processing of raw materials, see Gerald Nash, "Stages of California's Economic Growth, 1870–1970; An Interpretation," *California Historical Quarterly* 51 (Winter 1972): 317–19.

25. Oakland Tribune, *Alameda County, The Eden of the Pacific; the Flower Garden of California* (Oakland: Press of the Oakland Tribune, 1898), 150–63.

26. Edgar Hinkel and William McCann, eds., *Oakland: 1852–1938: Some Phases of the Social, Political and Economic History of Oakland, California* (Oakland: Oakland Public Library, 1939), 880. In 1929, Carnation Milk Products Company purchased Albers Brothers.

27. Arlington Otis, "Big Canning Industry Grows on Firm Foundation," *San Francisco Chronicle*, February 29, 1928.

28. E. T. H. Bunse, *Oakland Industries* (Oakland: Works Project Administration, 1939), 42–45; Beth Bagwell, *Oakland: The Story of a City*, 2nd ed. (Oakland: Oakland Heritage Alliance, 2012), 71–72.

29. Sue Shephard, *Pickled, Potted and Canned: How the Art and Science of Food Preserving Changed the World* (New York: Simon & Schuster Paperbacks, 2000), 246–47. See also Glenn Cunningham, "The Tin Can Industry in California," *Yearbook of the Association of Pacific Coast Geographers* 15 (1953): 11–16.

30. Justo Zavalla, *The Canning of Fruits and Vegetables* (New York: John Wiley & Sons, 1916), 3–9.

31. California Division of Public Employment Offices and Benefit Payments, *Employment Trends in California's Canning and Preserving Industry, 1950–1961* (Sacramento: California Department of Employment, 1962), 4–7.

32. On the evolution of the California canning industry, see Isidor Jacobs, "The Rise and Progress of the Canning Industry in California," in *A History of the Can-*

ning Industry by Its Most Prominent Men, ed. Arthur Judge (Baltimore: Canning Trade, 1914), 30–39.

33. Hans Christian Palmer, "Italian Immigration and the Development of California Agriculture" (PhD diss., University of California, 1965), 243.

34. Dean Witter & Co., *California Packing Corporation: A Study of Impressive Progress* (San Francisco: James H. Berry Co., 1950), 9.

35. Michelle Locke, "Canning History: Del Monte Still Canning after Long, Rocky Past," *Oakland Tribune*, September 20, 1991.

36. On the history of the Del Monte brand, see William Braznell, *California's Finest: The History of the Del Monte Corporation and the Del Monte Brand* (San Francisco: Del Monte Corporation, 1982), 28–30.

37. Dean Witter & Co., *California Packing Corporation*, 13.

38. *Del Monte Shield* 18 (September–October 1966).

39. Martin Brown and Peter Philips, "The Evolution of Labor Market Structure: The California Canning Industry," *Industrial and Labor Relations Review* 38.3 (1985): 395.

40. Ward Hill, "Del Monte Plant 35: A History of Emeryville's Most Fruitful Industry," *Journal of the Emeryville Historical Society* 3 (June 1992): 6–7.

41. Michael Grieg, "Fruit Cocktail Inventor Dies," *San Francisco Chronicle*, March 15, 1968.

42. Richard Walker, "Oakland Rising: The Industrialization of Alameda County" (2005), www.foundsf.org/index.php?title=Oakland_Rising:_The_Indus trialization_of_Alameda_County.

43. "New Building of Del Monte Food Co. Ready," *Oakland Tribune*, June 12, 1927.

44. Alan Olmstead and Paul Rhode, "The Evolution of California Agriculture, 1850–2000," in *California Agriculture: Dimensions and Issues* (Berkeley: University of California Giannini Foundation of Agricultural Economics, 2003), 7–9.

45. Beth Bagwell, "Inside Those Brick Walls," *The Montclarion*, February 14, 1979.

46. A. C. Griewank, "California Cotton Mills," *Architect & Engineer* 51.2 (1917): 17–74.

47. "Eastbay Destined to Be Textile Center," *Oakland Outlook* 3 (August 1924): 1.

48. Romaine Myers, "Pacific Coast Electro-Chemical Possibilities," *Journal of Electricity Power and Gas* 34 (March 27, 1915): 243–45.

49. Frank Kester, "Oakland Soap Firm Ships to Foreign Lands," *Oakland Tribune*, November 12, 1936.

50. On the equation of California's exploitation of natural resources with industrial later development, see Richard A. Walker, "California's Golden Road to Riches: Natural Resources and Regional Capitalism, 1848–1940," *Annals of the Association of American Geographers* 91.1 (March 2001): 167–99.

51. "Oakland Expects to Be Factory Center of the Pacific Coast," *San Francisco Chronicle*, December 8, 1917.

52. Willard Tim Chow, "The Context of Redevelopment in Oakland," *Urban Geography* 2.1 (1981): 46–48.

53. John Kenneth Turner, "105 National Concerns Choose Locations Here," *Oakland Post*, November 16, 1925.

54. Bunse, *Oakland Industries*, 62–63, 102.

55. On the role of the rail network in the formation of the manufacturing belt, see David Meyer, "Midwestern Industrialization and the American Manufacturing Belt in the Nineteenth Century," *Journal of Economic History* 49.4 (December 1989): 931–37.

56. On precision machining, see Simon Winchester, *The Perfectionists: How Precision Engineers Created the Modern World* (New York: Harper Collins, 2018).

57. Michael French, *U.S. Economic History since 1945* (Manchester: Manchester University Press, 1997), 55–60.

58. H. J. Brunnier, "Pacific Coast Shredded Wheat Factory," *Architect & Engineer* 47 (1916): 81.

59. On the evolution of factory design, see Betsy Hunter Bradley, *The Works: The Industrial Architecture of the United States* (Oxford: Oxford University Press, 1999).

60. Thomas O'Boyle, *At Any Cost: Jack Welch, General Electric and the Pursuit of Profit* (New York: Vintage, 1988), 25.

61. Leigh George, "The Sun's Only Rival: General Electric's Mazda Trademark and the Marketing of Electric Light," *Design Issues* 19.1 (Winter 2003): 63–66.

62. Clotilde Grunsky, "New Industrial Records on the Pacific Coast," *Journal of Electricity* 39 (November 15, 1917): 440–42.

63. "Oakland Lamp Plant," www.lamptech.co.uk/Documents/Factory%20-%2 0US%20-%20Oakland.htm.

64. Oakland City Planning Commission, "Staff Report on 5441 International Boulevard" (Oakland, 2012); Earl Ennis, "KGO on the Pacific: General Electric's Pacific Broadcasting Unit," *The Wireless Age* 11 (1923): 23.

65. John Schneider, "The History of KGO, Oakland, California," www.theradiohistorian.org/kgo.htm.

66. "Victor People Building Plant in Bay District," *San Francisco Chronicle*, December 25, 1923; "Victor Co. Start on New Plant," *Oakland Tribune*, October 7, 1923.

67. See William Nicholson, "Victor in the West: the Oakland Processing Plant," www.gracyk.com/oakland.shtml.

68. Billy Malone, *The Early History of the Magnavox Company* (Magnavox Government and Industrial Electronics Company, 1986), 94–97.

69. Alan Douglas, *Radio Manufacturers of the 1920s*, vol. 2 (Chandler, AZ: Sonoran, 1989), 133, 135.

70. "Merit of Oakland Firm's Product Wins For It Tremendous Success," *San Francisco Chronicle*, January 16, 1917.

71. James Cortada, *Before the Computer: IBM, NCR, Burroughs, and Remington Rand and the Industry They Created, 1865–1956* (Princeton, NJ: Princeton University Press, 1993), 171.

72. "Marchant Company Reorganizes," *Office Appliances: The Magazine of Office Equipment* 36 (September 1922): 45.

73. See Timothy Sturgeon, "How Silicon Valley Came to Be," in *Understanding Silicon Valley: Anatomy of an Entrepreneurial Region*, ed. Martin Kenney (Stanford: Stanford University Press, 2000).

74. Alfred D. Chandler, *The Visible Hand: The Managerial Revolution in American Business* (Cambridge, MA: Belknap Press of Harvard University Press, 1977), 376.

75. William Walters, "American Naval Shipbuilding: 1890–1989," *Geographical Review* 90.3 (July 2000): 419.

76. Hayes Hunter, "Oakland Shipbuilding Makes Strides," *Oakland Tribune*, May 8, 1952.

77. Frank Mulgrew, "Moore Shipbuilding Company," *Pacific Marine Review* 18 (July 1921): 468.

78. Wilbur Hall, "Ship Craftsmen of the Pacific," *Sunset* 39 (September 1917): 11–13.

79. Robin Bartoo and Harlan Barr, "A Brief History of Fifth Avenue Point," *Oakland Heritage Alliance News* 18.4 (Summer–Fall 1998): 2.

80. On Bethlehem Steel's shipbuilding, see Kenneth Warren, *Bethlehem Steel: Builder and Arsenal of America* (Pittsburgh: University of Pittsburgh Press, 2008), 102–15, 132–49.

81. Bill Brand, "The Place That Time Forgot," *Alameda Times-Star*, June 8, 1974; Woodruff Minor, "A Maritime History of Alameda: The Shipbuilders (Part 7)," *Alameda Journal*, February 3–9, 1989.

82. "Union Construction Company Holds High Place in Shipbuilding World," *San Francisco Chronicle*, January 15, 1919.

83. Bunse, *Oakland Industries*, 77–78.

84. Operations ceased altogether in 1948.

85. "Union Construction Company Enters Building Field for Structural Steel," *Architect & Engineer* 65 (June 1921): 111–13.

86. "Moore Shipbuilding Company Enters Construction Field," *Architect & Engineer* 64 (January 1921): 116–18.

87. E. T. Grether, *The Steel and Steel-Using Industries of California: Prewar Developments, Wartime Adjustments and Long-Run Outlook* (Sacramento: California State Printing Office, 1946), 19–20.

88. Ibid., 93.

89. Walter Isard and William Capron, "The Future Locational Pattern of Iron

and Steel Production in the United States," *Journal of Political Economy* 57.2 (April 1949): 119–20, 127.

90. Walter Isard, "Some Locational Factors in the Iron and Steel Industry since the Early Nineteenth Century," *Journal of Political Economy* 56.3 (June 1948): 215.

91. Hinkel and McCann, *Oakland: 1852–1938*, 830; "Steel from Battleship Used to Form Backbone of Great Aid to Public," *San Francisco Chronicle*, December 14, 1922.

92. Roger Lotchin, *Fortress California, 1910–1961: From Warfare to Welfare* (Oxford: Oxford University Press, 1992), 60–62.

93. Frederic Chapin Lane, *Ships for Victory: A History of Shipbuilding under the U.S. Maritime Commission in WWII* (Baltimore: Johns Hopkins University Press, 2001), 32–39.

94. "Bethlehem's Alameda Yard," *Pacific Maritime Review* 40 (August 1943): 66–71.

95. "Ship Building Boom Starts," *Oakland Tribune*, March 19, 1939; "$593,400,000 in Contracts Awarded Bay Shipyards," *Oakland Tribune*, January 9, 1941.

96. James Houlihan, *Western Shipbuilders in World War II* (Oakland: Shipbuilding Review, 1945), 23, 31.

97. "Army Prepares to Occupy Land," *Oakland Tribune*, January 17, 1941; "Huge U.S. Army Base Praised for War Job," *Oakland Post-Enquirer*, December 1945, annual issue; "Army Returns Port Area to Oakland," *Oakland Tribune*, April 2, 1946.

98. "Navy Selects Oakland Site for Supply Base," *Oakland Post-Enquirer*, December 29, 1937; "Oakland Naval Supply Center Is Twelve Years Old," *Oakland Tribune*, December 14, 1953; "Bases Battled Mud to Win the War," *Oakland Tribune*, December 11, 1966.

99. Abraham Lowenthal, *Global California: Rising to the Cosmopolitan Challenge* (Stanford: Stanford University Press, 2009), 24.

100. Marilynn S. Johnson, *The Second Gold Rush: Oakland and the East Bay in World War II* (Berkeley: University of California Press, 1996), 33–55, 146–48.

101. Stephen Horton, "Moore Shipbuilding Company: Reflections in Steel," *Sea Letter: National Maritime Museum Association* 44 (Fall–Winter 1991): 27. On the concurrent rise of employment for women at Bay Area shipyards, see Deborah Hirshfield, "Women Shipyard Workers in the Second World War," *International History Review* 11.3 (August 1989): 478–85.

102. "Ruling on Negroes' Plea Near," *Oakland Post-Enquirer*, June 5, 1944.

103. See also Cleveland Valrey, *Black Labor and Race: San Francisco Bay Area, World War II* (Church House, 2004), 29–30.

104. Katherine Archibald, *Wartime Shipyard: A Study in Social Disunity* (Berkeley: University of California Press, 1947), 61.

105. Hinkel and McCann, *Oakland: 1852–1938*, 886–87. On the reasons for midwestern dominance of automobile manufacturing, see Neil Hurley, "The Automotive Industry: A Study in Industrial Location," *Land Economics* 35.1 (February 1959): 1–3.

106. "The California Motor Car Company," *Sunset Magazine* 27 (July–December 1911): 599.

107. John Kenneth Turner, "Increase in Automotive Products Here to Clinch Title 'Detroit of West'," *Oakland Post*, November 17, 1925.

108. George Dammann, *Sixty Years of Chevrolet* (Glen Ellyn, IL: Crestline, 1972), 19.

109. Gene Gressley, "Colonialism: A Western Complaint," *Pacific Northwest Quarterly* 54 (January 1963): 2–3.

110. Charles Boas, "Locational Patterns of American Automobile Assembly Plants, 1895–1958," *Economic Geography* 37.3 (July 1961): 219.

111. "Motor Truck Manufacture: A Promising Industry," *Southwest Contractor and Manufacturer* 8 (February 17, 1912): 8.

112. "Auto Factory Builds Car in Eight Minutes," *San Francisco Chronicle*, December 8, 1917.

113. "New Automobile Plants Building near San Francisco," *Motor Age* 42 (July–December 1922): 30.

114. "Oakland Plant Turns Out 500 Autos per Day," *San Francisco Chronicle*, April 8, 1928.

115. Frank Kester, "Oakland Auto Plant Payroll Area's Largest," *Oakland Tribune*, December 4, 1936.

116. Steven Lavoie, "East Bay Once Center of West's Manufacturing of Automobiles," *Oakland Tribune*, June 2, 1996.

117. Leon Pinkson, "Coast Boasts of Big New Auto Plant," *San Francisco Chronicle*, June 10, 1917.

118. "Only as Good as the Man behind It," *Pacific Marine Review* 15 (August 1918): 154.

119. "Ground Broken for Fageol Plant," *Motor West*, June 1, 1917.

120. J. E. Beach, *Peterbilt: Long-Haul Legend* (Minneapolis: MBI, 2008), 16–20.

121. "Durant Plant Is Near Completion," *Motor West* 37 (May 15, 1922): 3, 23.

122. James Flink, *The Automobile Age* (Cambridge, MA: MIT Press, 1988), 106–8.

123. "Way Clear for Aerial Growth," *Oakland Post-Enquirer*, July 8, 1927.

124. Frederick Jones, "The Oakland Municipal Airport," *Architect & Engineer* 103 (November 1930): 61–64.

125. "Experts Laud City Airport as Finest of Any Country," *San Francisco Chronicle*, April 1, 1928. On the airport's early history, see Board of Port Commissioners, *Oakland Municipal Airport* (Oakland: Port of Oakland, 1928), 5–26.

126. Alastair Gordon, *Naked Airport: A Cultural History of the World's Most Revolutionary Structure* (Chicago: University of Chicago Press, 2008), 17.

127. Janet Bednarek, *America's Airports: Airfield Development, 1918–1947* (College Station: Texas A&M University Press, 2001), 41.

128. "California Leads Aviation," *San Francisco Chronicle*, September 26, 1929.

129. "Aviation in California," *The Commonwealth* 5 (October 1, 1929): 287.

130. Bednarek, *America's Airports*, 53–54.

131. Maurer, *Aviation in the U.S. Army, 1919–1939* (Washington, DC: Office of Air Force History, United States Air Force, 1987), 256–60.

132. Camille Allaz, *The History of Air Cargo and Airmail from the 18th Century*, trans. John Skilbeck (London: Christopher Foyle, 2004), 61–63.

133. Earle Soto, "Oakland—An Air Terminal," *Popular Aviation* 2.5 (May 1928): 35–36, 91.

134. Minor, *Pacific Gateway*, 92.

135. "Huge Airport Expansion Asked," *Oakland Tribune*, July 10, 1941.

136. John Walter Wood, *Airports: Some Elements of Design and Future Development* (New York: Coward-McCann, 1940), 130. On the tendency of airports to expand through unguided development, see Paul Barrett, "Cities and Their Airports: Policy Formation, 1926–1952," *Journal of Urban History* 14 (November 1987): 112–37.

137. Geza Szurvoy, *The American Airport* (St. Paul: MBI, 2003), 76, 83–84.

138. Minor, *Pacific Gateway*, 99.

CHAPTER 3. SPACE FOR AUTOMOBILES

1. Quoted in "The Growing Popularity of Automobiles in Oakland," *Oakland Enquirer*, November 7, 1903.

2. Stephen Goddard, *Getting There: The Epic Struggle between Road and Rail in the American Century* (Chicago: University of Chicago Press, 1994), 77.

3. "Survey Shows Rapid Growth of Oakland in Ten Years," *Oakland Tribune*, January 30, 1930.

4. Harland Bartholomew & Associates, *Oakland Master Plan: Transit Facilities and Mass Transportation* (Oakland: City of Oakland, 1947), 12.

5. Wilbur Smith & Associates, *Report on a Proposed Alameda County Highway Master Plan* (San Francisco, 1950), 15.

6. "Road Construction Lags Far behind Car Registration," *Automotive Industries: The Automobile* 46 (February 16, 1922): 427.

7. John Chynoweth Burnham, "The Gasoline Tax and the Automobile Revolution," *Mississippi Valley Historical Review* 48.3 (December 1961): 435–37.

8. Goddard, *Getting There*, 121–23.

9. Sappers, *Key System Streetcars*, 102, 105, 109.

10. Harre Demoro, "How Little Jitneys Bred the Mighty Trolley Killers," *Oakland Tribune*, December 13, 1974.

11. "The First Municipal Motor Bus Line for Street Service," *The American City* 18.6 (June 1918): 538–39.

12. Dykstra, "History of the Physical Development of the City of Oakland," 218–20.

13. Harland Bartholomew & Assoc., *Oakland Master Plan*, 40–43.

14. George Hilton, "The Rise and Fall of Monopolised Transit," in *Urban Transit: The Private Challenge to Public Transportation*, ed. Charles Lane (San Francisco: Pacific Institute for Public Policy Research, 1985), 45.

15. "Key Trackless Trolley Plan Is Broadened," *Oakland Tribune*, November 14, 1945.

16. David St. Clair, *The Motorization of American Cities* (Westport, CT: Praeger, 1986), 75–76.

17. "Streetcars to Bow to Buses," *Oakland Tribune*, May 16, 1946; "Removal of Tracks Approved," *Oakland Post-Enquirer*, March 2, 1949.

18. Stanley Fischler, *Moving Millions: An Inside Look at Mass Transit* (New York: Harper & Row, 1979), 79.

19. Jonathan Kwitny, "The Great Transportation Conspiracy," *This World*, March 1, 1981, 17.

20. St. Clair, *Motorization of American Cities*, 111–14.

21. Harre Demoro, *The Key Route: Transbay Commuting by Train and Ferry* (Glendale, CA: Interurban Press, 1985), 124.

22. "Bus Service Proposed on All Five Lines," *Oakland Tribune*, January 25, 1955.

23. Robert Gallamore and John Meyer, *American Railroads: Decline and Renaissance in the Twentieth Century* (Cambridge, MA: Harvard University Press, 2014), 81–85, 97.

24. Hinkel and McCann, *Oakland: 1852–1938*, 70–71.

25. Peter Norton, *Fighting Traffic: The Dawn of the Motor Age in the American City* (Cambridge, MA: MIT Press, 2008), 140.

26. Norton, *Fighting Traffic*, 75–78.

27. See the discussion in Douglas Harwood, *Effective Utilization of Street Width on Urban Arterials* (Washington, DC: Transportation Research Board, 1990), 14.

28. Christopher Wells, *Car Country: An Environmental History* (Seattle: University of Washington Press, 2012), 99–100.

29. Sam Staley and Adrian Moore, *Mobility First: A New Vision for Transportation in a Globally Competitive Twenty-First Century* (Plymouth, UK: Rowman & Littlefield, 2009), 145. See also Clay McShane, "The Origins and Globalization of Traffic Control Signals," *Journal of Urban History* 25 (March 1999).

30. Eric Klocko, "The Public-Private City: Automobile Parking and the Control

of Urban Space in San Francisco, 1920–1959" (PhD diss., University of California, 2006), 63.

31. Kerry Segrave, *Parking: Cars in America, 1910–1945, A History* (Jefferson, NC: McFarland, 2012), 117.

32. See the discussion in Alice Koch, "Curbstone Goldmine," *The Rotarian* 77 (September 1950): 15.

33. John Jakle and Keith Sculle, *Lots of Parking: Land Use in a Car Culture* (Charlottesville: University of Virginia Press, 2004), 48–51.

34. On the role of such associations in American cities, see Jerry Mitchell, *Business Improvement Districts and the Shape of American Cities* (Albany: State University of New York Press, 2008), 1–30; David Smiley, *Pedestrian Modern: Shopping and American Architecture, 1925–1956* (Minneapolis: University of Minnesota Press, 2013), 97–132.

35. Harland Bartholomew & Associates, *A Report on Off-Street Parking and Traffic Control in the Central Business District and Three Outlying Centers* (Oakland: City Council, 1947), 9.

36. Ibid., 24–39.

37. "Buildings to Be Wrecked for New Downtown Parking Lot," *Oakland Tribune*, December 30, 1958.

38. "Council OKs 1st Off-Street Parking Building," *Oakland Tribune*, June 6, 1958.

39. "Heliport, Parking Building Get Approval," *Oakland Tribune*, January 25, 1961.

40. Bartholomew & Assoc., *Report on Off-Street Parking*, 49.

41. D. Jackson Faustman, *Off-Street Parking Plan, City of Oakland* (Sacramento, 1961), 33.

42. "Planners Reject Lakeside Garage Plan," *Oakland Tribune*, January 23, 1970.

43. Norton, *Fighting Traffic*, 126, 162.

44. Miller McClintock, "How the City Traffic Problem Will Be Solved," *The Automobilist* (May 1927): 5–7.

45. "Street Widening Ordinance Passed," *San Francisco Chronicle*, July 15, 1923; "Twentieth Street Widening to Begin in Late August," *San Francisco Chronicle*, May 29, 1925.

46. "Improving of East 14th St. Approved," *Oakland Tribune*, December 30, 1924.

47. "Streets Are Big Problem, Says Expert," *Oakland Tribune*, February 18, 1924.

48. Harland Bartholomew & Associates, *A Proposed Plan for a System of Major Traffic Highways* (St. Louis, 1927), 21–23, 33.

49. Major Highway and Traffic Committee of One Hundred, *A Major Street Plan for Oakland* (Oakland, 1928).

50. "Wide Streets Urged in Oakland Major Street Plan," *Oakland Tribune*, March 26, 1928.

51. In 1972, a plan to further widen Skyline Boulevard was defeated. "Skyline Building Ban Compromise," *Oakland Tribune*, May 20, 1973.

52. Owen Gutfreund, *Twentieth-Century Sprawl: Highways and the Reshaping of the American Landscape* (Oxford: Oxford University Press, 2004), 78.

53. Jakle and Sculle, *Lots of Parking*, 25.

54. Ben Blow, *California Highways* (San Francisco: H. S. Crocker, 1920), 76.

55. Frank Lortie, "A Monument to Progress: The Posey Tube and the East Bay's Transition to the Age of the Automobile," *California History* 74.4 (Winter 1995): 431.

56. W. C. Names and William Wolfson, "Webster St. Tube," *California Highways and Public Works* (March–April 1962): 9–15.

57. "New Tunnel of Four Lanes Opens Today," *San Francisco Examiner*, December 5, 1937.

58. "Looking Back: Reporter Took Tunnel Road 41 Years Ago," *Oakland Tribune*, October 16, 1977.

59. "Low Level Tunnel Has Car Trouble—Too Many," *Oakland Tribune*, June 29, 1952.

60. Irwin Black and Oris Degenkolb, "The Caldecott Tunnels," *California Highways and Public Works* (July–August 1965): 12–18.

61. Fred Garretson, "Eastbay Dedicates New Tube Tuesday," *Oakland Tribune*, October 4, 1964. Amid ongoing development in Contra Costa County, traffic continued to increase, and a fourth bore was completed in 2013.

62. Harrison Robinson, "How Alameda County Will Gain by the SF-Oakland Bay Bridge," *Oakland Tribune Yearbook* (1934).

63. Karen Trapenberg Frick, *Remaking the San Francisco-Oakland Bay Bridge: A Case of Shadowboxing with Nature* (London: Routledge, 2016), 33–37. On overall planning, see Stephen Mikesell, *A Tale of Two Bridges: The San Francisco-Oakland Bay Bridge of 1936 and 2013* (Reno: University of Nevada Press, 2017), 29–60.

64. Donald McDonald and Ira Nadel, *Bay Bridge: History and Design of a New Icon* (San Francisco: Chronicle Books, 2013), 7, 23.

65. Mikesell, *A Tale of Two Bridges*, 62–66.

66. W. R. Cobb, "Traffic Engineer Reveals Interesting Facts about S.F.-Oakland Bay Bridge," *West Coast Shipper* (October 1948): 16.

67. "Distribution Structure for East Bay Approach," *San Francisco Chronicle*, November 12, 1936.

68. Jack Burroughs, "Omelet of Streets to Honor a Hero," *Oakland Tribune*, August 13, 1950.

69. Harland Bartholomew & Associates, *A Report on Freeways and Major Streets in Oakland, CA* (St. Louis, 1947), 29–35.

70. Frank Levy, Arnold Meltsner, and Aaron Wildavsky, *Urban Outcomes: Schools, Streets & Libraries* (Berkeley: University of California Press, 1974), 115–17, 120.

71. "Street Projects Held Revenue Aid," *Oakland Tribune*, November 3, 1958.

72. "City to Speed West Grand Ave. Widening Project," *Oakland Tribune*, July 7, 1957.

73. Levy, *Urban Outcomes*, 106–7, 130.

74. "Many Streets Torn Up for City Progress," *Oakland Tribune*, June 18, 1951; John Morin, "Major Arterial," *California Highways and Public Works* 34 (July–August 1955): 19.

75. James McCarty and Welton Follett, "Oakland Progress," *California Highways and Public Works* 37 (March–April 1958): 37.

76. "Face Lift to Beautify Lake Arm," *Oakland Tribune*, August 18, 1957.

77. Anastasia Loukaitou-Sideris and Renia Ehrenfeucht, *Sidewalks: Conflict and Negotiation over Public Space* (Cambridge, MA: MIT Press, 2009), 88, 241–42.

78. Nicholas Blomley, *Rights of Passage: Sidewalks and the Regulation of Public Flow* (Abington, UK: Routledge, 2011), 15, 21–22.

79. Robyn Spencer, *The Revolution Has Come: Black Power, Gender, and the Black Panther Party in Oakland* (Durham, NC: Duke University Press, 2016), 11–17.

80. Stephen Shames and Bobby Seale, *Power to the People: The World of the Black Panthers* (New York: Harry N. Abrams, 2016), 23.

81. "Traffic Calming in Berkeley" (Berkeley: City of Berkeley, Transportation Division, May 1998), www.ci.berkeley.ca.us/ContentDisplay.aspx?id=8238.

82. On the resident permit parking phenomenon, see James Andrews, "Don't Park Here: This Street Is for Residents Only," *Planning* 66 (October 2010): 20–23.

83. Christina Cielo, "Civic Sideshows: Communities and Publics in East Oakland" (Berkeley: Institute for the Study of Social Change, 2005), 20–23; Jennifer Tilton, *Dangerous or Endangered?: Race and the Politics of Youth in Urban America* (New York: New York University Press, 2010), 153–58.

84. Sandhya Dirks, "Sideshows: The Birth of Oakland's Hyphy Culture," *KQED News*, August 18, 2015.

85. H. Lavar Pope, "Hyphy Rap Music, Cooptation and Black Fanatics in Oakland, CA (1994–2010)," *Souls* 16.3–4 (2014): 246–47.

86. Traffic Calming Progress Report, *Planning* 75 (November 2009): 32–35.

87. On the related phenomenon of street narrowing, see Samuel Schwartz, *Street Smart: The Rise of Cities and the Fall of Cars* (New York: Public Affairs, 2015), 118–25.

88. Nate Berg, "From Parking to 'Parklets'," *Planning* 76.6 (July 2010): 5.

CHAPTER 4. THE POLITICS OF PARKS

1. Lionel Johnson, "New Industrial Features Being Developed in East Oakland," *Oakland Enquirer*, January 7, 1902.

2. Charles Mulford Robinson, *A Plan for Civic Improvement for the City of Oakland, California* (Oakland: Oakland Enquirer, 1906), 4.

3. Ibid., 6.

4. Terence Young, *Building San Francisco's Parks, 1850–1930* (Baltimore: Johns Hopkins University Press, 2004), 45.

5. Leo Jansen, "Mountain View," *Stone in America* 104 (June 1991): 261; Gaye Lenahan, "Mountain View Cemetery, 1863–1906," *Oakland Heritage Alliance News* 7 (Summer 1987): 2–4.

6. Charles Little, *Greenways for America* (Baltimore: Johns Hopkins University Press, 1990), 9.

7. Jon Peterson, *The Birth of City Planning in the United States, 1840–1917* (Baltimore: Johns Hopkins University Press, 2003), 116.

8. Heath Massey Schenker, *Melodramatic Landscapes: Urban Parks in the Nineteenth Century* (Charlottesville: University of Virginia Press, 2009), 118–28.

9. Galen Cranz, *The Politics of Park Design: A History of Urban Parks in America* (Cambridge, MA: MIT Press, 1987), 26–29.

10. Mel Scott, *American City Planning since 1890* (Berkeley: University of California Press, 1969), 13–16.

11. Howard Huselton, "Kansas City's Parks and Boulevards," *Arts and Progress* 3.1 (November 1911): 387–88; Matthew Gandy, *Concrete & Clay: Reworking Nature in New York City* (Cambridge, MA: MIT Press, 2002), 83–87. See also Catherine McNeur, "Parks, People and Property Values: The Changing Role of Green Spaces in Antebellum Manhattan," *Journal of Planning History* 16 (May 2017): 99.

12. Although majorities voted for the funds, the city's charter required a two-thirds supermajority for passage. "Park Bonds Voted Down," *San Francisco Chronicle*, October 30, 1898.

13. Robinson, *Plan for the Civic Improvement for the City of Oakland*, 12–15.

14. Mayor Frank K. Mott, "Plea for City Beautiful and for Public Parks," *Oakland Enquirer*, January 1, 1907.

15. On the history of Lake Merritt, see Richard Longstreth, "A Short History of Lake Merritt, 1850–1974" (University of California, 1974); Roland de Wolk, "The Jewel of Oakland," *Oakland Tribune*, March 24, 1991.

16. Other bold roadway plans, such as a 1938 idea for a bridge across the middle of the lake connecting 19th Street downtown to East Oakland's E. 18th Street, fortunately never came to fruition. Sandra Sher, "It Took Awhile: Boulevard around Lake Merritt," *The Museum of California* (November–December, 1987), 24.

17. Park Commission, *The Park System of Oakland, California* (Oakland, 1910), 15–52.

18. On Robinson's suggestions for parks in Oakland as well as Mott's successful creation of Lakeside Park, see Scott, *San Francisco Bay Area*, 125–32.

19. "Wildwood Park Plan Approved by Civic Clubs," *San Francisco Examiner*, December 29, 1913.

20. On Oakland park planning, see Richard A. Walker, *The Country in the City: The Greening of the San Francisco Bay Area* (Seattle: University of Washington Press, 2007), 62–63.

21. "Will Take Trip, Then Buy Parks," *San Francisco Chronicle*, January 14, 1914.

22. Hegemann, *Report on a City Plan*, 138.

23. Rhomberg, *No There There*, 43–45.

24. Edgar Sanborn, "Joaquin Miller Park," *Parks and Recreation* 22 (December 1938): 151–55.

25. "$210,000 Park Fund Voted over Protest," *San Francisco Examiner*, November 5, 1916; "Mayor Davie Opposes Park Appropriation," *San Francisco Chronicle*, November 18, 1919; "Trestle Glen Is Urged for Oakland Park," *Oakland Tribune*, January 6, 1920; "Trestle Glen Park Plan Now Seems Assured," *Oakland Tribune*, April 20, 1921.

26. "Oakland Lacking in Park Acreage Reports Expert," *Oakland Tribune*, August 20, 1922; "Oakland to Increase Parks," *Oakland Post-Enquirer*, May 19, 1923.

27. Carol Aronovici, "There Is Yet Time to Develop Parks," *Oakland Post-Enquirer*, January 31, 1923.

28. "Mayor Davie, Defeated in Park Fight, Is Undaunted," *San Francisco Chronicle*, May 26, 1927.

29. Chris Rhomberg, "White Nativism and Urban Politics: The 1920s Ku Klux Klan in Oakland, California," *Journal of American Ethnic History* 17.2 (Winter 1998): 39, 43–45.

30. E.B.M.U.D., *The Story of Water: A Brief History of the E.B.M.U.D.* (Oakland, 1932), 4.

31. John Wesley Noble, *Its Name Was M.U.D.* (Oakland: East Bay Municipal Utility District, 1970), 7–16. On the water wars and woes of the private companies, see Sherwood Burgess, "Oakland Water War," *California History* (Winter 1984): 35–41.

32. Philip Harroun, *Report of the Commission of the East Bay Cities on the Water Supply for the Cities of Oakland, Berkeley, Alameda and Richmond* (San Francisco: The Commission, 1920).

33. Sarah Elkind, "Industry and Water Distribution in California: The East Bay Municipal Utility District, 1920–1930," *Environmental History Review* 18.4

(Winter 1994): 69–70; "Water Plan Will Reduce Rates," *Oakland Post-Enquirer,* April 26, 1923.

34. "Sources of Water Now Cut to Four," *Oakland Tribune,* August 19, 1924. "Davis Attacks Foes of Mokelumne Project," *Oakland Post,* November 30, 1924.

35. Sarah Elkind, *Bay Cities and Water Politics: The Battle for Resources in Boston and Oakland* (Lawrence: University of Kansas Press, 1998), 137–40.

36. Noble, *Its Name Was M.U.D.,* 41.

37. Ed Salzman, "East Bay's Water Plan Threatened," *Oakland Tribune,* June 20, 1971.

38. "Meet Called to Map Plans for East Bay Chain Park," *San Francisco Chronicle,* December 10, 1929.

39. "Park Survey First Project of Kahn Fund," *San Francisco Chronicle,* January 25, 1931.

40. Olmsted Brothers and Ansel Hall, *Proposed Park Reservations for East Bay Cities* (Berkeley: Bureau of Public Administration of the University of California, 1930), 22.

41. Ibid., 16.

42. Ibid., 13.

43. James O'Connell, "How Metropolitan Parks Shaped Greater Boston, 1893–1945," in *Remaking Boston: An Environmental History of the City and Its Surroundings,* ed. Anthony N. Penna and Conrad Edick Wright (Pittsburgh: University of Pittsburgh Press, 2009), 171.

44. Frederick Kelsey, "Park System of Essex County, New Jersey," *Annals of the American Academy of Political and Social Science* 35.2 (March 1910): 50–55; Chas Doell and Gerald Fitzgerald, *A Brief History of Parks and Recreation Areas in the United States* (Chicago: Athletic Institute, 1954), 34–35.

45. Charles Eliot, *Report of the Board of Metropolitan Park Commissioners* (Boston: Massachusetts Metropolitan Park Commission, 1893), 1.

46. David Schuyler, *The New Urban Landscape: The Redefinition of City Form in Nineteenth-Century America* (Baltimore: Johns Hopkins University Press, 1986), 131–44; Steven Moga, "Marginal Lands and Suburban Nature: Open Space Planning and the Case of the 1893 Boston Metropolitan Parks Plan," *Journal of Planning History* 8.4 (November 2009): 308–29.

47. Mimi Stein, *A Vision Achieved: Fifty Years of East Bay Regional Park District* (Oakland: East Bay Regional Park District, 1984), 8–10.

48. Laura McCreery, *Living Landscape: The Extraordinary Rise of the East Bay Regional Park District and How It Preserved 100,000 Acres* (Berkeley: Wilderness Press, 2010), 5.

49. "Regional Park Plan Approved," *Berkeley Daily Gazette,* November 7, 1934.

50. In 1939, just a few years after the Lake Temescal Regional Park was established, a civic stadium seating 40,000 persons was proposed to occupy the land just south of the dam. It was dropped. Another idea that never came to fruition

surfaced in 1973, when the regional park was almost transferred to the City of Oakland because it was so small compared to other district parks. *Parkland Site Evaluations, Part 3 of Master Plan* (Oakland: East Bay Regional Park District, 1973), 68.

51. Malcolm Margolin, *The East Bay Out* (Berkeley: Heyday Books, 1974), 109.

52. Clay McShane, *Down the Asphalt Path: The Automobile and the American City* (New York: Columbia University Press, 1994), 33.

53. Paul Barrett, *The Automobile and Urban Transit: The Formation of Public Policy in Chicago, 1900–1930* (Philadelphia: Temple University Press, 1083), 71–72.

54. Glenn Orlin, "Roads and Parks in Harmony," *Washington History* 1.1 (Spring 1989): 60–62.

55. Olmsted Bros. and Hall, *Proposed Park Reservations for East Bay Cities,* 18, 33.

56. Elbert Vail, *East Bay Regional Park District Master Plan* (Oakland, 1940).

57. Lawrence Merriam, *A Preliminary Report upon the Proposed East Bay Regional Parks* (San Francisco: State Park Division of the National Park Service, February 1936), 19–29.

58. See the related discussion in Christian Zapatka, "The American Parkways," *Lotus International* 56 (1987): 115.

59. Carl Houtchens, "Oakland to Have Finest Park System," *Oakland Post-Enquirer*, July 27, 1946; "Park Director Enthusiastic over Expansion Program," *Oakland Post-Enquirer*, August 6, 1946; "Modernization Plans for Park System Near Completion," *Oakland Post-Enquirer*, August 7, 1946.

60. In 1958, Mott Jr. built two fly-fishing casting ponds in the Leona Park Trout Pond (now McCrea Park), the second largest installation of its kind in the world. In 1961, the Dimond Canyon Golf Center opened, a driving range alongside a pitch-and-putt course.

61. Al Kelley and Sharyn Gayton, "Lake Merritt Breakfast Club—The Sunnysiders Stylish Story" (Oakland: Lake Merritt Breakfast Club, 2004), 1–11.

62. "Children's Fairyland Soon," *Oakland Tribune*, February 17, 1949.

63. Mary Ellen Butler, *Prophet of the Parks: The Story of William Penn Mott Jr.* (Ashborn, VA: National Recreation and Parks Association, 1999), 39–46.

64. For a history of the evolving attraction, see Randal Metz and Tony Jonick, *Creating Fairyland: 60 Years of Magic at Children's Fairyland U.S.A.* (Oakland: Rapid Rabbit, 2011).

65. William Penn Mott Jr., "Magic Key to Your Park's Story," *Parks and Recreation* 42 (May 1959): 220–21.

66. Helen Kennedy, "Children's Fairyland," *National Motorist* (September–October 1953), 4–5.

67. "Where Fairy Tales Come to Life," *PG&E Progress* (May 1956), 54.

68. Butler, *Prophet of the Parks*, 52; "Playground Rocket Ride Creates Sensation," *Popular Mechanics* 112 (December 1959): 130.

69. Joe Frost and Sue Wortham, "The Evolution of American Playgrounds," *Young Children* 43.5 (July 1988): 21–22.

70. William Penn Mott Jr., "Dress Up Your Play Areas with Inexpensive Play Structures," *Parks and Recreation* 39 (May 1956): 4–5; Lee Elam and Leo Rosenhouse, "Playground with an Imagination," *Popular Mechanics* 106 (August 1956): 114–18.

71. In 1975, Knowland State Park was conveyed to the City of Oakland.

72. Donovan Bass, "Oakland Planning a Natural Zoo," *San Francisco Chronicle*, August 2, 1951. Mott Jr. may have anticipated the zoo movement to imitate natural conditions that began in the 1960s. On such attempts worldwide, see Eric Baratay and Elisa Beth Hardouin-Fugier, *Zoo: A History of Zoological Gardens in the West* (London: Reaktion Books, 2001), 265–80.

73. In 2015, ground was broken for a controversial 56-acre addition, the California Trail Project, atop land in Knowland Park. In order to make way for endangered grizzly bears and gray wolves, part of one of the few relatively undisturbed wild habitats in Oakland was bulldozed.

74. *Peralta Oaks Plan: A Plan for a Research and Conference Center in Hellman Park, Oakland, California* (Oakland: City Planning Commission, October 1963), 7–8

75. Ralph Craib, "Oakland's White Elephant," *San Francisco Chronicle*, March 8, 1971; "The Hellman Estate, Dunsmuir House Conference Center and Peralta Oaks Research Center" (Oakland: Office of the City Manager, January 15, 1971), 4–8.

76. "Oakland's Sculpture Garden Getting 12 Large-Scale Works," *San Francisco Chronicle*, June 25, 1982.

77. Stein, *A Vision Achieved*, 92.

78. Margot Patterson Doss, "Along the Huckleberry Trail," *San Francisco Chronicle*, March 16, 1986.

79. McCreery, *Living Landscape*, 36.

80. City Planning Commission, *Shoreline Development, Part of Master Plan* (Oakland, 1951), 12.

81. US Army Engineer District, *San Leandro Creek Flood Control Project* (San Francisco, March 1971), 2–3.

82. "Junky Shoreline Turning into Park," *Oakland Tribune*, May 4, 1978.

83. David Gates & Associates and Thurston Design Group, *Middle Harbor Shoreline Park: Master Plan* (Oakland: Port of Oakland, May, 1999).

84. Rick Pruetz, *Lasting Value: Open Space and Preservation Successes* (Chicago: American Planning Association, 2012), 15, 18.

85. DeMars & Wells and Jack Sidener, *Oakland's Form and Appearance* (Oakland: 701 Program of the City of Oakland, 1968), 5.

86. Dave Hope, "Oakland's Forgotten Creeks," *Oakland Tribune*, five-part series (January 28–31, February 1, 1947).

87. Walker, *The Country in the City*, 53; William Jordan III and George Lubick, *Making Nature Whole: A History of Ecological Restoration* (Washington, DC: Island Press, 2011), 132–34. For an in-depth discussion of East Bay creeks and restoration efforts, see Ann Riley, *Restoring Neighborhood Streams: Planning, Design & Construction* (Washington, DC: Island Press, 2016).

88. Barbara Falconer Newhall, "Oakland Rediscovers Its Web of Water," *Oakland Tribune*, April 13, 1986.

89. Gina Covina, "Up the Creeks," *East Bay Express*, June 5, 1998.

90. *Restoration of Peralta Creek at Cesar Chavez Park* (Berkeley: Urban Creeks Council, March, 2005), 1–3.

CHAPTER 5. MAJOR LEAGUE VENUE

1. O. P. Shelley, "A Municipal Auditorium for the City of Oakland," *Architect & Engineer* 38 (April 1914): 80–82.

2. Judith May, "Two Model Cities: Negotiations in Oakland," *Politics and Society* 2 (Fall 1971): 61.

3. William Wyckoff, *Creating Colorado: The Making of a Western American Landscape, 1860–1940* (New Haven, CT: Yale University Press, 1999), 116; Frederick Law Olmsted, "Plan of Developing Civic Center Outlined by Landscape Architect," *City of Denver* 1.13 (April 12, 1913): 1–2.

4. "Davie Opens Fight to Get Civic Center for Oakland," *San Francisco Chronicle*, March 3, 1930.

5. Homer Hadley, "Oakland's Monumental Courthouse," *Architect & Engineer* 126 (September 1936): 19.

6. For a discussion of Civic Center planning up to this point, see Geoffrey Bangs, "A Civic Center for Lake Merritt, Oakland, California," *Architect & Engineer* 160 (January 1945): 15–16.

7. City Planning Commission, *The Oakland Master Plan, The Civic Center and Lake Merritt Improvement* (Oakland, 1947), 17.

8. "Civic Center on Lakeshore Draws Committee Fire," *Oakland Tribune*, April 16, 1946.

9. "Civic Center Master Plans Face Change," *Oakland Tribune*, January 17, 1954.

10. "A Big New East Bay Hall of Justice," *San Francisco Examiner*, August 12, 1962.

11. "Municipal Museum Completed," *Oakland Tribune*, October 21, 1910.

12. For a discussion of the three earlier museums, see Marjorie Schwarzer, "Butterflies in the Basement: Requiem for the Snow Museum of Natural History," in *The Marvelous Museum: Orphans, Curiosities and Treasures*, ed. Mark Dion (San Francisco: Chronicle Books, 2010), 53–65.

13. Ibid., 58.

14. "Plans Finest Museum of Entire Coast," *San Francisco Chronicle*, September 3, 1916.

15. "Lake Merritt Scheme Told by Davie," *Oakland Museum*, November 21, 1970.

16. "Joint Committee Chosen to Finance a $1,000,000 Art Palace, Museum," *Oakland Tribune*, January 18, 1927.

17. "City Muffed Early Plan for Museum," *Oakland Tribune*, March 22, 1961.

18. Bill Fiset, "Oakland's Museums Far Outgrow Display Space," "City Outgrows Its Museums," "Rundown Mansion Holds 90,000 Museum Objects," *Oakland Tribune*, November 8–10, 1955.

19. "Attempt to Save Snow Museum Stalled," *San Francisco Examiner*, November 24, 1957.

20. Oakland Chamber of Commerce, "Comparison of Proposed Museum Sites in the City of Oakland" (Oakland, January 31, 1961).

21. "Charles Lineberger, "Lost Art," *East Bay Express*, February 15, 1985.

22. Bill Livingston, "Magic Carpet Designer's Dream for New Museum in Oakland," *Oakland Museum*, December 10, 1961.

23. "3-Level Design for Museum," *Oakland Tribune*, June 11, 1962.

24. Thomas Albright, "An Aware New Museum in Oakland," *San Francisco Chronicle*, May 9, 1969.

25. For architectural critiques, see "Terraces in Oakland," *Architectural Forum* 125 (October 1966): 64–65; "Oakland's Urban Oasis: New Oakland Museum," *Progressive Architecture* 50 (December 1969): 92–95; "The Oakland Museum," *Architectural Record* 147 (April 1970): 115–22.

26. Ed Salzman, "Museum Construction Job Delayed by Problems," *Oakland Tribune*, May 26, 1963.

27. See Paul Mills, "California Art at the Oakland Museum," in *Plein Air Painters of California: The North*, ed. Ruth Lilly Westphal (Irvine, CA: Westphal, 1986).

28. Nathan Hare, "She Always Stood by Me," *San Francisco Bay View*, March 29, 2019.

29. Michael Harris, "Oakland Museum Director Is Fired," *San Francisco Chronicle*, August 8, 1969.

30. Quoted in Charles McCabe, "A Bush League Decision (2)," *San Francisco Chronicle*, August 14, 1969.

31. "Julie Hare Urges New Museum Tack," *San Francisco Chronicle*, November 25, 1969.

32. "Oakland Backed by $30 Million," *San Francisco Chronicle*, January 31, 1960.

33. "Sports Stadium Plans Revealed," *Oakland Tribune*, November 3, 1960.

34. The other key members of Coliseum Inc. were William Knowland, Edgar Kaiser, and George Loorz, president of Stolte Construction.

35. Ed Schoenfeld, "Plans for Coliseum Taking Shape," *Oakland Tribune,* August 31, 1961.

36. "Stadium Entices Top Architects," *Oakland Tribune,* June 9, 1961.

37. "Rigney Sold on Layout of Coliseum," *Oakland Tribune,* February 6, 1962.

38. Quoted in John Lawrence, "Oakland Uses Sports to Give It an Image as a Big League City," *Wall Street Journal,* December 29, 1967.

39. Henry Super, "Coliseum Stadium Opens—It's a Dream Come True," *Alameda Times Star,* September 19, 1966.

40. On its history, see Robert Kessler and Chester Hartman, "The Illusion and Reality of Urban Renewal: A Case Study of San Francisco's Yerba Buena Center," *Land Economics* 49.4 (November 1973): 440–53.

41. Phil Gruen, "Postwar Stadiums: Will We Miss Them When They're Gone?," *Baseball Research Journal* 25 (1996): 19.

42. Alan Hess, "Coliseum Remodel a Fiasco," *San Jose Mercury News,* April 21, 1996.

43. On the Arena's inventive structure, see J. A. Diaz, "Prestressing: Technique and Innovation in 1950–1975 Architecture," in *Structures and Architecture: Concepts, Applications and Challenges,* ed. Pablo Cruz (Boca Raton, FL: CRC Press, 2013), 988.

44. "An Elegant Sports and Recreation Center," *Architectural Record* 143 (June 1968): 121–28. See also the discussion of the complex in the issue devoted to SOM, *A + U: Architecture & Urbanism* 37.4 (January 1974).

45. Bill and Nancy Boyarsky, *Backroom Politics: How Your Local Politicians Work, Why Your Government Doesn't, and What You Can Do about It* (New York: J. B. Tarcher, 1974), 189.

46. Dean Baim, *The Sports Stadium as a Municipal Investment* (Westport, CT: Greenwood Press, 1994), 95–98, 157.

47. Maria Veri, "Sons of Oakland," in *San Francisco Bay Area Sports: Golden Gate Athletics, Recreation and Community,* ed. Rita Liberti and Maureen M. Smith (Fayetteville: University of Arkansas Press, 2017), 217.

48. Roger Noll and Andrew Zimbalist, "Build the Stadium—Create the Jobs," in *Sports, Jobs and Taxes: The Economic Impact of Sports Teams and Stadiums* (Washington, DC: Brookings Institution Press, 1997), 7, 28.

49. Ibid., 24–25; Michael Hiltzik and Lisa Dillman, "Who Wins in Stadium Shootout," *Los Angeles Times,* July 13, 1997.

50. Robert Trumbour, *The New Cathedrals: Politics and Media in the History of Stadium Construction* (Syracuse, NY: Syracuse University Press, 2007), 39–40.

51. "Hegenberger Road—The Golden Corridor," *San Francisco Examiner,* October 10, 1971. On the phenomenon of commercial districts and industrial parks locating around airports, see Douglas Karsner, "Aviation and Airports: The Impact on the Economic and Geographic Structure of American Cities, 1940s–1980s," *Journal of Urban History* 23 (May 1997): 407.

52. "Airport Hotel Project Starts in 90 Days," *Oakland Tribune* (February 2, 1960); "Edgewater Inn Opens with Charity Dance," *Oakland Tribune*, October 29, 1961.

53. Lawrence, "Oakland Uses Sports to Give It an Image as a Big League City."

54. In 2005, the site became the Hegenberger Gateway shopping center.

55. Eugene Moran, "Eastbay Cultural Upsurge," *Oakland Tribune*, November 22, 1964.

56. "Performing Arts Center Eventually," *Oakland Tribune*, February 28, 1963.

57. J. B. S. Cahill, "The Paramount Theater, Oakland," *Architect & Engineer* 108 (March 1932): 11–28.

58. Steven Levin, "Paramount Theatre of the Arts," *Marquee* 4 (1973).

59. Lester On, "It Was a Very Good Year," *Oakland Tribune*, November 11, 1976.

60. On the plight of other symphony orchestras around the nation, see Robert Commanday, "Trouble in Symphonyland," *San Francisco Chronicle*, October 26, 1986.

61. James Phills, *Integrating Mission and Strategy for Nonprofit Organizations* (Oxford: Oxford University Press, 2005), 50.

62. "St. Mary's Considers Move from Oakland as $3 Million Drive Fails," *Oakland Tribune*, April 26, 1927; "St. Mary's Site Plan Change Reasons Told," *Oakland Tribune*, May 10, 1927.

63. "$4,000,000 Holy Names Campus Project to Start," *Oakland Tribune*, December 30, 1955; "Holy Names Sisters Show Campus at Open House," *Oakland Tribune*, April 7, 1957.

64. On the historical underpinnings of the plan, see John Aubrey Douglass, *The California Idea and American Higher Education: 1850 to the 1960 Master Plan* (Stanford: Stanford University Press, 2000).

65. Donna Jean Murch, *Living for the City: Migration, Education and the Rise of the Black Panther Party in Oakland, CA* (Chapel Hill: University of North Carolina Press, 2010), 111.

66. Concerning the rise of the Black Panther Party in Oakland, see Sean Malloy, *Out of Oakland: Black Panther Party Internationalizing during the Cold War* (Ithaca, NY: Cornell University Press, 2017), 48–55.

67. Bobby Seale, *Seize the Time: The Story of the Black Panther Party and Huey Newton* (New York: Random House, 1970), 13–15.

68. Jeffrey Ogbar, *Black Power: Radical Politics and African American Identity* (Baltimore: Johns Hopkins University Press, 2004), 126.

69. Ishmael Reed, "Ethnic Studies in the Age of the Tea Party," *Amerikastudien/American Studies* 55.4 (2010): 747.

70. Murch, *Living for the City*, 71, 106, 112–14.

71. Ernie Cox, "A Merritt Student's Plea," *Oakland Tribune*, May 5, 1969.

72. John Keane, "An Assault Bewilders College," *San Francisco Chronicle*, November 18, 1972.

73. Bill Wyman, "Roots: The Origins of Black Politics in the East Bay," *East Bay Express*, August 7, 1987.

74. Murch, *Living for the City*, 216–20.

75. On the emergence of black political power, see Frederick Douzet, *The Color of Power: Racial Coalitions and Political Power in Oakland* [2007], trans. George Holoch (Charlottesville: University of Virginia Press, 2012), 56–63, 128–44.

76. Robert Stanley Oden, *From Blacks to Brown and Beyond: The Struggle for Progressive Politics in Oakland, California, 1966–2011* (San Diego: University Readers, 2012), 41–51.

77. J. Phillip Thompson, III, *Double Trouble: Black Mayors, Black Communities, and the Call for a Deep Democracy* (Oxford: Oxford University Press, 2006), 69–71.

78. Nina Mjagkij, ed., *Organizing Black America: An Encyclopedia of African American Associations* (New York: Garland, 2001), 190.

79. Andrea Alison Burns, "'Show Me My Soul!': The Evolution of the Black Museum Movement in Postwar America" (PhD diss., University of Minnesota, July 2008), 14–15, 23.

80. Carl Hall, "Nothing but Space: What If You Built a Big, Beautiful Observatory and Nobody Came?," *San Francisco Chronicle*, March 2, 2003.

81. For background on the AAMLO and Chabot Space and Science Center, see Ishmael Reed, *Blues City: A Walk in Oakland* (New York: Crown, 2003), 74–76, 185–86.

CHAPTER 6. THE PROMISE AND THE REALITY OF FREEWAYS AND BART

1. Jon Carroll, "Best Roads," in *The Best of California* (Santa Barbara: Capra Press, 1986), 32.

2. John Krich, *Bump City: Winners and Losers in Oakland* (Berkeley: City Miner Books, 1979), 89.

3. Joint Fact-Finding Committee on Highways, Streets and Bridges, *Study for the California Legislature: Engineering Facts of a Future Program* (Sacramento: State Printing Office, 1946), 9–10.

4. Richard Weingroff, "Federal-Aid Highway Act of 1956: Creating the Interstate System," *Public Roads* 60.1 (Summer 1996): 1–2.

5. Message from the President of the United States, *Interregional Highways* (Washington, DC: Government Printing Office, 1944), 7, 78, 85. A subsequent study by the American Institute of Planners and the American Transit Association, *Urban Freeways* (1947), proposed combining rail and bus transit with the upcoming urban freeway system. In the following decades, this approach usually came to naught, as mass transit planning was still not regarded as a public responsibility requiring federal funding. Joseph DiMento and Cliff Ellis, *Chang-*

ing Lanes: Visions and Histories of Urban Freeways (Cambridge, MA: MIT Press, 2013), 43, 80.

6. The state gas tax had been raised in 1933, and would be increased again in 1953. Daniel Mitchell, "Earl Warren's Fight for California Freeways: Setting a Path for the Nation," *Southern California Quarterly* 88.2 (Summer 2006): 205.

7. David W. Jones, *California's Freeway Era in Historical Perspective* (Berkeley: Institute of Transportation Studies, July 1989), 17.

8. "Proposal to Break Traffic Funnel," *Oakland Tribune*, July 31, 1937.

9. "Freeway to Ease Oakland Traffic," *Architect & Engineer* 143.2 (November 1940): 45.

10. On Bartholomew's career in highway planning, see Jeffrey Brown, "A Tale of Two Visions: Harland Bartholomew, Robert Moses and the Development of the American Freeway," *Journal of Planning History* 4 (February 2005): 4–27.

11. Bartholomew, *A Report on Freeways and Major Streets in Oakland, CA*, 1–27.

12. "Freeway Key to County's Huge Industrial Growth," *Oakland Tribune*, July 4, 1954.

13. E. J. Carter, "Rapid Progress: Eastshore Freeway in Oakland Nearing Completion," *California Highways and Public Works* 28 (May–June 1949): 8.

14. Newell Grover, "Cooperation" Community Planning Spurs Freeway Progress in Alameda County," *California Highways and Public Works* 29 (1950): 9–11.

15. "Freeway Sector to Be Opened," *Oakland Tribune*, July 17, 1949. See also John Rae, *The Road and Car in American Life* (Cambridge, MA: MIT Press, 1971), 221.

16. Donald Hauser, "The Cypress Structure and the West Oakland Black Community," *From the Archives* 1.1 (Winter 1990).

17. Gar Smith, "Freeways, Community and 'Environmental Racism,'" *Race, Poverty and the Environment* 1.1 (April 1990): 7.

18. DiMento and Ellis, *Changing Lanes*, 126. For further reflection on this issue, see E. Michael Jones, *The Slaughter of Cities: Urban Renewal as Ethnic Cleansing* (South Bend, IN: St. Augustine's Press, 2004), 341.

19. Brian Ladd, *Autophobia: Love and Hate in the Automobile Age* (Chicago: University of Chicago Press, 2008), 105–6.

20. "$41 Million for Roads in Two Counties," *Oakland Tribune*, October 30, 1959.

21. Raymond Mohl, "The Expressway Teardown Movement in American Cities: Rethinking Postwar Highway Policy in the Post-Interstate Era," *Journal of Planning History* 11.1 (February 2012): 90–96.

22. Joseph Rodriguez, *City against Suburb: The Culture Wars in an American Metropolis* (Westport, CT: Praeger, 1999), 55–67.

23. Carol Minyard, "Huge Cypress Project Pushing Forward to Meet 'Fast Track' Finish," *Construction Management Magazine* (September 1995): 12–13.

24. Brett Jackson, "Replacing Oakland's Cypress Freeway," *Public Roads* 61 (March–April 1998).

25. Chris Thompson, "City Unveils New Plan for West Oakland's Mandela Parkway," *East Bay Express*, February 27, 1998.

26. B. W. Booker, "Bay Area Freeways," *California Highways and Public Works* 33 (March–April 1954): 10–11.

27. "Oakland Hill Protest on Freeway," *San Francisco Chronicle*, May 9, 1953.

28. "Prayer Vigil in Oakland for Freeway," *San Francisco Chronicle*, October 18, 1956.

29. On the history of the system, see Thomas Karnes, *Asphalt and Politics: A History of the American Highway System* (Jefferson, NC: McFarland, 2009), 85–92.

30. State Division of Highways, *The California Freeway System* (Sacramento: State Printing Office, 1958); Jeffrey Brown, "Statewide Transportation Planning: Lessons from California," *Transportation Quarterly* 56 (Spring 2002): 56–57; Katherine Johnson, "Captain Blake versus the Highwayman: Or, How San Francisco Won the Freeway Revolt," *Journal of Planning History* 8 (February 2009): 63.

31. Brian Taylor, "Public Perceptions, Fiscal Realities, and Freeway Planning: The California Case," *Journal of the American Planning Association* 61.1 (1995): 46.

32. "New Cross-Town Freeway Outlined," *Oakland Tribune*, August 26, 1953.

33. "Traffic on Nimitz Held State's Worst," *Oakland Tribune*, August 15, 1965.

34. Richard Zettel, *Urban Transportation in the San Francisco Bay Area* (Berkeley: Institute of Governmental Studies, 1963), 30–31.

35. "$31 Million Trans-Oakland Freeway Project Outlined," *Oakland Tribune*, April 7, 1954.

36. "Commission Hearing Here Tomorrow on Route for MacArthur Freeway," *Oakland Tribune*, November 11, 1954.

37. "City OK's MacArthur Freeway," *Oakland Tribune*, June 19, 1957.

38. "Freeway Would Ruin Mills College," *San Francisco Chronicle*, March 28, 1962.

39. Mark Rose, *Interstate: Express Highway Politics, 1939–1989* (Lawrence: University of Kansas Press, 1990), 102.

40. Tom Lewis, *Divided Highways: Building the Interstate Highways, Transforming American Life* (Ithaca, NY: Cornell University Press, 2013), 169.

41. Bill Stroebel, "Lost: One Shopping Center," *Oakland Tribune*, October 9, 1960.

42. L. M. Peterson, "U.S. 50 Freeway," *California Highways and Public Works* 39 (March–April 1960): 8–9.

43. "MacArthur Project Receives Send-Off," *Alameda Times-Star*, April 9, 1966.

44. Oakland Chamber of Commerce, *Oakland and the MacArthur Freeway* (1966).

45. City of Oakland, City Planning Department, *Scenic Highways: An Element of the Oakland Comprehensive Plan* (Oakland, 1974), 6.

46. Ibid., 7.

47. "Report from Mills," *Bulletin of Mills College* 52 (November 1962).

48. Department of Public Works, Division of Highways, *Report on Feasibility of Providing an Alternative Truck Route So That Truck Traffic May Be Eliminated from the MacArthur Freeway through the City of Oakland* (Sacramento: State of California, 1962).

49. "Oakland Freeway Network Expedited," *Oakland Tribune*, May 25, 1958.

50. Jeff Norman, *Temescal Legacies: Narratives of Change from a North Oakland Neighborhood* (Oakland: Shared Ground, 2006), 74–77, 91–92.

51. "North Area Fights Route for Thruway," *Oakland Tribune*, January 17, 1957; "North Oakland Freeway Disputed," *San Francisco Chronicle*, March 26, 1958; "Sue to Block Oakland Freeway," *San Francisco Examiner*, February 27, 1959.

52. Gerald Sturges, "Chabot Canyon Assn. Fights Wide Fill Plan for Freeway," *Oakland Tribune*, February 23, 1964.

53. Frank Piazzi, "BART New Freeway Opposed," *San Francisco Chronicle*, November 19, 1967.

54. Frank Piazzi, "Oakland Residents Organize," *San Francisco Chronicle*, November 19, 1967.

55. Bruce Bishop, C. H. Oglesby, and Gene Willeke, *Socio-Economic and Community Factors in Planning Urban Freeways* (Washington, DC: US Department of Transportation, September 1970), 2.

56. H. Marshall Goodwin Jr., "Right-of-Way Controversies in Recent California Highway-Freeway Construction," *Southern California Quarterly* 56.1 (Spring 1974): 61–65.

57. Jones, *California's Freeway Era*, 23.

58. Tom Lewis, *Divided Highways: Building the Interstate Highways, Transforming American Life* (New York: Viking Books, 1997), 234–37.

59. "Board Kills Plans for Six SF Freeways," *San Francisco Chronicle*, January 27, 1959. See also William Lathrop, "The San Francisco Freeway Revolt," *Transportation Engineering Journal of the American Society of Civil Engineers* 97 (February 1971): 133–44.

60. William Issel, "Land Values, Human Values, and the Preservation of the City's Treasured Appearance: Environmentalism, Politics and the San Francisco Freeway Revolt," *Pacific Historical Review* 68.4 (November 1999): 616.

61. Assembly Interim Committee on Natural Resources, Planning & Public Works, *Highway and Freeway Planning* (Sacramento: State of California, 1965), 23.

62. Rose, *Interstate*, 105.

63. Taylor, "Public Perceptions, Fiscal Realities, and Freeway Planning," 44, 47–50.

64. "Shafter Freeway Protested," *Oakland Tribune*, July 20, 1971.

65. "Four Freeway Routes Hit by Oakland," *Oakland Tribune*, August 27, 1959.

66. "Shepherd Canyon Freeway Opposed," *Oakland Tribune*, May 21, 1972.

67. Oakland City Planning Department, *Shepherd Canyon Corridor Study* (Oakland, October 1975).

68. Seymour Adler, "The Political Economy of Transit in the San Francisco Bay Area, 1945–1963" (PhD diss., University of California, 1980), 35.

69. Sy Adler, "Infrastructure Politics: The Dynamics of Crossing the San Francisco Bay," *Public Historian* 10.4 (Autumn 1988): 23–29.

70. Ibid., 36–39.

71. Parsons, Brinckerhoff, Tudor, and Bechtel, *Engineering Report to the San Francisco Bay Area Rapid Transit District* (San Francisco, June 1961), 5.

72. John Marr, *The Transit Problem in the East Bay* (Oakland: City of Oakland Planning Commission, March 1950), 19.

73. Alameda–Contra Costa Transit District, *Preliminary Report on Transbay Transit* (San Francisco: De Leuw, Cather, 1957), iv, vi.

74. "Key System Will Curtail Service on Eight Bus Lines," *San Francisco Chronicle*, March 24, 1949; "Cuts Planned in Local Coach Lines," *Oakland Tribune*, June 28, 1954.

75. "District Is Climax of 10-Year Effort," *Oakland Tribune*, September 30, 1960.

76. "Special Issue," *AC Transit Times*, October 1960.

77. De Leuw, Cather & Company, *Summary of a Public Transit Plan for Alameda-Contra Costa Transit District* (San Francisco, August 27, 1958); Alameda–Contra Costa Transit District, *Annual Report 1959/1960* (Oakland, 1960).

78. "AC Buses Are Running in the Red," *Oakland Tribune*, January 12, 1969.

79. Alameda–Contra Costa Transit District, Annual Report 1969/1970 (Oakland, 1970); Alameda–Contra Costa Transit District, Annual Report 1975/1976 (Oakland, 1976).

80. Harre Demoro, "AC Transit Trims Service Schedules," *Oakland Tribune*, June 7, 1971.

81. Michael Looney, "Attacks on Bus Drivers—It's Almost Routine," *Oakland Tribune*, July 30, 1978.

82. Stephen Zwerling, *Mass Transit and the Politics of Technology: A Study of BART and the San Francisco Bay Area* (New York: Praeger, 1974), 18.

83. Ibid., 92–94.

84. Richard Marcantonio and Angelica Jongco, "From the Back of the Bus to the End of the Line: The Discriminatory Funding of Public Transit in California," *Human Rights* 34.3 (Summer 2007): 10.

85. William Middleton, *Metropolitan Railways: Rapid Transit in America* (Bloomington: Indiana University Press, 2003), 115–20.

86. William Middleton, "Trouble-Plagued BART Brings in a New Team of Problem Solvers," *Railway Age* (April 12, 1976): 27.

87. David Jones, *Mass Motorization and Mass Transit: An American History and Policy Analysis* (Bloomington: Indiana University Press, 2008), 100–101.

88. Harre DeMoro, "BART: 10 Years After," *San Francisco Chronicle*, September 9, 1984.

89. P. R. Hutchinson, "A Rapid Transit System for San Francisco," *Geography* 59.2 (April 1974): 150.

90. One regional idea that did not pan out was the creation of a regional transportation authority to administer all bridges, seaports and airports, and rapid transit. See *Report of the Golden Gate Authority Commission, Final Report on the Feasibility of a Regional Agency to Coordinate Transportation Facilities Serving the People of a Nine-County Metropolitan Region* (Sacramento: California State Legislature, February 1, 1961), 16–20.

91. For a critique of BART's corporate ties, see John Gilber, "BART, GM & Bechtel: Protecting Property Values in the San Francisco Financial District," *Race, Poverty and the Environment* 12.1 (Winter 2005–6): 24–25; Greg DeFreitas, "BART: Rapid Transit and Regional Control," *Pacific Research and World Empire Telegram* 4 (November–December 1972): 12–17. For a viewpoint stressing regional planning factors as key to the system's structure, see *Critical History of Transit Planning and Decision Making*, 10–17, www.princeton.edu/~ota/disk3/1976/76 09/760905.PDF.

92. Gilber, "BART, GM & Bechtel," 26.

93. Melvin Webber, "The BART Experience—What Have We Learned?" *The Public Interest* (Fall 1976): 83.

94. Aaron Golub, Richard Marcantonio, and Thomas Sanchez, "Race, Space and Struggles for Mobility: Impacts on African Americans in Oakland and the East Bay," *Urban Geography* 34 (May 2013): 717, 721. See also Harold Frye, Pat Gelb, and David Minkus, *BART Impacts on Travel by Ethnic Minorities* (San Francisco: Metropolitan Transportation Commission, 1977).

95. 95 "BART Memorandum to Board of Directors from General Manager," October 21, 1966, 6.

96. Initially, the downtown Oakland 19th Street station was planned further north, at Grand Avenue. It was relocated at the behest of the city's large department stores and theaters.

97. On BART's history, see William Middleton, *Metropolitan Railways: Rapid Transit in America* (Bloomington: Indiana University Press, 2003), 115–23; Michael Healy, *BART: The Dramatic History of the Bay Area Rapid Transit System* (Berkeley: Heyday, 2016).

98. "UC Wants 2nd Berkeley Rapid Transit Station," *Oakland Tribune*, November 11, 1960.

99. Richard Grefe and Richard Smart, *A History of the Key Decisions in the Development of the Bay Area Rapid Transit District* (San Francisco: Metropolitan Transportation Commission, 1975), 109.

100. Ed Salzman, "Most Land for Transit in Oakland," *Oakland Tribune*, March 29, 1964.

101. Joseph Rodriguez, *City against Suburb: The Culture Wars in an American Metropolis* (Westport, CT; Praeger, 1999), 48, 60.

102. Edward Myers, "BART Is New from the Rails Up," *Modern Railroads Rail Transit* (February 1972).

103. Carl Irving, "Bay Area Advised to Buy Land," *Oakland Tribune*, March 6, 1964.

104. City Planning Department, *BART Impact: 5 Oakland Stations* (Oakland, 1969), 14–24.

105. Ibid., 45.

106. Ibid., 92.

107. Ibid., 115–16.

108. Harre DeMoro, "Unfinished Symphony or Broken Record," *Oakland Tribune*, August 14, 1977.

CHAPTER 7. IN THE WAKE OF DEINDUSTRIALIZATION

1. Warren Hinckle, "Metropoly: The Story of Oakland, California," *Ramparts* (February 1966): 26.

2. Ibid., 26.

3. J. W. Cowart, *A Report on the Economic Growth and Development of the Metropolitan Oakland Area* (Oakland: Oakland Chamber of Commerce, 1948). See also Self, *American Babylon*, 27.

4. "Ship Building Shut Down at Moore Yards," *Oakland Tribune*, February 21, 1961.

5. "California Cotton Mills to Close Historic Plant," *Oakland Tribune*, June 30, 1954.

6. Arthur Hepner, "Cotton Dethroned," *Challenge* 3.3 (December 1954): 27–28.

7. "Oakland Area Is Industrial Giant," *Oakland Tribune*, October 10, 1954.

8. Paul Griffin, "Recent Land-Use Changes in the San Francisco Bay Area," *Geographical Review* 47.3 (July 1957): 399.

9. George Ross, "Old Peralta Tract Just Keeps Dividing Along," *Oakland Tribune*, September 5, 1955; George Ross, "Rubber-Tired Migration Burying Bay Area Growers," *Oakland Tribune*, September 4, 1955.

10. On the disastrous coincidence of the migration with deindustrialization,

see Stewart Tolnay, "The African American 'Great Migration' and Beyond," *Annual Review of Sociology* 29 (2003): 218–22.

11. Elmont Waite, "Bay Racial Forecast-Clashes," *San Francisco Chronicle*, May 15, 1963.

12. "San Leandro—City Famed for Tax Cuts," *Oakland Tribune*, January 10, 1965; Robert Self, "California's Industrial Garden: Oakland and the East Bay in the Age of Deindustrialization," in *Beyond the Ruins: The Meanings of Deindustrialization*, ed. Jefferson Cowie and Joseph Heathcott (Ithaca, NY: Cornell University Press, 2003), 168–70.

13. Randy Leffingwell, *History of the Farm Tractor* (Osceola, WI; MBI, 1996), 9–12. The plant, at 800 Davis Street, remained in operation until 1985.

14. Richard McKenzie, *Fugitive Industry: The Economics and Politics of Deindustrialization* (Cambridge, MA: Ballinger, 1984), 20–22.

15. Richard Walker, "Industry Builds Out the City: The Suburbanization of Manufacturing in the San Francisco Bay Area, 1850–1940," in *Manufacturing Suburbs: Building Work and Home on the Metropolitan Fringe*, ed. Robert Lewis (Philadelphia: Temple University Press, 2004), 92, 110.

16. Bill Stokes, "Decentralization Changes Course of Alameda County's Expansion," *Oakland Tribune*, May 14, 1954.

17. See Oakland Chamber of Commerce, *A Report on the Economic Growth and Development of the Metropolitan Oakland Area* (Oakland, 1948).

18. Van Beuren Stanbery, *Projected Growth of the Bay Area* (San Francisco: San Francisco Bay Area Council, 1957), 16.

19. Self, "California's Industrial Garden," 161.

20. Sally Denton, *The Profiteers: Bechtel and the Men Who Built the World* (New York: Simon & Schuster, 2016), 21–22, 45–52.

21. For a biography, see Mark Foster, *Henry J. Kaiser: Building in the American West* (Austin: University of Texas Press, 1989).

22. Rhomberg, *No There There*, 33, 126.

23. Edward C. Hayes, *Power Structure and Urban Policy: Who Rules in Oakland?* (New York: McGraw Hill, 1972), 40.

24. On the city's struggles within the bay region, see Darrell Hoerter and Michael Wiseman, "Metropolitan Development in the San Francisco Bay Area," *Annals of Regional Science* 22 (November 1988): 22.

25. "Oakland's Chevrolet Plant Pioneered Assembly Line," *Oakland Tribune*, November 23, 1954.

26. Harry Martin, "Auto Industry Growth Linked to the East Bay," *Oakland Tribune*, January 27, 1974.

27. B. P. Birch, "Locational Trends in the American Car Industry," *Geography* 51.4 (November 1966): 375.

28. James Rubenstein, "Changing Distribution of the American Automobile Industry," *Geographical Review* 76.3 (July 1986): 288–93.

29. Michael Teitz and Philip Schapira, "Growth and Turbulence in the California Economy," in *Deindustrialization and Regional Economic Transformation: The Experience of the U.S.*, ed. Lloyd Rodwin and Hidehiko Sazanami (Boston: Unwin Hyman, 1989), 87.

30. Stanford Research Institute, *Economic Projections for Oakland to 1975 and 1985* (Menlo Park, CA: Stanford Research Institute, 1968), 5–12.

31. Robert Douglas, "A Brief History of West Oakland: Adapted from Olmsted and Olmsted (1994)," 46, www.sonoma.edu/asc/cypress/finalreport/Chapter02 .pdf.

32. Abby Cohn, "East Bay Once Had a Cannery Row of Its Own," *San Francisco Chronicle*, May 26, 2000.

33. "Del Monte Closing Plant in Oakland," *Oakland Tribune*, August 25, 1984. The last building was torn down in 1992, and the site later became home to Pixar.

34. Rebecca Smith, "Clorox to Shut Its Historic Oakland Plant," *Oakland Tribune*, May 27, 1992. A thousand people continued to be employed at the Oakland headquarters downtown.

35. Leslie Guth, "Granny Goose to Close if No Buyer Is Found," *Contra Costa Times*, May 13, 1995.

36. Barry Bluestone and Bennett Harrison, *The Deindustrialization of America: Plant Closings, Community Abandonment and the Dismantling of Industry* (New York: Basic Books, 1982), 6.

37. Richard Peet, "Relations of Production and the Relocation of United States Manufacturing Industry since 1960," *Economic Geography* 59.2 (April 1983): 130.

38. Quentin Skrabec, *Fall of an American Rome: De-industrialization and the American Dream* (New York: Algora, 2014), 62, 69.

39. Steven High, *Industrial Sunset: The Making of North America's Rust Belt, 1919–1984* (Toronto: University of Toronto Press, 2003), 9.

40. Oakland Chamber of Commerce, *Community Economic Profile for Oakland, Alameda County* (Oakland, September 1985).

41. Charles Wollenberg, *Berkeley: A City in History* (Berkeley: University of California Press, 2008), 156–58.

42. Michael Storper, Thomas Kemeny, Philip Makarea, and Taner Osman, *The Rise and Fall of Urban Economies: Lessons from San Francisco and Los Angeles* (Stanford: Stanford University Press, 2015), 32.

43. Meredith Wadman, "Aviation Depot Put on Hit List," *Oakland Tribune*, June 27, 1993. The Naval Hospital had been rebuilt in 1968 as a nine-story concrete block with a 650-bed capacity.

44. Delores Nason McBroome, *Parallel Communities: African Americans in California's East Bay, 1850–1963* (New York: Garland, 1993), 65.

45. Quintard Taylor, *In Search of the Racial Frontier: African Americans in the American West, 1528–1990* (New York: W. W. Norton, 1998), 224.

46. Gretchen Lemke-Santangelo, "Deindustrialization, Urban Poverty, and

African American Community Mobilization in Oakland, 1945 through the 1990s," in *Seeking El Dorado: African Americans in California*, ed. Lawrence De Graaf, Kevin Mulroy, and Quintard Taylor (Los Angeles: Autry Museum of Western Heritage, 2001), 345–49.

47. Lemke-Santangelo, "Deindustrialization, Urban Poverty," 352.

48. Thomas J. Sugrue, "Labor, Liberalism, and Racial Politics in 1950s Detroit," *New Labor Forum* 1 (Fall 1997): 23.

49. Thomas J. Sugrue, "Affirmative Action from Below: Civil Rights, the Building Trades, and the Politics of Racial Equality in the Urban North, 1945–1969," *Journal of American History* 91 (June 2004): 147, 173.

50. William Woodson and Susan Sheffield, *Second Interim Report of the Oakland Adult Project Follow-Up Study* (Oakland: Department of Human Resources, 1966), 116.

51. William Henry Brown, "Class Aspects of Residential Development and Choice in the Oakland Black Community" (PhD diss., University of California, Berkeley, 1970), 169.

52. Hayes, *Power Structure and Urban Policy*, 52.

53. See Department of Industrial Relations, Division of Fair Employment Practices, *Negro Californians: Population, Employment, Income, Education* (Sacramento: State of California, 1963).

54. Joseph Hochstim, Demetrios Athanasopoulos, and John Larkins, "Poverty Area under the Microscope," *American Journal of Public Health* 58 (October 1968): 1827.

55. "Oakland's Minority Unemployment Problem," *Oakland Post*, May 22, 1965.

56. "Ward's Goes Part-Way with Core," *San Francisco Chronicle*, May 17, 1963.

57. "Oakland Restaurants Picketed," *San Francisco Chronicle*, February 20, 1965.

58. Joseph Rodriguez, *City against Suburb: The Culture Wars in an American Metropolis* (Westport, CT: Praeger, 1999), 61–63. While many of these struggles were covered in the mainstream press and black newspapers like the *Oakland Post*, other venues appeared. *The Flatlands* was published by Alexandra Close and Lynn Phipps from March to December of 1966, covering housing, employment, and social conditions in the city's black neighborhoods.

59. "Council Forum on Minorities," *Oakland Tribune*, September 1, 1965.

60. Hugh Pearson, *The Shadow of the Panther: Huey Newton and the Price of Black Power in America* (Cambridge, MA: Perseus, 1994), 116. See also Jane Rhodes, "Black Radicalism in 1960s California: Women in the Black Panther Party," in *African American Women Confront the West, 1600–2000*, ed. Quintard Taylor and Shirley Ann Wilson Moore (Norman: University of Oklahoma Press, 2003), 347.

61. Jennifer Smith, *An International History of the Black Panther Party* (New York: Garland, 1999), 37.

62. Donald Hausler, *Blacks in Oakland, 1852–1987* (self-pub., 1987), 131–32.

63. Hayes, *Power Structure and Urban Policy*, 130–32.

64. Jeffrey Pressman and Aaron Wildavsky, *Implementation: How Great Expectations in Washington Are Dashed in Oakland* (Berkeley: University of California Press, 1973), 13–14.

65. Amory Bradford, *Oakland's Not for Burning* (New York: David McKay, 1968), 26.

66. Pressman and Wildavsky, *Implementation*, 140.

67. "U.S. Invests $1,085,000 to Create 43 Oakland Jobs," *Oakland Tribune*, March 16, 1969; Judith May, "Two Model Cities: Negotiations in Oakland," in *The Politics and Society Reader*, ed. Ira Katznelson, Gordon Adams, Philip Brenner, and Alan Wolfe (New York: David McKay, 1974), 68–100.

68. Arnold Meltsner, *The Politics of City Revenue* (Berkeley: University of California Press, 1971), 15.

69. In 1960, Matsons's *Hawaiian Citizen* was converted into the Pacific Ocean's first full-time containership. Rene de la Pedraja, *A Historical Dictionary of the U.S. Merchant Marine and Shipping Industry* (Westport, CT: Greenwood Press, 1994), 380.

70. John Davies, "40 Years Later, Boxes Rule," *Journal of Commerce* (April 26, 1996): 1–2.

71. Mike McGrath and Michele Thomas, "The Rise and Fall of the Port of Oakland," *East Bay Express* 13 (July 5, 1991): 19–20.

72. Mark Rosenstein, "The Rise of Maritime Containerization in the Port of Oakland: 1950 to 1970" (master's thesis, New York University, 2000), 48.

73. Woodruff Minor, "A Maritime History of Alameda: the Shipbuilders (Part 13)," *Alameda Journal*, March 17–23, 1989.

74. "Huge Dockside Container Crane Being Built Here," *Alameda Times-Star*, August 28, 1958. On the crane's significance, see Paul Graves Brown, "The Box and the Encinal Terminal: An Archaeology of Globalization," *Post-Medieval Archaeology* 47.1 (2013): 254–55.

75. Paul Sorensen, *Development of Containerization at the Port of Oakland, 1962–1974* (Oakland: Port of Oakland, 1975), 507.

76. "New Look for Shipping," *Oakland Tribune*, January 23, 1966.

77. On the terminal, see Port of Oakland, Public Relations Dept., "7th Street Terminal Issue," *Port Progress* (May 1971).

78. Minor, *Pacific Gateway*, 50–51. See also "Mitsui O.S.K. Lines," *The Compass* 4 (1979): 2.

79. Jasper Rubin, *A Negotiated Landscape: The Transformation of San Francisco's Waterfront since 1950* (Chicago: Center for American Places at Columbia College, 2011), 86–87.

80. On the Port of Oakland's advantages over San Francisco regarding containerization, see Yehuda Hayuth, "The Port-Urban Interface: An Area in Transition," *Area* 14.3 (1982): 220–21.

81. Quoted in Bill Bancroft and Bill Eaton, "Port Stuck Its Neck Out—and Won," *Oakland Tribune*, October 2, 1974.

82. Norm Hannon, "Oakland's Container Port World's Second Largest," *Oakland Tribune*, May 4, 1969.

83. Allan Temko, "A Work of Engineering on the Bay," *San Francisco Chronicle*, February 27, 1978.

84. Brian Cudahy, *Box Boats: How Container Ships Changed the World* (New York: Fordham University Press, 2006), 247.

85. Bill Eaton, "Port Plans New Terminal Despite Tonnage Decline," *Oakland Tribune*, May 9, 1976. On Oakland's position within national trends, see also Yehuda Hayuth, "Rationalization and Deconcentration of the U.S. Container Port System," *Professional Geographer* 40 (1988): 279–88.

86. Stephen Maita, "Port of Oakland Playing Its Trumps," *Oakland Tribune*, December 16, 1984; John Gulick, "The Urban Ecological Contradictions of the Port of Oakland Globalism," *Capitalism Nature Socialism* 13.3 (2002): 2–3.

87. Psyche Pascual, "Rising Tide," *Contra Costa Times*, January 18, 1998.

88. For a discussion of the size and capacity of each port terminal, from Sea-Land in 1962 to Tra Pac in 1994, see Minor, *Pacific Gateway*, 52–57.

89. Board of Port Commissioners, *Port of Oakland at Sixty Years: A Chronicle of Progress* (Oakland, 1987). The channel would again be deepened in 1998, this time to 48 feet, and again in 2004 to 50 feet.

90. Port of Oakland, *Vision 2000: Expansion and Modernization Programs* (April 1994).

91. James Goode, "Flying High: The Origin and Design of Washington National Airport," *Washington History* 1.2 (Fall 1989): 24.

92. Oakland Postwar Planning Committee, *Oakland's Formula for the Future* (Oakland, September 1945), 22–23; Fred Dubois, "Wartime Changes Boomed Oakland Airport Growth," *Oakland Tribune*, April 20, 1952. On airports' standards, see Paul Barrett, "Cities and Their Airports: Policy Formation, 1926–1952," *Journal of Urban History* 14.1 (November 1987): 113–23.

93. Bill Eaton, "Oakland's Airport Soars with the Jet Age," *Oakland Tribune*, September 19, 1965.

94. James Turner, "San Francisco's New International Airport," *California— Magazine of the Pacific* (June 1954): 201–11.

95. Board of Port Commissioners, *Port of Oakland: Sea-Air-Rail-Truck Center of San Francisco Bay* (Oakland, 1954), 9.

96. Knappen-Tippetts-Abbett-McCarthy, *Master Plan: Development Plan: Metropolitan Oakland International Airport* (Oakland: Port of Oakland, 1954). See also Port of Oakland, *Oakland International Master Plan* (Oakland, 2006), 8.

97. It would henceforth be used primarily for general aviation.

98. Al Reck, "Domestic Airline Hops from Oakland Show 10-Year Drop," *Oakland Tribune*, November 30, 1960.

99. Ralph Craib, "Jet-Age Airport with No Jets," *San Francisco Chronicle*, September 18, 1962.

100. Minor, *Pacific Gateway*, 102.

101. "Oakland Is Charter Capital, Birthplace of Low Air Fare," *Oakland Tribune*, June 2, 1974.

102. Richard de Neufville, "Planning for Multiple Airports in a Metropolitan Region," *Built Environment* 10.3 (1984): 162–63.

103. Port of Oakland, *Airport Master Plan, Draft EIR*, 3 vols. (Oakland, 1974), 8–13.

104. Ben Jesse Clarke and Hana Baba, "Port of Oakland: Private Industry or Public Agency?," *Race, Poverty & the Environment* 12.1 (Winter 2005/2006): 35–38.

105. Oden, *From Blacks to Brown and Beyond*, 181.

106. Bill Eaton, "Airport Expansion Snagged by BCDC," *Oakland Tribune*, January 31, 1972.

107. Herman Boschken, "The Demands of Conflicting Change on Public Enterprise: West Coast Seaport Development and Environmental Legislation," *Public Administration Review* 42.3 (May–June 1982): 220–22.

108. Allan Temko, "Danger to Our Great Bay," *San Francisco Chronicle*, November 18, 1963.

109. Betty Thompson, "Portrait of a Man with a Plan," *Western Construction News* (November 1947): 89.

110. Ralph Craib, "Bay Development Fight," *San Francisco Chronicle*, July 28, 1972. In 1977, construction began on the 3,200-unit Harbor Isle development, a real estate land grab that ate up a large expanse of wetlands and conflicted with the flight patterns of the Oakland airport.

111. "Bay Fill Would Add 100 Docks," *Oakland Tribune*, February 12, 1965.

112. Mel Scott, *The Future of San Francisco Bay* (Berkeley: Institute of Governmental Studies, 1963), 27.

113. Ibid., 24–25.

114. Office of Area Development, *Future Development of the San Francisco Bay Area, 1960–2020* (Washington, DC: US Department of Commerce, 1959), 79.

115. Janine Dolezel and Bruce N. Warren, "Saving San Francisco Bay: A Case Study in Environmental Legislation," *Stanford Law Review* 23.2 (January 1971): 349–52.

116. On related regional struggles to limit growth and environmental damage, see Stephanie Pincetl, *Transforming California: A Political History of Land Use and Development* (Baltimore: Johns Hopkins University Press, 1999), 144–149.

117. San Francisco Bay Conservation and Development Commission, *San Francisco Bay Plan* (San Francisco, 1969), 1–7.

CHAPTER 8. HOUSING INJUSTICE

1. Oakland City Planning Department, *Oakland's Housing Supply: Cost, Condition, Composition, 1960–1966* (Oakland, 1968), 11.

2. "Planner Sees New Oakland as Dream City," *Oakland Tribune*, December 12, 1954.

3. Oakland City Planning Department, *Oakland Residential Area Analysis: A Quality Evaluation by Census Tracts* (Oakland, 1956); Bill Stokes, "24% of Homes in City Blighted," *Oakland Tribune*, July 22, 1956.

4. John Jakle and David Wilson, *Derelict Landscapes: The Wasting of America's Built Environment* (Savage, MD: Rowman & Littlefield, 1992), 152–53.

5. On housing inequality, see Xavier de Sousa Briggs, ed., *The Geography of Opportunity: Race and Housing Choice in Metropolitan America* (Washington, DC: Brookings Institutions Press, 2005), 1–10.

6. Residential Development Committee, *The Demand for Houses* (Oakland: Oakland Chamber of Commerce, 1937).

7. Oakland City Planning Commission, *Need for a Low-Rent Housing Project in Oakland, California* (Oakland, 1938), 11–18.

8. Jennifer Donnelly, "Myth, Modernity, and Mass Housing: The Development of Public Housing in Depression-Era Cleveland," *Traditional Dwellings and Settlements Review* 25.1 (Fall 2013): 58–59.

9. Oakland City Planning Commission, *Preliminary Report of the Oakland City Planning Commission to the City Council: Need for a Low-Rent Housing Project in Oakland, California* (Oakland, 1938). See also National Association of Housing Officials, *Housing Yearbook* (Washington, DC, 1941).

10. On public housing, urban renewal, and reactions to those efforts in West Oakland, see Elaine-Maryse Solari, "The Making of an Archaeological Site and the Unmaking of a Community in West Oakland, California," in *The Archaeology of Urban Landscapes: Explorations in Slumland*, ed. Alan Mayne and Tim Murray (Cambridge: Cambridge University Press, 2001), 22–35.

11. Lawrence Vale, *Purging the Poorest: Public Housing and the Design Politics of Twice-Cleared Communities* (Chicago: University of Chicago Press, 2013), 6.

12. For a discussion of the impact of Campbell Village on its neighborhood, see Glenn Robert Lym, "Effect of a Public Housing Project on a Neighborhood: Case Study of Oakland, California," *Land Economics* 43.4 (November 1967): 461–66.

13. Fred Jones, "Oakland's Low-Rent Housing Projects," *Architect & Engineer* 151.1 (October 1942): 15–24.

14. "Housing Project Protested by Residents of East Oakland Area," *Oakland Tribune*, April 4, 1941.

15. Johnson, *The Second Gold Rush*, 84–90.

16. Housing Authority of the City of Oakland, California, *11th Annual Report* (Oakland, 1951).

17. Johnson, *The Second Gold Rush*, 98–109.

18. Steven Lavoie, "War Brought Segregated Housing to the East Bay," *Oakland Tribune*, August 21, 1994.

19. Housing Authority of the City of Oakland, California, *10th Annual Report* (Oakland, 1950).

20. "City Council Receives Plan for 500 Housing Units," *Oakland Tribune*, September 23, 1954.

21. Housing Authority of the City of Oakland, California, *13th Annual Report* (Oakland, 1953).

22. Housing Authority of the City of Oakland, California, *17th– 18th Annual Report* (Oakland, 1965). *Public Housing in Oakland* (Oakland: Bay Area Social Planning Council, 1966).

23. Oakland City Planning Department, *Oakland's Housing Supply*, 61.

24. Oakland Redevelopment Authority, *Summary of Oakland Redevelopment Projects* (Oakland, 1973), 1–5.

25. Vale, *Purging the Poorest*, 13, 17.

26. Margery Turner, Susan Popkin, and Lynette Rawlings, *Public Housing and the Legacy of Segregation* (Washington, DC: Urban Institute Press, 2009), 4–5.

27. Karen Franck, "Changing Values in U.S. Public Housing, Policy and Design," in *New Directions in Urban Public Housing*, ed. David Varady, Wolfgang Preiser, and Francis Russell (New Brunswick, NJ: Center for Urban Policy Research, 1998), 86–87.

28. Betty Segal, "West Oakland's Housing Blues," *Berkeley Barb*, December 19–25, 1975.

29. Michael Looney, "Mayor Hears Housing Gripes," *Oakland Tribune*, November 8, 1977.

30. See Melvin Bobier Associates, *A Plan for the Distribution of Scattered Turnkey Housing Units, Report to the Housing Authority* (Oakland, 1968); Jill Griffin, *An Assessment of the New Turnkey Program in Oakland as Seen by Turnkey Residents* (Oakland: Oakland City Planning Department, 1969); *Oakland's Turnkey Housing: Its Impact on the Community* (Oakland: Oakland City Planning Commission, January 1970).

31. "First Move on Homes Project," *Oakland Tribune*, December 5, 1967; Pearl Stewart, "Rainy Days Pour Trouble on Turnkey Housing Units," *Oakland Tribune*, February 12, 1978.

32. By 1990, almost 5,000 units in Oakland qualified for Section 8 subsidies, alongside another 1,845 units whose residents received housing vouchers. Housing Authority of the City of Oakland, California, *54th Annual Report* (Oakland, 1990).

33. Oakland Housing Authority, *Lion Creek Crossings Master Plan* (Oakland, 2004).

34. Rod Henmi and Brenda Nasio, "Home Is Where Hope Is: The Architecture of Affordable Housing," *African American Architect: Magazine of the National Organization of Minority Architects* (Fall 2004, Convention Issue): 21.

35. Samuel Zipp, "The Roots and Routes of Urban Renewal," *Journal of Urban History* 39.3 (May 2013): 367.

36. C. Louis Knight, "Blighted Areas and Their Effects upon Urban Land Utilization," *Annals of the American Academy of Political and Social Science* 148 (March 1930): 134.

37. Robert Klove, "A Technique for Delimiting Chicago's Blighted Areas," *Journal of Land & Public Utility Economics* 17.4 (November 1941): 483.

38. Jon Teaford, *The Rough Road to Renaissance: Urban Revitalization in America, 1940–1985* (Baltimore: Johns Hopkins University Press, 1990), 11.

39. Marc Weiss, "The Origins and Legacy of Urban Renewal," in *Federal Housing Policy and Programs: Past and Present*, ed. J. Paul Mitchell (New Brunswick, NJ: Rutgers Center for Urban Policy Research, 1985), 254–56.

40. Ashley Foard and Hilbert Fefferman, "Federal Urban Renewal Legislation," *Law and Contemporary Problems* 25 (Fall 1960): 652–55, on 662–65.

41. Oakland City Planning Administration, *Redevelopment in Oakland* (Oakland, 1949).

42. Bill Stokes, "City to Clean Up 78-Block Section," *Oakland Tribune*, October 26, 1955. Amendments, written into the Housing Acts of 1954 and 1956, introduced the term "urban renewal," where redevelopment agencies undertook projects in slums and areas deemed blighted or soon to become blighted, and where efforts expanded from housing to other building types. Alexander von Hoffman, "A Study in Contradictions: The Origins and Legacy of the Housing Act of 1949," *Housing Policy Debate* 11 (2000): 312–14.

43. The city council's vote was 8–1; the dissenting vote came from the West Oakland councilman, representing one of the areas targeted for redevelopment. *Oakland Tribune*, October 12, 1956.

44. Bill Stokes, "Oakland Urban Renewal Team Ends Inspection Tour," *Oakland Tribune*, December 2, 1956.

45. Department of Urban Renewal, *Clinton Park Urban Renewal Plan* (Oakland, November 1957), 2–6.

46. Ibid., 15–19.

47. Don Steward, "Oakland Attacks Its Blight," *San Francisco Chronicle*, March 22, 1959.

48. "Slum Stop Aim Is End of Bad Housing," *Oakland Tribune*, November 17, 1963.

49. "Urban Renewal Project Launched," *Oakland Tribune*, July 1, 1957.

50. Department of Urban Renewal, *Clinton Park Urban Renewal Plan*, 10–12.

City of Oakland, Building and Housing Department, *Final Report of the Clinton Park Urban Renewal Rehabilitation Project* (Oakland, 1962), 17.

51. "Gigantic Apartment Project Set for Urban Renewal Area," *Oakland Tribune*, June 25, 1958.

52. Building and Housing Department, *Final Report of the Clinton Park Urban Renewal*, 26, 38.

53. *The Clinton Park Plan* (Oakland: Urban Ecology, August 1999), 9–10.

54. Redevelopment Agency of the City of Oakland, *West Oakland General Neighborhood Renewal Plan* (Oakland, 1958), 13–15. Eighty-six percent of the buildings were subsequently deemed substandard, most of which were scheduled for clearance. Redevelopment Agency of the City of Oakland, *Acorn Urban Renewal Project, Progress Report to City Council* (Oakland, October 1959), 1.

55. Oakland Redevelopment Authority, *Summary of Oakland Redevelopment Projects*, 1–5. Self, *American Babylon*, 148.

56. Jim Wood, "Acorn Project Aims to Attract Whites," *Oakland Tribune*, May 26, 1968.

57. Bradley Inman, "Acorn Housing Project: Tenant, Owner Pride Rise after Years of Neglect," *San Francisco Examiner*, February 23, 1992.

58. Rick DelVecchio, "Tenants' Group Takes Leadership," *San Francisco Chronicle*, May 15, 1995.

59. Larry Spears, "Huge Facilities in Oakland," *Oakland Tribune*, May 14, 1967.

60. Rod Mabe, *History of Oakland, California Post Office* (Oakland: Oakland Post Office, 1975), 14–18.

61. Moriah Ulinskas, "Imagining a Past Future: Photographs from the Oakland Redevelopment Agency," *Places* (January 2019).

62. June Lee Gin, "We're Here and We're Not Leaving: Framing, Political History & Community Response to Gentrification in the San Francisco Bay Area" (PhD diss., University of Michigan, 2007), 88.

63. These complexes included Oak Village, Taylor Memorial Homes, and Oak Center Towers, an 11-story highrise for seniors. Oakland Redevelopment Authority, *Summary of Oakland Redevelopment Projects*, 1–5.

64. "Additional Oak Center Cash Sought," *Oakland Tribune*, June 5, 1969; Oakland Redevelopment Agency, *Oak Center Redevelopment Plan* (Oakland, September 15, 1970).

65. James Bailey, "Oakland Presents Its Case for Salvaging a Ghetto," *Architectural Forum* 126 (April 1967).

66. See Michael J. White, *Urban Renewal and the Residential Structure of the City* (Chicago: Community and Family Studies Center, 1980), 149–209.

67. Oakland City Planning Department, *Oakland's Housing Supply*, 19; Self, *American Babylon*, 155.

68. Martin Anderson, *The Federal Bulldozer: A Critical Analysis of Urban*

Renewal, 1949–1962 (Cambridge, MA: MIT Press, 1964), 220–21; Hayes, *Power Structure & Urban Policy*, 119–20.

69. "Sheffield Village," *Architect & Engineer* 143 (December 1940): 22–24.

70. Andrew Hope, "Evaluating the Significance of San Lorenzo Village, A Mid-20th Century Suburban Community," *CRM: The Journal of Heritage Stewardship* 3 (Summer 2005): 52–56.

71. John Stahura, "Suburban Development, Black Suburbanization and the Civil Rights Movement since World War II," *American Sociological Review* 51.1 (February 1986): 133.

72. "East Bay Slum Is Doomed," *San Francisco Chronicle*, October 5, 1961.

73. Johnson, *The Second Gold Rush*, 214–15.

74. Governors Advisory Commission on Housing Problems, "Report on Housing in California," (Sacramento, January 1963), 6, 38–42.

75. Jones-Correa, "Origin and Diffusion of Racial Restrictive Covenants," 565.

76. Amy Hillier, "Redlining and the Home Owners' Loan Corporation," *Journal of Urban History* 29.4 (2003): 398.

77. Amy Kantor and John Nystuen, "De Facto Redlining: A Geographic View," *Economic Geography* 58.4 (October 1982): 309–10. See also Marc Weiss, "Richard T. Ely and the Contribution of Economic Research to National Housing Policy, 1920–1940," *Urban Studies* 26 (1989): 115–26.

78. Eric Brown, *The Black Professional Middle Class: Race, Class and Community in the Post–Civil Rights Era* (London: Routledge, 2014), 24.

79. Annette Sorensen, Karl Taeuber, and Leslie Hollingsworth, "Indices of Racial Residential Segregation in 109 Cities in the United States, 1940–1970," *Sociological Focus* 8 (1975): 128–30.

80. Douglas Massey and Nancy Denton, *American Apartheid: Segregation and the Making of the Underclass* (Cambridge, MA: Harvard University Press, 1993), 46.

81. Kenneth Kusmer, "African Americans in the City since World War II: From the Industrial to the Post-Industrial City," *Journal of Urban History* 21.4 (May 1995): 461–62.

82. Delores Nason McBroome, *Parallel Communities: African Americans in California's East Bay, 1850–1963* (New York: Garland, 1993), 97.

83. For further commentary on how government programs often worked against the housing aims of black citizens, see Patricia Fernandez-Kelly, "Land, Race, and Property Rights in American Development," in *Race and Real Estate*, ed. Adrienne Brown and Valerie Smith (Oxford: Oxford University Press, 2016), 64–86.

84. See Keeanga-Yamahtta, *Race for Profit: How Banks and the Real Estate Industry Undermined Black Homeownership* (Chapel Hill: University of North Carolina Press, 2019), 55–92.

85. As interviewed by Sean Illing in "The Sordid History of Housing Discrimination in America," *Vox*, December 4, 2019.

86. N. D. B. Connolly, *A World More Concrete: Real Estate and the Remaking of Jim Crow South Florida* (Chicago: University of Chicago Press, 2016), 4.

87. Floyd Hunter, *Housing Discrimination in Oakland, California* (Oakland: Mayor's Committee on Full Opportunity & Alameda County Council of Social Planning, 1964), 31–72.

88. See the discussion on postwar white attitudes on housing in David Freund, *Colored Property: State Policy and White Racial Politics in Suburban America* (Chicago: University of Chicago Press, 2007).

89. R. Bryce Young, *Oakland's Changing Community Patterns* (Oakland: City Planning Department, 1961).

90. Gene Ayres, "Bias Charge on Housing in Oakland," *Oakland Tribune*, July 28, 1964.

91. W. Edward Orser, *Blockbusting in Baltimore: The Edmondson Village Story* (Lexington: University Press of Kentucky, 1994), 4.

92. William Frey, "Central City White Flight: Racial and Nonracial Causes," *American Sociological Review* 44.3 (June 1979): 444.

93. Luigi Laurenti, *Property Values and Race: Studies in Seven Cities* (Westport, CT: Greenwood Press, 1960), 124–26.

94. "Brookfield Tract Opens," *Oakland Tribune*, September 27, 1942.

95. Laurenti, *Values and Race*, 133–35.

96. "Brookfield, Sobrante Areas in Civic Betterment Move," *Oakland Tribune*, January 1, 1957.

97. Calvin Whitaker, "The Abandonment of Housing in East Oakland" (master's thesis, San Jose State University, 1992), 30.

98. Martha Taylor, *From Labor to Reward: Black Church Beginnings in San Francisco, Oakland, Berkeley and Richmond, 1849–1972* (Eugene, OR: Resource, 2016), 56–59, 129, 137–41, 161–62.

99. Laura Henze, Edward Kirshner, and Linda Lillow, *An Income and Capital Flow Study of East Oakland, California* (Oakland: Charles Stewart Mott Foundation, November 1979), 8, 21–22.

100. Fran Dauth, "Citizen Groups on the Move in East Oakland Districts," *Oakland Tribune*, April 28, 1974.

101. Larry Spears, "East Oakland's Housing Plan Gains Support," *Oakland Tribune*, June 15, 1975.

102. Eric Brown, "The Black Professional Middle Class and the Black Community: Racialized Class Formation in Oakland and the East Bay," in *African American Urban History since World War II*, ed. Kenneth Kusmer and Joe Trotter (Chicago: University of Chicago Press, 2009), 272–73.

103. George Lipsitz, "The Racialization of Space and the Spacialization of

Race: Theorizing the Hidden Architecture of Landscape," *Landscape Journal* 26.1 (2007): 12.

104. Ishmael Reed, "My Oakland: There Is a There There, Part I," *California Magazine* (March 1983).

105. Laurenti, *Values and Race*, 151–66; Wallace Smith, *Filtering and Neighborhood Change*, Research Report No. 2 (Berkeley: University of California Center for Real Estate and Urban Economics).

106. William Henry Brown, "Class Aspects of Residential Development and Choice in the Oakland Black Community" (PhD diss., University of California, Berkeley, 1970), 184–215. On the correlation between higher black household income and higher level of integration with whites, see Julia Hansen, "Residential Segregation of Blacks by Income Group: Evidence from Oakland," *Population Research and Policy Review* 15.4 (August 1996): 386–87.

107. Brown, *Black Professional Middle Class: Race, Class and Community*, 103.

108. Oakland City Planning Commission, *Modern Zoning for Oakland: A Summary and Guide for the Proposed Oakland Zoning Regulations* (Oakland, August 1963), 4, 18.

109. Hayes, *Power Structure and Urban Policy*, 61.

110. "Growing Opposition to Merritt Apartments," *Oakland Tribune*, May, 23, 1963; "City Planners OK Condominium Apartment," *Oakland Tribune*, September 13, 1962.

111. "New Silhouettes in Merritt Skyline," *Oakland Tribune*, June 5, 1964.

112. "Something New for Skyline," *Oakland Tribune*, August 20, 1964.

113. John Dengel, "Lake Highrise Nearly Ready," *Oakland Tribune*, July 28, 1968.

114. Citizens Committee on Residential Development, *A Report on Residential Development in the City of Oakland* (Oakland, 1942), 15.

115. "New Hillside Residential Tract Planned Here," *Oakland Post-Enquirer*, April 22, 1947.

116. Dave Hope, "Hill Area Growth Crowds Schools," *Oakland Tribune*, May 31, 1956.

117. Dick Ricca, "Integration Battle at Skyline High," *Oakland Tribune*, August 26, 1962. On the controversy in the context of Oakland attempts at school desegregation, see David Kirp, "Race, Schooling, and Interest Politics: The Oakland Story," *School Review* 87.4 (August 1979): 359–62.

118. "Skyline High to Get More Outsiders," *Oakland Tribune*, February 17, 1965.

119. David Weingarten and Lucia Howard, *Ranch Houses: Living the California Dream* (New York: Rizzoli, 2009), 14–19.

120. Matthei Kuruvila, "Fight over Oakland Trees, Views not Over," *San Francisco Chronicle*, September 18, 2012.

121. City of Oakland, City Planning Department, *Oakland Hills: A 701 SubArea Report* (Oakland, May 1969), 26–29.

122. On providing less expensive and more diverse types of housing via PUDs, see Andrew Whittemore, "The New Communalism: The Unrealized Mid-Twentieth Century Vision of Planned Unit Development," *Journal of Planning History* 14 (August 2015): 246–48.

123. Frank Pizzi, "High-Rise Apartment Warfare," *San Francisco Examiner*, August 25, 1963.

124. "Apartment Clusters in Hills Rapped," *Oakland Tribune*, November 11, 1969; Fran Dauth, "City OKs Mountain Village," *Oakland Tribune*, November 1, 1972.

125. Bernard Frieden, *The Environmental Protection Hustle* (Cambridge, MA: MIT Press, 1979), 58.

126. David Dowall, *The Suburban Squeeze: Land Conversion and Regulation in the San Francisco Bay Area* (Berkeley: University of California Press, 1984), 141–42.

127. Pearl Stewart, "The Battle over Oakland's Last Frontier—North Hills Development Is at Issue," *San Francisco Chronicle*, July 21, 1986.

128. Peter Charles Hoffer, *Seven Fires: The Urban Infernos That Reshaped America* (New York: Public Affairs, 2006), 264–87.

129. Roger Kemp, *Coping with Proposition 13* (Lexington, MA: Lexington Books, 1980), 85. On the connection between Proposition 13, reduction in fire department services, and the destruction, see Gregory Simon, *Flame and Fortune in the American West: Urban Development, Environmental Change and the Great Oakland Hills Fire* (Oakland: University of California Press, 2017), 68, 75.

130. Hoffer, *Seven Fires*, 304–6.

131. Sally Woodbridge, "Missed Chances in the Oakland Hills," *Progressive Architecture* 75 (July 1994): 23.

132. Cathy Lang Ho, "Rebuilding the East Bay," *Metropolis* 15 (July–August 1995): 68–87.

CHAPTER 9. DOWNTOWN RENEWAL AND RUIN

1. Irving Morrow, "The Packard Building at Oakland," *California Arts and Architecture* 35 (February 1929): 55–56.

2. "Landmarks Preservation Law Would Save Oakland's Past," *The Montclarion*, May 30, 1973.

3. "Building Wrecked but Memorial Sought for Site," *The Montclarion*, October 10, 1973.

4. Fran Dauth, "Eight Historic Sites Approved," *Oakland Tribune*, December 28, 1974.

5. Oakland City Planning Department, *Oakland General Plan: Historic Preservation Element* (Oakland, 1993), 2.1.

6. It is also a sad fact that practically all traces of Oakland's major shipyards, its three military bases, and many of its industrial plants are gone.

7. For an earlier version of the City Center saga, see Mitchell Schwarzer, "Oakland City Center: The Plan to Reposition Downtown within the Bay Region," *Journal of Planning History* 14.2 (May 2015): 88–111.

8. Irving Kahn, "Downtown Oakland Modernized," *Architect & Engineer* 128 (October 1944): 33.

9. "Remodeled, Enlarged J. C. Penney Store Opens Here Tomorrow," *Oakland Tribune*, June 18, 1940. The store expanded again in 1948 to 183,000 square feet, taking up the entire block on Washington Street between 11th and 12th Streets. "Rebuilt Penney Store to Open," *Oakland Tribune*, June 1, 1948.

10. "Streamlining of 32nd Business Property Downtown Complete," *Oakland Tribune*, August 17, 1939; "Hale Bros. Modernized Store Opens Officially Tomorrow," *Oakland Tribune*, November 6, 1940.

11. M. Gottdiener, "Understanding Metropolitan Deconcentration: A Clash of Paradigms," *Social Science Quarterly* 64 (June 1983): 238–42.

12. "Lakeside Colossus," *Architect & Engineer* 220 (December 1960): 17–21.

13. While initial plans called for a luxury hotel, Henry Kaiser was soon convinced that Oakland couldn't compete with San Francisco for the tourist trade. Marlea Graham, "Mid-Century Modern: The Kaiser Roof Garden Comes of Age," *Journal of the California Garden & Landscape History Society* 12 (Summer 2009): 2–3.

14. Fifteen years later, the 371-foot Lake Merritt Plaza consolidated the lakeside office district.

15. Gerald Adams, "Bay Area Trilogy," *Planning* 60 (February 1994): 12. See also Roberto Brambille and Gianni Longo, *For Pedestrians Only: Planning, Design and Management of Traffic-Free Zones* (New York: Whitney Library of Design, 1977), 124–44. While offices thrived in the new lakeside setting, stores did not; the White House store closed in 1965.

16. Allan Temko, "A Dream of Splendor for Oakland," *San Francisco Chronicle*, April 30, 1960.

17. Robert Fogelson, *Downtown: Its Rise and Fall, 1880–1950* (New Haven, CT: Yale University Press, 2001), 318.

18. Dick Ricca, "Battle on Blight Leaves Vacant, Locked Eyesores," *Oakland Tribune*, November 5, 1961.

19. Paul Groth, *Living Downtown: The History of Residential Hotels in the United States* (Berkeley: University of California Press, 1994), 273.

20. Jeffrey P. Levin, "Residential Hotels in Downtown Oakland" (master's thesis, University of California, Berkeley, 1985), 11, 30–31. By 2016, the number of residential hotel rooms had plummeted to 1,311 and many of these were

threatened with conversion to market-rate apartments, condominiums, or tourist hotel rooms. Darwin BondGraham, "Affordable No More," *East Bay Express*, May 18–24, 2016.

21. Groth, *Living Downtown*, 7–8, 131–33.

22. Willard Tim Chow, "The Context of Redevelopment in Oakland," *Urban Geography* 2.1 (1981): 52.

23. George Sternlieb, "The Future of Retailing in the Downtown Core," *Journal of the American Institute of Planners* 29 (May 1963): 104.

24. Shirley Weiss, "The Downtown Mall Experiment," *Journal of the American Institute of Planners* 30 (February 1964): 66–68.

25. *Oakland Tribune*, October 20, 1963.

26. Jeff Morgan, "Failure of a Downtown Mall," *Oakland Tribune*, June 24, 1974.

27. "Heart of Gruen's Fresno Plan," *Progressive Architecture* 46 (January–February 1965): 184–86.

28. Kent Robertson, "Downtown Retail Revitalization: A Review of American Development Strategies," *Planning Perspectives* 12 (1997): 389–90.

29. Kent Robertson, "The Status of the Pedestrian Mall in American Downtowns," *Urban Affairs Review* 26 (December 1990): 268–69.

30. Bob Heisey, "City's Dream Downtown Gets Backing," *Oakland Tribune*, November, 30, 1965.

31. Oakland Redevelopment Agency, *City Center, Oakland California* (Oakland, 1965).

32. From 1970 through the mid-1990s, redevelopment priorities shifted to less intrusive retailing, sports, and entertainment complexes. John Rennie Short, *Alabaster Cities: Urban United States since 1950* (Syracuse, NY: Syracuse University Press, 2006), 50, 54–55.

33. Jeffrey Hardwick, "A Downtown Utopia? Suburbanization, Urban Renewal and Consumption in New Haven," *Planning History Studies* 10 (Winter 1996): 41–49.

34. Lizbeth Cohen, "Buying Out Downtown Revival: The Centrality of Retail to Postwar Urban Renewal in American Cities," *Annals of the American Academy of Political and Social Science* 611 (May 2007): 85–85.

35. Bob Heisey, "City Welcomes New Renewal Director," *Oakland Tribune*, December 2, 1964. Bell was asked to resign over disagreement on the standards for rehabilitation at the Oak Center urban renewal project. *Oakland Tribune*, May 13, 1964.

36. Redevelopment Agency of the City of Oakland, *A Weekly Summary of Redevelopment Activities* (August 5, 1966); Redevelopment Agency of the City of Oakland, *Oakland Redevelopment News* (May 1968).

37. "Vision of the City: An Interview with John B. Williams, Oakland Redevelopment Director," *The Montclarion*, September, 13, 1967.

38. Environmental Impact Planning Corporation, *Oakland City Center: Environmental Impact Report Prepared for the Oakland Redevelopment Agency* (San Francisco, 1973), 7–8.

39. Redevelopment Agency of the City of Oakland, *A Report on Current Activities* (Oakland, April 1965), 38–44; Oakland City Planning Commission, *Presenting Telegraph Square* (Oakland, 1963), 7.

40. Two other redevelopment projects were designated outside of downtown: Elmhurst, 20 blocks of commercial buildings along East 14th Street, from 81st to 100th Avenue, along with some adjacent blocks of residences; and Stanford/Adeline, four mixed-use blocks in North Oakland. Oakland Redevelopment Authority, *Summary of Oakland Redevelopment Projects* (Oakland, 1973).

41. Backing for the plan came from federal urban renewal funds, the city-sponsored capital improvement program as well as the Central Business District Association, headed by Senator William Knowland, publisher of the *Oakland Tribune*. Bill Martin, "Facelifting for Oakland Proposed," *Oakland Tribune*, February 16, 1966; *Oakland Tribune*, March 3, 1966.

42. Oakland City Planning Commission, *Oakland Central District Plan* (Oakland, 1966), 8–10.

43. Ed Salzman, "Oakland's Central Area Is 'Too Big,'" *Oakland Tribune*, August 26, 1963.

44. *Oakland Central District Plan*, 38–40.

45. On the ideology behind such efforts, see Samuel Zipp, "The Roots and Routes of Urban Renewal," *Journal of Urban History* 39 (May 2013): 366.

46. Redevelopment Agency of the City of Oakland, *City Center* (May 1967), 3–6; Redevelopment Agency of the City of Oakland, *Weekly Summary* (June 16, 1967).

47. *Oakland Tribune*, January, 17, 1968.

48. Oceanic Properties, *Preliminary Oakland City Center Proposal* (Honolulu, 1968); Redevelopment Agency of the City of Oakland, *Oakland Redevelopment News* (May 1968).

49. *Oakland Tribune*, October 2, 1968.

50. Bill Martin, "$50 Million City Center Plan OK'd," *Oakland Tribune*, February 14, 1969.

51. The land and engineering construction company had earlier been responsible for the Bunker Hill urban renewal project in Los Angeles.

52. Bill Martin, "$93 Million City Center Project," *Oakland Tribune*, October 2, 1969.

53. Redevelopment Agency of the City of Oakland, *Central District Urban Renewal Plan* (Oakland, 1969), 5.

54. The original $3.8 million commitment by HUD for the Corridor Redevelopment Project was now augmented by $9.8 million in federal dollars. "Federal Go-Ahead Given City Center," *Oakland Tribune*, March 23, 1970.

55. Additional urban renewal sites south of 11th Street and east of Broadway brought the number of demolished blocks up to 23.

56. Some Victorian residences from here and elsewhere were relocated on the western edge of the project site—Preservation Park.

57. "A Weekly Summary of Redevelopment Activities," *Redevelopment Agency of the City of Oakland* (August 5, 1966); Environmental Impact Planning Corporation, *Oakland City Center: Environmental Impact Report Prepared for the Oakland Redevelopment Agency*, 22.

58. Jon Teaford, "Urban Renewal and Its Aftermath," *Housing Policy Debate* 11.2 (2001): 450–51.

59. Eugenie L. Birch, "Downtown in the 'New American City,'" *Annals of the American Academy of Political and Social Science* 626 (November 2009): 139.

60. Heather MacDonald, "Jerry Brown's No-Nonsense New Age for Oakland," *City Journal* 9 (Autumn 1999): 33. For an analysis of many of these federal programs, see Oakland Task Force and San Francisco Federal Executive Board, *Federal Decision-Making and Impact in Urban Areas: A Study of Oakland* (New York: Praeger, 1970).

61. "Consultant Hits City Center Plan," *Oakland Tribune*, October 14, 1972.

62. "Challenge to City Center," *The Montclarion*, June 6, 1973.

63. Cobb later went on to head OCCUR. Hayes, *Power Structure and Urban Policy*, 112.

64. Gail Berkley, "Developers Defend City Shopping Center," *Oakland Post*, April 12, 1978.

65. Grubb & Ellis Development Company, *Oakland City Center: Completing the Change, Beginning the New City* (Oakland, 1972).

66. Edwin Daniel, "Oakland's Dream Downtown Moves toward Reality via Renewal," *Journal of Housing* 32 (September 1975): 392.

67. "Report Paints Grim Picture for City Center," *The Montclarion*, September 10, 1975.

68. Richard Spencer, "Air of Confidence at City Center Despite Proposition 13," *Oakland Tribune*, August 20, 1978.

69. *Oakland Tribune*, June 16, 1982.

70. A related 68,000-square-foot retail project, City Square, opened in 1988. Stephen Maita, "Oakland Pushes City Center," *San Francisco Chronicle*, December 1, 1986.

71. Bernard Frieden and Lynne Sagalyn, *Downtown Inc.: How America Rebuilds Cities* (Cambridge, MA: MIT Press, 1989), 171–73.

72. Alison Isenberg, *Downtown America: A History of the Place and the People Who Made It* (Chicago: University of Chicago Press, 2004), 176–80.

73. Mark Blackburn, "Is Oakland's Office Building Boom All It's Cracked Up to Be?" *California Business* (November 1982): 49–50.

74. Allan Temko, "Empty Spaces in Oakland's City Center," *San Francisco Chronicle*, November 7, 1977.

75. On the stark postwar geography dividing inner-city black slums from white suburbs, see Eric Avila and Mark Rose, "Race, Culture, Politics, & Urban Renewal," *Journal of Urban History* 35 (March 2009): 339.

76. Katherine Bishop, "Oakland: A Twist in the Revival of Downtowns," *New York Times*, January 31, 1988; Lonnie Isabel, "Oakland: Is It There Yet?" *Oakland Tribune*, September 18, 1988; Wayne Attoe and Donn Logan, *American Urban Architecture: Catalysts in the Design of Cities* (Berkeley: University of California Press, 1994), 102–5.

77. Quoted in Brian Johns, "Starting Over," *Oakland Tribune*, May 4, 1992.

78. John Oliver, "Breuners: At 125, One of the Nation's Largest Furnishers," *Daily Review*, October 1, 1981.

79. Not surprisingly, that event sparked talk of yet another retail renaissance. Carl T. Hall, "Sears May Take Emporium's Place," *San Francisco Chronicle*, November 17, 1995.

80. The three years of BART excavation and construction, from January 1967 to November 1969, also contributed to the economic disruption of the northern retail district. *Oakland Tribune*, December 6, 1970.

81. Redevelopment Agency of the City of Oakland, *Oakland City Center Study: Towards a Restructuring of the Central Business District* (Oakland, 1968).

82. Redevelopment Agency of the City of Oakland, *City Center Urban Renewal Plan* (Oakland, 1968), 2.

83. Oceanic Properties and Kidder Peabody Realty Corporation, *Preliminary Oakland City Center Project* (Oakland, 1968).

84. Self, *American Babylon*, 152.

85. Brian Godfrey, "Urban Development and Redevelopment in San Francisco," *Geographical Review* 87 (July 1997): 315–18.

86. This creation of a *cordon sanitaire*, or transition zone that separates affluent districts from poorer ones, within and without the redevelopment zones, contributed greatly to San Francisco's emergence as a city of the wealthy. See Chester Hartman with Sarah Carnochan, *City for Sale: The Transformation of San Francisco* (Berkeley: University of California Press, 2002), 53–54.

87. *Design Resources in the Oakland Central District* (Oakland: Oakland City Planning Department, 1963), 16; Oakland City Planning Department, *Victorian Row: A Report on the Potential for Revitalizing Ninth Street in Oakland* (Oakland, 1967).

88. Lester On, "Oakland's Tarnished Treasures," *Oakland Tribune*, December 7, 1975.

89. Peter Bosselman and Stefan Pellegrini, *Rebuilding the Urban Structure of the Inner City: A Strategy for the Repair of Downtown Oakland, California* (Berkeley: Institute for Urban and Regional Development, 2003), 25.

90. Bill O'Brien, "Old Oakland Languishes: Retailers Remain Unimpressed with Victorian Row Development," *East Bay Express*, May 6, 1988.

91. Competing with upscale Union Square in San Francisco wasn't a formula for success, nor was ignoring outreach to nearby Chinatown. Jane Bower, "The Payoffs of Inclusion," *Urban Land* 54 (September 1995): 60–61.

92. Ed Salzman, "Fifth Downtown Department Store Urged by Economic Expert," *Oakland Tribune*, August 27, 1963.

93. Carl Abbott, "Five Strategies for Downtown: Policy Discourse and Planning since 1943," in *Planning the Twentieth-Century American City*, ed. Mary Corbin Sies and Christopher Silver (Baltimore: Johns Hopkins University Press, 1996), 408–409.

94. Alex Greenwood and Patrick Lane, "Oakland's 10K Race for Downtown Housing," *Planning* 68 (August 2002): 14, 17.

95. Similar efforts were undertaken in those years across the country. See Frederick A. Steinmann, "The Use of Retail Development in the Revitalization of Central Business Districts," *Economic Development Journal* 8 (Spring 2009): 14–22.

96. Quoted in Cathy Lang Ho, "Hope for Oakland," *Architecture* 88 (November 1999).

97. Alex Greenwood and Patrick Lane, "Oakland's 10K Race for Downtown Housing," *Planning* 68 (August 2002): 14, 17.

98. Thaai Walker, "Tough Transition in Old Oakland: Low-Income Residents Fear Displacement as Downtown Gets Upscale Makeover," *San Francisco Chronicle*, August 26, 1997.

99. James Temple, "Economy Casts Shadow on Oakland 10k Plan's 10th," *San Francisco Chronicle*, July 12, 2009; Zuscha Elinson, "As Mayor, Brown Remade Oakland's Downtown and Himself," *New York Times*, September 2, 2010.

100. City of Oakland, *Central District Redevelopment Area: Project Update* (Oakland, 2008), 4.

101. Chloe Veltman, "Oakland's Journey from Seedy to Sizzling," *New York Times*, April 30, 2010. On how the arts and culture can help restore a downtown, see Ann Markusen and Greg Schrock, "The Artistic Dividend: Urban Artistic Specialization and Economic Development Implications," *Urban Studies* 43 (2005): 1661–86.

102. Chase Billingham, "The Broadening Conception of Gentrification: Recent Developments and Avenues for Future Inquiry in the Sociological Study of Urban Change," *Michigan Sociological Review* 29 (Fall 2015): 79–82.

103. See the discussion on the improvements gentrification can bring to minority neighborhoods in Lance Freeman, *There Goes the 'Hood: Views of Gentrification from the Ground Up* (Philadelphia: Temple University Press, 2006), 156–87.

104. Neil Smith, "Gentrification and Uneven Development," *Economic Geography* 58.2 (April 1982): 152.

105. Just Cause, *Development without Displacement: Resisting Gentrification in the Bay Area* (Oakland: Just Cause, 2012), 14–15.

106. James Richardson, Bruce Mitchell, and Jad Edlebi, *Gentrification and Disinvestment 2020* (Washington, DC: National Community Reinvestment Coalition, 2020), 14, 25.

CHAPTER 10. SHOPPING CENTERS AND STOREFRONT STREETS

1. *New Shopping Areas: San Francisco Bay Area Market* (San Francisco: San Francisco Examiner Marketing Division, 1956).

2. "Drug Chain to Open New Store," *Oakland Tribune*, October 10, 1951.

3. David Oliver, "Location Theory and Practice: A Case Study of Safeway Stores" (master's thesis, University of California, Berkeley, 1966), 3, 17.

4. Avijit Ghosh and Sara McLafferty, "The Shopping Center: A Restructuring of Post-war Retailing," *Journal of Retailing* 67.3 (Fall 1991): 254. On the emergence of shopping center planning, see Michael Southworth, "Reinventing Main Street: From Mall to Townscape Mall," *Journal of Urban Design* 10 (June 2005): 153–54; Howard Gillette Jr., The Evolution of the Planned Shopping Center in Suburb and City," *Journal of the American Planning Association* 51.4 (1985): 448–60.

5. "Bridging the Retail Gap," *Redeveloping Oakland* 3.1 (Fall 2008), www2.oaklandnet.com/oakca1/groups/ceda/documents/webcontent/dowd007813.pdf.

6. See the discussion on store modernization in Richard Longstreth, *The American Department Store Transformed, 1920–1960* (New Haven, CT: Yale University Press, 2010), 41–47.

7. "Oakland Unit 350th Link of Chain in U.S.," *Oakland Tribune*, March 12, 1930.

8. Tevere MacFadyen, "The Rise of the Supermarket," *American Heritage* 36 (October–November 1985): 23–29.

9. "Andrew Williams Super Market Opens," *Oakland Tribune*, March 19, 1937.

10. "Andrew Williams Store," *Architect & Engineer* 170.1 (July 1947): 22–38. The market resembled other multipurpose stores of the time. Simon's on lower Broadway downtown started as a hardware store, and over the years added items like liquor, jewelry, clothing, and food products.

11. "The First Decade," *Safeway News* (February–March 1976).

12. David Appel, "The Supermarket: Early Development of an Institutional Innovation," *Journal of Retailing* 48.1 (Spring 1972): 40.

13. Peter Albert Allen, "A Space for Living: Region and Nature in the San Francisco Bay Area, 1939–1969" (PhD diss., University of California, Berkeley, 2009), 182–84.

14. Supermarket News, *The New Way at Safeway* (New York: Fairchild, 1958), 6–7.

15. Ibid., 188–89.

16. James Mayo, *The American Grocery Store: The Business Evolution of an Architectural Space* (Westport, CT: Greenwood Press, 1993), 169.

17. "The Story of Safeway Stores, Inc.," *Safeway News* 6 (March–April 1951): 2–3.

18. "Two Unusual California Supermarkets," *Architectural Record* 133 (June 1963).

19. Richard Longstreth, *The Drive-In, the Supermarket and the Transformation of Commercial Space in Los Angeles, 1919–1941* (Cambridge, MA: MIT Press, 1999), 158, 162.

20. "Hillside Area Developers Reveal Shopping Center Plans," *Oakland Tribune*, January 11, 1961.

21. Lance Owen, "How the Mall Made Walnut Creek: Retail Planning Dynamics in a California Suburb," *Journal of Planning History* 15 (November 2016): 290–95.

22. "Broadway Plaza Turns the Big 6-0," *Walnut Creek Patch*, June 13, 2011.

23. "Bay-Fair Shopping Project," *San Francisco Chronicle*, August 26, 1954; "$6,000,000 Unit in Bay-Fair Shopping Area Will Be Erected by Macy's San Francisco," *New York Times*, April 8, 1953; Jim Ritch, "Freeways, Industry Transform South County," *Oakland Tribune*, January 1, 1957.

24. "Two Gruen Shopping Centers," *Progressive Architecture* 34 (October 1958): 142.

25. Victor Gruen and Larry Smith, *Shopping Towns, USA: The Planning of Shopping Centers* (New York: Reinhold, 1960), 161.

26. Vicki Howard, *From Main Street to Mall: The Rise and Fall of the American Department Store* (Philadelphia: University of Pennsylvania Press, 2015), 133–34, 138.

27. "Center Planned for Oakland," *Los Angeles Times*, November 12, 1961; "Two Large Shopping Centers Will Open Here," *Oakland Tribune*, March 18, 1962.

28. "New Oakland Shopping Center Set," *Oakland Tribune*, August 4, 1961; "$3.5 Million Shop Center Proposed," *Oakland Tribune*, October 26, 1961.

29. "28-Story Building to House Store," *Oakland Tribune*, March 5, 1954.

30. "New Ideas in Oakland Center," *San Francisco Examiner*, October 18, 1964.

31. "Unique Features Planned for $10 Million Center," *Oakland Tribune*, May 26, 1963.

32. There was also parking for 250 cars at the ground level. "$10 Million Broadway Shop Center," *Oakland Tribune*, May 16, 1963.

33. The center limped on for a few decades, its facilities gradually taken over by the Kaiser Permanente Medical Center, to the point where it was demolished for a new hospital that opened in 2014.

34. $11 Million Mall Addition," *Oakland Tribune*, August 4, 1968; "New East-

mont Mall Opens, Beauty in Terazzo and Tile," *Oakland Tribune*, November 17, 1970; "Eastmont Mall Near 4th Phase," *Oakland Tribune*, June 12, 1974.

35. Richard Longstreth, *City Center to Regional Mall: Architecture, the Automobile and Retailing in Los Angeles, 1920-1950* (Cambridge, MA: MIT Press, 1997), 307-9.

36. Fred Garretson, "Eastmont Leads Pack," *Oakland Tribune*, July 25, 1977.

37. "Swat Team Cleans Up Oakland Mall," *San Francisco Chronicle*, September 19, 1976.

38. Joan McKinney, "Norman Spaulding: Young Man in a Hurry," *Oakland Tribune*, November 14, 1976.

39. "$500,000 Modernization Plan for Lakeshore Avenue," *Oakland Tribune*, June 20, 1963.

40. For an overview of the street's history, see Jennifer Soliman, "The Rise and Fall of Seventh Street in Oakland," www.foundsf.org/index.php?title=The_Rise_and_Fall_of_Seventh_Street_in_Oakland.

41. Michael Maly, *Beyond Segregation: Multiracial and Multiethnic Neighborhoods in the United States* (Philadelphia: Temple University Press, 2005), 166.

42. Christopher Gunn and Hazel Dayton Gunn, *Reclaiming Capital: Democratic Initiatives and Community Development* (Ithaca, NY: Cornell University Press, 1991), 40-41.

43. The mail order business shuttered in 1986 and, after a long preservation battle, the building was demolished in 2001 to make way for a school.

44. Lon Carlston, "Elmhurst Residents Involved in Rehabilitation Program," *Oakland Tribune*, June 23, 1974; Laura Henze, Edward Kirshner, and Linda Lillow, *An Income and Capital Flow Study of East Oakland, California* (Oakland: Charles Stewart Mott Foundation, November 1979), 52.

45. Chester Liebs, *Main Street to Miracle Mile: American Roadside Architecture* (Boston: Little Brown, 1985), 184.

46. "Golden Gate Business Walking Tour," *Oakland Heritage Alliance News*, August 29, 1999.

47. Jennifer Cooper, *Golden Gate Neighborhood Commercial Revitalization Report* (Oakland: Office of the City Manager, 1994), 8-10.

48. Milton Rube Research, *North Oakland Neighborhood Commercial Revitalization Project Market Analysis* (Oakland: Office of Economic Development and Employment, 1979).

49. "West Oakland Protest on Market," *Oakland Tribune*, January 17, 1978.

50. George Williamson, "Anger over Closing of a Safeway," *San Francisco Chronicle*, March 29, 1978.

51. Elizabeth Eisenhauer, "In Poor Health: Supermarket Redlining and Urban Nutrition," *Geojournal* 53.2 (2001): 127-28.

52. Brian McKenzie, "Access to Supermarkets among Poorer Neighborhoods," *Urban Geography* 35.1 (2014): 136.

53. Quoted in "The Supermarket Shuffle," *Mother Jones* 9.6 (July 1984): 7.

54. Nathan McClintock, "From Industrial Garden to Food Desert: Demarcated Devaluation in the Flatlands of Oakland," in *Cultivating Food Justice: Race, Class, and Sustainability*, ed. Alison Alkon and Julian Agyeman (Cambridge, MA: MIT Press, 2011), 104, 111.

55. On the issue of food security, see Camille Tuason Mata, *Marginalizing Access to the Sustainable Food System: An Examination of Oakland's Minority Districts* (Lanham, MD: University Press of America, 2013), 56–69.

56. Anne Short, Julie Guthman, and Samuel Raskin, "Food Deserts, Oases or Mirages?," *Journal of Planning Education and Research* 26 (March 2007): 352–53.

57. Ron Michael Donohue, "Abandonment and Revitalization of Central City Retailing: The Case of Grocery Stores" (PhD diss., University of Michigan, 1997), 37.

58. *Oakland Tribune*, April 25, 1951; *Oakland Tribune*, May 1, 1951; Board of Port Commissioners, *Port of Oakland* (Oakland, 1954), 16–17.

59. On the history of Jack London Square, see Mitchell Schwarzer, "A Tale of Two Waterfronts: Oakland's Jack London Square Competes with San Francisco," *California History* 91 (Fall 2014): 6–30.

60. "AC Transit to Build Mall Transfer Hub—Oakland Hopes to Improve Eastmont Town Center," *San Francisco Chronicle*, December 19, 1997. Similarly, the Foothill Square shopping center was practically abandoned by the early 2000s.

61. Joan Obra, "Mall Adjusted, Welcome to Eastmont Center," *East Bay Express* 22 (July 14, 2000): 1–14.

62. Dashka Slater, "A Tale of Two Cities: Emeryville, Oakland and the Swiftly Changing Face of East Bay Commerce," *East Bay Express* 16 (May 20, 1994): 14.

63. "Huge Bayside Complex Starts," *Oakland Tribune*, August 2, 1970.

64. Julie Smith, "Emeryville Tries to Get Itself Together," *San Francisco Chronicle*, September 28, 1976.

65. Kenneth Stone, *Competing with the Retail Giants: How to Survive in the New Retail Landscape* (New York: John Wiley & Sons, 1995), 109.

66. Laura Evenson, "Huge Retail Project for East Bay," *San Francisco Chronicle*, April 26, 1991.

67. See the discussion of big box aesthetics in Sam Lubell, "Is There Hope for the Big Box," *Architectural Record* 193.8 (August 2005).

68. Morris Newman, "A Onetime Industrial Field Now Sprouting Storefronts," *New York Times*, January 7, 2004.

69. Alex Schafran, *The Road to Resegregation: Northern California and the Failure of Politics* (Oakland: University of California Press, 2018), 135.

70. WalMart pulled out in 2016, the company claiming it did not perform well enough. Another reason may have been Oakland's higher minimum wage.

71. "White People Protest against Chinese Influx," *Oakland Herald*, June 13, 1906.

72. William Chow, *The Reemergence of an Inner City: The Pivot of Chinese Settlement in the East Bay Region of the San Francisco Bay Area* (San Francisco: R & E Research Assoc., 1977), 60–76.

73. L. Eve Armentraut Ma, *Hometown Chinatown: The History of Oakland's Chinese Community* (New York: Garland, 2000), 75, 100.

74. Edwin Lee, "Displacement and Dislocation of Low-Income Asians from Low-Cost Housing Units Due to Urban Redevelopment: San Francisco and Oakland Experience," in *A Sheltered Crisis: The State of Fair Housing in the Eighties* (Washington, DC: US Commission on Civil Rights, 1983), 200–203.

75. For a discussion of the differences in Chinatown before and after the Immigration Act, see William Wong, "American Dream: Chinatown Branch," in *Yellow Journalist: Dispatches from Asian America* (Philadelphia: Temple University Press, 2001), 10–23.

76. "The Changing Face of the City's Chinatown," *Oakland Tribune*, March 2, 1974.

77. Michael Dorgan, "Oakland's Chinatown: Renaissance Evokes Some Fears," *San Jose Mercury News*, June 1, 1983.

78. Thomas Mullen, *Immigrants and the American City* (New York: New York University Press, 1993), 127–54.

79. Ai Hosokawa, "Migration and Culture: Vietnamese Communities in Oakland, California" (master's thesis, California Institute of Integral Studies, 2000), 42–43; Aihwa Wong, *Buddha Is Hiding: Refugees, Citizenship, the New America* (Berkeley: University of California Press, 2003), 242–44.

80. See the discussion on ethnic ownership and employment in Ivan Light and Steven Gold, *Ethnic Economies* (San Diego: Academic Press, 2000), 27–58. For more analysis on ethnic retailing, see Steven Gold, *The Store in the Hood: A Century of Ethnic Business and Conflict* (Lanham, MD: Rowman & Littlefield, 2010), 123–53.

81. Areeya Chumsai, "San Antonio District: A True Blend of Cultures," *Oakland Tribune*, September 14, 1992.

82. Michael Robinson, "Immigration Boom Spurs Emergence of New Oakland Chinatown," *Chinatown News* 43.1 (October 3, 1995): 11.

83. Elizabeth Hollander, "Oakland's Eastlake District Experiences a Renaissance," *East Bay Express*, February 9, 2001.

84. Fernan Ramirez, "Eastlake's Makeover," *San Antonio Unity*, March, 2002. On the revival of the Eastlake district, see Maly, *Beyond Segregation*, 201–5.

85. Mona Younis, "San Antonio and Fruitvale," *Cityscape* 4.2 (1998): 226–27.

86. Robert Lemon, *The Taco Truck: How Mexican Street Food Is Transforming the American City* (Champaign: University of Illinois Press, 2019), 20, 22–23.

87. Manuela Silva, "The Fruitvale Village," *Economic Development Journal* 1.3 (Summer 2002): 31–36.

88. Stacy Finz, "Mi Pueblo Food Centers Success Story for Immigrant," *San Francisco Chronicle*, June 12, 2011.

89. On the early emergence of Koreatown, see Elaine Kim, "Between Black and White: An Interview with Bong Hwan Kim," in *The State of Asian America: Activism and Resistance in the 1990s*, ed. Karin Aguilar-San Juan (Boston: South End Press, 1994), 77–79.

90. Chuck Squatriglia, "Oakland's Got Seoul: Koreatown Emerges as Hub of Asian Culture and Downtown's Rebirth," *San Francisco Chronicle*, June 12, 2002.

91. Kathleen Richards, "Oakland's Koreatown Isn't Your Typical Ethnic Enclave," *East Bay Express*, May 6, 2009.

92. Margot Patterson Doss, "Continental Ways in Berkeley," *San Francisco Examiner*, April 14, 1977.

93. Bertram Gordon, "Shifting Tastes and Terms: The Rise of California Cuisine," *Revue Francaise d'etudes Americanes* 27/28 (February 1986): 112–15.

94. Liza Bercovici, "For Them, Haute Cuisine Beats Higher Learning," *New York Times*, November 12, 1975).

95. R. B. Read, "There and Now," *San Francisco Chronicle*, February 8, 1976.

96. Gerald Nachman, "There Is No Quiche There: It's a Paradise for Beefeaters," *San Francisco Chronicle*, April 22, 1984.

97. "Rockridge Residents Cheer Temporary Building Ban," *The Montclarion*, June 5, 1974.

98. "Hearing Slated on Rockridge Zoning," *Oakland Tribune*, September 27, 1974.

99. Ed Aust, "Market Hall: Architect's Addition to Rockridge," *The Voice*, November 23–24, 1987.

100. Deborah Hallberg, "A Developer Builds His Dream in Rockridge," *Oakland Tribune*, July 27, 1987.

101. Sharon McCormick, "Oakland's Former Little Italy Is Re-Emerging as Thriving Neighborhood," *Oakland Tribune*, August 31, 1986. On Greater Temescal in the 1980s, see Ishmael Reed, "My Oakland: There Is a There There," in *West of the West: Imagining California: An Anthology*, ed. Leonard Michaels, David Reid, and Raquel Scherr (Berkeley: University of California Press, 1989), 252–56.

102. Bradley Inman, "New Life for Oakland's Upper Telegraph," *San Francisco Examiner*, July 26, 1987.

103. Rob Baedeker, "A New Gourmet Ghetto," *Wall Street Journal*, December 29, 2007.

104. Sarah Henry, "Behind the Boom: The Finances Fueling Oakland's New Wave of Restaurants," *Edible East Bay* (Summer 2014).

105. Bryan Miller, "But Is It Near a Restaurant?" *New York Times*, July 17, 2016.

CODA

1. See Richard Walker, *Pictures of a Gone City: Tech and the Dark Side of Prosperity in the San Francisco Bay Area* (Oakland: PM Press, 2018).

2. Phillip Sprincin, "If You Let Them, They Will Build: Oakland Shows How to Expand Housing Supply," *City Journal*, November 29, 2019.

3. For an extended discussion of this phenomenon, see Mitchell Schwarzer, "Privatizing the City: Oakland's Lopsided Boom," *Places* 30 (June 2019).

4. Marisa Kendall, "Oakland Isn't Even Close to Meeting Its Lofty Affordable Housing Goal," *East Bay Times*, March 12, 2019.

5. Lance Freeman, *A Haven and a Hell: The Ghetto in Black America* (New York: Columbia University Press, 2019), 220.

Select Bibliography of Books about Oakland

Bagwell, Beth. *Oakland: The Story of a City*. Novato, CA: Presidio Press, 1982; 2nd edition, Oakland: Oakland Heritage Alliance, 2012.

Cummings, G. A., and E. S. Pladwell. *Oakland: A History*. Oakland: Grant D. Miller, 1942.

Douzet, Frederick. *The Color of Power: Racial Coalitions and Political Power in Oakland*. Charlottesville: University of Virginia Press, 2012.

Evanosky, Dennis. *Oakland's Laurel District*. Alameda, CA: Stellar Media Group, 2007.

Gutman, Marta. *A City for Children: Women, Architecture, and the Charitable Landscapes of Oakland, 1850–1950*. Chicago: University of Chicago Press, 2014.

Hayes, Edward C. *Power Structure and Urban Policy: Who Rules in Oakland?* New York: McGraw Hill, 1972.

Hinkel, Edgar, and William McCann, eds. *Oakland: 1852–1938: Some Phases of the Social, Political and Economic History of Oakland, California*. Oakland: Oakland Public Library, 1939.

Johnson, Marilynn. *The Second Gold Rush: Oakland and the East Bay in World War II*. Berkeley: University of California Press, 1993.

Ma, L. Eve Armentrout. *Hometown Chinatown: The History of Oakland's Chinese Community*. New York: Garland, 2000.

Marshall, Amelia. *East Bay Hills: A Brief History*. Charleston, SC: History Press, 2017.

Minor, Woodruff. *Pacific Gateway: An Illustrated History of the Port of Oakland*. Oakland: Port of Oakland, 2000.

Murch, Donna Jean. *Living for the City: Migration, Education, and the Rise of the Black Panther Party in Oakland, CA*. Chapel Hill: University of North Carolina Press, 2010.

Norman, Jeff. *Temescal Legacies: Narratives of Change from a North Oakland Neighborhood*. Oakland: Shared Ground, 2006.

Oden, Robert Stanley. *From Blacks to Brown and Beyond: The Struggle for Progressive Politics in Oakland, California, 1966–2011*. San Diego: University Readers, 2012.

Reed, Ishmael. *Blues City: A Walk in Oakland*. New York: Crown, 2003.

Rhomberg, Chris. *No There There: Race, Class, and Political Community in Oakland*. Berkeley: University of California Press, 2004.

Sappers, Vernon. *Key System Streetcars: Transit, Real Estate, and the Growth of the East Bay*. Wilton, CA: Signature Press, 2007.

Self, Robert. *American Babylon: Race and the Struggle for Postwar Oakland*. Princeton, NJ: Princeton University Press, 2003.

Simon, Gregory. *Flame and Fortune in the American West: Urban Development, Environmental Change, and the Great Oakland Hills Fire*. Oakland: University of California Press, 2017.

Spencer, Robyn. *The Revolution Has Come: Black Power, Gender, and the Black Panther Party in Oakland*. Durham, NC: Duke University Press, 2016.

Index